American Honor

CRAIG BRUCE SMITH

American Honor

The Creation of the Nation's Ideals during the Revolutionary Era

The University of North Carolina Press *Chapel Hill*

This book was published with the assistance of the Anniversary Fund of the University of North Carolina Press.

© 2018 The University of North Carolina Press
All rights reserved
Set in Arno Pro by Westchester Publishing Services
Manufactured in the United States of America

The University of North Carolina Press has been a member of the Green Press Initiative since 2003.

Library of Congress Cataloging-in-Publication Data
Names: Smith, Craig Bruce, author.
Title: American honor : the creation of the nation's ideals during the
    revolutionary era / Craig Bruce Smith.
Description: Chapel Hill : University of North Carolina Press, [2018] |
    Includes bibliographical references and index.
Identifiers: LCCN 2017033928| ISBN 9781469638836 (cloth : alk. paper) |
    ISBN 9781469638843 (ebook)
Subjects: LCSH: United States—History—Revolution, 1775–1783—Social
    aspects | United States—Civilization—Philosophy. | United States—
    History—Philosophy. | Adams, John, 1735–1826—Philosophy. |
    Franklin, Benjamin, 1706–1790—Philosophy. | Jefferson, Thomas,
    1743–1826—Philosophy. | Washington, George, 1732–1799—Philosophy.
Classification: LCC E209 .S65 2018 | DDC 973.01—dc23
LC record available at https://lccn.loc.gov/2017033928

Jacket illustration: *The Resignation of General Washington, December 23, 1783* by John Trumbull. Photo courtesy of the Yale University Art Gallery.

For Tiffany

Contents

Acknowledgments

This book's long progression from thoughts to pages could not have been completed without the help of many individuals. Those named here are only a few among the many deserving of thanks. So to anyone who ever listened to me ramble on about honor, please accept my utmost gratitude and apologies.

David Hackett Fischer has done more for me than he will ever know, and I lack the words to express my thanks. His effortless grace and generosity have been the surest proof that honor still exists in this world. In no uncertain words, Jason M. Opal's and David L. Preston's insights made this a better book. The late Bertram Wyatt-Brown was an inspiration, as was Gordon S. Wood, who both served as invaluable commenters. Additional thanks go to Jane Kamensky for her continuing support throughout the writing process.

The book's research and writing were immeasurably eased by the generous support of the Boston Athenaeum, Brandeis University, the Colonial Williamsburg Foundation, the Crown family, the Fred W. Smith National Library for the Study of George Washington, the Society of the Cincinnati, the Massachusetts Society of the Cincinnati, the Mellon Foundation, the Robert H. Smith International Center for Jefferson Studies, and the Smith Richardson Foundation.

Thank you to Lucas Morel and Andrew Jackson O'Shaughnessy, both fine gentlemen who have provided me with tremendous opportunities. The highest regards go to Joyce Antler and Paul Jankowski, who have been unwavering in championing me. Doug Bradburn, Ellen McCallister Clark, Stephen McLeod, and Mary Warnement have also been immensely supportive of this project.

Many thanks are reserved for the editors and staff of the University of North Carolina Press, especially Jad Adkins, Dino Battista, Kim Bryant, Catherine Cheney, Susan Garrett, Chuck Grench, and Jay Mazzocchi, who made my first book a reality. Credit is also due to the staff at Westchester Publishing Services, especially Erin Davis, Melody Negron, and Ashley Moore, and Jessica Ryan for copyediting, proofing, and generally keeping my text safe from unintentional error. I also owe additional gratitude to Anna Berkes, Elizabeth Frengel, Rachel Jirka, Doug Mayo, Carolle Morini, Sarah Myers, Jack Robertson, Valerie Sallis, Mark Santangelo, Michelle Lee Silverman, and all of the other librarians and archivists who had the misfortune of reading my nearly illegible call slips.

I am a historian because of Ron Vallar, and I was aided at St. John's University by Mauricio Borrero, Timothy Milford, and Konrad Tuchscherer. In addition, David Ekbladh, Jeffrey Fortin, Mark Gibney, Erik Hillskemper, and Javier Marion have helped throughout my career. I'm still thrilled to have been a part of the 2011 West Point Summer Seminar in Military History, and thankful that it created friendships with Sally Burt, Robin Conner, Ross Mahoney, Nadejda Popov Williams, and Judy Van Buskirk. Judy and the late Caroline Cox were also both research inspirations to me as an undergraduate, and it has been an honor to know them.

All of my current and former colleagues and students at William Woods University (especially the Society of Historians), Tufts University, Brandeis, Emmanuel College, Lesley University, and Suffolk University are deserving of acknowledgment (even those who have commented that "honor is stupid"). Additional thanks to Jeffrey Pasley, Jay Sexton, and the faculty, fellows, and grad students of the Kinder Institute on Constitutional Democracy at the University of Missouri for the continued warm welcome. To the audiences at BOLLI and the Washington and Lee University Institute of Honor Symposium, it has been my pleasure and I hope to give you an encore. Thanks also to Kayleigh Whitman, my first teaching assistant.

My parents (biological, step, and in-law) were all immensely supportive (even though they still have no clue exactly what I do). This book is the product of Kathy Kissane's kindness. Lincoln and Abby Mullen, digital historians extraordinaire and all-around genuinely good people, are always deserving of acknowledgment for their friendship. I also received tremendous encouragement from my friends Jodie Austin, Georgia Luikens, the Plaza family, Rachel Rhame, Aly Sheehan, Sarah Sutton, and the Walters family. To all of my other family and friends, thank you.

Most of all, none of this would have been possible without my wife. Tiffany is the best thing that ever happened to me. During the entire research and writing process (and our whole life together, actually), she could not have done more. Her love, compassion, and tireless support cannot be described. Also, she just happens to be a professional editor (one of the many perks of our marriage), and she read, edited, and then reread and reedited every word of this book. In so doing, she became every bit as much of an expert on the topic as I am. Her name should also be on the title page. Tiffany, I love you more than anything.

American Honor

What Are Honor, Virtue, and Ethics and How Did They Influence the American Revolution?

From the Sons of Liberty to the Son of Thunder, crisis had brought them to Philadelphia. Years of resentment and demands of liberty sparked the rattle of carriages and the thump of horseshoes from all corners of the thirteen colonies. Delegates from each of the colonies gathered in the Pennsylvania capital for a "general congress" ready to resist Great Britain and, if necessary, to "risque [risk] their all." Each morning they arose for a purposeful stroll along Chestnut Street that brought them down a cobblestoned alleyway. Although flanked by buildings on either side, it was still wide enough for the gentlemen to continue their conversations side by side. Every inch of their nearly two-hundred-and-fifty-foot approach framed their destination: an elegant Georgian building of vibrant red brick, accented in crisp white and crowned with a rising spire. Once inside, all fifty-six individuals had to saunter down "a long Entry" before turning east. Each then sat on a wooden Windsor chair facing a small writing desk on which he would help to decide the future of his country. Despite the hour, the chamber was dark, illuminated only by the dancing flicker of candles. The shutters had been drawn—all inside understood the gravity of their task and the moment. "This Assembly [was] like no other that ever existed," remarked John Adams of Massachusetts, for "Every man" in that packed twenty-by-thirty-foot room was "a great Man." Sequestered inside, the delegates "debate[d]" theorists Emer de Vattel, Jean-Jacques Burlamaqui, John Locke, and Montesquieu "like philosophers." Using these texts to inform their conceptions of colonial "rights" and "justice," each ultimately made a pledge based on "sacred" "honor."

The date was October 20, 1774.

The American patriots gathered in Carpenter's Hall and unanimously declared themselves "associate[d], under the sacred ties of virtue, honour and love of our country."

At the signing of the Declaration of Independence in July 1776, roughly two years and a thousand feet away, many of the same patriots, now delegates of the Second Continental Congress, repeated and expanded on the sentiments of the first when they "pledge[d]" their "Lives, our Fortunes, and our sacred

Honor." These words offered at the Pennsylvania Colonial Legislature (soon to be known as the State House or Independence Hall) formed the foundation of a new nation, and they are arguably the most famous reference to honor in American history. However, the earlier invocation of honor, virtue, unity, and the willingness to hazard virtually everything suggests a unity of thought that existed prior to independence. After only fifty-one days, the delegates of the First Congress, most of whom had never actually met before, displayed a "common cause." They came from diverse origins and held varied religious beliefs. Was less than two months together enough to form a like mind? Or was it something else? There already seemed to be a commonality that allowed them to equate "sacred rights and privileges" with "sacred" virtue and honor. Before independence, even before the war itself, Americans' understanding of and belief in honor and virtue had united them.[1]

From the Old World to the New, many people understood the importance of the preservation of honor. Honor, virtue, and ethics are powerful ideas that have governed society for centuries and remain continually relevant even in the modern day. However, these three ideas are often understood as disparate concepts, with little intersection. Furthermore, virtue and honor, more especially, are often dismissed as antiquated and only applicable to the upper echelons of society, particularly white males. But just how crucial were these concepts in the formation of America and early American identity? Themes of honor and virtue emerged from all areas of American society beginning in the seventeenth century. Although the origins of these ideas lay across the Atlantic, Americans from expansive gender, social, and racial categories transformed them as their own.[2] As Thomas Jefferson remembered, "Before the establishment of the American states, nothing was known to History but the Man of the old world."[3] In the New World, people developed modified notions, both individuated and collective, of what it meant to be honorable, virtuous, and ethical.

Despite today's popular perception, honor in early America was not synonymous with dueling; nor did honor and virtue exist with standardized, black-and-white definitions. Many interpretations of these ideas subsisted throughout society, but their existence and importance were unquestioned. While there are subtle distinctions between the terms, in contrast to the traditional historiography on the pathology of honor, early Americans came to understand honor and virtue as akin to, and often indistinguishable from, morality and ethics.[4] However, "ethics" as a term (aside from references to classical and moral philosophy) was largely absent from colonial America, especially during the Revolutionary era. In fact, it doesn't regularly appear until the early republic at the earliest, which is indicative of the use of the terms "honor" and "virtue" to express the same ideals.[5] Still, the early Americans' discussion of ethics reflects their understanding of honor and virtue. One's honor and virtue depended on right or proper conduct. How that was judged was a matter of each person's own ethical and cultural understandings. Thus, these ideas evolved into more than just a traditional domain of the elite. As they became understood as synonymous with ethics, people up and down the social hierarchy were capable of embracing these concepts and using them to direct their lives.

From America's infancy, honor and virtue had been stereotypically the domain of white males. From the elites to the middling class, these ideals were often the bar to which all men were held. They governed their beliefs, their careers, their social interactions—their entire lives. In *Common Sense*, Thomas Paine reminded readers, "When we are planning for posterity, we ought to remember that virtue is not hereditary."[6] It was each individual's actions alone, and not his or her birth status, that determined whether that individual was virtuous. Similarly, Connecticut-born patriot spy Nathan Hale believed, "Every kind of service, necessary to the public good, becomes honorable by being necessary."[7] Through a duty to the nation, regardless of the contribution, honor was bestowed. And white men during this time often inherently considered these ideas as linked to ethics and morality. Bostonian Samuel Adams warned, "A general Dissolution of Principles & Manners will more surely overthrow the Liberties of America than the whole Force of the Common Enemy. While the People are virtuous they cannot be subdued."[8] Adams believed that the only way America could lose the war was if they morally failed themselves. Patriots thought that only through superior ethical conduct could America be preserved.

Honor and virtue were also not inherently masculine or feminine. Both concepts were manifestations of ethical principles that could be embraced by either sex. Through this ethical lens, a picture emerges of feminine honor and virtue that represents more than just chastity retained or lost, as illustrated by Samuel Richardson's depictions of his heroines in his mid-eighteenth-century epistolary novels *Pamela* and *Clarissa*.[9] In *A Treatise on the Immutability of Moral Truth*, Catharine Macaulay, an English historian whose ideas resonated in America, contended that by 1783 "virtue" was an "inseparable union of moral causes."[10] With similar individuality, Judith Sargent Murray (an early American women's rights activist) proclaimed in her 1790 publication, *On the Equality of the Sexes*, that women held an "innate" conception of honor that allowed them to serve their nation.[11] Women thought of honor and virtue in ways that were both reminiscent of those of their male counterparts and personalized. What other divides could ethics help bridge?

While hierarchy and birth status were crucial components of early modern European honor, we see greater variance on the other side of the Atlantic. Eighteenth-century pirates, dismissed by cultivated society as the lowest of the low and nothing more than outlaws, maintained a distinctive and egalitarian sense of honor and virtue. Pirates placed an enormous value on oaths of honor that required a new sailor to "swear to true to the Crew" in order to gain full acceptance. On their ships, pirates valued their own sense of "Conscience" and "Honor"; they may steal and kill, but there were still rules of justice and fairness—each man got what he deserved.[12] Along the hierarchical scale, honor still guided conduct.

Honor and virtue as ethical concepts were also not limited by race. In his encounters with Native Americans, eighteenth-century traveler William Bartram found that "as moral men they certainly stand in no need of European civilization." He concluded that Native Americans had "the most delicate sense of honour and reputation of their tribes and families." Their ethical codes were not unlike those of white Americans, for "in order to inculcate morality, and promote human happiness, they applaud praise worthy actions, as commendable and necessary for the support of civil society, and maintain the dignity and strength of their nation or tribe."[13] Similarly, on an expedition to the western frontier, former soldier Jonathan Carver described their "character" as "possessed of virtues which do honour to human nature." Furthermore, he declared their understanding of these concepts as consistent with the "honour of their tribe, and the welfare of their nation . . . not as a personal qualification, but as a national characteristic."[14] Native American honor centered on moral deeds and the collective good. But what about when race was coupled with a lack of independence?

While honor was clearly present at the top rungs of society's ladder, it was also just as important at the bottom. Despite the common Anglo-American perception that a slave was inherently without honor, Aphra Behn's 1688 novel, *Oroonoko: or, The Royal Slave*, offered a rare counterpoint. In this tale of an enslaved African prince, Behn cast the titular character as possessing "those refin'd Notions of true Honour." This work of fiction suggests an alternative perception, even though she credits his honor to a moral education administered by a French tutor and his interactions with the English and Spanish while still a freeman and a royal.[15] However, African American slaves possessed an ethical code based on their own understanding of morality.[16]

Honor and dependence have always been understood as mutually exclusive, thereby seeming to remove enslaved African Americans from the discussion. However, eighteenth- and nineteenth-century slave narratives reveal a complex and individuated sense of honor that existed, despite bondage. In Africa, honor and slavery were not necessarily disjunctive, and that tradition was brought to America.[17] Slaves considered the merit and value of their deeds, and they believed that they still had to maintain an ethical foundation. Even more, morality and proper conduct became the principle means by which slaves judged not only themselves but also other slaves and even their masters.[18] Olaudah Equiano, a former Virginian slave who went on to become an early abolitionist leader, recounted in his autobiography, "Reflecting on my past actions, I began to think I had lived a moral life," and he concluded that his ideas were acquired through personal experience, as "almost every event of my life made an impression on my mind, and influenced my conduct."[19] Equiano's ideals were a widespread concept that crossed racial boundaries— regardless of one's status, this sense of progression was a constant.

For more than just Equiano, slaves' careful attention to morality was at the heart of the honor code. The inherent subjugation of slavery in many ways actually reinforced a more internal and lofty sense of honor and virtue, often in direct opposition to slaves' white masters. In 1838, Frederick Douglass (then a slave) was hired out by his master, who on rare occasions would offer Douglass a few pennies "to encourage" him. Based on his own ethical principles, Douglass "always felt worse for having received any thing; for I feared that the giving me a few cents would ease his conscience, and make him feel himself to be a pretty honourable sort of robber."[20] This story illustrates that both men entertained ideas of honor, but with starkly different interpretations. A slave often had limited tools to combat his master, but Douglass sought to shame his owner's false sense of honor through the language of honor.

Slaves had their own way of thinking. As Charles Ball (a slave who lived in both Maryland and Georgia before escaping) claimed, "I was never acquainted with a slave who believed that he violated any rule of morality by appropriating to himself any thing that belonged to his master, if it was necessary for his comfort." Yet contrary to what he himself presented as the general rule, Ball dismissed this principle as "the too common rule of moral action" and personally and "solemnly declare[d] . . . that I never deprived any one of all the masters that I have served, of anything against his consent." For him, stealing was dishonorable, no matter one's status; the only exceptional theft was of food, which should then be shared with other slaves in a Robin Hood fashion.[21]

Even within slave communities, there was a diversity of independent moral thought that mirrored that of white colonial society.

Deprived of legal rights, slaves, like pirates, used the principle of honor as a conception of a higher law above that of their white masters.[22] Kentucky slaves Henry Walton Bibb and Malinda married by "clasping each other by the hand, pledging our sacred honor that we would be true." For Bibb, who went on to become a well-known author and abolitionist, "there was nothing that could be more binding upon us as slaves than this."[23] Harriet Jacobs's grandmother was another firm believer in honor, lending saved money to her destitute mistress; as the former-slave-turned-abolitionist Jacobs recounted, "She trusted solely to her honor. The honor of a slaveholder to a slave."[24]

Most surprisingly of all, honor was even more valuable than freedom to some slaves. Passing through the free state of Ohio during the antebellum era, Josiah Henson refused his chance at freedom out of a sense of honor because he had promised to make a delivery in Kentucky for his master; Henson explained that his decision was the only honorable one: "What advantages I may have lost, by thus throwing away an opportunity of obtaining freedom, I know not; but the perception of my own strength of character, the feeling of integrity, the sentiment of high honor, I have experienced,—these advantages I do know, and prize; and would not lose them, nor the recollection of having attained them, for all that I can imagine to have resulted from an earlier release from bondage."[25] His word was his bond, and he dared not break it and lose his honor for any reward—even freedom. Such thinking was not isolated. Maryland native James Roberts similarly passed up the chance for escape out of "a sense of honor and justice."[26] Henson's and Roberts's concept of ethics illustrates two distinct points: for some, honor was the highest goal, and it was accessible to all people, regardless of their status.

Honor and virtue became a means by which one could advance in American society. Far from being divisive, honor and virtue became inclusive ideas. The obvious sense of honor that Native Americans possessed led Thomas Jefferson to regard the failure to recognize the rights of this population as "a principal source of dishonour to the American character."[27] It also allowed Venture Smith, a former slave, to be called "an ornament and an honor to human nature" on par with "a Franklin and a Washington, in a state of nature, or rather in a state of slavery."[28] In post-Revolutionary America, social mobility was possible based on ethics.

But while the ideas of honor, virtue, and ethics were clearly present during early America, how intrinsic were they? How necessary were they to people's lives? And how did those ideas change with time in America?

American Honor tells the history of the American Revolution through an ethical lens. But within this broad scope, it engages in two simultaneous inquiries, one on the ethical ideology of early America and the other on the Revolution's causes. In essence, this book shows that a colonial ethical transformation caused and became inseparable from the American Revolution, creating a continuing ethical ideology. As highlighted in the opening, the patriots famously "pledge[d] . . . our Lives, our Fortunes, and our sacred Honor" during the 1776 signing of the Declaration of Independence.[29] But before this, even before Lexington and Concord, Americans felt bound by ethics. For by 1774, they already believed themselves "associate[d], under the sacred ties of virtue, honour and love of our country."[30] These ethical changes occurred before the war and influenced its outbreak; the Revolution, in turn, allowed for these ideas to be broadly instituted in society. Thus, this work offers an ethical history and a new causation narrative of the American Revolution.

As an ethical history of early America, it examines honor, virtue, and, obviously, ethics from the coming of the American Revolution through the early republic. It centers on several generations of Americans who shared common and defining experiences. These founders are remembered for their contribution to American independence and the creation of a new nation, but while they were forming this new republic, they also carefully and continuously reflected on the ethics of their deeds. They were deeply concerned with the principles behind their own actions and the consequences for the fledgling nation. They wanted to win, but win well. They wanted the new country to succeed, but not at the cost of honor or virtue. These concepts of honor and virtue were at the forefront of the American founders' minds as they traveled the precarious road to independence. They were considered the highest ideals to which every person—and country—should aspire. However, these twin pillars of ethics manifested themselves in very distinct ways in the minds of America's founders. And it is from these thoughts that we have much to learn.

This book asks questions that have been absent, or at least less central, in more contemporary historical literature. In February 2015, Pulitzer Prize–winning historian Gordon Wood controversially complained, "A new generation of historians is no longer interested in how the United States came to be."[31] The historiography over the past half century has transitioned to questions of change rather than cause. While a worthy pursuit, the past three-plus decades have created an opportunity for a new look at an old question. This book intends to reopen debate and allow for a more complete vision of the Revolution.[32] Its causes are undeniably varied, and this book doesn't dispute this fact. Historical studies have accurately relayed that the Revolution was caused by numerous economic, political, and social considerations. This ethical interpretation is not meant to overturn, reject, or even argue with these diverse models but rather to offer a new, complementary narrative of causality.[33]

Admittedly, this book pays close attention to many leaders of the founding era, most notably John Adams, Benjamin Franklin, Thomas Jefferson, and George Washington, precisely because these individuals were directly responsible for writing on and implementing changing ethical ideas. In addition, their understanding of honor and virtue influenced their personal and public thoughts and actions. The acts and thoughts of a leader have always been, and continue to be, deeply relevant to many other people. Religious historian Mark Noll agrees, stating that "many nonpublishing citizens read, pondered, and considered themselves part of the circles of debate" created by the elite and that "most residents" still felt involved in the same "public realm of discourse."[34] Thus, through these leaders, a great deal about broader societal values and ideals can be discovered.

Contrary to a great deal of recent historical work, this book presents these leaders' ethical ideology as crucial to decision making. In *Sentimental Democracy*, historian Andrew Burstein examines the Revolutionary language of liberty and happiness, and he notes the creation of a new national vocabulary in which words (including "honor" and "virtue") were expanded and developed to express sentiment. Although he describes the Revolution as a "moral crisis," Burstein concludes that such words were rhetorical or an emotional expression. While he is correct in identifying the rise of such language and the ideals it represented (and its implications for national character), he dismisses the deep-seated beliefs and calls to action that were directly linked to such words.[35] However, historian Richard Beeman contends that patriotic action and legislation "were not a mere exercise in rhetoric."[36] Ethics were a driver of personal and political thought and action, not a tool for the rationalization of material interest or simply an overly dramatic metaphor. The Revolutionary ethos of honor, virtue, and ethics was not rhetorical; it was not intended to disguise economic motivation. As opposed to recent and often jaded trends aimed at debunking the founders, this book invites the reader to take the American Revolution and its participants' statements of moral purpose seriously. By examining the Revolutionary generation's words and thoughts as they intended and understood them, a new perspective on the creation of the American republic emerges.

Acknowledging the accuracy of the recent causation narratives, the central focus on the American elite is supplemented by the inclusion of middling and lower-class views and ethical understandings. It engages groups and individuals usually sidelined by studies of honor, such as African Americans and women, and shows that honor and virtue were not reserved only for white males. By discussing how this area has largely been ignored in the historiography, this project explores the prevalence of honor, virtue, and ethics within diverse groups.

The Revolution allowed for new ideas of honor and virtue to be instituted in society. These ethics fundamentally challenged their older conception, in which they were exclusively based on rank and status. While hierarchy did not vanish, the egalitarian shift in ethics suggests the opening of a social system in which honor and virtue were at least attainable—although not necessarily given outright. These ethical changes allowed for the greater possibility of an ascent through the ranks. More people were able to claim honor and virtue through service to the nation and the ideology of the Revolution, thereby making it difficult for these assertions to be ignored. In this respect, the term "American founders" refers to more than just the typical founding fathers; it denotes a collection of all of those individuals who thought ethically and contributed to the cause of the Revolution and the formation of the United States.

In the modern world, honor is often dismissed due to the violent, hierarchical, and oppressive aspects of honor culture, incorrectly viewed as honor itself. The ideals of honor and virtue discussed here are ones that were attainable across American society—perhaps not equally, but still representative of a democratic shift.

Because of the diversity of individualized ethical thought, it is exceedingly difficult to apply a singular theoretical model to this study. Sociologist Pierre Bourdieu's *Distinction* notes that cultural perceptions can bring about social mobility. However, he was looking at twentieth-century France, and other theorists would instead argue that you cannot apply universal theories to every time and place; for example, political scientists Patrick Chabal and Jean-Pascal Daloz insist on the connections between national culture and politics.[37] Also, unlike Eric Hobsbawm and Terrence Ranger's *Invention of Tradition*, which primarily centers on the postindustrial world, this book presents ethical interpretations of honor and virtue that predated the Revolution and thus cannot be simply used for "establishing or symbolizing social cohesion." While there is a certain "vague[ness]" and individualized meaning to honor and virtue, they lack the "compulsory" aspect of invented tradition.[38] Honor and virtue were paths to social mobility, not necessary elements of being American. Because of Anglo-American cultural similarities, it is possible to observe change in America, with Britain serving as a counterpoint.

Thus, national and cultural differentiation emerges from the sources themselves, rather than as an applied preexisting theoretical framework. Still, as this study is primarily situated in the late eighteenth century, the dawn of nationalism, there are parallels to Benedict Anderson's *Imagined Communities* in that in Revolutionary American cultural beliefs became grafted onto national ideals. As Anderson expressed, "Nation, nationality, nationalism—all have proved notoriously difficult to define, let alone analyze."[39] This same issue of the difficulty of definition also arises in relation to honor, virtue, and ethics.

In relation to the foregoing plan to study the founders' words and thoughts as they intended and understood them, the question of rhetoric needs to be addressed. On first glance, the constant invocation of the terms "honor" and "virtue" may appear suggestive of philosopher of language J. L. Austin's "performative utterances," which would reduce such usages to linguistic turns of phrase.[40] Naturally, certain individuals, such as Aaron Burr, employed the terms as rhetoric in order to advance their own purposes. However, mentions of honor and virtue were so pervasive in the writings and speeches of the Revolutionary era that it is difficult to dismiss all of the mentions as simply rhetoric—especially when an expression of these thoughts culminated in corresponding action. There is such a high volume of these references that they simply cannot be ignored or brushed aside. What happens if the founders' discussion of honor and virtue are not dismissed as symbolic, rhetorical, or figurative? Furthermore, Austin's theory doesn't account for ethical beliefs, since they cannot be definitively stated as true or false in his estimation. Far from suggesting the universalist views of anthropologists James George Frazer or Claude Lévi-Strauss, ethics are undoubtedly surrounded by murky depths of gray, but one would be hard pressed to find a culture without some form of an ethical basis. This book invites the reader to be open to taking the founders at their word (coupled with evidence, of course) and seeing how ethics played a role in the story of the Revolution.

The interconnection between the Revolution and ideological thought are also apparent in early American religious history. In the words of historian Thomas Kidd, religion during the Revolutionary era was a belief system that was "both diverse and thriving" and "not mere slogans."[41] Much like the changes to honor and virtue, eighteenth-century religious awakenings illustrated "a shift away from European theological traditions" and led to "the democratization of Christianity" by manifesting faith-based beliefs within "popular culture."[42] Within colonial America, the Great Awakening resulted in the formation of a powerful dissenting tradition positioned against an older order of thinking and belief. Dissenting religious figures, such as Jonathan Edwards, advanced a "new moral philosophy" akin to a concept of "universal morality" or a "common sense tradition," which, it was claimed, no "rational person" could dismiss. This new dissent, combined with broader Enlightenment thought, led to religion's direct intersection with honor and virtue from the colonial era into the antebellum era.[43] This book explores similar ideological transformations that show honor and virtue as being understood and accessible across societal boundaries. However, this inquiry focuses on the more expansive understanding of ethics, spurred by the Great Awakening's new moral philosophy, that allowed these terms to be understood apart from dogmatic theology while forming the core of a "civil religion" that arose in relation to the Revolution.[44] Still, this approach, like these religious studies, aims to show how thought (religious or moral) brought about tangible changes in society.

This work presupposes and builds on the vast societal acceptance of ethical principles in early America (although not universal in belief) and examines the tangible actions governed by them. In evaluating the ethicality of individual and national deeds, especially in regard to the limits of violence leading up to and during the Revolution, this book shares a great deal of communality with just war theory. Drawing on a diverse literature, ranging from theologians Saint Augustine and Thomas Aquinas to diplomat and philosopher Emer de Vattel, this work examines the belief that war and its combatants must be judged and limited by ethical principles.[45] As an eighteenth-century theorist, Vattel is especially important for looking at ethics during this time period. He concluded before the Revolution, "True glory . . . is acquired by virtue, or the qualities of the mind and the affections, and by the great actions that are fruit of these virtues."[46] Vattel understood honor, virtue, and glory as inherently linked through an ethical waging of warfare. Saying the words alone was not enough; actions spoke their value. As such, this work evaluates the ethics of the causes and consequences of the war through an intellectual lens that the founders would have understood. Thus, it examines the ethics of the causes and actions of the Revolution.

In addition to the ethical causes of the Revolution, *American Honor* addresses the following four interwoven questions.

How did honor and virtue evolve into ethics and change from the coming of the Revolution to the early republic? This issue is the focal point of the book. Recent work, such as Kwame Anthony Appiah's *The Honor Code: How Moral Revolutions Happen*, has noted that honor can spark change, but virtually no study has illustrated how honor and virtue themselves have changed over time or how they evolved into ethics.[47] For instance, by 1723, Benjamin Franklin had already started challenging European values with his concept of "ascending honor," which advanced merit and ethics over birth status.[48] Meanwhile, the life of George Washington follows an arc that is indicative of the development of American honor culture. His early years reveal a clear regard for and acceptance of British notions of honor, gentility, and social hierarchy that exalted birth, military valor, and social graces.[49] However, slights suffered at the hands of the British and the perceived tyranny of the king and Parliament resulted in a complete transformation of these traditional concepts into more egalitarian ones based on moral and ethical character. This work tracks the changes to honor and virtue in select individuals, and looks at these ideas throughout society as a whole. On the one hand, the conventional, British-based, eighteenth-century notions of honor stressed external rank and reputation—epitomized by Washington's early preoccupation with status. On the other hand are Jefferson's unique ideas about honor, which he described as centering on inner virtue based on ethical choices rather than public recognition. This inquiry shows how the standard ideals of honor and virtue were supplanted by a conception of ethics consistent with Jefferson's decidedly modern philosophy—societal acceptance alone was no longer the benchmark of honor or virtue. Honor and virtue did not consistently advance at the same pace during this time period. The evolution moved in a wavelike fashion that saw periods of dramatic transformation during the Revolution but usually was characterized by gradual change. In fact, some of the changes didn't hold for long but were reinterpreted by later generations and individuals.

How did regionalism affect ethical factors and differentiate honor and virtue within America? In order to explore the roots and variations of American honor and virtue, this book's regional focus emerges organically based on the founders' points of origin. Unlike in previous historians' works, this study will not concentrate primarily on the South; it will look at honor and virtue equally within the South, New England, and the middle colonies. These three regions provide a lens through which to assess ethical conduct from diverse socioeconomic, cultural, and religious parameters. In his groundbreaking work, *Southern Honor*, Bertram Wyatt-Brown argues that virtue and honor are inseparable; however, the New England–based John Adams asserted the supremacy of virtue.[50] Adding to the confusion is eighteenth-century author (and Franklin acquaintance) Bernard Mandeville's claim, "The Invention of Honour has been far more beneficial to the Civil Society than that of Virtue."[51] This work will illustrate the dramatic variances among the American conceptions of ethics.[52]

Rather than interpreting honor and virtue within these three regions as isolated entities, this project examines American ethics as a whole. In order to accomplish this goal, each region is examined through a core sampling of localized individuals. This shows individuated thought processes and removes the rigidness of a strict adherence to a regional model. This approach hopefully provides the reader with a personal and narrative ethical view while simultaneously removing a great deal of the inherent confrontation and awkwardness that arise when simply comparing the Northern and Southern colonies. Honor and virtue historically and historiographically become a way to unite diverse regions under a common ethical framework.

To what extent was the American Revolution an ethical clash over matters of honor and virtue? Honor in America changed from a distinctly British concept into something that was more ethically centered as a nascent proto-nationalism developed in the new United States. This book contends that the patriots viewed the American Revolution as a matter of honor and a test of virtue caused by a British ethical failing. Patriots felt that British policy had attacked their honor, and they were forced to react. America would win or lose based on its ability to maintain its virtue. The Revolution, in turn, influenced dynamic societal and ethical change; as Continental-congressman-turned-historian David Ramsay recorded, "It called forth many virtues, and gave occasion for the display of abilities which, but for that event, would have been lost to the world."[53] The war created both the need and opportunity for broad sections of the American people to band together with a shared ideology. Thus, the Revolution and its ethical changes are not an example of American exceptionalism but rather an exceptional moment in history.

How were honor, virtue, and ethics collectivized and nationalized, and how did their understandings influence American society, government, and policy? How did Americans come together based on their ethical thinking? What were the roles of personal experience, literature, schools, organizations, and occupations? How did a colonial collectivization of ethical thinking in turn lead to revolution and nationalization? Personal honor gave way to national honor, in the sense of duty to the greater good. Thus, during the Revolution, we also see a democratization of honor influenced by military necessity and the defense of the home front. But can one still maintain personal honor while espousing the honor of the nation as paramount? What happens if personal and national honor conflict? Washington held the nation's honor above his own, but how did other individuals and organizations, such as the Society of the Cincinnati, navigate the gray area between personal and collective honor? The theme that generally emerges is an exaltation of national honor, but one with varying definitions and ethics behind individual understandings—how an Alexander Hamilton differs from a Thomas Jefferson.[54]

American Honor traces honor chronologically, geographically, and personally. By employing a braided narrative that features storytelling and academic analysis, this work sheds new light on how honor contributed to the foundation of the American republic. Other works have discussed the significance of honor regionally or with regard to certain individuals, events, or other parameters, but never following a clear, advancing trajectory through both time and space; this book does just that, thereby showing a change in the conception of honor, from one that purely pertains to rank and reputation to one that concerns a more modern sense of moral rightness.[55]

Methodologically, this study primarily involves a chronological examination of the founders' private and public papers from the early eighteenth century through the early nineteenth century. As stated previously, the narrative and research revolve around Adams, Franklin, Jefferson, and Washington because they had extensive societal impact, their papers have great depth and breadth, and they are representative of different regions. Other individuals from various races, classes, and genders also emerge, but it is usually more difficult to consistently track change in the same way. Wherever possible, the ethical ideals throughout a person's entire life were investigated to note progression and avoid taking a quotation out of context. This results in a form of collective biography and an accurate representation of individual change. Seizing on the recent digitization of many prominent figures' papers, it was possible to read virtually every written mention they made of honor, virtue, and ethics. Using traditional archival research and new digital techniques, including keyword searches and Google Ngrams, the usage of the words "honor," "virtue," and "ethics" (and related words such as "right," "good," "moral," "duty," "valor," "reputation," and so on) was traced during the long eighteenth century. At times the founders do not actually use the words "honor" or "virtue" but instead use synonyms that express the same ethical principles. In no way is this problematic to the narrative; instead, it offers an opportunity to look at the extensive nature of American ethical thought. These techniques allowed for the uncovering of changing perceptions in America, in contrast to the more static ones that were present in Britain. Thus, the progression of honor and virtue discussed within this book is a representation of personal and cultural transformation.

As the founders' words alone cannot reveal everything central to their ethics, this book also uses interdisciplinary sources, such as novels, moral and religious texts, college records, governmental debates, and so on, to show the expansive impact of ethical ideals on society. Naturally, their ideals didn't just happen, and, thus, equally important are the factors that helped to form their ethical mind-sets. As Anderson states, "The printer's office emerged as the key to North American communications and community intellectual life."[56] Furthermore, literary historian David S. Shields has asserted that books had "an influence as broad as Britain's empire of the seas."[57] These changes were not class specific. Literary scholar Michael McKeon concludes that through novels, "the predominate meaning of the word 'honor' as a term of denotation shifts from 'titles of rank' to 'goodness of character.'"[58] Meanwhile, in 1748's *Principles of Natural and Politic Law*, Swiss political philosopher Jean-Jacques Burlamaqui connected "honour" with "conscience," illustrating a further link with ethical concepts.[59] In this respect, period books and other printed materials are essential sources and an effective gauge of ideas, learning, and culture. These sources and their discussions of honor and virtue were not arbitrary selections but rather reflect research into texts that the patriots actually owned and read (often in the same edition). While it is impossible to know with certainty the influences on a person's mind, the focus on printed materials that can be connected with certain individuals and society (usually based on their popularity) offers the most potential to fill in evidentiary gaps. Other influencers, from individuals to schools, are analyzed in much the same way. How did the beliefs of a parent, teacher, or family member alter an individual's perception? Discovering the mixture of ideas that circle the founders was essential and fruitful, as there are direct correlations among these influencers, their lives, and their deeds.

Applying the same lens beyond these four individuals, this book also looks at ethics among the lower classes, women, and African Americans. As these groups often lacked the scale of the elite's writings, it is more difficult to track the progression of ideas. Instead, it involved first searching for a baseline of what was considered honorable and virtuous within the groups, then looking for individual examples to help narrate the story. But after in-depth research, these cases conformed, much like the other founders', with a belief in the righteousness of the Revolution and the possibility for advancement through service.

Finally, this book reinvestigates the key documents associated with the American Revolution and early republic. As questions of causation have waned, fresh eyes on an old question were used to discern this ethical pattern that has hidden in plain sight. As a result, the seven chapters unfold chronologically, examining the ethical history of early America before, during, and after the Revolution. Still, the most complicated aspect of the project remained defining honor and virtue—a process that has been challenging scholars for centuries.

In early America, there were no universal definitions of honor and virtue. The greatest difficulty in studying these concepts stems from the debate surrounding the meaning of the terms, due to the great diversity in thought and practice. Historian Kenneth Greenberg has called the study of honor "a work of translation . . . a reconstruction and interpretation of a 'dead' language," but one that "cannot be accomplished in dictionary form, since dictionaries usually reduce context: they isolate words and connect them to other isolated words."[60] In 1754, Cambridge professor Rev. Thomas Rutherford expressed the same lamentation about the word "honor": "It is no easy undertaking to explane a word, which is used by all men very unsteadily, and by most without any meaning at all."[61] Even fictional characters entered the debate, with Richardson's Pamela challenging her male antagonist, Mr. B, "I too much apprehend, that *your* Notions of Honour and *mine* are very different from one another."[62]

While most sources agree that virtue is directly related to morality or ethics, there is similar conflict over the subtle nuances of the meaning of "true" virtue. As historian Christopher Grasso has stated, " 'Virtue' was everywhere in the political talk and writing of the 1770s, though historians have disagreed about what it all meant."[63] At nearly the same time, authors Mandeville and Alexander Pope came to similar opinions with distinctly opposite conclusions. In 1732, Mandeville stated, "Honour owes its Birth" to "Passion" and was a form of "Self-liking."[64] The next year, Pope argued that "the surest virtues thus from passions shoot" and linked them with "self-love."[65] Was human emotion the foundation of honor and virtue? In his posthumous 1765 publication, *An Essay on the Nature of True Virtue*, Great Awakening preacher Jonathan Edwards addressed this issue on the "controversies and variety of opinions . . . about the nature of Virtue" and worried over "an inconsistence in some writers on morality," particularly regarding the debate over its religious or secular origins.[66] Historically, individuals frequently bandied about claims of "true" and "false" honor, which further complicated the connection with "true" virtue. Honor's and virtue's definitions were never static, as they constantly evolved based on individual and societal understandings.[67]

Over two centuries later, historian Wyatt-Brown contributed the most to untangling these concepts in 1982, while acknowledging the "many meanings that the word 'honor' has been given." For Wyatt-Brown, honor could essentially be boiled down to a "moral code," one intimately tied to "the evaluation of the public," "self-worth," "public morals," "respect," and "social order." But Wyatt-Brown also struggled with providing a singular, solid definition and instead turned to period literature and sources to piece together his understanding.[68]

When relying on a similar technique of investigating period writings and publications, different versions of honor and virtue arise. Regional, religious, and societal variants have historically influenced the definitions. To this point, the 1761 *Essay on the Art of War* explains that "Honour is a vague Expression, to which Custom has given different Meanings."[69] Honor was ever changing, as it varied based on time and place. Meanwhile, virtue has traditionally been understood as morality and often been linked to religion, while honor is typically seen as more secular and a judge or guide of a person's conduct. Historical sources reveal over and over that the terms are very closely related. Honor was often considered to be the reward of virtue, but dissension still exists. Adding to the confusion, during the American colonial, Revolutionary, and early republican eras, "honor" and "virtue" were often used interchangeably as two words representing the same ethical ideal. Even the term "ethics" was open to interpretation; moral philosopher Adam Smith concluded that morality was equal to ethics but still "does not admit of the most accurate precession," despite still being "highly useful and agreeable."[70] Even on the eve of the Revolution, the *Virginia Gazette* called ethics a "plaguy [troublesome] hard word."[71]

Honor, virtue, and ethics are ancient concepts; in his *Nicomachean Ethics*, the classical Greek philosopher Aristotle asserted that honor was bestowed by others and was linked with pride, while virtue was excellence.[72] But the Aristotelian definitions did not hold, for, as John Adams complained, ethics was "a field too vast," and many alternatives existed.[73] The *Pennsylvania Herald* explained that "no sooner had Sir Richard Steele [one of the founders of the *Spectator*, a prominent gentlemen's magazine that paid particular attention to morals] given the example at the beginning of this century, than ethics, philosophy, and politics, were reduced into the pithy form of periodical essays."[74] Although classical texts were available throughout the Atlantic World, early Americans were more apt to look to contemporary authors. It was through diverse, largely Anglo-American, literary and societal understandings that they came to evaluate honor and virtue by the same criteria as moral philosophy, ethics, and proper conduct. In this respect, changes to honor and virtue could have transpired in Britain, but the unique moment of the

Revolution sparked an American cultural shift.[75] Democratized honor and virtue are not inherently American, but they were a product and a cause of the American Revolution.

The changing understanding of honor and virtue occurred gradually throughout the eighteenth century, and it was accelerated during the Revolutionary era, by which time they could be considered the same as modern ethics.[76] The pervasiveness of this theory is strongly suggested by the fact that the first American dictionary, produced by the Connecticut-born Samuel Johnson Jr. in the late eighteenth century, contains no formal entry for either "honor" or "virtue" but instead uses these terms to define other words.[77] Early Americans already comprehended these terms, but the definitions of "honor" and "virtue" were in constant motion.

From the early eighteenth through the nineteenth century, "ethics" was a seldom-used word in America. Still, its definitions illustrate a near-identical similarity to those of "honor" and "virtue." Ethics could be "moral philosophy," "a system of morality," or simply anything "moral" or even "relating to manners or morals." But despite this transition, "honor" and "virtue" often were used as representative of the same ideals. Period dictionaries only added to this confusion, with virtue even assuming martial characteristics, such as "bravery" and "valour," in addition to its general moral constructs. Conversely, "honor" became defined in accordance with traditional interpretations of "virtue," such as "moral rectitude."

Illustrating the development between the early and mid-eighteenth century, Nathan Bailey's *Universal Etymological English Dictionary* labeled "honour" simply as "reputation," but Thomas Dyche's *New General English Dictionary* described "honour" as being "commonly joined with virtue." Virtue, as mentioned previously, was usually tied with morality, but it also increasingly came to be understood as proving "advantageous to society in general," basically a conception of the greater good. In fact, by 1800, a miniature edition of Dr. Samuel Johnson's dictionary simply defined "honour" as "virtue," while in 1828 Noah Webster concluded that "honor" was "any particular virtue much valued."[78]

Because concepts of honor and virtue have consistently changed and been understood in a variety of ways throughout American history, it is exceedingly difficult to offer a brief, historically accurate definition. Drawing on the many praiseworthy studies of honor that have been written, particularly over the past four decades, honor does not have a singular definition; rather, its meaning is united around central points. Numerous scholars have advanced varied perceptions and manifestations of honor that are all fundamentally correct. Historians Wyatt-Brown's and Joanne Freeman's versions were "primal" and centered on revenge and shame; others, such as historian Caroline Cox, cast the ideas as those of rank and status. The value and accuracy of their work are undisputed, and each presents a different component of the historical conceptions of honor. In turn, this inquiry presents honor and virtue as ethical concepts of right conduct and moral action. Much like the Revolutionary causation narrative, this approach functions not as an alternative to its predecessors but as an addition to them. The placement of this book alongside others is meant to offer a fuller picture of honor in America, not to contradict the existing literature.

Despite the inherent difficulty of defining these ethics, for the sake of clarity, the terms discussed usually conform to the following definitions. Honor, in its most basic form, is understood as right conduct, but what is understood as being "right" varies greatly based on the individual's ethical and cultural beliefs. Thus, there can be a great degree of variance. Personal honor, by far the most recognizable form, conforms to Wyatt-Brown's, Freeman's, and Cox's models and is understood as reputation based on an individual's proper or right conduct. Collective honor, on the community or organizational level, or national honor, when viewed in light of the country as a whole, are virtually synonymous with personal honor, just manifested on a wider scale. Collective and national honor are a reflection of the actions of an individual, the citizenry, or the government on that person's or entity's reputation. For one to advance the principle of national honor over personal honor means that the individual is more concerned with the welfare of the nation than his or her own standing. This does not mean that personal honor and national honor did not exist at the same time, but there was an expectation that the personal had to be secondary to the collective good.

More specifically, "democratized honor" or "egalitarian honor" refers to the recognition that anyone on the social ladder can possess honor, consistent with their status, actions, service, and morality, usually in relation to support of the Revolution or the new nation. It is reflective of the emergence of other classes into prominence during the early republic. The use of the words "democratized" and "egalitarian" does not mean that rank and class distinctions vanished; it instead illustrates the potential for social mobility. Throughout this text, such a dynamic may occasionally be referred to as the "Americanization" of honor, but again it is not indicative of American exceptionalism.

Certainly, war (and revolution) has consistently allowed for a degree of societal ascent, and, thus, similar changes could and did occur elsewhere.

European writers and political theorists reflected on the possibility of advancements in honor and social mobility, as shall be discussed in relation to the American Revolution. The French Revolution also engaged with hierarchy and ethics, as did the British arming of the citizenry in response to Napoleon, which illustrated that patriotism "could *for a time* smoothe over social divisions." Yet France descended into terror, empire, and a return to monarchy; and Britain, although altering the viewpoints of the lower classes for the purposes of national defense, still raised soldiers who "abhor republican tyranny."[79] In many ways, the old order in Europe, even if altered, still remained, while America was the first to enact and retain changes in social hierarchy based on ethics.

Thus, "Americanized honor" is used as a term to differentiate it from the hierarchical European conceptions. For, as French-officer-turned-American-farmer John Hector St. John de Crèvecœur wrote, after observing the Revolutionary era, even an "enlightened Englishman" who visited the New World would "take some time ere [before] he can reconcile himself to our dictionary, which is but short in words of dignity, and names of honour." Europeans recognized honor across the Atlantic as something different. As St. John de Crèvecœur further contended, Americans were "strangers to the honours of monarchy" and lacked a devotion to "vain luxuries," "sounding titles," and "frivolous names!"[80] Virtue, on the whole, is much more straightforward than honor. It was predominantly the same as morality, but it was often connected with religion, varying regionally.[81] Overall, honor and virtue are best understood as ethics.

A good general rule in colonial America is that the farther north one travels, the greater the separation between honor and virtue (with virtue taking prominence, usually due to religion); the farther south you look, the reverse is true, with honor and virtue becoming essentially synonymous. However, as this book shows, the American Revolution played a vital role in linking these terms across the nation, changing people's perceptions, and exposing them to a more national consciousness, thus making the previous rule obsolete.

Despite the usefulness of a concise definition, honor and virtue continually seem to defy specific categorization. In fact, throughout their history in America, these ethical concepts are much more akin to Alexis de Tocqueville's notion of "the habits of the heart." Examining the interplay between American customs and democracy, in *Democracy in America*, the Frenchman applied the term "habits of the heart" "to the various notions and opinions current among men and to the mass of those ideas which constitute their character of mind. I comprise under this term, therefore, the whole moral and intellectual condition of a people." Honor and virtue exist in much the same way; they are an ever-changing matter of morals and ethical thought. Tocqueville concluded that these "habits of the heart" were "favorable to the maintenance of [American] political institutions"—so too are honor and virtue.[82]

The Revolution was a matter of hearts and minds. As John Adams reminisced to Thomas Jefferson, "The Revolution was in the Minds of the People, and this was effected, from 1760 to 1775, in the course of fifteen years before a drop of blood was drawn at Lexington."[83] For Adams, the Revolution was at its core an intellectual movement; the war was simply a tangible representation of internal changes that had already occurred. Coinciding with this evaluation, the transformation of honor and virtue into ethics in America also began before the outbreak of fighting against Great Britain. These new ideals served as a galvanizing force, uniting the colonies in a shared moral and intellectual vision. Just as Adams said, the war was conducted with a clear regard to thought, led by these new ethical principles, while the early republican years represented their formal instillation into a fundamentally new government and society. Even before independence, patriot Arthur Lee proudly declared, "We consider ourselves as bound in honour . . . to share one general fate with our sister colonies, and should hold ourselves base deserters of that union to which we have acceded, were we to agree on any measures distinct and apart from them."[84] A democratized understanding of honor and virtue based on merit, morality, and service to the cause united the American people. What followed was a matter of ethical thought spurring revolutionary action.

CHAPTER ONE

The Old World Meets the New

Colonial Ethical Ideals before the Revolution

In the idyllic French village of Passy, a short distance from Paris and a stopping point en route to the royal splendor of Versailles, a seventy-eight-year-old Benjamin Franklin sat within the palatial Hotel de Valentinois. He had been a nonpaying resident of "le petit hôtel," as a guest of Donatien le Rey de Chaumont (a friend of King Louis XVI), for all nine years of his diplomatic stay in France; it was a mission that culminated in his successful negotiation of the Treaty of Paris, which ended the American Revolution and legitimized the United States of America. From his terrace, the manicured, tree-lined gardens beckoned, but the January cold likely kept the elder diplomat comfortably inside. It was now 1784, only four months after the official conclusion of a war that had ravaged his native country. One could excuse the oldest American statesman a moment of respite to watch, from his room situated high atop a grass-lined hill, the shimmering waters of the Seine as it flowed past the Ile de Cygnes. A low-lying, single-tiered fence framed the scene, as if captured by an artist's brush. But inside, Franklin did not meander as the river did—inside he wrote.[1] As Franklin's quill scratched out a reply to his first-born daughter, Sarah Bache, his words revealed a fundamental shift not only in the progression of his own life but in the perception of his country as a whole.

Franklin wrote, "For Honour worthily obtain'd . . . is in its Nature a personal Thing, and incommunicable to any but those who had some Share in obtaining it. . . . Honour does not *descend* but *ascends*. . . . His Parents are immediately intitled to all the same Ceremonies of Respect from the People."[2] In only a few lines, Franklin had reversed the traditional European, largely British, perception of the importance of honor through lineage and status. This was by no means a sudden shift or dramatic conversion; rather, it was indicative of a change in the notions of honor and virtue over time both in Franklin's personal life and in post-Revolution America. These words reveal a sense of egalitarianism within the honor code that was quite novel, and they are symbolic of the evolution of Franklin and a nation. Honor was now the product of an individual's actions, not one's birth status.

Fifteen years later and an ocean away, storms of snow, ice, and hail rocked the estate of Mount Vernon.[3] George Washington lay dying in his bed, his body tortured by the pain of infection, yet, fully awake, he sensed his fate. His loving wife, Martha; his physicians; and several slaves were by his side. Steadily losing control of his body, he uttered one of his last commands—for the comfort of a slave. Washington, the man who defined America in the eighteenth century, would not live to see the nineteenth. But how is it that a Virginia slaveholder's final thoughts were directed to the care of a slave, a person legally considered property? The answer: his honor.

Two very different men, from even more disparate backgrounds, shared a joint belief in the importance and value of honor and virtue in daily life and government. Although bred in different regional and economic locales, Washington's and Franklin's developmental paths from youth to adulthood bear strikingly similar patterns that reflect the ideas of honor held within the British Empire. They both came of age in, and accepted, the hierarchical world they were born into and sought to navigate it by advancing through the acquisition of honor and virtue. Each man approached this task with a different perspective. Franklin was born, raised, and grew to prominence in the Northern colonies, and his sensibilities reflect this location. He sought out virtue as the highest goal a man could achieve and used it as the central means to advance in the world. The Southerner Washington was immersed in an honor culture that viewed virtue and honor as fundamentally the same ideal. But, by the outbreak of the American Revolution, they both believed in and exemplified a stark new version of democratized honor and virtue—one open to all Americans. Through a combination of social interaction, literature, and life experience, Washington and Franklin developed in similar ways. Ideals shared during their youth transformed again to find continued common ground in their later years.

In many respects, Franklin would come to resemble the self-made man of traditional American folklore. He was born in Boston on January 17, 1706, as (he would later record in his *Autobiography*) "the youngest Son of the youngest Son for 5 Generations back," during a time in which birth order and inherited honor could pave the way for advancement or cast one down toward a comparatively lowly existence.[4] His father, a candle- and soap-maker, could only afford to provide Franklin with two years of formal education. Franklin's real learning came from whatever book he could get his hands on. It was through the cultivation of his youthful "Bookish Inclination" that he was consistently exposed to lessons and examples of honor and virtue.[5]

Franklin was not unique in adopting the various authors of the printed word as his mentors. This motif was common in colonial America, especially in New England, where roughly three-quarters of the population could read, and it helped fill the gaps left by little to no formal schooling. As a relatively poor boy who spent virtually every sum he possessed on a modest collection of books (and borrowed when he lacked the funds), Franklin cherished books, and their influence on him was unmistakable.

In Puritan-dominated Boston, many of Franklin's first experiences with honor and virtue were unsurprisingly from a religious perspective. Since the days of founder John Winthrop, Boston's notion of honor was consistent with a "condition of Christian sanctification" invested in a man of "Learning, Breeding, and Virtue."[6] Honor was subservient to religious virtue, consistent with one's birth and education. From John Bunyan's *Pilgrim's Progress*, Franklin was taught that "a man may cry out against sin, of policy; but he cannot abhor it but by virtue of a godly antipathy against it. I have heard many cry out against sin in the pulpit, who yet can abide it well enough in the heart, house, and conversation."[7] In order to preserve virtue, the young Franklin was instructed to be a man of action rather than of words. It was not enough to state a belief in virtue; one had to live a virtuous life and be the enemy of vice. Many of the religious-oriented texts offered Jesus Christ as the perfect example of "a person of honour."[8] Franklin found Bunyan's themes of honor and virtue to be echoed, in discussion of Jesus's words and deeds, by Boston's own Cotton Mather, a minister from a prominent local family, who asserted that Jesus made the performance of good works "honourable" and that "without Christ all virtue is but vice."[9] In Puritan New England, the conventional belief held that honor and virtue were inseparable from Christianity. While Franklin was born a Congregationalist, he was a deist at best, as his later life does not show any favorable opinion of organized religion. But he still continued to hold a belief in God and in the value of religions for "their contributions to virtue or morality."[10] Thus, Mather's emphasis on the necessity of an "education" based on "the principles of *reason* and *honour*" certainly took hold in the young Bostonian.[11]

In addition to the looming presence of New England Puritanism, Franklin grew up in a hierarchical world in which birth, parentage, and status were crucial in deciding an individual's ability to even claim notions of honor and virtue, let alone a reputation for them. While a great deal of Boston society and available literature reinforced these principles, Franklin undoubtedly embraced works that offered any alternative to birth as a means to personal advancement.[12] Years later, Franklin recalled fondly the influence of one such book, Plutarch's *Lives*, "which I read abundantly, and I still think that time spent to great Advantage."[13] Plutarch's *Lives* is a collective history and biography of the prominent figures of ancient Greece and Rome, a subject that was all the rage in eighteenth-century Anglo-American society. Through tales of Alexander the Great, Cato, Pompey, and others, Franklin was introduced to the classical understanding of virtue. While the text certainly contains traditional concepts of hierarchy, more inclusive ideas would have undoubtedly attracted the interest of the lower-class Franklin.[14] Contained within the tale of King Agesilaus II of Sparta is an ancient account of the elevation of "persons of worth and virtue, but miserably poor," to high status, regardless of wealth and instead based on internal qualities. Moreover, "this popular act gained general good-will and reputation" for Agesilaus.[15] Here was a model Franklin could aspire to; virtue and its usual companion, honor, could overcome his birth and provide the path for him to follow while making his way in the British Empire. Within Plutarch's writings, he found the classical basis for his ascent in society. Certainly these ancient heroes provided an archetypal example, but the question remained, how could Franklin acquire honor and virtue himself?

Unsurprisingly, the answer came in the form of literature. But this time, the authors were of a more contemporary lineage. In his teenage years, Franklin first became acquainted with the British gentlemen's magazine the *Spectator*, published by Joseph Addison and Richard Steele. This eight-volume collection of over six hundred essays educated the literate of all classes in virtue, honor, and the more fashionable aspects of society.[16] Franklin became "delighted" by the *Spectator* and "wish'd if possible to imitate it."[17] In his spare moments each morning and night, he would devise exercises to mimic its writing and tone, all the while consciously and unconsciously absorbing Addison's views on honor and virtue.

Much like Plutarch's, Addison's writing reinforced traditional ideas of honor and virtue, coupled with critiques on the restrictiveness of society. Contained within volume 3 alone, the first volume young Franklin discovered, are blatant references to a more egalitarian notion of honor and virtue. The *Spectator* remarks, "In the Founders of great Families, such Attributes of Honour are generally correspondent with the Virtues of that Person to whom they are applied; but in the Descendants they are too often the Marks rather of Grandeur than of Merit."[18] Addison's language is rather pointed in that it traditionally regards the aristocracy and gentry as being created by men of honor and virtue, but he is dismissive of the idea of these characteristics descending to their progeny simply based on birth. Instead, he favors the acquisition of honor and virtue based on personal experience, merit, and quality. Addison insists that "both in great and ordinary Affairs, all Superiority which is not founded on Merit and Virtue, is supported only by Artifice and Stratagem."[19]

The virtuous actions of the individual alone could make them esteemed as honorable, not the deeds of their parents. Honor was simply the public validation of a virtuous life. From the *Spectator*, as from Plutarch's *Lives*, Franklin developed an understanding of virtue as the highest goal, even above honor.[20] In Franklin's mind, honor could be gained only through virtue. Amid his fervent candlelight scribbling, the young printer's apprentice was unlikely to have missed an idea that provided him with the inspiration and means to advance himself in the British world.

Throughout his life, Franklin strove to measure up to the ideas of virtue espoused by Addison. But, because of his low birth, his views on virtue tended to favor a bit more egalitarianism than was common in British society. He looked on virtue as his means to enter the upper strata of society and gain honor. Still, he seems to have harbored a bit of class resentment in his early years, which would subside as he grew in stature—ultimately remerging with a vengeance on the eve of the Revolution.

In 1722, as his older brother, printer, and boss, James, satirized Boston society by cloning the style of Addison and Steele in his newspaper, the *New-England Courant*, Franklin entered the fray in the guise of a middle-aged widow named Silence Dogood.[21] Purposefully borrowing the name from Mather's *Essays to Do Good*, a sixteen-year-old Franklin went on to reveal his sentiments on honor and virtue and their proper methods of acquisition and cultivation. This series of letters begins with a simple introduction, which reveals that Franklin both understood the circle of honor and wished to be accepted into it. Franklin "observed, that the Generality of People . . . are unwilling either to commend or dispraise what they read, until they are in some measure informed who or what the Author of it is, whether he be *poor* or *rich, old* or *young,* a *Scholar* or a *Leather Apron Man,* &c."[22] Even in an anonymous letter, Franklin's style shows a carefully contrived word choice that implies an acceptance of the implicit nature of reputation and status. Franklin extended his opening parley with an even more pointed statement: "I shall conclude this with my own Character, which (one would think) I should be best able to give. *Know then,* That I am an Enemy to Vice, and a Friend to Vertue."[23] This line reflects Franklin's understanding of the importance of reputation, for how could one be believed if he or she were not virtuous?

Despite his acceptance of the basic principles of honor and virtue, Franklin advanced a clear disregard for gaining them through any measures but one's own merit and actions. As Dogood (a character that he also later used for his first written mention of "Ethicks"), Franklin was dismissive of the true worth of a formal education, and he quickly took aim at Harvard College. He declared that a college education was built on parents' "own Purses instead of their Childrens [*sic*] Capacities," which resulted in students who "were little better than Dunces and Blockheads." There was certainly a twinge of jealousy in Franklin's words, as he saw men without distinction or character being raised up only by wealth. Still, Franklin viewed a college education as essentially lacking, concluding that the only thing graduates learned was "how to carry themselves handsomely, and enter a Room genteely," and how to be "more proud and self-conceited."[24] Franklin opposed the external qualities of gentility in favor of the internal ethic of virtue, which he found absent at Harvard. Literature appeared to be the most direct and formative way for people of different stations to gain self-improvement and the instillment of ideas of honor and virtue. And so Franklin used his brother's newspaper as an educational exercise for himself and the rest of society.

Franklin continued to be caught between his quest for reputation and his lowly birth and occupation. Still, as early as 1723, adolescent signs of Franklin's 1784 thinking on honor and virtue are visible. In a *New-England Courant* article entitled "On Titles of Honour," Franklin, in the form of a fictional debate held within a gentlemen's club, first asserts that "*Honour* . . . properly ascends, and not descends." As mentioned previously, this is a radical departure from a British system that stressed birth and hierarchy above all, but here Franklin is not only speaking of birth. His use of the words "ascends" and "descends" is not just reserved for parentage but rather pertains as well to the type of honor. The terms themselves point to Franklin's mind-set. Ascending honor is an elevated principle, something inherently noble, while descending honor is earthbound and fundamentally tied to human self-interest. Franklin mocks the emulation of "hat honor," a common term that referenced doffing one's hat (or gentility), which stresses etiquette and manners over ideals. In a rather farcical rationale, he states, "There can be no Honour in it. Besides, Honour was from the *Beginning*, but Hats are an Invention of a *late Time*, and consequently true Honour standeth not therein." Despite the obvious satirical nature of his statement, it does touch on a deeper truth—hat honor, or gentility, and its trappings are a creation of man. Therefore, for Franklin, true honor was something loftier, something that ascends—an internal ethic of virtue.[25]

Franklin was clearly uncomfortable with the eighteenth-century aristocratic and religious titles bestowed on those who, in his view, lacked inner virtue. This was reminiscent of a lesson he first learned in the *Spectator*, which stated, "As Virtue is the most reasonable and genuine Source of Honour, we generally find in Titles an Intimation of some particular Merit that should recommend Men to the high Stations which they possess."[26] Titles should be an external manifestation of internal qualities; without a regard for honor and virtue in one's deeds, the title was hollow. Echoing the words of Addison, Franklin remarked on inner virtue's holding more importance than titular status when he claimed "that tho' Abraham was not styl'd *Right Honourable*, yet he had the Title of *Lord* given him by his Wife Sarah, which he thinks entitles her to the Honour of *My Lady* Sarah."[27] Franklin was not dismissive of aristocratic titles; rather, he felt that they were granted too liberally to the less worthy.

As Franklin's notoriety increased in Boston due to his literary accomplishments, it also contributed to the worsening of his relationship with his brother—never the best to begin with—and, within the city's religious establishment, his rise prompted joint accusations against him of vanity and atheism.[28] And so the seventeen-year-old left the city of his birth, running away from his apprenticeship, for Philadelphia in order to raise himself "from the Poverty & Obscurity in which I was born & bred, to a State of Affluence & some Degree of Reputation in the World."[29] With dreams of grandeur, a travel-weary, hungry, and filthy Franklin, humbly attired in his "Working Dress," arrived in Philadelphia. He had next to no money in his pockets and he "knew no Soul," he would later reminisce.[30] But before long, Franklin would advance in the world through the patronage of more established men.

Unfortunately, the runaway apprentice carried with him no letters of recommendation or introduction, which were both a courtesy and a crucial gateway into a city's business and polite society.[31] Such letters, written to officials, clergymen, and prominent gentlemen, were commonplace throughout the eighteenth century. They vouched for a person's reputation and merit and helped establish personal connections that could make or break any hope of advancement. The absence of any established connections forced Franklin to be self-reliant in forging a reputation based on his own character. Luckily, he was not lacking in this regard. Franklin ultimately gained employment at Samuel Keimer's print shop (Keimer also acquired him lodging through John Read, his future father-in-law) through equal parts his own qualifications and recommendations forged from newly made relationships with father and son printers William (of New York) and Alexander Bradford (of Philadelphia).

As in Boston, it would be Franklin's literary skill that first gained him the notice of prominent men. A chance encounter between Franklin's brother-in-law, ship captain Robert Holmes, and Sir William Keith, lieutenant governor of Pennsylvania, exposed the governor to one of Franklin's letters. He marveled at its prose, was "surpriz'd when he was told [Franklin's] Age," and declared that Franklin "appear'd a young Man of promising Parts, and therefore should be encouraged." Franklin stated, "For his Part, he would procure me the publick Business, and do me every other Service in his Power."[32] Before long the governor was paying social calls on Franklin and offering patronage "with a Condescension and Politeness I had been quite unus'd to."[33] Franklin considered this practice to be a mark of "the *true Gentleman*, who is well known to be such, can take a Walk, or drink a Glass, and converse freely . . . with any honest Men of any Degree below him, without degrading or fearing to degrade himself in the least."[34] Franklin believed that one should be able to interact with all classes. Although the governor's promises were never fully realized, Franklin was soon strutting about in a "genteel new Suit from Head to foot, a Watch, and my Pockets lin'd with near Five Pounds Sterling in Silver," and conversing with prominent men such as New York governor William Burnet and Cotton Mather.[35]

Shortly thereafter, Franklin set sail for London to procure the necessary tools to start his own printing business. It was there that he felt his first slight at the hands of the British government. Keith, who had promised to supply Franklin with a letter of credit, reneged on the arrangement, leaving Franklin despondently stating, "But what shall we think of a Governor's playing such pitiful Tricks, and imposing so grossly on a poor ignorant Boy!"[36] It was a hard lesson to learn, but one that did not sour him on the advantages that could be gained through patronage or the British system, unlike many other future patriots. Although Franklin was in London during "an age of luxury, fashion, and wit" in which the city's residents boasted Isaac Newton, Lord Chesterfield, Voltaire, Henry Fielding, Daniel Defoe, and Samuel Richardson, historian Carl Van Doren remarks that he "was little closer to it at first hand than if he had been in Boston or Philadelphia."[37]

As in America, Franklin's exposure to honor and virtue would be only in literature, not in formal interaction with the elites of British society. His knowledge of the pleasures of the big city would be gained from experience, and from them he came to conclude that "from the Attributes of God . . . nothing could possibly be wrong in the World, and that Vice and Virtue were empty Distinctions, no such Things existing."[38] Franklin would not be the first, or the last, young man to make such a claim (or at least wish for it to be true), but we do see a certain distinction even in the 1720s between British conceptions of virtue and the more intellectual perceptions held in America.

After his return to Philadelphia, Franklin continued to receive patronage from prominent citizens, such as merchants Thomas Denham, William

Allen, and lawyer Andrew Hamilton, although none as eminent as a governor. This custom of British hierarchy remained of use to Franklin, so he readily accepted it, and it helped to establish him as a prominent Philadelphia printer. However, his understanding of virtue seems to have reverted back to a less rakish interpretation, as he wrote that his former view was "not so clever a Performance as I once thought it." He came away from London with a heightened sensitivity to morality and virtue, likely brought on by sinner's remorse due to an excessive indulgence in London's wine and women. Franklin "grew convinc'd that *Truth, Sincerity and Integrity* in Dealings between Man and Man, were of the utmost Importance to the Felicity of Life" and vowed "to practice them ever while I lived." He now viewed virtue and morality as consistent with the greater good, rather than as religious doctrine, as "Actions might not be bad *because* they were forbidden by it, or good *because* it commanded them; yet probably those Actions might be forbidden *because* they were bad for us, or commanded *because* they were beneficial to us."[39] Dogmatic religious principles alone were not the determination of what was ethical; for Franklin, only an action's positive or negative impact on society determined its morality.

Franklin was a man who both influenced and was influenced by his surroundings. In some ways he reflected the nature of the community he lived in, exalting virtue in Puritan Boston and Quaker Philadelphia, while appearing more hedonistic in London. Franklin clearly held some higher ethic, but his environment during his youth played a profound role. Though Franklin was not overtly religious, still, in part due to the constant presence of Puritan ethics in Boston, virtue took precedence over honor.

This motif continued in Quaker-friendly Philadelphia, as Quakers rejected traditional notions of honor as worldly and instead advanced the necessity of virtue and duty.[40] Quaker "honor," largely referred to as "virtue" or "duty," represented a combination of love of God with "good neighborhood" and "doing good to others."[41] Franklin built on this theme, but he did so "to promote nonsectarian virtue."[42] In this way, we see Franklin being formed by his environment and then affecting others in his exaltation of virtue as for society's best interest.

Franklin's personal changes came to influence others through relationships, group membership, and the literature he wrote or printed. Before long, Franklin became for many Americans what Addison had been for the young Bostonian. By the late 1720s, Franklin assembled a "mutual improvement" group called the Junto that consisted of tradesmen and gentlemen. Every Friday the members of the Junto would meet, usually at a local tavern, to discuss ways to improve life in Philadelphia through virtue, morality, and politics. Led by Franklin, the Junto borrowed a great deal from similar church societies established by Cotton Mather in various Boston neighborhoods. Groups like Mather's and Franklin's were not uncommon in colonial America, but the fact that the Junto existed for over three decades under the same leader, and gave birth to subsidiary societies and a subscription library (the Library Company of Philadelphia), makes it exceptional and gave it a lasting influence on Philadelphia. The Junto advanced virtuous actions by individuals and society, as well as guarded personal reputations.[43] In essence, it instituted the principle that "self-love and social be the same," from Alexander Pope's *Essay on Man*, which had been adopted by the group. Bettering the individual also helped to advance society as a whole.[44] With such lessons in place, Franklin regarded the Junto as "the best School of Philosophy, Morals and Politics that then existed in the Province."[45]

Perhaps the most influential contribution of the Junto was the Library Company of Philadelphia, which continually grew under Franklin's watch and is still in existence. The library was originally composed of the joint collections of the members of the Junto, and, since the organization was particularly interested in virtue and morality, these ideas were prominently represented within it. For the relatively low price of forty shillings up front and ten shillings per year subsequently, Franklin boasted that his subscription library (and those that would follow) "improv'd the general Conversation of the Americans, made the common Tradesmen and Farmers as intelligent as most Gentlemen from other Countries."[46] In essence, Franklin was offering Americans the same opportunities that he had; they could overcome a lowly birth through self-education and literary immersion.

Through his writings and publications, Franklin attempted to standardize a general definition of and plan for acquiring virtue. He complained of the confusion created by varying definitions of terms, a problem that still persists in understanding honor and virtue today. He wrote, "In the various Enumerations of the moral Virtues I had met with in my Reading, I found the Catalogue more or less numerous, as different Writers included more or fewer Ideas under the same Name."[47] Franklin was determined to explain "the *Means* and *Manner* of obtaining Virtue, which would have distinguish'd it from the mere Exhortation to be good, that does not instruct."[48] Through his newspaper the *Pennsylvania Gazette* and his *Poor Richard's Almanac*, which he viewed as a "Means of Communicating Instruction," Franklin made ideas of virtue more readily accessible and dispersed them among the people—chiefly to those who had not read Addison or Plutarch.[49] *Poor Richard*, with its homespun proverbs, and the *Gazette*, with original pieces by Franklin and excerpts from authors of morality like Addison, continuously advanced the cause of virtue.

In addition, Franklin sold a variety of texts by numerous authors on "moral Virtue," which he labeled "Books of Ethics"; his advertisement for them marks one of the earliest newspaper uses of the word "ethics."[50] He also printed books such as Samuel Richardson's *Pamela*, which he would gift to his daughter Sarah, being his single novel (and the first one published in America). In the *Gazette*, Franklin, quoting the wordy title page, made sure to describe the text as a work "to cultivate the Principles of Virtue . . . in the Minds of the Youth of both Sexes."[51] Despite its overt theme of chastity, Franklin would have been struck by its simultaneous advancement of merit, as its introduction summarized, "Advantages from Birth, and Distinction of Fortune, have no Power at all, when consider'd against those from Behavior, and Temper of Mind."[52] After all, Franklin believed that ethics were accessible throughout society by one's deeds.

Franklin came to understand virtue in the same context as notions of the greater good. For him, virtue benefited society without doing it or the practicing individual any harm, or as little harm as possible. This trend remained a consistent theme throughout the Revolutionary era. More specifically, Franklin determined that there were "Thirteen Names of Virtues": (1) Temperance, (2) Silence, (3) Order, (4) Resolution, (5) Frugality, (6) Industry, (7) Sincerity, (8) Justice, (9) Moderation, (10) Cleanliness, (11) Tranquility, (12) Chastity, and (13) Humility. Franklin's theory was that one should master one type of virtue at a time in order to gain them all. His concept of virtue was a reflection of his own ideas and those of literature, his youth in Boston, and even the Quaker influence of Philadelphia.[53] The perfection of each virtue would enhance and ease the transition to the next, and he thus ranked them from the easiest to the most difficult. Although Franklin's system of perfecting virtue was not widely known before the publication of his *Autobiography* in 1791, and thus was not significantly influential to the general public, he claimed to have followed his ascending scale and monitored his results every day in a rotating thirteen-week cycle. Franklin's technique used the creation of tables and charts to track his progress: "I made a little Book in which I allotted a Page for each of the Virtues. I rul'd each Page with red Ink, so as to have seven Columns, one for each Day of the Week, marking each Column with a Letter for the Day. I cross'd these Columns with thirteen red Lines, marking the Beginning of each Line with the first Letter of one of the Virtues, on which Line and in its proper Column I might mark by a little black Spot every Fault I found upon Examination to have been committed respecting that

Virtue upon that Day."[54] Through this ritual Franklin believed that he could seek to master each of his thirteen virtues.

Although he focused on the perfection of virtue, his understanding of perfection opened up the notion to include more practical applications. He believed that one could not undertake to improve every virtue at once, "and like him who having a Garden to weed, does not attempt to eradicate all the bad Herbs at once, which would exceed his Reach and his Strength, but works on one of the Beds at a time . . . so I should have, (I hoped) the encouraging Pleasure of seeing . . . the Progress I made in Virtue."[55] Even when practicing these virtues one at a time, Franklin allowed for a bit of unorthodox leeway; for example, his version of the virtue of chastity allowed for extramarital affairs and premarital sex, so long as they did not cause "Injury of your own or another's Peace or Reputation."[56] Although Franklin's ideas of virtue were based on traditional notions of classical and British learning, his own interpretations were often visibly original.

Building on his one-step-at-a-time path to virtue, in a departure from what he viewed as the restrictiveness of organized religion, he boldly declared in the *Pennsylvania Gazette* "*that* Self-Denial *is not the* Essence of Virtue."[57] Franklin instead claimed that proper action is always commendable, and choosing to refrain from an inclination toward vice is not any more virtuous than acting morally. He rejected the passive restraint in favor of the active practice of habit, a nonreligious take on the teachings of John Bunyan. For Franklin, in sharp contrast with the tenets of many organized faiths, self-denial and self-flagellation in the context of Christianity did not guarantee a virtuous life. Instead, Franklin chided that anyone believing in "the Notion of taking up the Cross . . . is not practising the reasonable Science of Virtue, but is lunatick."[58]

To what end did Franklin hope this education and revival of virtue would lead? Franklin envisioned forming a "united Party for Virtue" to govern society. He wanted to form "the Virtuous and good Men of all Nations into a regular Body, to be govern'd by suitable good and wise Rules, which good and wise Men may probably be more unanimous in their Obedience to, than common People are to common Laws." While Franklin's international conglomerate was never to be, his discussion of it shows a clear recognition that government and its members should be founded on the basis of virtue. He even prophesied that "whoever attempts this aright, and is well qualified, cannot fail of pleasing God, and of meeting with Success."[59]

Meanwhile, some 150 miles farther south, George Washington was born into the Chesapeake gentry on February 22, 1732. He was an immediate member of the upper echelons of American colonial society, where honor was a crucial part of the culture.[60] Both Franklin and Washington had to deal with the disadvantages of not being firstborn sons. But, in stark contrast to Franklin, Washington did not have to combat his birth status; in fact, it gave him a decided advantage within hierarchical society. Whereas Franklin's early life, due to his New England heritage and Northern sensibilities, reflected a greater attention to virtue than honor, Washington in his youth focused almost exclusively on the acquisition of honor. The roots of Washington's conception of honor reached far back into European antiquity.[61] Specifically, the English view of honor had a dramatic impact on the hierarchy of the American colonies.[62] Like most eighteenth-century Virginians, Washington was concerned with emulating genteel English culture.[63] Unlike Franklin, he did not have to depend solely on his own self-cultivation to advance. Both men learned much from study, but Washington's introduction to honor also came from male role models.

Washington's father, Augustine, died when Washington was eleven. Documentation on Augustine is scarce, but reasonable assertions regarding his influence on Washington can still be made.[64] As a member of Virginia's gentry, Augustine would have been concerned with personal independence, or the ability to maintain oneself economically.[65] Augustine sought to preserve his family within the gentry by sending Washington's older brothers to school in England, thus establishing their genteel status in matters of the mind.[66] Based on Augustine's concern over gentility, it is not unreasonable to assume that he was equally devoted to honor, a trait that his sons then sought to replicate.

After Augustine's death, Washington sought an alternative male influence to fill the void in his life. He did not have to look far. His older half brother, Lawrence Washington, served as a "surrogate father" and was charged with establishing young Washington in the hierarchical world in a way that James Franklin could never dream of.[67] Washington's half brothers had been educated in England, but Augustine's death forced Washington to receive more humble schooling in Virginia.[68] This education failed to deliver the cultivation of etiquette prized by gentlemen.[69] Washington remained self-conscious of his "defective education" for the rest of his life and turned to literature as a substitute.[70]

Despite the tremendous influence effected by masculine notions of honor, Washington's earliest known introduction to honor and virtue came from his mother, Mary Ball Washington, and her daily readings from Sir Mathew Hale's *Contemplations Moral and Divine*.[71] His mother's and Hale's understandings of honor and virtue would differ greatly from many of the ideas he would cultivate in later years, but they certainly laid a foundation of morality and character in the young boy. The ideas advanced by his mother, in the typical feminine fashion of the period, centered more on virtue. She recounted Hale's maxims, very similar to the treatment Franklin received from Mather and Bunyan, that honor came from and was due to God, not man, and that even "the best kind of Honour imaginable . . . degradest into Vanity."[72] For Hale and Mary Washington, honor was of the secular world (virtue was of the spiritual) and tied to personal interest and reputation. Vanity was an indictment of selfishness over the greater good.

While a young Franklin embraced the exaltation of virtue described in his readings, Washington was less receptive. Whether it was youthful rebellion, grief over the loss of his father, or typical angst, Washington made a conscious effort to separate himself from his mother's ideals. As she advanced religious virtue, he sought out manly honor free of dogmatic conditions and gentility without the scorn of vanity. Thus, one could actually credit Mary Washington with a tremendous influence on Washington's sense of honor. The differing views of mother and son drove Washington to become even closer to his brother and to make his own literary choices.

Washington became an avid reader—though not quite at Franklin's level—with his tastes focusing more on genteel literature (against the wishes of his mother), which stressed codes of conduct, hierarchy, and social graces.[73] Fashionable throughout the Anglo-American world, this literature provided an outlet for provincials to experience English aristocratic culture and "infuse[d] into the untainted youth early notices of . . . honour."[74] Gentlemen's magazines such as the *Spectator*, novels such as the *History of Tom Jones*, and etiquette guides such as Lord Chesterfield's *Letters to His Son* stressed the necessity of honor and gentility in solidifying one's rank through proper conduct, conversation, and appearance.[75] Lord Chesterfield instructed that the "ambition" to acquire honor and virtue was positive and healthy, and that "however trifling a genteel manner may sound, it is of very great consequence toward pleasing in private" and in gaining reputation.[76] These priorities resonated with the teenage Washington and reinforced the ideal "that the strictest and most scrupulous honour and virtue can alone make you esteemed and valued by mankind."[77] Despite their different initial hierarchical standings, the young Washington, like the young Franklin, understood that honor and virtue were the means to advance in society. Washington eagerly copied down such social maxims in what became his *Rules of Civility and Decent Behavior in Company and Conversation*.[78] Like Franklin's "Thirteen Names of Virtues," Washington had a formalized set of principles by which to live his life. In this book, the recognition of rank was crucial: "In writing or speaking, give every person his due title according to his degree and the custom of the place."[79] While Washington was not its writer, *Rules* grounded him in a genteel world dependent on social etiquette.[80]

Although Washington read many of the same works and authors as Franklin, his attention seems directed to more traditional representations of honor and virtue. From the *Spectator*, Washington learned that "the great Point of Honour in Men is Courage" and "Shame is the greatest of all evils."[81] It was a clear example of the author's words being read and interpreted by both men in vastly different ways. Washington's understanding was influenced by Southern society, which championed these ideas of masculine honor, reputation, and etiquette. The other works Washington read also reinforced such ideas, specifically *Tom Jones*, a novel he consumed religiously. In *Tom Jones*, author Henry Fielding professes that "true Honour and true Virtue are almost synonymous."[82] Decades later, Thomas Jefferson would remark that fiction taught morality "more effectually . . . than by all the dry volumes of ethics and divinity that ever were written."[83] This maxim seems to have applied, as the perception of honor and virtue as equals became a mainstay in Washington's life; he would use both words, but they were essentially interchangeable for him. Another Fielding-influenced notion of honor that Washington adopted was that honor was capable of existing independently of religion—thus, honor was virtue, and virtue was honor, with neither dependent on theological dogma.[84]

Literature may have provided a reference for Washington's honor, but the most significant portion of his honor was enhanced through personal relationships. He followed the mandate in *Rules*: "Associate yourself with men of good quality, if you esteem your own reputation."[85] Both Lawrence and Washington benefited from the generosity of their neighbors, the Fairfaxes.[86] Lawrence linked the Washingtons to the Fairfaxes through his marriage to Ann Fairfax, the daughter of Colonel William Fairfax, a cousin and agent of Lord Thomas Fairfax.[87] As members of the British aristocracy, the Fairfaxes possessed unquestionable status and gentility, and they served as the role models that Franklin had hoped to encounter in London.[88] William, his son (George William), and Lord Fairfax admired Washington and accepted him as an intimate of the family.[89] Without ever leaving Virginia, Washington experienced all the trappings of British society; his presence among the aristocratic family exposed him to individuals worthy of emulation, the comforts of luxury, the importance of appearance, and the thrill of the foxhunt.

Through the Fairfaxes, Washington became accustomed to the traditional components of British honor: the importance of birth, hierarchy, and gentility. He also was indoctrinated in Stoicism, a classical philosophy that combined virtue with self-control and reserved emotions. For Washington, the ideals of gentility and Stoicism, what Addison termed "the Pedantry [or application] of Virtue," became inseparable.[90] He was not ignorant of this philosophy, as it had been a theme in many of the works of genteel literature that he had previously read, yet William Fairfax urged him to study classical texts.[91] Stoicism instilled in him the belief that "virtue is the perfect good" and that it was his intentions, or "virtue, that make the action good or ill."[92] He became a self-proclaimed "Stoic," often quoting or paraphrasing *Cato*, a drama written by Addison that was based on Plutarch's biography of the Roman republican, and aspiring to the role of Cato himself.[93] Seneca's Stoic sense of obligations between benefactors and recipients underscored Washington's ascent to a high position through the patronage common in the Anglo-American world.[94] But, as mentioned earlier, virtue for him was always a matter of honor. After all, Addison had written that honor, virtue, and morality were the same idea—just confused by terminology. In the *Spectator*, he stated, "I understand by the Word Virtue such a general Notion as is affixed to it by the Writers of Morality, and which by devout Men generally goes under the Name of Religion, and by Men of the World under the Name of Honour."[95] Morality and honor were the same ethical concepts, just separated between religious and secular thought.

As Washington was nearing manhood, back in Philadelphia, Franklin had established himself as one of the city's premiere intellectuals and was on his way to becoming one of the wealthiest men in the Northern colonies. Despite this, Franklin's profession as a printer and his low birth continuously denied him entrance into the gentry. One could not simply buy passage to being a gentleman; the idea that honor and status derived exclusively based on wealth is a modern one and highly anachronistic to the eighteenth century. As a printer, Franklin remained merely a tradesman, albeit a highly skilled and educated one, in the eyes of the gentry.

If anything, it was Franklin's intellect and knowledge that made his status in Philadelphia more contested than his growing fortune. Yet Franklin made sure that he did not overstep his bounds. Trying to enter the gentry was one thing; completely denigrating the social hierarchy and its customs was quite another. Franklin would ultimately become a gentleman, but not before he retired from labor, thus free of the shackles that his trade imposed and able to be recognized by society.

On the other hand, there was never any doubt as to Washington's status as a gentleman. With the Fairfaxes as patrons, and his place within the gentry uncontested by both birth and bearing, Washington began his career as a surveyor, a "respectable and lucrative" profession that granted him a degree of personal independence, though nowhere near Franklin's earning capacity.[96] When Lawrence died, his position of adjutant general of Virginia fell into the lap of an unqualified twenty-year-old Washington—with help from the Fairfaxes, of course.[97] As Washington filled part of his brother's post, Governor Robert Dinwiddie assumed the role of patron, expediting the ascent of the newly promoted major Washington.[98]

As a counterpoint, Franklin, nearly thirty years Washington's senior, would also enter the military ranks consistent with his new genteel status. Military rank was regularly understood to be a reflection of one's civilian status; as one rose in the army, one rose in society. However, Franklin would become a colonel in the militia in 1756 three years after Washington assumed his command in Virginia, clearly illustrating that in midcentury British America, honor through birth and patronage still counted for more than virtue earned by merit, knowledge, and skill combined.[99]

In 1753, Washington would again rely on the benefits of patronage to become an emissary to the French commander at Fort LeBoeuf in the upper Allegheny Valley, although he did not even speak French.[100] Dinwiddie had again elevated the status of an underqualified Washington. By advancing within the military, Washington was solidifying his standing in society; his uniform outwardly displayed the inner merit that he possessed. He now had a reputation to enhance and—more importantly—to protect.[101] This was consistent with British honor, as Addison remarked, "The first Step towards Virtue that I have observed in young Men . . . has been that they had a regard to their Quality and Reputation."[102] Recalling the lessons of genteel literature, Washington realized that his reputation was tied to the status of his honor; as Fielding had said, "I would not be thought to undervalue reputation. . . . To murder one's own reputation is a kind of suicide, a detestable and odious vice."[103] In Washington's world, the failure of a man to maintain and advance his own reputation was an unthinkable evil.

Rank was also a recognized outward expression of honor. Growing up amid the Fairfaxes, Washington was unprepared for offenses to his rank. His continued fervent defense of his honor reveals that he had not yet solidified the social position that Stoic gentility required.[104] He wished to serve his country, but not at the expense of his honor.[105]

The menacing French presence on the frontier gave Washington an opportunity to advance in rank again, this time as a lieutenant colonel.[106] The higher his rank became, the greater Washington's opportunity to gain honor and glory.[107] But his forays on the western frontier were marked by numerous challenges to his honor. The first insult that Washington faced concerned the inferior pay of colonial officers with respect to their British counterparts: "We should be treated as gentlemen and officers, and not have annexed to the most trifling pay, that ever was given to English officers."[108] Lower pay was not only a slight to the colonial officers' status within the British Empire; it also had the potential to infringe on their personal independence, undermining their gentility. If they couldn't afford to act the part of a gentleman, how could they expect to maintain their reputation? Washington, as senior officer, took up the cause and unsuccessfully petitioned Governor Dinwiddie.[109] Though offended by what he considered dishonorable pay, he still displayed a Stoic sense of honor and fulfilled his military duties and his duty to his country. He even offered to serve without pay or resign his commission; while serving as a volunteer would garner praise, he believed continuing to accept payment under such conditions would bring dishonor. He ultimately remained in service, but the offense would not be forgotten.[110]

Washington pressed his men forward to meet the French, and on May 28, 1754, he was involved in a skirmish with international repercussions. The British and their Indian allies overwhelmed a surprised French force and accidentally killed a diplomat, French commander Joseph Coulon de Villiers, Sieur de Jumonville.[111] Washington's inability to understand French was the main culprit, which magnified his insecurity about his "defective education."[112] Washington's Indian ally, Tanacharison, who spoke French fluently, understood Jumonville's diplomatic mission but still killed him, stating "that their intentions were evil."[113] And Washington could not overcome the language barrier.[114] Two months later, this affair culminated in a challenge to Washington's honor.

Genteel reservation was set aside when Washington's rank was directly challenged. Slights of pay were an insult; a slight of rank was much worse. Without his rank, he would lose his desired status.[115] Washington became locked in a power struggle with Captain James Mackay, the commander of an independent company and holder of a king's commission, over who possessed the higher rank.[116] Nominally, Washington did, but Mackay was a "gentleman" commissioned in the British regular army and felt that he outranked any colonial.[117] This slight of rank, combined with the effrontery of Mackay, motivated Washington to separate his troops from royal officers—for the preservation and expansion of his own honor.[118] In early July 1754, superior French forces under Jumonville's brother pinned the recently promoted colonel Washington behind the walls of Fort Necessity.[119] Washington found himself in this unfortunate situation for "being too ambitious of acquiring all the honour, or as much as he could, before the rest joined him."[120] He was forced to surrender and sign an improperly translated document acknowledging that he had assassinated Jumonville.[121]

Washington attempted to justify the death of Jumonville to himself and his superiors by claiming that he had been told of the diplomatic nature of the French mission only after the skirmish, and that he was not quick to believe French testimony. Washington penned in his journal, "They had informed me that they had been sent with a summons to order me to retire—A plausible pretence to discover our camp, and to obtain knowledge of our forces and our situation!"[122] He speculated further, with his honor informing his suspicions and clouding his judgment: "Besides, an Embassador has princely attendants, whereas this was only a simple petty *French* officer; an Embassador has no need of spies, his person being always sacred."[123] Washington belonged to a genteel world in which appearance, conduct, and manners were outward displays of inner virtue. Jumonville's external appearance failed to conform to Washington's model of a gentleman and thus hindered Washington's acceptance of his status.

Critics attacked Washington for signing "the most infamous [document] a British subject ever put his hand to."[124] For the newly minted colonel, who "was inordinately sensitive to criticism and strongly blame-aversive," these attacks were viewed as threats to his honor.[125] Luckily for him, the French assertions were dismissed.[126] Thanks in large part to the intervention of William Fairfax and Dinwiddie, Washington emerged "with honor" from the affair as a "noble" hero who defended Virginia against French invasion.[127]

Soon after, Washington landed on the wrong side of Dinwiddie's military reorganization. Dinwiddie stated, "As there have been some disputes between the regulars and the officers appointed by me . . . there will be no other distinguished [colonial] officer above a captain."[128] Unfortunately for Washington, his earlier complaints would be his undoing, as his rank of colonel would be downgraded to that of captain if he continued in service. Washington's Stoic honor to country gave way to the preservation of his personal honor. Washington was interested in his "own Honour, and Country's welfare," in that order.[129] He refused to risk his personal reputation. His new fame forced him to be conscious of the effects of a demotion on his honor.[130] Washington resigned, even though his "inclinations [were] strongly bent to arms."[131]

While Washington was leaving the service of his country over a matter of honor, Franklin was focusing on public service and the greater good out of a sense of virtue. He wrote, "When I disengag'd myself as above mentioned from private Business, I flatter'd myself that by the sufficient tho' moderate Fortune I had acquir'd, I had secur'd Leisure during the rest of my Life . . . but the Publick now considering me as a Man of Leisure, laid hold of me for their Purposes; every Part of our Civil Government, and almost at the same time, imposing some Duty upon me."[132] Since his retirement in 1748, Franklin had been attempting to better the people of Philadelphia in all manner of ways: through science (his famous electrical experimentation), education (the founding of the Academy and Charitable School in the province of Pennsylvania), politics (as a member of the Common Council, alderman, burgess, postmaster, and justice of the peace), and defense (as an officer in the militia).

As Washington waited for another chance to secure honor by combating the French, Franklin hoped to establish a lasting peace on the western frontier through his Albany Plan of Union, which would join all the colonies together for the purposes of common defense. It was here in Albany, New York, during the summer of 1754 that Franklin first became acquainted with forty-two-year-old Thomas Hutchinson, a Massachusetts native with whom he collaborated in drafting the proposal. In the coming years, it would be Hutchinson who would go on to directly and indirectly create a challenge to Franklin's honor that ultimately became one of the pivotal moments of both men's lives. Although the Albany Plan would ultimately fail, it represented a nascent moment of colonial unity and introduced Franklin to other distinguished figures and to the higher realms of imperial power.

Since distancing himself from the odor of trade, Franklin boasted a list of acquaintances that now included British aristocrats, royal governors, and the colonial elite. His growing stature within Pennsylvania and the British Empire saw him acting less the lowborn printer and more the "proud . . . overbearing and rather insolent" gentleman.[133] His political and military positions came to be viewed as outward reflections of his inner virtuous merit. Franklin's public recognition coincided with his developing a sense of his own honor. After being named colonel of the Pennsylvania Regiment, some forty mounted soldiers flanked Franklin and, as he recalled, "drew their Swords, and rode with them naked all the way. . . . No such Honour had been paid . . . to any of his Governors; and [an anonymous critic] said it was only proper to Princes of the Blood Royal." Franklin claimed he was "ignorant of the Etiquette, in such Cases," but his pride in the public recognition of his honor still shines through in his *Autobiography*, which was penned significantly later in his life.[134] What is clear is that Franklin was growing accustomed to the privileges of status, following a path of virtue had gotten him there, and, as he had learned from the *Spectator*, "Titles and Honour are the Rewards of Virtue."[135]

Just as the elder Franklin began to surpass Washington in military rank and stature, the young Virginian ended his absence from military life. General Edward Braddock, commander in chief of the British forces in North America, arrived to lead a campaign against the French. Braddock needed officers with firsthand knowledge of the frontier, and Washington was a well-known and respected figure.[136] Washington became part of Braddock's staff as a volunteer and gained the protection of a patron. As an aide-de-camp, his status was preserved by his connection to Braddock, preventing it from being contested by junior British officers and allowing him to feel safe in his honor.[137]

On July 9, 1755, in a battle that had long-lasting repercussions and influenced the careers of multiple Revolutionary War participants, the British were routed and the wounded Braddock died.[138] Though Washington lost the backing of an influential patron, his own honor was advanced immeasurably. Washington had been ill with dysentery, but he still conducted himself valiantly on the battlefield and emerged unscathed. He regaled, "I luckily escapd witht a wound, tho' I had four Bullets through my Coat, and two Horses shot under me."[139] Fortune, or fate, had validated his claim to honor.[140] Washington's bravery in rallying the remnants of the British force and his seeming invincibility led many officers to refer to him as a "favorite of the gods."[141] He gained public recognition through valor on the battlefield, a crucial component of honor. Washington's preservation of his honor through valor would not waiver, and his bravery remained virtually unchallenged throughout the rest of his career. He wrote, "Who is there that does not rather Envy, than regret a Death that gives birth to Honour & Glorious memory."[142] An honorable death was something to be admired. With this new recognition, his status increased and he became more protective of his honor, fearing any action that could cause him to "loose [*sic*] what at present constitutes the chief part of my happiness, i.e. the esteem and notice the Country has been pleas'd to honour me with."[143]

Following the now-familiar pattern, Washington's next commission as a colonel resulted from his patrons' petitions and Dinwiddie's revival of the Virginia Regiment.[144] He was "always ready, and always willing, to do my Country any Services . . . but never upon the Terms I have done, having suffer'd much."[145] In other words, he would serve, as long as his status was commensurate with his rank. But it did not take long for Washington to become entangled in yet another challenge to his honor. Captain John Dagworthy, a provincial Maryland officer with a nullified king's commission, refused to recognize Washington's seniority and claimed that instead he was the highest-ranking colonial officer.[146] For Washington, Mackay, an actual British regular, had been bad enough; he was not about to suffer any further dishonor at the hands of a mere colonial captain. Washington complained to the governor, furiously proclaiming, "I can never submit to the command of Captain Dagworthy, since you have honoured me with the command of the Virginia Regiment."[147] Dinwiddie took Washington's protest to Maryland governor Horatio Sharpe, but the attempt proved fruitless.[148] The uncertainty of the matter led to further challenges to Washington's honor, including another slight against his rank, this time by Lieutenant William Stark.[149]

Washington was permitted to present his case personally before William Shirley, the Massachusetts governor, commander in chief of British North America, and a Franklin acquaintance, and hoped to settle the matter once and for all by obtaining a royal commission, thereby making him a British regular officer.[150] He traveled to Boston, complete with a gentlemanly retinue of subordinate officers and servants "calculated to create the impression of merit, dignity, and high estate."[151] Shirley restored the supremacy of Washington's command over Dagworthy, but no royal commission was granted.[152] When Shirley was replaced by John Campbell, Earl of Loudoun, as commander in chief, Washington wrote to Lord Loudoun and again attempted to gain a royal commission.[153] In Washington's addresses to Loudoun and Dinwiddie, he is often argumentative and sensitive to any slights against his rank. But while one may see this as a break from genteel behavior, one must keep in mind that Washington was acting in defense of his honor.[154] If he did not follow the maxims of his *Rules of Civility*, it does not necessarily mean that he was acting dishonorably; after all, Bernard Mandeville and Pope both agreed that honor and virtue were based on passion.[155] Washington held firm to Seneca's principle that "if a man does not live up to his own rules, it is something yet to have virtuous meditations and good purposes. . . . There is something of honor yet in the miscarriage; nay, in the naked contemplation of it."[156] In this instance, Washington seems to have agreed that honor was in the intent, not necessarily the result.

His defense of his honor was not an abandonment of his genteel principles but rather a confrontation with his own insecurities of status. A gentleman was expected to defend his honor.[157] The lack of civility that Washington exhibited during this stage of his life was due to the internal tension between Stoic gentility and personal honor. For much of the war, it is his personal honor that proved paramount to him. But his continued espousal of Stoic honor to country illustrates that he was uncomfortable with his own defensive actions.

Washington was continuously becoming disillusioned with patronage.[158] Within the Virginia Regiment, he began to grant commissions based on merit and seniority rather than patronage.[159] His orders to the troops read, "Remember, that it is the actions, and not the Commission, that make the Office—and that there is more expected from him than the *Title.* . . . I shall make it the most agreeable part of my duty, to study merit, and reward the brave, and deserving."[160] After moments of feeling degraded by the British army, Washington's experience in the military had taught him that proper conduct was the only true path to advancement. By this point, he was beginning to understand that honor did not simply apply to gentlemen. While these changes first occurred in a martial setting, Washington would soon adapt this new form of social mobility to his perception of civilians as well.

Washington's newfound devotion to advancement by merit conflicted with the system of patronage that had accounted for his own rise.[161] William Fairfax asked Washington to commission his sons, Bryan and Billy, as lieutenants.[162] Washington felt a sense of duty to his pseudo-father, but he was grieved over the process.[163] He sought to circumvent such an open display of patronage and requested that Dinwiddie grant the commission instead, because "making him Lt over many old Ensigns, will occasion great confusion in the corps, and bring censure on me; for the Officers will readily conceive, that my friendship and partiality to the family were the causes of it."[164] This was a sharp turn for Washington. Although he still respected hierarchy, he was now disposed to a more meritorious method of advancement.[165]

Meanwhile, Franklin was coming to appreciate the British government, the patronage system, and what personal relationships could do for him. Gordon Wood remarks, "By 1756 Franklin must have thought he was on top of the world. No one had seen more of America, and no one knew more people in the colonies, than he. He was in a position, he thought, to accomplish extraordinary things."[166] Franklin had done a great deal to put himself in a position to accept patronage; it would be foolish to argue that he was the product of great men. Instead, it is more accurate to note that Franklin was aided and his ascent eased by his patrons. Aside from the snub received by Franklin from William Keith nearly three decades earlier, he had no reason to criticize the patronage system. Certainly it should be reserved for men of virtue, but there was no harm in claiming a reward. And so, the poor boy from Boston began exercising his own form of patronage though his various offices and arranged employment for his near and distant relatives alike, most notably his illegitimate son, William Franklin, who was named the royal governor of New Jersey largely through his father's relationship with Lord Bute.

Embracing merit-based advancement over traditional patronage and hierarchy was a new step for Washington, but it had been a core value for Franklin since his youth. While he accepted and appreciated patronage, he still retained his original regard for virtue and merit. In his pamphlet *Proposals Relating to the Education of Youth in Pennsylvania*, he declared, "*True Merit*, should also be often presented to Youth ... as consisting in an *Inclination* join'd with an *Ability* to serve Mankind, one's Country, Friends and Family ... and should indeed be the great *Aim* and *End* of all Learning."[167] He accepted that any person of virtue, character, and merit should be able to advance in the British world by upholding a conception of the greater good.

Still, Franklin tried not to overstep his bounds in the hierarchy. He consented that good breeding was still "most agreeable to all," but one must deserve the status of a gentleman before acting the part.[168] He wished for people to "always have the Grace to know my self [*sic*] and my Station."[169] He was always conscious of public recognition, which shows he had a clear understanding of honor culture. Although in much of Franklin's early years he seems to have had a desire to advance himself rather than forge new hierarchical foundations, he still maintained a sense of interclass equality that became evident in a more mature Washington.

After the war, each man embarked on a different path. Washington retired to the life of a country gentleman, husband, and stepfather. He secured his personal independence and was elevated into the upper levels of the gentry after his marriage to Martha Custis, one of the wealthiest widows in Virginia. The honor he gained through valor and his personal independence contributed to securing his rank within the civilian hierarchy.[170] Washington's view of honor had adapted in response to the degradation he faced at the hands of his British superiors and even inferiors.[171] He became more willing to accept a degree of mobility within the social hierarchy based on merit. In doing so, he exhibited a departure from the traditional form of honor practiced in the Anglo-American world. He was still a loyal British subject, but his trust in the empire had been shaken by what he viewed as personal slights to his honor.

Franklin, on the other hand, had become absolutely mesmerized by the British Empire. He had moved to London in 1757 and become celebrated by the major British institutions of learning, such as Cambridge and Oxford— another reward of honor for his virtue. The ever-sociable Franklin struck up friendships with prominent figures in academia, science, government, and the aristocracy. He kept company with many of Britain's enlightened thinkers, including moralists Adam Smith and William Robertson. He embraced the fashionable culture of London, residing in a handsome brick building near the government center at Whitehall and joining clubs that further drew him into the metropolitan lifestyle. Unlike some Americans abroad in Britain who viewed London as a den of vice (such as future patriot John Dickinson), Franklin saw the city as a bastion of virtue that he wished his colonial homeland could mimic. In 1763 he wrote, "That little Island, enjoy[s] in almost every Neighbourhood, more sensible, virtuous and elegant Minds, than we can collect in ranging 100 Leagues of our vast Forests."[172] By the early 1760s, George III and Britain had no firmer American friend than Benjamin Franklin.

The development of Franklin and Washington followed two very different courses. Through these two individuals we are able to peer into regional differences between the colonial North and South, but, more than that, they allow us to examine how European concepts of honor and virtue began to become transformed. The spread of understandings of honor and virtue through literature and personal interactions is a microcosm of the wider progression of colonial America. Even before the coming of the American Revolution, a change between the colonists and the mother country was already visibly evident through an ideological lens.

CHAPTER TWO

A Shared Identity

Colonial Colleges and the Shaping of
Pre-Revolutionary Thought

Benjamin Franklin and George Washington were, in large part, a product of their own efforts and environments. Meanwhile, most of the prominent American Revolutionary leadership had formal schooling, and even attended college; some were educated in Britain, but the vast majority remained in the colonies for school.[1] Colleges throughout the British world were founded on principles of virtue and honor, and these ethics represented the core of the colonial curriculum. While Franklin and Washington first learned of these ideals from personal reading, the bulk of the Constitution's framers, such as John Adams and Thomas Jefferson, were exposed through the combined influences of reading, instruction, and examination.[2] Early American colleges came to function as both centers of learning and models of the outside world. Colleges reflected their regional, religious, and societal ideals and were responsible for directly influencing the Revolutionary generation.

British colleges were long regarded as bastions of honor, and all American colleges were founded on some basis of honor or virtue.[3] In the decades before the American Revolution, regardless of region, religion, or date of founding, each college actively sought to adopt these ideas not only as the foundation of the school but also as the fundamental basis for each student's education. A substantial emphasis was placed on solidifying each student's moral character, which allowed for a collectivized identity.

This approach represented one of the earliest, though not necessarily deliberate, attempts in America to institutionalize, or standardize, ideas of honor and virtue. Through assigned readings, lessons, and codes of conduct, American college students were exposed to similar ways of thinking. Furthermore, the overt encouragement of students to emulate the best among them (and similar examples to be found among the faculty and archetypal ideals) created a culture in which young men strived to be well regarded.[4] While, obviously, the individual interpretation of these principles by the different schools varied, there was a degree of consistency in the core elements. As classes of students were subjected to these comparable ideas, a collective understanding of honor and virtue was fostered that in many cases came to influence the young men far into adulthood. Students were almost invariably Christian white males from fairly well-off families, and it was not a drastic step for them to develop such camaraderie. In addition, unlike today, students could enter college in their early teens, making them more impressionable to the lessons imposed on them than a young man would be. Thus, colleges in many ways became the principal breeding ground for honor culture and the formation of a sense of identity based on virtue and morality.

Unlike Franklin and Washington, John Adams developed directly due to the regimented ethics and morality imparted by formal education. Adams was born on October 30, 1735, in Braintree, Massachusetts, not far from Boston, to a middling family made so by "Industry and Enterprize." Like Franklin, Adams grew up within the Puritan tradition and came to favor virtue over honor. But, unlike Franklin, Adams actively sought to continue the legacy of his Puritan ancestors throughout the eighteenth century. He followed the example of his father, John Adams Sr., who was "a Select Man, a Militia Officer and a Deacon in the Church" and who possessed such an unblemished character that Adams regarded him as "the honestest Man I ever knew."[5] Adams was taught to admire virtue and avoid the presence "of disgrace, of baseness and of Ruin." He concluded that this familial education had given him a guiding principle to follow throughout the rest of his life, writing that "the Happiness of Life depends more upon Innocence" and that all he learned throughout his life and travels "would serve to confirm what I learned in my Youth in America, that Happiness is lost forever if Innocence is lost."[6] This youthful sentiment bears within it the basic tenets of honor and shame and expresses Adams's belief that if honor is lost, it is irrecoverable.

Despite the importance of the lessons learned at home, Adams was carefully guided into formal education at the wishes of his father, and he first attended the public Latin school under Joseph Cleverly, a teacher whom Adams disliked. Nevertheless, he was forced to admit reluctantly that Cleverly was a gentleman. Contrary to the wishes of his father and the later image of the elder statesman and president, Adams did not initially take to books or education— partly because of an affinity for the outdoors, combined with a mixture of distaste for the "indolent" Cleverly. His dominant father, out of a sense of paternal duty and a desire to live vicariously through his son, insisted Adams be educated and attend college. Only after transferring to the inspirational tutelage of Joseph Marsh, who ran a private school only a couple of doors from his home, did Adams become a devoted student.[7] Adams committed himself so fully to his studies that in 1751, at age sixteen (the roughly standard age for admittance into college), he entered Harvard College, just as his older cousin Samuel Adams had done fifteen years prior.

Adams's experiences at Harvard mirrored those of so many other students of the era in curriculum, discipline, and regulation. As previously mentioned, there was congruity among many of the ideas on honor and virtue espoused across America's colleges. In the 1763 petition for Rhode Island College (now Brown University) to the colonial assembly, the officers of the college declared, "Institutions for liberal Education are highly beneficial to Society by forming the rising Generation to Virtue Knowledge and usefull Literature and the preserving in a Community a Succession of men qualified for discharging the offices of Life with usefulness and Reputation."[8] The idea that college was to instruct students in honor and virtue in order to make them good citizens was accepted across all institutions. Before admittance to college was possible, an understanding of honor and virtue was essential; entrance was frequently limited to students who could prove that they had lived a "blameless life," as it was stated that "none shall be admitted to the Honours of College without Testimonials of their good moral Conduct . . . signed by Two or more Gent. Of Note & Veracity."[9] Men of reputation had to publicly vouch for the reputation of the applicant in order for him to even be considered.

Honor and virtue were central components of the college curriculum. They appeared in classes on moral philosophy, ethics, religion, and history. History and ethics classes both built on many of the same classical works that had influenced Franklin and Washington, most prominently Plutarch's *Lives*. Courses in religion were more varied, based on regional denominations.[10] But overall, colleges were fairly consistent in their use of texts, adopting them exclusively from British sources; this was particularly true in the study of moral philosophy, which included Adam Smith's *Theory of Moral Sentiments*, Lord Shaftesbury's *An Inquiry concerning Virtue*, and Francis Hutcheson's *Short Introduction to Moral Philosophy*.

Each author imparted significant interpretations of the nature of honor and virtue to Americans. Lord Shaftesbury was a proponent of the idea that religion and virtue were not inherently linked. He mused about "HOW FAR COULD VIRTUE ALONE GO." Virtue was goodness toward others, and one could be virtuous without religion and vice versa.[11] It was this disassociation that seems to have limited Shaftesbury's influence in religious America, especially in the largely Puritanical New England.[12] Smith, though he disagreed with Shaftesbury's assertions on virtue, was in favor of morality administered by each person's conscience.[13] Still, Smith posited, quite similarly to Shaftesbury, that honor was based on selflessness.[14] Even more clearly, for Smith, virtue was equal to greatness acquired by merit, while honor was an adherence to the general rules of society.[15] These authors' influence would be felt in the colonies, but on a more moderate scale in comparison to that of Hutcheson.

Frances Hutcheson, a student of Shaftesbury, became the backbone of college moral philosophy.[16] His concepts of honor and virtue were closely related. They lacked any inherent tension or division, as illustrated in the lives of Franklin and Washington. Honor, for Hutcheson, was based on virtue, and "all true virtue must have some nobler spring than any desires of worldly pleasures or interests."[17] Thus, virtue became associated with something loftier than personal interest; it was described and taught as "true goodness" and happiness achieved through moral sense and duty to the greater good.[18] Hutcheson espoused that "moral sense is naturally connected . . . [to] Honour and Shame, which makes the approbations, the gratitude, and esteem of others who approve of our conduct, matter of high pleasure; and their censures, and condemnation, and infamy, matter of severe uneasiness."[19] While he connects honor with morality, Hutcheson still maintains elements of a European focus that advanced public recognition as a crucial component of honor.

But Hutcheson went further than any traditional model when he contended that honor was not just a creation of man but rather was an inherent part of human nature that was linked with virtue. He separated manmade components of "civil honours," such as titles, deference, and condescension, from what he termed "natural honour." Natural honor was based on each person's moral sense and "plainly designed as a guardian not only to moral virtue." In a rather lighthearted but surprisingly acute observation, he declared that blushing was an act of "natural modesty" and proves the inherent notion of honor in humanity.[20]

College professors imparted the ideas of these texts, combined with their own personal interpretations—which accounts for a bit of variety among the different schools. John Witherspoon, a professor of moral philosophy at the College of New Jersey, was so celebrated in America that his lectures functioned as texts for newer colleges.[21] Witherspoon quite impartially conducted his classes from differing points of view and debated the merit of the multiple definitions. Students copied down, and were expected to know, "The Nature of Virtue," which consisted of a list of a diverse cross section of explanations and definitions from multiple authors: "Virtue is said by different Authors to consist (1) in acting according to the Reason & Nature of Things; Or (2) in Public Affectation; or (3) in Truth; or (4) in Self Love; or (5) in Sympathy; or

(6) in whatever is agreeable; or (7) in the Love of Being as such[;] Again (8) others found Virtue on Piety[;] Of the Foundation of Virtue. This according to different Authors is (1) The Will of God; or (2) The nature of Things; or (3) Public; or (4) Private Interest." According to Witherspoon, "All [definitions] are to be included" in the examination of virtue. Despite this variety, he did teach some consistent standards. Virtue was "true Goodness" and "True Virtue certainly promotes the General Good." Furthermore, virtue was a duty each man owed, not a desire to fulfill his own personal interests; for this professor, "this Sense of Duty is the primary Notion of Law & Right taken in their most extensive Sense."[22]

Virtue determined right and wrong, but what maintained these principles? To Witherspoon, honor was a valuable notion both personally and professionally.[23] He determined that honor was a part of nature, but more than just a communal system of worth and reputation; it was the "Guard to Virtue." He did not dismiss the notion that elements of public acceptance and shame were a part of honor culture but rather believed that these trappings played a bigger role "by making us apprehend Reproach from others for that which in itself is worthy of Blame." Honor made a person dutiful and virtuous. It is not surprising that Witherspoon's conclusions were remarkably similar to Hutcheson's, illustrating the tremendous influence the author and the subject had on the education of American youths.[24]

King's College in New York (now Columbia University) was an epicenter for the personal reinterpretation of ideas of moral philosophy. The Yale College–educated Samuel Johnson, as both president and professor, based a portion of each student's ethical education on his own text, *Ethices Elementa*. Johnson subdivided the idea of virtue into three refined definitions and duties. He concluded that man had an obligation to "behave suitably" for oneself (*"Human Virtue"*), God (*"divine Virtue"*), and all of humanity (*"social Virtue"*).[25] Though differentiated from others' standard understandings of virtue, each of these definitions supported an idea of proper conduct designed to promote goodness and happiness. Johnson's ideas lived on at King's College long after his presidency was over, as his book became a required text on the school's curriculum.[26] And, like Witherspoon, his work had an effect beyond King's College, as it was adapted by the College of Philadelphia and sold more broadly, including by Benjamin Franklin.[27] Johnson's successor, Myles Cooper, retained the book, as well as adding Hutcheson and his own work *Ethics Compendium*, in which he concluded, "The essence of human happiness consists in acting according to the best and most perfect virtue."[28]

Despite the careful attention given to honor and virtue through traditional coursework, the principal means of instilling a devotion to these ethics in students was through the establishment of codes of conduct, or laws of the college. This was in stark opposition to customs at British schools, particularly Eton College. There, exposure to honor and virtue was through formal instruction, while students enjoyed a "freedom from supervision" and "independence of any visible control."[29] As concluded by Shaftesbury, American codes of conduct became a tangible way for students to understand and practice the tenets of honor and virtue.[30]

Outside academia, a great deal of confusion often existed as to exactly what was proper, honorable, and virtuous. The world outside college lacked the close monitoring that was consistent with a student's world. Within the halls of the Ivory Tower, the rules were more clearly defined and regulated from above for the advancement of the greater good of the community. This enabled more unified, collective ideas to grow within the student population and also for a core system of ethics to be shared by a prominent proportion of the American leadership at the dawn of the American Revolution.

Many of the colleges' codes of conduct were synonymous with each other, just varying in degree. From Massachusetts to Virginia, there was an inherent hierarchy from the college president down to the lowly first-year students; in this respect, it was an accurate reflection of the British world. Students were ranked in their incoming class upon entrance into the school. During the early and mid-eighteenth century, ranking was not based on academic merit. High grades could still earn one the title of valedictorian or salutatorian, but rankings were a reflection of the existing social hierarchy. Colleges determined each student's class rank exclusively by "the presumed official or social rank of their parents."[31] Samuel Adams, a future patriot, suffered such a degradation of rank at Harvard College, due to the fact that President Benjamin Wadsworth "disliked the idea that the two top positions in the class would go to the sons of men who . . . possessed neither a gentleman's education nor other special distinctions."[32] With this hierarchy came traditional outward manifestations, as students were expected to demonstrate respect for the officers, professors, and all personnel of the college in words and deeds, "showing all those laudable expressions of honour & Reverence that are in use," including tipping their hats and keeping their heads uncovered in the presence of one of a more exalted rank.[33]

Harvard was the earliest proponent of such a system. It would in later years draw criticism from Franklin as a vain perpetrator of hat honor. Though Harvard drew Franklin's personal ire, all pre-Revolutionary colleges embraced such practices. Rhode Island College and the College of New Jersey (now Princeton University) even used a ranking system to determine the order students would get their meals in the dining hall or walk on campus.[34] Such measures were far from uncommon; class rank ordered a student's life throughout his academic career, from his assigned seat in classes to his pew during religious services. Historian Brooks Mather Kelley relates, "Thus a man's place in his class was far more important than just his position on a piece of paper. He had to act out his ranking every day of his college life."[35] Even more stringently, students were forbidden from speaking out against their superiors or their superiors' reputations. Since 1741, Yale had a law that stated that a student could be expelled if he "directly or indirectly" called into question the character or morals of any college officer (administrator, trustee, or faculty).[36] Within the decade, other colleges followed suit, thus instilling a social hierarchy that was consistent with the outside world.[37]

While administrations often felt that an internal hierarchy would govern all such behavior, students often saw shades of gray. As the Revolution drew nearer, colleges frequently had to adapt their rules to reflect changes within society and the student body. For instance, by the 1770s, the ranking of students based on "*the supposed Dignity of the Families*" started to be abandoned, with even Harvard favoring the more democratic alphabetizing of the freshman class.[38] This certainly is indicative of an ideological dissent in colonial society that suggested heightened equality but still attempted to maintain hierarchy among classes, faculty, and administration.[39] Even more generally, changes in student behavior often forced colonial colleges to adjust for instances that were not explicitly covered by their laws.[40] Other colleges would usually adopt comparable measures themselves—lest they face a similar circumstance.

The codes of conduct were instilled not simply to run the institution more efficiently but to improve the moral character of its students. Named offenses were fairly consistent among colleges and (given the nature, gender, and ages of the students involved) leaned heavily toward gambling, drunkenness (combined with simply visiting taverns), fornicating, fighting, and lying. There were greater offenses as well, but those crimes judged by the common law were more infrequent and generally recognized as dishonorable and unvirtuous.

The methods of enforcement were also harmonious; colleges were fairly consistent in their methods of punishment. Monetary fines were by far the most minor sentence for an infraction. The codes of conduct were largely enforced based on principles of honor, mainly through oath taking and public shaming. Students were expected to know their school's codes of conduct, which were prominently displayed; some colleges even mandated that students carry around rulebooks. Trivial offenses were dismissed with a fine of several shillings; larger infractions or repeated behavior resulted in students being forced to admit publicly their crimes before the assembled students and faculty. This form of public shaming, common in honor culture, proved an effective means of maintaining student discipline. Yale president Thomas Clap wrote, "The passions of fear shame & dishonour are most proper to be wrought upon and set as a counter balance against the practice of those vices and disorders."[41] Some students would even seek to leave school rather than face the shame and dishonor of such a punishment, and Yale thus instituted a policy that no student could be released without parental permission—thereby forcing students to face their shame.[42]

The most insidious transgressions were met with degradation in class rank (even to a lower rank in a lower class—the worst rank downgrading), rustication (suspension), or expulsion, in effect an extreme form of public shaming that traveled not just within the college but also into the surrounding community and beyond. It became commonplace for a college to inform other schools of an infraction and the lack of character of an expelled student.[43] Thus, expulsion not only removed an individual from college, shamed him in front of his peers, and reflected on his family, but it also blackened his reputation throughout the colonies as a whole. As historian Samuel Eliot Morison explains, "Expulsion was not a mere matter of telling the culprit to pack up his things and leave; it was a very solemn business, like breaking an army officer."[44] College students learned that their behavior could have tangible and long-lasting effects on their ability to rise in a hierarchical world founded on a system of honor.

Despite the seeming rigidity of the standards of punishment, students could often find a way to return to good standing in the college if they learned the rules and the language of honor. It was fairly common for students, even those expelled, to be reinstated to their former status, provided they would swear an oath and pledge on their honor to not duplicate the behavior. Sometimes their oath would hold, and sometimes continued lapses in behavior prompted swift and disproportionate measures, as a word of honor had been broken.[45]

Although honorable and virtuous behavior was exalted, the college officers did not entirely trust the students' still-developing morals and characters. Since the 1740s, an overabundance of regulations were passed to keep students out of situations that could result in unfavorable activity, rather than letting them rely on their own personal judgment to steer them from vice.

Since the early days of the College of New Jersey, students were banned from taverns, from "Places of publick Entertainment," and even from having a relationship with anyone "of known Scandalous Lives."[46] The College of William and Mary and Dartmouth College also instituted such bans, hoping to spare their students from interaction with "unsavory" characters who would "corrupt their morals and draw away their minds from a strict adherence to virtue."[47] Other colleges, such as Yale, passed comparable laws, as well as deals with local merchants to restrict students' purchases to only what was deemed a necessity by the college officers.[48] Yale even named official shops and proprietors, including the appropriately named Nathan Beers, who was the sole alcohol distributer to students who possessed a permit signed by the college president.[49]

Such an emphasis was placed on honor culture in colleges because of the sense of collective identity that formed within them. Students came to view their classmates as something closer to brothers than peers, thereby forming pseudo-kinship ties.[50] Such sentiments were part organic and part contrived, as some emerged from a natural sense of affection and camaraderie, while others were a result of the continued espousal from college officers that the character of the individual influenced the reputation of the institution. The College of Philadelphia (now the University of Pennsylvania), a school founded by Franklin, proclaimed as its first code of conduct, "The Honour and Reputation of this Institution depend on the good morals and behaviour of the Youth who are educated at it."[51] Still, such devotion to a collective sense of honor existed independent of school authority, as expelled King's College student George Rapalje begged forgiveness from "my fellow Students for the Disgrace I have brought upon the Seminary of which they are Members by my unguarded and ungenteel Behaviour."[52] Even in the less regimented British intuitions, such as the legal training ground of the Inns of Court, collective and profession-specific conceptions of honor developed that were undoubtedly understood by many of the future patriots in attendance.[53]

It was not only students who were expected to adhere to these tenets of virtuous conduct; all members of the college were held to this standard and bound by oaths.[54] Yale-educated minister Samuel Seabury wrote to King's College president Samuel Johnson, "The Reputation of any Seminary of Learning depends upon the Abilities, and virtuous Conduct of the Persons employed as Instructors."[55] From the trustees to the professors to the servants, a good character was crucial to securing and maintaining a position. In Williamsburg, Virginia, during the spring of 1760, Jacob Rowe, the Oxford-educated

master (or chair) of philosophy at William and Mary, had started overindulg-
ing in alcohol in public situations—in effect casting a negative light not only
on himself but on the college as well. While Rowe's drunkenness was problematic, the board of visitors (trustees) was more concerned by the philosopher's proclivity for swearing oaths while inebriated. Drunkenness was a
character flaw, but swearing oaths and subsequently breaking them called
into question his and the school's honor. The board, protective of their own
reputation, summoned Rowe in the same manner in which they summoned
students to be chastised and issued "strong Admonitions," which elicited "solemn Promises of future good Behaviour."[56] Professors were not only required
to teach on the importance of the subjects of honor and virtue, they were expected to display them in their daily lives.

Administrations were not the only ones enforcing these codes of conduct;
students began to take initiative and used similar elements of honor and shame
to regulate their peers and even their teachers. Six years after Rowe's disgrace,
the fate of King's College professor Robert Harpur became a more public
mockery from an unlikely source, as a cartoon of his misdeeds began to circu-
late, courtesy of his students. The crudely drawn cartoon—possibly by the
hand of future patriot and King's College student Gouverneur Morris—was
distributed by several students, led by college senior and future faculty member John Vardill. It depicted Harpur's scandalous acts of fornication, which
resulted in his mistress's unplanned pregnancy and subsequent abortion. Although the portrayed character was given the pseudonym of Pagan, obviously to illustrate his loss of Christian virtue and honor (as well as protect the
authors from reprisals), the depiction was known to be Harpur. The academ-
ically robed, dark-haired Harpur is shown paying for and forcing an abortion
on his fearful mistress, who laments that he has "ruined" her.[57] In an accompanying play, the King's College students insinuated that Harpur had fallen
from the path of true honor and virtue, and they accused him (and his mistress, by connection) of simply trying to allow their "reputation[s]" to "flourish
Midst the Frowns of Fortune!"[58] Although the charges were never definitively
proved, thereby allowing Harpur to retain his position, he lost a great deal of
his current and future students' respect; his reputation was weakened to such
a point that a student publicly "insult[ed him] with the most indecent language."[59] Within pre-Revolutionary colleges, elevated notions of honor and
virtue were used to measure one's reputation. Harpur's attempt to maintain
his reputation did not remove the blackness attached to his character for his
alleged moral deficiency.

While there was consistency between the ideological origins of America's colleges and their rules, there was still a fair amount of individualized thought and regional interpretation. These divisions influenced the development of individuals and their understanding of honor and virtue. John Adams was shaped in part due to the geographic and religious constraints of his schooling at Harvard College. Adams was already deeply interested in religion and the Puritan tradition. Harvard, situated just outside Boston, was a perfect location for him; like many New England colleges, it made a conscious effort to tie religion and virtue together synonymously.

While there was an acceptance of the principles of honor at the school, Harvard was also the most outwardly resistant to students aspiring to gentility. Contrary to Franklin's youthful admonitions against Harvard, there seems to have been a belief that gentility was selfish and devoid of elevated principles. Harvard, in particular, was concerned that students would dishonor themselves, their parents, and the college by placing themselves in debt while attempting to live a genteel life beyond their means. Harvard College declared, "Exorbitant Expenses . . . are not only highly dishonorable to the college, but also prejudicial to the Parents of such extravagant youths."[60] This attack on gentility went beyond financial concerns, as the administration resisted showy displays that they considered foppery and inconstant with virtue, banning "any Gold or Silver Lace, Cord or Edging, upon their Hats, Jackets, or any other Parts of their Clothing, nor any Gold nor Silver Brocades in the College, or Town of Cambridge."[61] This planned resistance to gentility would have been less regulated and accepted in New York or New Jersey and completely foreign to the students at William and Mary in Virginia. Yet it greatly influenced the students in Cambridge.[62] Throughout his life, Adams came to denigrate notions of gentility as being decidedly feminine.[63] His concept of honor possessed a touch of humility that seemed dependent on recognition of his own good fortune, along with a desire to not overextend himself or his family.[64] This idea seems to have a great deal to do with the importance placed on virtue over honor by Adams and the colleges.

In Northern colleges, particularly those in New England, virtue and religion were often inseparable, and honor was viewed as an outward, lesser manifestation of these ideals. Students were frequently admonished for not only their dishonoring of the college but also their "dishonor[ing] of God."[65] These ideas were bolstered in large part due to the prominent presence of clergymen in high-ranking college positions. Rev. Aaron Burr Sr., father of the patriot of the same name and president of the College of New Jersey, spoke of true honor being consistent with proper Christian ethics and the promotion of the glory of God.[66] Dartmouth president and founder, Rev. Eleazer Whee-lock, governed the college based on his own personal understanding that "as to my own character I would have no respect to that any further than the Glory of God and the Cause of the Redeemer may be affected by it."[67] Religion and virtue were considered the highest goals for a person to aspire to, and irreli-gion could be punished—with blasphemy resulting in possible expulsion.[68] The lesson of religiously tinted virtue over honor stuck with Adams through-out his life, as he deduced that "our proper Business in this Life is, not to ac-cumulate large Fortunes, not to gain high Honours and important offices in the State, not to waste our Health and Spirits in Pursuit of the Sciences, but constantly to improve our selves in Habits of Piety and Virtue."[69]

Still, honor was viewed by Adams and the colleges as a secular alternative to religious virtue; Yale president Clap wrote, "So far as scholars are not influ-enced by true Religion, they ought to be influenced [by] . . . a true Sense of Honor and Reputation."[70] Adams, though exalting virtue as superior, still un-hesitatingly asked, "Which, dear Youth, will you prefer? A Life of Effeminacy, Indolence and obscurity, or a Life of Industry, Temperance, and Honour?"[71]

Honor and virtue were often presented as a secular or civic religion. As college halls were filled with religious figures in teaching and leadership posi-tions, this focus on honor and virtue seems representative of Great Awakening dissent and a belief in universal morality. These ethical concepts thus existed as a reflection of a more inclusive religious morality. This shift resulted in honor and virtue being presented in more secular or civic terms. The more secular language didn't mean irreligion in colonial colleges, but rather a new focus on nondenominational ethical concepts that represented a challenge to an older order.[72]

Despite this overt emphasis in Northern colleges on religion and virtue, with honor as a subsidiary, there was still a major focus on establishing hier-archy and proper conduct befitting one's rank. Harvard was one of the most active colleges in disciplining students by lowering their class rank for of-fenses ranging from public insults to disobedience to noise infractions.[73]

Within New England colleges, such as Dartmouth and Rhode Island, an unofficial enforcement of an honor code also existed. Students implemented these regulations on other students. The sense of a belief in the greater good of the college community and its reputation as a whole seems to have driven these students to police themselves. At Rhode Island College, seniors were expected to correct the faulty behavior of lower classmen and keep watch over them to ensure their compliance, as it reflected on the reputation of the entire student body.[74] Meanwhile, the students of Dartmouth were much more vigorous in their approach. In 1775, five students wrote a pronouncement to the board of trustees that they wished to rid the school of "the influence of Gentlemen (so called) or persons of prophane and unsavory Conversation" who had corrupted their fellow youths, and whose continued behavior "would much mar and sully the honor, and entail great and lasting reproach upon this School of the Prophets, the reputation of which we earnestly desire may be preserved and transmitted to the latest posterity." The students claimed that all were "united" in their efforts to maintain the honor of Dartmouth College, and they only asked for assistance in instances in which their censures would not prove formidable enough.[75] There was a clear sense of collective honor in New England, in that the honor or dishonor of one could influence the reputation of the whole. Thus, the students became proactive in their guarding of their own personal and institutional honor and reputation.

In the South, the College of William and Mary stood virtually alone as the center for colonial higher education.[76] At William and Mary, a different understanding of honor existed—one more consistent with traditional notions of Southern honor. Unlike the students at Northern institutions who regulated the honor code and sought assistance from and coordinated with the administration, the Southern students banded together and formed a wall of silence to protect each other and themselves from interlopers. Their collective understanding of honor existed, but it was also very personal.[77] In April 1769, a riot broke out on the grounds of the college, orchestrated in large part by a student named Thomas Byrd; before the night was done, shattered glass and debris were scattered about the campus. The faculty quickly began their inquiry, and while they ascertained that Byrd was the ringleader, they were unable to identify a significant number of the participants. The faculty was left with only one offender, and they begrudgingly bemoaned their students' "false Sense of Honour."[78] Instead of keeping the student rioters in check, other fellow students held their tongues out of a sense of collective honor, independent from the reputation of the institution. Thus falsehoods, lies, and lies of omission could be considered perfectly acceptable, even honorable, to the Virginia student. This concept was directly at odds with the traditional view held by the administration that stressed morality and the supremacy of the greater good as honor.

While in New England the reputations of the students and the college were inseparable, in Virginia the two were mutually exclusive. Such behavior was apparently not that uncommon; since the 1730s, William and Mary was forced to employ both "Publick and Clandestine" student informers to manage infractions viewed as dishonorable.[79] It is unclear how effective these measures were, as many students had a very real "fear of being beaten & abused by the Delinquents among them."[80] In this respect, the students again established an honor code that was outside the wishes of the administration but used the same tenets of shame and disgrace among one's peers.

The point of honor was a bit sharper—or duller, depending on which side one stood on—in Williamsburg than it was in any of the other collegiate cities. William and Mary was the most English in style and sentiment of all of America's colleges. Again reflective of the growing dissenting belief in universal morality, students were not browbeaten with the religious overtones of honor and virtue (although virtually all of the professors were Anglican clergymen), and in general there were fewer defined rules than could be found anywhere on this side of the Atlantic. There was clearly a greater emphasis placed on each student's personal sense of honor, but ironically it was at William and Mary that the differences between the students', faculty's, and administration's understandings were greatest. While rules were less clearly defined, punishments were considerably harsher, with "imprudent" or "insolent" acts toward a superior chastised with expulsion.[81] Beatings were also not uncommon at the college for more egregious offenses, a disciplinary action that was less vigorously employed elsewhere in America during the mid-eighteenth century.

The more draconian nature of punishment seems to have existed in direct correlation with the unprecedented displays of violence perpetrated by students and faculty of William and Mary. In a system in which students were supposed to be able look to their teachers as models of virtue and honor, many were left wanting by the personage of Jacob Rowe, the aforementioned chair of moral philosophy. Only a couple of months after he was censured by the college, Rowe's behavior deteriorated from drunken rants to gunshots, as he led his students against the town's young apprentices in "a pitched Battle with Pistols and other Weapons." So-called riotous behavior was quite common in all American schools, but nothing near this level. Government and college officials tried to stay the violence, but they were met with hostility— some from Rowe personally. The disgraced professor placed the barrel of his pistol to the chest of John Campbell before taking aim at future patriot Peyton Randolph, a member of the board of visitors and a Williamsburg magistrate (though, luckily for Randolph, Rowe didn't fire). This little Williamsburg war was eventually quelled, but Francis Fauquier, William and Mary's rector and Virginia's future governor, was afraid of subsequent battles and instituted a strict confinement to campus for all of the students. Upon hearing this, Rowe became incredulous and argumentative. With seemingly no fear, likely from alcohol-induced courage, he "insulted" the William and Mary president and rector for questioning his authority and impugning his honor. Rowe was immediately stripped of his position and ordered removed from the campus—by force if necessary.[82] This incident illustrates just how individualized honor was in Virginia before the Revolution, as both sides believed they were acting in accordance with the principles of honor. The event demonstrated the practical applications of these principles, as it forced the board of visitors to institute a new professor of moral philosophy, one who would have a substantial impact on one of America's greatest thinkers.

The sudden vacancy left by Rowe's departure saw William Small taking over as professor of moral philosophy. Small, a native of Scotland and one of the few laymen on the faculty, was still only five years removed from Marischal College in Aberdeen, Scotland, where he studied under classicist and philosopher William Duncan; he had been a professor of natural philosophy at William and Mary since 1758.[83] Despite his relative inexperience in the classroom, Small was a welcome change, as he possessed "eminent Virtues" and was described as "a Gent[lema]n of great Worth, Integrity & Honour."[84] In addition to these qualities, he became the pioneer of the lecture system in America and the first teacher to offer "regular lectures in ethics, rhetoric, and Belles Lettres [artistic literature, novels, and so on]."[85] Small fit the mold of an eighteenth-century morality teacher, in that he was able to effectively convey an understanding of the material and he actually possessed qualities worthy of his students' emulation. Through a combination of fate and luck, Small's appointment as professor of moral philosophy virtually coincided with a young Thomas Jefferson's entrance into William and Mary.

Jefferson was born on April 13, 1743, as the eldest son of a gentry family that had been well established in Virginia since the seventeenth century. Jefferson's father, Peter, much like Lawrence Washington, had elevated his already comfortable status when he married Jane Randolph, a member of the eminent Randolph family, and ultimately became a prominent squire in the Piedmont region of Virginia and a member of the state's House of Burgesses. A great deal of Jefferson's early learning came at the hands of his father, an avid reader, who exposed him to many of the same works known to the young Franklin and Washington, particularly the *Spectator*. Peter Jefferson, a rough-and-tumble bear of a man, also instructed his son in manly physical trappings, from riding to hunting. Jefferson did not take particularly well to such masculine behavior, but he did become enthralled with books, and at the age of five he began the start of his extensive formal education, attending a one-room schoolhouse with his siblings and Randolph cousins. Throughout his life, Jefferson believed that novels could prove just as educational as serious tomes and treatises—though he would still continue his formal education well past the traditional age dictated by the norms of society. By age nine, he was boarding with his Scottish tutor, Rev. William Douglas. For five years, Douglas, who was previously the tutor for the Monroe family, was charged with teaching Jefferson the skills that marked an educated gentleman: French, Latin, and Greek. However, not to discredit his teachers, Jefferson still considered his father to be his most defining influence.

In 1757, Peter Jefferson died at age forty-nine and left his son grief-stricken and angry. The teenage Jefferson lashed out at his mother, unfairly blaming her for his father's untimely demise. For the next two years, Jefferson lived with his new tutor, Rev. James Maury, an arrangement he welcomed if only to escape his mother's gaze. Despite the pragmatic reason for his continued education, Maury's tutelage was extensive. He would impart the "virtues" of "force and elegance" and further exposed Jefferson to classical and Enlightenment authors.[86] Although at this point Jefferson was as well educated as nearly anyone in Virginia, he still feared he was stagnating under his mother's guidance and trifles, and that his "schooling was falling into discourse." He needed to escape. A college education was a crowning achievement for a young gentleman, and the answer to both of his problems. It was not long before his relative Col. Randolph reaffirmed and encouraged Jefferson's wish to attend William and Mary, and so off he went.[87]

Jefferson arrived in the colonial capital of Williamsburg in May 1760, possibly with just enough time to witness and be suitably shocked by Rowe and his band of gentry students' public street battle. For a shy seventeen-year-old from the fringes of the Virginia frontier, the spectacle of the scandal surrounding Rowe's termination (let alone the battle itself) would have proved an inauspicious beginning and a poor introduction to the character of the school and its students. Williamsburg was the cultural hub of Virginia society, and, aside from a young aspiring lawyer named Patrick Henry, whom he had befriended en route to the college, he did not know a soul for nearly a hundred miles.

It was under these circumstances that an impressionable Jefferson met William Small, the man who would become his pseudo-father, despite being only nine years older. Small relished his new role as professor of moral philosophy, was an eager proponent of Enlightenment ideas, and personally introduced Jefferson to the great French philosophers, including Montesquieu. French nobleman Charles-Louis de Secondat, baron de Le Brède et de Montesquieu, first published his immensely influential work the *Spirit of the Laws* in 1748, which put forth novel interpretations of honor and virtue. Through Montesquieu's *Spirit of the Laws*, Jefferson learned the Frenchman's self-proclaimed "new" theory that virtue was a political idea, and that honor—though admirable—could be easily corrupted and become divisive. Still, Montesquieu imparted the wisdom that honor itself could inspire virtue, a principle that was the opposite of that taught to Adams—and one that would have a tremendous impact on all of society in the coming decade.[88] Though Jefferson had a command of the French language, it was the translations of Montesquieu's work into English during the 1750s that made it a crucial text for the American Revolution. Subsequently, Small was also responsible for introducing Jefferson to other renowned men of status. They included famed trial attorney George Wythe and Virginia governor Francis Fauquier. Jefferson became a frequent guest at the governor's table, and he imbibed the words of these lofty figures long into the night.

Jefferson's relationship with Small was a crucial step to solidifying himself in the hierarchical world. But just how comfortable Jefferson was with embracing the system of patronage, a common motif in honor culture, remains debatable. On the one hand, Jefferson, like Washington with the Fairfaxes, used his Randolph connections to ease his transition into Williamsburg high society. His lineage made it quite easy for him to befriend other well-off young men, including John Page and John Tyler. Jefferson found himself participating in the typical activities of the young men of William and Mary. He ran up large debts, frequented taverns, fancied women, and even engaged in "town and gown" brawls (locals versus students) similar to the one he likely experienced upon his arrival. On the other hand, Jefferson—though a member of the Randolph family—was not a Randolph. This may have weighed on him, as he chose to separate himself from claims of nepotism as he took up legal studies under Small's friend Wythe, rather than his attorney cousins Peyton and John Randolph. Such thought and actions show Jefferson's remarkable degree of self-assured independence and resistance to the unearned rewards of lineage, which only become apparent in a more mature, battle-hardened Washington.

In 1762, Jefferson left the College of William and Mary to study law privately with Wythe. Law was deemed an honorable profession for a gentleman, and this type of legal education was common in America. Adams had gone the same route under Worcester lawyer James Putnam and later Boston attorney Jeremiah Gridley. In fact, private study represented the only method of legal education available to colonists, outside of attending the Inns of

Court in London (as the Randolphs had done). An education at London's Inns of Court was both costly and, by the eighteenth century, negatively acknowledged by Americans abroad (such as John Dickinson) and famed British lawyer William Blackstone as devoid of any "regard to morals," which were "found impracticable and therefore entirely neglected."[89] Another American student in London (and future signer of the Declaration of Independence), Charles Carroll, nearly identically remarked, "Few young gentlemen here to be found of sound morals."[90] Luckily for Jefferson, Virginia native Wythe, who would go on to become America's first law professor, was considered to be one of the finest legal minds in the colony. Wythe also made a name for himself as, according to one acquaintance, "the only honest lawyer I ever knew" because he would dismiss clients and refund fees if he deemed them at fault in a case.[91] He was also so well versed and practiced in the classical ideas of honor and virtue that it was claimed that he had greater virtue and selflessness than any found in ancient Greece or Rome.[92] Jefferson was instructed in the law, Enlightenment philosophy, and Hutcheson's morality. Unlike modern-day stereotypes, lawyers were expected to and needed to behave ethically. Gridley similarly taught Adams, "Indeed a Lawyer through his whole Life ought to have some Book on Ethicks or the Law of Nations always on his Table. They are all Treatises of individual or national Morality and ought to be the Study of our whole Lives."[93] Through guided readings and courtroom and personal observation, Wythe became a model worthy of emulation for Jefferson, for, as one former student claimed, "such a man casts a light upon all around him."[94] Thus, it was not surprising when mentor and pupil came to similar conclusions on the state of the British Empire at the close of the French and Indian War.

Education in early America instructed young men in honor culture from an ethical perspective. American colleges and schools became instrumental in establishing a commonality of thought and a sense of camaraderie based on honor culture that helped to translate into unity during the Revolution. The lessons taught in classes and the rules that governed the colleges became a guide and foundation for the continued progression of honor as an ethical concept throughout early America. It was a first step on the path from thought to action.

CHAPTER THREE

A Matter of Honor and a Test of Virtue

*Riots, Boycotts, and Resistance
during the Coming of the Revolution*

The year 1763 marked the end of the French and Indian War, a conflict that fundamentally changed the British Empire's relationship with the American colonies. The colonists initially viewed the British victory in the war as an opportunity to improve their standing within the empire. What resulted was stricter regulation and subjugation. Americans had fought with their British brethren, and their efforts had helped defeat the French; remove the previous, ever-present fear of hostility along the frontier; and claim large expanses of land for the Crown. For many Americans, it was a moment of triumph— they had proved their valor and gained honor through battle. At the close of the war, most Americans, like Benjamin Franklin, would have considered themselves British. While the war may have been a unifying event for the colonists, its aftermath quickly became divisive. Britain was left with the daunting task of paying the bill for the latest chapter of its centuries-old struggle with France. To the British Parliament, the taxation of the colonies in order to offset the costs of the war and administer Britain's new territories seemed a viable solution. What began as a matter of money became a matter of honor.

As Britain began to pass invasive legislation, levy taxes, and assert control over colonial commerce, Americans started to question the ethics of their mother country. The idea that Britain has failed in its duty to its subjects, and thus sacrificed its honor, slowly took root in the minds of the colonists. They began to examine every British action through the lens of honor. Honor had always existed in the colonies, but during the period between the French and Indian War and the American Revolution, it became a unifying element that was less hierarchical and dominated political and social life.

With the French threat removed from the borders of the American colonies after the French and Indian War, many real estate speculators lustily eyed the newly opened lands west of the Allegheny Mountains. For Virginians— George Washington chief among them—land denoted wealth, power, and gentility. The greater the Virginia planters' lands, the more crops they could yield, which in turn made them more money. It allowed them to live the life of country gentlemen. As a result of service in the French and Indian War,

Washington and other officers of the Virginia Regiment had been promised extensive land grants on the western frontier. While these grants were sizeable, they were not enough for a land-hungry Virginian. In September 1763, Washington and nineteen speculators formed the Mississippi Land Company, which laid claim to 2.5 million acres of western lands as far away as Illinois. The foundation intended to expand the influence and wealth of the Virginia gentry far across the horizon.

However, Britain feared that Anglo-American expansion would incite Indian hostility, as Pontiac's Rebellion did on the western frontier six months earlier, thereby disrupting trade and creating the expense of additional troop deployments. Less than a month after Washington and his associates made their claims, the British Parliament issued the Proclamation of 1763, banning all expansion between the Appalachian Mountains and the Mississippi River. With the stroke of a quill, Britain had taken the spoils of war from the waiting hands of the colonists. Washington felt that he had spent the duration of the French and Indian War suffering denigrations of pay and status at the hands of the British; now, instead of being rewarded for his efforts, he was again dismissed.

While Washington was being robbed of his anticipated earnings, his London creditors, Robert Cary and Company, came calling for the payment of his debts. It was common for gentleman planters to contract with London merchants to sell their crops (largely tobacco in Virginia) and acquire British goods for them on credit to be paid from the season's harvest. As a gentleman planter, Washington was a subscriber to this system and relied on these middlemen to both sell his crops and obtain luxury items. The Virginian desired all the trappings of gentility—from fashion to silverware to wine—and he managed to accumulate a considerable debt in the process.

Debt was a fact of life for planters, and Washington's indebtedness was not the matter at issue. It was perfectly acceptable (though not desirable), and even expected, that Virginia's gentlemen farmers would have debts; there was no dishonor attached to it. In the eighteenth century money did not dictate one's honor. Quite the contrary, debts of money were always considered to be in reality "debts of honor."[1] Debt actually bestowed a level of honor on the individual, as it was a sign of trust that indicated that the individual's reputation alone could be counted on to ensure future payment. To society, those who regularly incurred debt clearly possessed honor, since they were obviously thought of as capable of making good on their promises.

For Washington, the problem was that, in 1764, Robert Cary dared to ask for immediate payment of his debts.[2] This was an affront to Washington's honor, as it implied that he was not good for the money or would not pay. Washington responded, in what he regarded as "terms equally sincere and direct," that the ability to pay was "not in my power . . . to make remittances faster than my Crops . . . will furnish me with the means." Thus, the debts were not a reflection on him but rather were the result of a poor showing of his crops due to weather and, in a more than slightly accusatory manner, Cary for not securing better prices for his harvest. Washington was clearly sensitive regarding Cary's demands, as he complained that "if notwithstanding, you cannot be content with this mode of payments you have only to advise me of it and I shall hit upon a method . . . that will at once discharge the Debt, and effectually remove me from all further mention of it." He announced that he would settle his debt, but the mere "mention" of the requested payment made Washington noticeably uncomfortable and forced him to become protective of his honor and reputation. He was genuinely shocked that his character would be called into question, stating, "I must confess, I did not expect that a corrispondant so steady, & constant as I have proovd . . . woud be reminded . . . how necessary it was for him to be expedious in his payments." Washington was incensed that he would be reminded of his obligation, lecturing Cary that he would always choose to do what was "right" and that the merchant should "have rested assured, that so fast as I coud make remittances without distressing myself too much, my Inclinations woud have prompted me to it."[3] Washington took the matter very personally, adding to his growing list of insults at the hands of the British.

While Washington was lamenting London's interference in his personal finances, the British Parliament was concerned with the empire's own staggering (and still growing) debt of just under £130,000,000. Strapped for ready cash to pay down the debt's nearly £5,000,000 annual interest, in addition to the £200,000 yearly cost of garrisoning the colonies, the British resorted to a form of direct revenue taxation that had never before been implemented in America.[4] Taxation had always existed as a voluntary gift from the subjects to the king, but it was never directly enforced in America. The colonists, with a few exceptions, took for granted the long tradition that they could only be directly taxed by colonial legislatures.

Spurred by the debt of the war, the British imposed revenue taxation legislation in 1764 in the form of the Sugar Act (a tariff on sugar, cloth, wine, and coffee, partially designed to eliminate smuggling). As this act was viewed simply as trade regulation, its impact was quickly surpassed by the specter of the Stamp Act, which had a profound effect on the psyche of the colonists.

While the American uproar against the Stamp Act is mostly credited with producing the immortal words "no taxation without representation," there were concurrent matters of honor in the balance as well. The Stamp Act placed a duty on all printed articles, which required them to bear the British treasury's stamp. As it is commonly and correctly understood, the act represented a conflict between Parliament and the colonies over the powers of taxation, issues of direct versus virtual representation, and exactly what rights Americans had as English subjects. However, the colonists were just as concerned with how the Stamp Act infringed on their honor—individually and collectively.

As noted by historian Bertram Wyatt-Brown and anthropologist Julian Pitt-Rivers, involuntary taxation and honor have always been at odds with each other. Contributing money as a gift by subsidy, as the colonies had done since their founding, denoted a sense of equality. Colonists viewed direct taxation as a form of tribute that denigrated them to the position of "defeated enemies and inferior people." The American colonists had just fought valiantly for the glory of the British Empire, and they were now being tangibly and symbolically treated as something other than English subjects.[5] Bostonian James Otis Jr. stated that the only distinction that should be made between the colonies and Britain was that they owed "deference and dutiful submission" to the Crown—being taxed as a conquered people was a form of shaming and dishonor.[6]

After the passage of the Stamp Act, nine colonial assemblies adopted resolutions affirming their opposition to the tax based on their lack of representation and Parliament's lack of rights to direct taxation. At the same time, showing just how expansive the notion of honor was in the American colonies, the outrage aimed at the Stamp Act based on honor was equally exhibited across regional lines, with references being made from Massachusetts to Georgia (the latter of which did not issue a formal resolution). While honor is popularly considered as a Southern ideal, New England actually led the charge in accusing Britain of wounding the colony's honor. The Harvard-educated, Boston-based Samuel Adams, in conjunction with the House of Representatives of Massachusetts, formally declared that the Stamp Act infringed on their "warm sense of honor, freedom and independence" and that "they esteem it sacrilege for them to ever give them up: and rather than lose them, they would willingly part with every thing else."[7] The members of the Massachusetts legislature made it clear that this was a principled resistance rather than a financial one. They were willing to give up "everything else," provided they did not have to sacrifice their ideals. The linkage between the words "honor," "freedom," and "independence" was a conscious choice, one that underpinned the nature of honor itself. Honor required freedom and independence in order to exist; to remove them made a person a slave, a status that, in the eighteenth century, was widely considered devoid of any form of honor. During the years leading up to the American Revolution, Americans continually linked the ideas of honor and virtue with liberty, freedom, and independence; in many ways, these ideas became inseparable and have only been distanced in the linguistics of the modern era. Within the next few years, colonial newspapers, such as the *Pennsylvania Chronicle* and *Providence Gazette*, would report that "independence" was the source of "a life of virtue" and that "men of virtue" were followers of "ethics."[8] The terms "honor" and "virtue" became representative of much more than they had previously. John Adams, Samuel's younger cousin, specifically regarded "Liberty" as "the complication of real Honor, Piety, Virtue, Dignity, and Glory."[9] The colonists resented the Stamp Act because it made them feel subservient and unequal. In even more pointed terms, Samuel Adams and Massachusetts assemblyman Thomas Cushing explained that Parliament's demand for taxes, rather than its acceptance of them as the traditional gift, reduced the colonists to an inferior status and robbed them of their "Honor or Safety, as Subjects!"[10]

John Adams, a lawyer and another student of Harvard's virtue-over-honor curriculum, also felt that he was "under all obligations of . . . Honour" to contend with the illegality of the Stamp Act. The religious Adams, keeping in mind his youthful education, made the Stamp Act an offense against not only the honor of man but also the honor of God. Adams wrote that accepting the Stamp Act was synonymous with "consenting to slavery," which "is a sacrilegious breach of trust, as offensive in the sight of God, as it is derogatory from our own honor or interest or happiness; and that God almighty has promulgated from heaven, liberty, peace, and good-will to man!"[11] Despite the religious overtones, Adams's point remained that to accept the taxation would dishonor them. This rationale was understood and believed throughout the colonies, as its people came to resent this British slight.[12]

A collective sense of honor developed in response to the Stamp Act, paving the way for a common identity regardless of societal status.[13] Since as early as 1761, Adams understood that Boston's honor was dictated by the combined actions of its citizens.[14] By 1765, it was not a leap for him, and others, to begin to imagine the colonies as part of one large whole. Adams spoke of the "Infant Country" of America as being the inheritors of the virtue of ancient Rome, and he asserted that Americans were a "People" who "merited Honour and Happiness" and possessed a "radical sense of Liberty."[15] Adams's views found support in the American press; an article in the *Connecticut Courant,* symbolically written under the pseudonym of the Roman hero Cato, contended that Americans are "a virtuous People unjustly sunk and debased by Tyranny and Oppression."[16]

In 1765, the Eton-, Cambridge-, and Middle Temple–educated Maryland lawyer and politician Daniel Dulany wrote a scathing pamphlet, *Considerations on the Propriety of Imposing Taxes in the British Colonies for the Purpose of Raising a Revenue by Act of Parliament,* attacking Parliament's right to impose the Stamp Act. He saw America's honor at stake, honor that its people had a duty to defend even against the mother country. He wrote, "Any oppression of the colonies would intimate an opinion of them I am persuaded they do not deserve, and their security as well as honour ought to engage them to confute." This was not a symbolic defense of honor; Dulany insisted that some form of action be taken—to fail to do so would indicate that the colonists had already lost their honor. He instructed, "When contempt is mixed with injustice, and insult with violence, which is the case when an injury is done to him who hath the means of redress in his power; if the injured hath one inflammable grain of honour in his breast, his resentment will invigorate his pursuit of reparation, and animate his efforts to obtain an effectual security against a repetition of the outage." Dulany declared that America must act in order to avoid dishonor, and he suggested the way to accomplish this was through a boycott of British-made goods. He urged, "Let the manufacture of America be the symbol of dignity, the badge of virtue, and it will soon break the fetters of distress."[17] The colonies had been a source for Britain's raw materials, but the actual manufacturing took place across the Atlantic, with the colonists forced to pay high prices for the finished goods. Dulany wanted to defend American honor by hurting Britain's purse, just as it had injured America's.

By only using American-made products, they would be defending and embracing their honor and collective ideals, and also distancing themselves from the hierarchical, showy accouterments of gentility. For "a garment of linsey-woolsey, when made the distinction of real patriotism, is more honourable and attractive of respect and veneration, than all the pageantry, and the robes, and the plumes, and the diadem of an emperor without it." Dulany urged Americans to view their honor as separate from merely the external trappings of appearance and embrace a deeper ideal.[18] Wearing simple garments became a symbol of honor through patriotism and resistance. These ideas spread throughout the colonies. As historians Edmund Morgan and Helen Morgan explain, "Dulany's pamphlet was bought by his countrymen as they had scarcely bought any pamphlet before."[19] Hundreds of American merchants from throughout the colonies signed on to support such a nonimportation agreement. From the start, it was recognized as a valid means for the colonists to illicit a response and defend their honor from Britain. These actions even garnered sympathy from their English merchant counterparts, due to a sense of understanding and their own financial woes caused by the boycott.

Nonimportation agreements and boycotts of British goods became common tools for the colonists throughout the run-up to the Revolution. They became tried-and-true responses to all manner of British legislation, always framed by the language of honor and cast as "a public virtue."[20] In Virginia it was declared, "We do hereby engage ourselves, by those most sacred ties of honour and love to our country, that we will not, either . . . hereafter import within the true meaning of this association, [or] make any advance in price, with a view to profit by the restrictions hereby laid on the trade of this colony."[21] In refusing to sell or import British goods, colonists were uniting their personal senses of honor with one another for a higher cause, devoid of economic interest. The nonimportation agreements fostered a collective sense of honor, and Samuel Adams regarded them as "very solicitous for the Honor of the Merchants of Boston, my fellow Citizens, but much more for my Country."[22]

Adams's "fellow Citizens" were not only the men of the colonies; they were also the women. In 1764, Otis had publicly recognized that "women" were "born as free as men" and therefore equals in the quest for colonial rights.[23] Women—frequently overlooked in discussions of honor—played an important role in protesting the actions of the British. Female participation in the boycott of British goods, particularly during the Tea Act, helped women gain equality in terms of honor, even if they still lacked social equality. Writing after the conclusion of the war, Mercy Otis Warren, Otis's sister, recalled that "all the American continent was involved in one common danger" and that the boycotts were "solemn agreements" that "plighted their faith and honor to each other, and to their country."[24] Women stopped consuming and serving British tea, gave up luxurious clothes and fineries, and instituted home manufacturing, particularly of cloth, for the cause. They thereby engaged in both personal and collective matters of honor and illustrated their "Harmony and union," as well as their "industry and virtue."[25] Philadelphia poet Hannah Griffitts wrote,

> Let the Daughters of Liberty, nobly arise,
> And tho' we've no Voice, but a negative here,
> The uses of the Taxables, let us forbear,

(Then Merchants import till yr. Stores are all full
May the Buyers be few and yr. Traffick be dull.)
Stand firmly resolved and bid Greenville to see
That rather than Freedom, we'll part with our Tea
And well as we love the dear Draught when adry,
As American Patriots,—our Taste we deny.[26]

As women denied their desires for the greater good, it became a tangible sign of honor, with honor also expanding its meaning. Women demonstrated these values in a variety of ways, from personally making their own cloth to refusing a cup of tea.

But women's sense of honor also became collectivized, like that of their male counterparts, and in turn expanded their public and political roles. In Newport, Rhode Island, nearly one hundred women, recognized as "daughters of Liberty," engaged in a "voluntary Bee or Spinning Match" to produce bolts of homespun cloth as a sign of resistance. Such actions by "Ladies of Character" were not isolated incidents and were conspicuous to the "Eyes of the World" as "contributing to bring about the political Salvation of the whole Continent." Furthermore, this collective action was regarded as "a credit to their fair Sex, and an Honour to America."[27] Their actions were considered not only to benefit women collectively but also to be representative of united colonial sentiment. Boycotting British goods and making their own clothes became an external sign of their inner qualities and so matched the ethic of honor perfectly. Again the Tea Act provided the most prominent examples of collective female honor. On October 25, 1774, in Edenton, North Carolina, fifty-one ladies led by Penelope Baker held their own tea party in which they forswore the beverage as a "duty we owe not only to our near and dear connections . . . but to ourselves" and for "the peace and happiness of our country."[28] The affair was directly organized by women, independent of male influence, and spoke to their conceptions of personal and collective honor. In turn, Warren attempted to galvanize all women into taking action for the cause:

Let us resolve on a small sacrifice
And in the pride of Roman matrons rise;
Good as Cornelia, or Pompey's wife,
We'll quit the useless vanities of life.[29]

Warren appealed to virtue based on classical sentiments; just as the men had their Roman heroes, such as Cato, women could look to antiquity for shining examples of honor and virtue to which they could aspire.[30]

All of these actions brought women into the public and political sphere.[31] Before this, women were infrequent political actors. Their deeds rarely entered them into the conversation of honor and thus were not typically talked about in such terms. Through political action, they gained honor for themselves and their sex collectively. By offering a degree of political inclusion, the boycotts represented a moment of stark departure from the traditional references to women's honor and virtue as being confined only to chastity. For some, boycotts served as a gateway to even more patriotic behavior. In the Massachusetts countryside, a tall young lady named Deborah Sampson gained her first taste of honor by weaving cloth for the cause—and she would come to desire more.[32]

The boycotts included women from all classes, including those of "Rank and Influence." Women publicly spoke up against the British infringement on liberty, saying it could reduce America to slavery.[33] These concepts, already firmly tied to honor, became the backbone of the female protest. Quaker planter and future abolitionist Robert Pleasants celebrated the fairer sex, saying that "in Consequence of this resolution the use of Tea is declined in great measure, and with credit to our Women, it may be said they seem as forward to promote the cause in that respect as the Men."[34] This was not simply rhetoric; the idea that women were active participants in the resistance movement was held broadly in colonial society. Hannah Winthrop, wife of Harvard professor John Winthrop, reveled in the story of a gentleman remarking to a young boy that his mother was a "fine lady." The boy accepted the compliment but added his own stipulation, "I know my mama is a fine lady, but she would be much finer if she were a Daughter of Liberty."[35] This anecdote illustrates that in America during the 1760s and 1770s, it was understood that a woman could possess all of the traditional female attributes associated with gentility but would be improved by the honor of taking up the cause of America. Not only did men recognize the honor that women possessed, but women also came to see themselves as patriots and began to utilize much of the same language of honor as men.[36] America's females believed that "honor," "virtu[e]," and "noble resolution" were demanded of both men and women. They became active participants in the fight for freedom, and they wanted "it known unto Britain, even American daughters are politicians and patriots and will aid the good work with their female efforts."[37]

On the other side of the debate, those colonists who defied the agreement were considered to be acting dishonorably and as a result were shunned, vilified (often in scathing newspaper articles), or publicly shamed (possibly even through tarring and feathering) by their patriotic neighbors.[38] British-educated lawyer Arthur Lee regarded opposition as "treachery," and it made him fear that "there was not virtue enough in America."[39] Samuel Adams, under the pseudonym Determinatus, roused the people against such nonconformity, stating, "Where then is the honor! Where is the shame of these persons, who can look into the faces of those very men with whom they have contracted, & tell them Without Blushing that they resolved to Violate the contract! Is it obstinacy, perverseness, pride, or from what root of bitterness does such an unaccountable defection from the laws of honor, honesty, and even humanity spring?"[40]

For some colonists, the Stamp Act and the boycott of British goods became personal. Washington, still in the midst of his continuing feud with Cary, began to link his own predicament to the legislation imposed by Parliament. Washington added a slew of additional grievances to his argument with Cary. He accused the merchant of cheating him on the profits for the sale of his tobacco crops, as well as supplying him with inferior goods at disproportionate prices. He linked these personal slights with those suffered by America as a whole. The Stamp Act became an "ill Judgd," "unconstitutional method of Taxation" and "a direful attack upon their Liberties." Washington concluded, like Dulany, that the only way to combat such offenses was to disengage from commerce with Britain. Washington's sense of America's honor was born from his own personal honor, but over time collective honor took precedence. In a letter to Cary that could have just as easily been addressed to Parliament, he wrote, "The Eyes of our People (already beginning to open) will perceive, that many of the Luxuries which we have heretofore lavished our Substance to Great Britain for can well be dispensed with whilst the Necessaries of Life are to be procurd . . . within ourselves."[41] The colonists were waking up and thinking alike. The boycott was a way for America to defend its honor without sacrificing its virtue by descending to violence.

For many, however, this form of action was not enough; tempers began to overflow and more public and violent displays soon sprang up within the colonies. Displeasure over the Stamp Act was aimed largely at government officials, who were viewed as supporting or at least collaborating with Parliament. Violence was soon directed at the city's stamp distributer and secretary of Massachusetts, Andrew Oliver, and his brother-in-law Chief Justice and Lieutenant Governor Thomas Hutchinson. Oliver and Hutchinson had been accumulating titles and offices for themselves for years, though they claimed this rise to power was not out of interest but rather out of duty. Outrage over their nepotistic familial networks and hereditary advancement made them a target for the green-tinged eyes of others. Future patriots, such as John

Adams and Otis, viewed the preferential treatment of these families as an attempt to institute aristocratic rule, a prospect that was "humiliating," especially after Hutchinson was given the position of chief justice, despite not being a lawyer.[42] Heredity had conquered merit, and the patriots of Boston would not forget the insult. Jealousy and slights over personal matters again combined with the political realm to create a storm of hostility focused on the two relatives.

Oliver and Hutchinson became representative of the old style of advancement, which was based on heredity and patronage. Hostility toward them was in effect also a protest against this old system of non-merit-centered, descent-oriented hierarchy. Such animosity showed an evolving understanding of the nature of honor, both personally and professionally. Both men viewed themselves as behaving honorably in the typical manner of the British Empire, but such a style was now less acceptable in American society. Hutchinson was conscious of the American resistance to hereditary advancement; he recognized that the "appointment of natural sons to places of honour had an ill effect upon people's minds in America."[43] Still, he considered himself as behaving properly given his station and office.

Hutchinson viewed himself as firmly American; his family was made up of successful Congregationalist merchants (although he was more Anglican in belief) who were considered to be among the founders of Massachusetts. He was born in Boston in 1711 and attended the Boston Latin School (his father, Colonel Thomas Hutchinson, donated its building on School Street) and Harvard College. He was "well-to-do, well born, and of good character" and married into an equally prominent family: the Sanfords of Rhode Island, whose patriarch was also that colony's governor.[44] It was through this marriage that Hutchinson and Oliver became linked, as they both married Sanford daughters. Oliver came from a similar background to Hutchinson's; he was also Harvard educated and from a successful merchant family. As a result, Oliver and Hutchinson moved in virtually identical familial, political, and social circles, linking them inseparably in the minds of Bostonians. By the late 1730s, Hutchinson had entered Boston politics, and he remained ensconced in them for the next four decades.

The patriots resented Hutchinson as a representative of the old ideals of honor and hierarchy, but he was more an amalgamation of his Puritan upbringing and royal offices. Hutchinson was no stranger to the value of reputation, the necessity of virtue, and the laws of honor, and he was begrudgingly regarded as a "very good gentleman" by Otis.[45] The former Massachusetts governor Jonathan Belcher called him "a young gentleman of exact virtue."[46]

Like John Adams, Hutchinson rejected ostentatious displays of wealth and rank in favor of a subtler form of gentility. He possessed "self-respect" and "restraint" created by his "reputation and honor."[47] But these attributes did not stop many colonists from casting Oliver and Hutchinson as the villains behind the Stamp Act; Otis even suggested that Hutchinson had personally negotiated it.

On August 13, 1765, violence erupted. Spurred by the Loyal Nine, a collection of artisans, merchants, and shopkeepers (later renamed the Sons of Liberty), the lower classes of Boston's North and South Ends lashed out against the city's stamp distributor, Oliver. Despite the seemingly anonymous face of this collection, the influence of Ebenezer Mackintosh, "Commander of the South," would have been apparent (the events of the evening may have been influenced by Samuel Adams and Otis). Mackintosh, a cordwainer (shoemaker) by trade, was representative of Boston's less exalted residents. In a microcosm of colonial society, often divided, the North and South End mobs formed a "Union" and put aside personal interests for "patriotic principles," as they too understood the dictates of honor. (Only months later, Mackintosh; Samuel Swift, the "Commander of the North"; and their subordinates made an agreement "engaged upon their Honor," and there is no reason to believe similar promises did not occur here.) Illustrative of this point about speaking in terms of honor, Peter Oliver, a loyalist author, writes unfavorably about Mackintosh but still declares him to be a man of "superior Honor." In addition, Mackintosh's actions may have been due in part to his realization that the Stamp Act would negatively affect all tradesmen. Thus, his and the mobs' involvement may represent an early form of occupational or professional honor.[48]

With Mackintosh and Swift at the helm, the mob (led by a soon-to-be beheaded effigy of Andrew Oliver) broke through Oliver's front door and windows and ransacked his house near Fort Hill, all the while searching for the official with obvious malevolent intentions.[49] Oliver escaped that night, but his patriot neighbors soon threatened him into resigning his official commission. The event clearly left Oliver shaken, as years later he continued to denounce the evening's organizers as the "sons of Violence." He viewed the actions taken against him in his official capacity as both a personal insult and a slight to the British government. And he offered a solution: "If the honour of an insulted Government should require some examples of justice, the men could be easily pointed out, and ought to be offered as victims, if it might be a means of saving the community."[50]

The following night, a crowd surrounded Hutchinson's handsome white Georgian three-storied Boston mansion and demanded that he publicly swear he disapproved of the Stamp Act. The leaders of the mob claimed, "Since . . . they respected Hutchinson's private character they would accept his personal assurance that he did not favor the act." This ultimatum, though inherently threatening, showed that the colonists at least understood Hutchinson to be a man of honor, as they only questioned his public office. Hutchinson was set against answering such a charge on principle. He was spared by the shouts of an old tradesman in the crowd, who "charged" the mob with "ingratitude in insulting a gentleman who had been serving his country all his days."[51] The crowd dispersed, as this impassioned plea based on honor seemed to shame them, or at least momentarily satisfy their demands. However, less than two weeks later, another mob returned. The elegant governor remained determined to face the oncoming swarm personally and not withdraw from the danger, until his twenty-one-year-old daughter Sarah pleaded with him to flee. As he ran out the rear entrance, the mob descended, split his front door with axes, looted his family's possessions, and completely ravaged his home.[52] Before long, mobs and threats of violence sprang up throughout the colonies, and stamp distributors promptly withdrew from office.

The rage and violence employed by some colonists seems consistent with the nature of primal honor. Primal honor, as defined by historian Wyatt-Brown, involves the act of avenging a slight to one's honor through force. In many ways, these riots followed the same architecture as a duel, forcing capitulation or contrition by threat of violence. While these riots, which targeted Crown officials, had the same intended purpose as the nonimportation agreement, they were less readily accepted as an appropriate means of defense. As many came to view honor as consistent with ethics, the condemnation of violence was diverse. According to Boston pastor Charles Chauncy, the assault on Hutchinson's home "was so detested by town and country, and such a spirit at once so generally stirred up, particularly among the people, to oppose such villanous conduct, as has preserved us ever since in a state of as great freedom from mobbish actions as has been known in the country."[53] South Carolinian slave trader Henry Laurens denounced rioters, especially the Sons of Liberty, as enactors of "pretended Patriotism" who were filled with purely selfish and economic motivations. He argued that riots were not done to help relieve the burdens of America but rather were "unbounded acts of Licentiousness & at length Burglary & Robbery." Laurens then went one step further and denounced the riots' leaders as only hoping "to pay their debts or at least to obtain a Credit during their own pleasure by the destruction of the Stamp'd Papers."[54]

Washington also disapproved of this mob justice, as did Pennsylvanian John Dickinson. Dickinson went to great lengths to defend American honor by distancing the majority of the colonists from their more rambunctious brethren. He stated that he resented being grouped with "those few of the lower rank, who disturbed us with two or three mobs in some of the provinces," and lamented that critiques of America were not limited "to any other particular class of people; but that the censure is designed for ALL the inhabitants of these colonies."[55] Coinciding with this thinking was the idea that nonviolence also could even lead to social mobility for those of lower rank.[56] Dickinson spoke out against mob violence in order "to vindicate the honour of my country, which I think grossly and wantonly insulted."[57] Those using violence, in Dickinson's view, were acting against the best interest of America and weakening their ethical position.

In many ways Dickinson was an odd champion of honor, as he was born into a Quaker family, married a Quaker, and held many Quaker beliefs (though he was not formally a member of their meeting). Quakers were largely opposed to the notion of honor. Honor was owed to God; it was not the possession of man but humanity's duty to its creator. There was no concept of honor for men; it was only for God. Despite this belief, there was a heightened sense of duty and virtue in the Quaker faith. They were consistent with the very understanding of honor that they publicly shunned. The Quaker conception of the duty to act virtuously conformed to many of the traditional values. Quakers still had a complex understanding and acceptance of shame and disgrace—and, in turn, dishonor.[58] They did not believe dishonor should be avenged through violence, but rather by public affirmations. The mere use of the term "honor" and its conception by Dickinson in light of his religion are significant, and they show the widespread acceptance and importance of the concept, even despite specific attempts to curtail its influence. Even Quakers, who were technically opposed to the notion of honor, realized its importance in colonial affairs. Dickinson's stance in regard to colonial violence also suggests that in embracing the concept of honor, he was speaking of its ethical variant rather than the older form in opposition to Quaker beliefs.

Despite opposition from many of the exalted men of American society, these Stamp Act riots were not simply the actions of the rabble; they were conducted by those from diverse social stations who sought to take action in defense of their honor and liberty—in the same way as those who supported the nonimportation agreements. Throughout the colonies, men from all walks of life contributed to the riots. Gentlemen usually took the helm, with those of humbler origins in tow. In Williamsburg, Virginia, stamp distributer George Mercer was forced from his post by a group that Governor Francis Fauquier gasped, "I should call a Mob, did I not know that it was chiefly if not altogether Composed of Gentlemen."[59] Thus, the matter was not inherently an issue of class division but rather a disagreement on the interpretation of morality.

Violence was not limited to mobs. In January 1766 in New Haven, Connecticut, a brash young merchant and bookseller who had been continuing to illegally trade as if the Stamp Act did not exist and who had already shown a penchant for settling personal slights through duels led a less extravagant public assault against Peter Boles, one of his own merchant sailors who attempted to inform on his employer's smuggling.[60] The twenty-five-year-old, named Benedict Arnold, viewed the Stamp Act and Boles's conduct as an infringement on his business and as a personal slight. Arnold likely charged Boles with ingratitude, one of the worst offenses against a man of honor. The incident intimately tied the political with the personal. Arnold dragged Boles from his apartment, ripped the clothes from his back, and tied him to the town whipping post. Then Arnold "did with the same force & violence then & there assault . . . beat & abuse in a most cruel shocking & dangerous manner" the unfortunate Boles, who suffered forty lashes "to his grievous damage" and was forced out of New Haven. Arnold was charged for the crime by Justice Roger Sherman, who nearly a decade later would be an architect and signer of the Declaration of Independence. He received barely a slap on the wrist—a sign of the broad acceptance of Arnold's actions.[61] Arnold used the language of honor to justify actions that were clearly extreme. While the fervor of the Stamp Act made his assault slightly more justifiable in the eyes of his neighbors, Arnold's continued leaps in the defense of honor would place him in a more serious predicament during the Revolution.

The dual nature of the resistance to the Stamp Act is illustrative of the varied interpretations of honor by society. There was agreement among patriotic Americans that Parliament's actions imposed on the colonists' and the colonies' honor, but differences arose as to how to defend or reclaim it. Could a defense of honor justify violence?

At first, Laurens took special pleasure in the fact that such physical outbursts were not native to South Carolina. Laurens delighted in the fact that his colony would be free of "disturbance to the expected Stamp Officer" and of all "riot and Mobbing & every mark of tumult & sedition" against the Stamp Act; even though it was "oppressive," the act would not be opposed through lawlessness. He even looked on the legislation as an opportunity for South Carolina to show its ethical and ideological superiority to the other colonies, as he claimed, "We in Carolina have now a glorious opportunity of standing distinguished for our Loyalty, which we have sometimes boasted of very much, an opportunity of standing single in the only cause wherein singularity merits commendation, the cause of Virtue."[62]

Unfortunately for him, under a midnight sky, a sudden pounding on his door drowned out his boasts as a mob of about fifty people demanded to search his house for stamped paper under the cries of "*Liberty.*" Despite protesting and giving his "word & honour" that he possessed no such materials, Laurens did not sway them from searching his home (only to find nothing incriminating) amid the "shrieking" of the ill and pregnant Mrs. Laurens.[63]

Primal honor clearly existed within society, but it did not represent the only view of the ethic. Dickinson perceived such actions as unjustifiable for a nonphysical slight to America's honor. John Adams regarded primal honor, as its name would indicate, as barbaric and a quality of primitive man. Dickinson and Adams both associated this form of honor with the lower class. In addition, Adams long feared that an unchecked proclivity toward primal honor in society would compromise virtue, a view that was not dissimilar from Laurens's notion of South Carolinian virtue. In 1763, Adams had prophetically written before the Stamp Act violence that "whole armed Mobs shall assault a member of the House—when violent Attacks shall be made upon Counsellors—when no Place shall be sacred."[64] Though opposition to primal honor existed throughout the colonies, it was only the violent methods that were being criticized, not the rationale. Primal honor would find acceptance and resistance throughout the colonies, illustrating that such a concept of honor existed throughout all of America, not simply the South, as is traditionally perceived. Furthermore, some Southerners resented this notion of primal honor as inconsistent with virtue.

The Stamp Act was repealed in 1766, a year after it was first initiated, in no small part due to the joint resistance of the colonists. It was this resistance, and the methods employed under it, that united the colonists in defending the honor of their individual colonies. Over time, this cause would be combined with that of the defense of the honor of the colonies as a whole. Personal honor became linked to the collective honor of the colonies, which would become national honor by the outbreak of the Revolution. This display of unity prompted Georgia reverend and religious dissenter John Joachim Zubly to remark that "the unanimous, steady, and prudent union of the Americans, does honour to the present generation."[65] In Boston, Chauncy spoke of the "honor" of American resistance, and he illustrated its diversity by stating, "There was never, among us, such a collection of all sorts of people upon any public occasion."[66] Likewise, Samuel Adams wrote in the *Boston Gazette*, "Their [the colonies'] united and successful struggles against that slavery with which they were threatened by the stamp-act, will undoubtedly be recorded by future historians to their immortal honor."[67] The successful opposition to the legislation showed that by combining their efforts and viewing the honor as collective, they could bring about change.

From the Stamp Act onward, the defense of collective honor remained a constant motif in Anglo-American politics. Colonial reaction to ensuing Parliamentary legislation, such as the Declaratory Act, the Quartering Act, the Townshend Acts, the Tea Act, and the Intolerable Acts, all became matters of honor in the same way as first exhibited toward the Stamp Act. Illustrating this point, Dickinson's *Letters from a Pennsylvania Farmer*, written in 1768 in response to the Townshend Acts, was "a lively resentment of every insult and injury offered to your [an American's] honour and happiness." As Dickinson stated, "honour and welfare will be, as they now are, most intimately concerned" with the opposition to British legislation, and these notions would allow the people to be "cemented by the dearest ties" into a "band of brothers."[68] His message was twofold: resistance was a matter of honor, and honor was the link between the colonists. It was this shared commonality of honor that would make union a possibility.

When people failed to uphold the boycotts, it was not considered a failure of honor culture. Even loyalist New York minister Samuel Seabury, while he accused merchants of seeking profit over "honour, virtue, and courage," simply considered the individual as having "prostitute[d] his honor."[69] In fact, as Warren noted, although it was "not uncommon to see virtue, liberty, love of country, and a regard to character, sacrifice[d] at the shrine of wealth," it was viewed as an individual not upholding "ties of honor, or the principles of patriotism," rather than a reduction of these ethics in society as a whole.[70] Thus, it actually shows that the joint principles of honor and virtue were indeed viewed as the means to judge right and wrong. While the importance of these ideals was never doubted, the debate over whether violence was a justifiable defense of honor continued on the streets of Boston.

Honor and virtue were always understood as ethical matters, and they were constantly considered throughout the coming of the Revolution. For example, the *Essex Journal* asked its readers to consider the "justness" of British legislation to enable the colonists "to determine with ethical certainty" whether they "violated the principles of equity with the destruction of the tea, or whether it was warrented by a prime law inherent, being wrote indeli-ble characters on the table of the heart."[71] The individual and society were expected to ethically measure their deeds in order to retain moral superiority. The limits of honorable resistance as an ethical matter would largely domi-nate the contested meaning of the ideal. How far could honor go while still being viewed as ethical?

Well-known Bostonian Otis grew more resentful of British legislation—and, as the decade progressed, he became bolder (possibly because of his progressively worsening undiagnosed mental illness). Otis had become ob-sessed with the fact that British agents and supporters were conspiring against him. Like Washington, Otis linked his personal slights with those of the people as a whole. On September 4, 1769, he lashed out in an advertisement in the *Boston Gazette*, vilifying a number of officials—particularly Boston-based customs commissioner John Robinson—and saying that they "frequently and lately treated the character of all true *North Americans* in a matter that is not to be endured, by *privately* and *publically*, representing them as *Traitors* and *Rebels*."[72]

But words were not enough for Otis; the following evening, he burst into the British Coffee House on King Street with designs to extract "a Gentle-man's satisfaction" (a duel) from Robinson. Dueling was illegal in Boston, but this did not dissuade Otis, who instead opted to use his fists. Otis invited Robinson to join him outside to settle the matter and was turning toward the door when Robinson attempted to tweak his nose (a substantial eighteenth-century insult). Otis struck back with his cane, and for the next minute they fought, Robinson armed with a stick. Unfortunately, Otis had failed to con-sider his surroundings, and the Coffee House's patrons (mostly British mili-tary or officials) shoved at him the entire time. Passerby John Gridley denounced this gang assault as a dishonorable "dirty Usage" and leapt into the fray to aid Otis, but was promptly beaten as well. Despite the assistance of his would-be savior, Otis was thrown through the door onto King Street. Robinson stalked his prey, pummeling Otis with his bare hands to the crowd's chorus of "Kill him." His assault was so furious that the beaten attorney's hat and wig flew off and were lost among the mass of feet circling the area (or possibly stolen or hidden by British officer Captain Bradford).

Otis was left a bloodied mess, lying in the street amid the cheers of British officers, who felt that he "deserved" his "Drubbing."[73] The *Boston Gazette* of-fered a competing view of the heroic Otis and Gridley, lauding them for standing up against British insults despite being greatly overmatched in num-bers. The newspaper made them an example to be followed, as it declared that both men "acquitted themselves with a Spirit and Resolution becoming Gentlemen and Men of Honor."[74] Warren acknowledged the public acclaim and speculated, "[Do] we have men among us under the guise of officers of the Crown, who have become assassins?" She denounced Robinson and his British brethren as dishonorable, for they "attacked a gentleman alone and unarmed with a design to take away his life."[75]

While Warren showed genuine sisterly concern for her brother's injuries and ordeal, her views on honor continued to show a polarization over the use of violence. Warren's idea of honor was closely tied to conscience. She mocked the "laws of honour," meaning the trappings of primal honor (dueling and so on), as nothing more than "false honour." For Warren, true honor was consistent with the will of God and "promoting the greatest good."[76] This view again shows the more typical New England understanding of virtue as the highest goal, as opposed to Otis's less common reaction. Though Warren and Otis were from the same family, divisiveness over what could be justified by honor was just as prevalent as within society as a whole.

Less than a year later and only three hundred feet west, a crowd of angry colonists encircled a patrol of eight British soldiers and one officer on a clear and cold March night. The affair was sparked by a minor dispute over a debt and quickly escalated as a mob began to form in the shadow of the State House. Threats of death and various projectiles were hurled at the British. As the circle drew tighter, tensions and fear rose. A well-aimed piece of ice struck the head of a soldier and triggered the first shot. After a moment of pause, perhaps of disbelief, a British volley of fire commenced. Three colonists fell on the spot; two more were carried from the scene but died soon after. Church bells sounded the alarm for fire (flames, not bullets), drawing John Adams from the South End to help fight a blaze—but to his shock he saw not the crimson glow of flames but the shimmer of fresh blood. The blood of the fallen and the blood of countless other wounded stained the blanket of freshly fallen snow—a symbol of America's fractured innocence.

From a dockside brawl to five bodies littering the Boston streets, both sides of the affair agreed that honor was at the heart of these killings. Colonists argued that the Boston Massacre, as it was termed by Samuel Adams, was the result of the shame a British soldier in the Twenty-Ninth Regiment suffered, as he was bested in a fight with a Boston rope maker.[77] This earlier one-on-one fight deteriorated into a free-for-all between citizens and soldiers that saw the British retreating after being driven back. It was claimed that the events of September 5 were an attempt to reclaim their lost honor from the previous fight. The publication of *A Short Narrative of the Horrid Massacre in*

Boston, authored by a committee made up of James Bowdoin, Joseph Warren, and Samuel Pemberton, supported the fact that this initial scuffle "made a strong impression on the minds of the soldiers in general, who thought the honour of the regiment concerned to revenge those repeated repulses. For this purpose, they seem to have formed a combination to commit some outrage upon the inhabitants of the town indiscriminately."[78] Boston looked on the affair as a display of false honor at the hands of the British troops. Although this depiction did not prove to be accurate, it still dominated the minds of Boston's citizens. For a people who had been using the defense of honor as justification for combating parliamentary legislation, this incident complicated what actions were ethically permitted by honor yet again.

John Adams defended the accused soldiers, even though he had commented to Samuel Adams, Otis, and John Hancock less than a year earlier that "common Decency, as well as the Honour, and Dignity . . . will require a Removal of those Cannon, and Guards."[79] John Adams, joined in the defense by attorneys Josiah Quincy Jr. and Robert Auchmuty, was no friend to the recent British legislation. He believed that the accused needed a fair trial to show the world the true virtue that America possessed; against general preconceptions, the most vocal patriot leaders, including Samuel Adams and Hancock, likewise supported the soldiers' defense on these grounds.[80] Quincy centered his opening statements on the nature of honor and virtue. He claimed that the actions of the colonists led to each British soldier being "touched in the Point of Honour, and in the Pride of Virtue, when he saw and felt these Marks of Disrespect."[81] But Quincy was adamant that "words . . . are no *justification* of blows, but they serve as the grand clues to discover the temper and the designs of the agents: they serve also to give us light in discerning the apprehensions and thoughts of those who are the objects of abuse." The threats, snowballs, and clubs of the colonists questioned the honor of the soldiers. Quincy equated the slight of the soldiers' honor with that of the colonies at the hands of Parliament when he asked the jury, "Would you not spurn at that spiritless institution of society, which tells you to be a *subject* at the expence of your *manhood*?" Quincy claimed that it was impossible for one to remain "calm and moderate" when "every passion of which the human breast is susceptible" is stirred. The defense insisted that "fear, anger, pride, resentment, revenge, alternately, take possession of the whole man" and were not only understandable but expected—making the firing on the civilians a justifiable action provoked by the behavior of the victims.[82]

The defense illustrated that there were limits to what could be done in defense of honor, but physical slights could be returned in kind. In many respects, the trial set limits on American resistance to British legislation and established honor and virtue as ethical principles. Before, all patriot actions had been billed as a defense of honor against Parliament. But after the conclusion of the trial, when all but two of the soldiers (who were guilty only on a lesser charge) were acquitted, society accepted that only violence could justify violence. More importantly, the trial and verdict illustrated to the colonists and the world that America was a land of honor and virtue, not one of selfishness and revenge. These were not show trials or witch burnings but a real attempt to seek truth and act justly. Adams reminisced on his role in defending the soldiers, "It was, however, one of the most gallant, generous, manly and disinterested Actions of my whole Life, and one of the best Pieces of Service I ever rendered my Country." He continued, "Judgment of Death against those Soldiers would have been as foul a Stain upon this Country as the Executions of the Quakers or Witches, anciently."[83] Adams, Quincy, the jury, and all those who had behaved properly in seeking justice rather than vengeance, proved themselves capable of Roman disinterested virtue—a form that would serve them well in the years to come.[84] The trial was a matter of honor and the first real test of American virtue. And in it, Americans proved themselves to be ethical.

Across the Atlantic, Benjamin Franklin watched the events in the colonies from London with detached optimism. He interpreted the Sugar Act as acceptable and the Stamp Act as regrettable but justifiable. Franklin maintained that Britain "cannot hurt [the colonists] without hurting [itself]."[85] Franklin was personally opposed to the Stamp Act; he was willing to allow "a great many debts due to me in America" to "remain unrecoverable by any law, than submit to the stamp act. They will be debts of honour."[86] He also recognized that a tax on paper would hurt him more than anyone, as he was still a partner in several printing firms, although no longer a printer by trade. Still, he dismissed this imposition as a necessary evil in order to maintain the empire. He declared that it would provide the colonies with a chance to cultivate the virtues of "Frugality and Industry."[87] Franklin, as a colonial agent, maintained a spirit of classical disinterestedness. His position made him unpopular among many colonists. Throughout the passage of the Townshend Duties, he sought to bring the colonies and England closer together in understanding. At the same time, he moved to advance himself in government.

By the end of 1772, according to Gordon Wood, "Franklin was as optimistic as he had ever been" about the British Empire.[88] As Franklin was busy trying to reconcile the colonies and solidify his own position with Britain, he made a political misstep. And it had profound consequences for his honor and the perception of the colonies. Private correspondence between his old acquaintance Governor Hutchinson, Lieutenant Governor Oliver, and British undersecretary Thomas Whately came into Franklin's hands through a third party. The letters were written between 1767 and 1769. They incriminated Hutchinson, whom Franklin hoped the colonists would regard as the true villain behind the treatment of the colonies, not the British government. Franklin believed that if America could have a few key villains to focus on, it would turn its attention away from its anger toward Parliament.

Although the letters possessed incendiary verses, they were not conclusive evidence or even devoid of sympathy for the colonies. Franklin showed he was well aware that he was using both Oliver and Hutchinson, whose guilt was dubious at best, as "scape-goat[s]," when he wrote a cover letter included with his intercepted documents that stated, "But if they are good Men, and agree that all good Men wish agood [sic] Understanding and Harmony to subsist between the Colonies and their Mother Country, they ought the less to regret, that at the small Expence of their Reputation for Sincerity and Publick Spirit among their Compatriots, so desirable an Event may in some degree be forwarded."[89] Franklin's choice was made in favor of what he regarded as the greater good. He was willing to trade Hutchinson's and Oliver's honor and reputations to maintain the empire.[90] Even more so, he expected that if they really were truly "good" men (meaning men of honor and virtue), they would willingly sacrifice themselves and their honor for the greater good of America and the empire.

In 1772, Franklin sent these letters to Massachusetts with the intent of privately and anonymously sharing them with a limited number of the colonial leadership. Almost immediately their reach went further than Franklin wished. The papers quickly passed into the hands of John and Samuel Adams, who made their contents broadly known before they were openly debated in the Massachusetts House of Representatives. Within the year, the messages were published in a pamphlet, entitled *The Representation of Governor Hutchinson and Others*, and readily available to the volatile population as a whole. Alarming passages written by Hutchinson, accompanied by instructions to "keep secret every thing I write," seemed to support the idea of a conspiracy being plotted against American's rights, and more importantly seemed to prove the accusations leveled against Hutchinson seven years earlier.[91]

In the letters, Hutchinson, like a latter-day Thomas Hobbes, concluded that the proper solution for the colonies "must be an abridgment of what are called English liberties." He stated, "I relieve myself by considering that in a remove from the state of nature to the most perfect state of government there must be a great restraint of natural liberty." The American-born Hutchinson was intent on maintaining the subservience of the colonies to Britain, stating, "I wish to see some further restraint of liberty." He wrote of the tensions of Boston's "crisis" that Britain must do what "is absolutely necessary to maintain . . . the *dependance* which a colony ought to have upon the parent State; but if no measures shall have been taken to secure this dependance, or nothing more than some declaratory acts or resolves, *it is all over with us.*"[92] This threat against liberty and independence (not necessarily in a political sense), both necessary components of honor, was especially startling to many Americans. Such actions could stop or at least delay a growing sense of American honor, and the colonists took the possibility seriously.

The reaction to the letters was swift and severe in both America and Britain. The Massachusetts House of Representatives found Hutchinson and Oliver to be nothing more than two-faced liars "chargeable with the great Corruption of Morals" and out "to raise their own Fortunes and advance themselves to Posts of Honor . . . at the Expence of the Rights and Liberties of the American Colonies."[93] They were vilified for seeking personal gain rather than the greater good of the colonies. They were held up as examples of a false sense of honor, due to their lack of a collective spirit. By their behavior, they had proved themselves dishonorable and unvirtuous. Americans blamed Franklin's chosen villains, but it did not abate the animosity toward Parliament, which they considered in league with the two men. They petitioned Parliament for the immediate dismissal of Hutchinson and Oliver from their official positions.

Almost concurrently, on December 16, 1773, colonists protested the tax on tea by throwing the cargo of three ships that belonged to the British East India Company into Boston Harbor. For many, especially Hutchinson and those in the British government, the two events were inseparably linked—the Tea Party was the result of the publication of the letters. Throughout the whole affair, Hutchinson professed that he was acting "to save the honour of the Government" and was behaving according to his duty of office.[94] It was in this tumultuous environment that Franklin, acting in his role as a colonial agent, appeared before Britain's Privy Council and represented Massachusetts's bid to remove Hutchinson and Oliver. Even before news of the latest events in Boston arrived, the fact that private correspondence had been betrayed cast doubt and dishonor on innocent parties. Oliver frantically wrote that it was "an affair w[hi]ch much effect my peace & honour, the peace & honour of my best fr[ien]d the Gov[erno]r, & the Hon[o]r of your family [the Whatelys]."[95]

In England, William Whately, Thomas's brother, took the matter just as seriously and fought a duel against Member of Parliament John Temple, which resulted in minor injuries, over Temple's suspected involvement in releasing the papers, prompting Franklin to publicly admit his role in the affair to avoid future violence.[96]

On January 29, 1774 (nine days after news of the Tea Party reached London), Franklin was called before the Privy Council in White Hall Chapel and excoriated by Solicitor General Alexander Wedderburn for behaving "dishonourably" in his acquisition of the letters, his dispersal of them, and his secrecy and attempted anonymity. Wedderburn accused Franklin of breaking the "sacred" bond of "private letters of friendship" that was "precious to Gentlemen of integrity," with a design to satisfy his own personal motives of inflaming the colonies against Britain. Franklin remained silent as he "stood the butt of his invective and ribaldry for near an hour."[97] This sense of indignation mounted as the Privy Council assented to Wedderburn's argument and declared "that nothing has been laid before them, which does or can, in their opinion, in any manner or in any degree impeach the honour, integrity or conduct of the said Governor or Lieutenant Governor." In London, Hutchinson and Oliver retained their honor, but Franklin did not. Though Franklin attempted to remain stoic and hide his emotions, he was badly shaken. He had been publicly humiliated, his honor had been discredited, and he was declared to be a man only of personal interests.[98]

Just two days later, the British further shamed Franklin when he was stripped of his position of deputy postmaster in America and virtually barred from future advancement in government.[99] He was overtly disgraced yet again when William Whately filed a civil suit against Franklin for the return of the original letters.[100] To Franklin and his supporters it was clear that this barrage "was to wound the Doctor's character."[101] Franklin believed that he "indecently suffered" and that the lambasting he received in London had insulted his reputation, character, and honor.[102] He insisted that his actions were ethical, since he "came by them [the letters] honourably," and his "intention of sending them virtuous."[103]

It was a moment that fundamentally changed Franklin's perception of the British Empire and placed him firmly on a path to becoming a patriot. He felt that his actions had served the greater good, and his degradation convinced him of a disconnect between his own and British thought. Like Washington before him, this personal slight to Franklin's honor exacerbated a shift away from Britain. At first glance, this change appears immensely selfish, but it took firsthand experiences of slights to honor to open both men's eyes and give them a new appreciation for America's position.

In America, Franklin received quite a different reception. Instead, people lashed out against Wedderburn and the Privy Council and praised Franklin's actions. His reputation grew immensely in the colonies, from its low point during the Stamp Act crisis to its resurrection as patriotic hero. The budding patriots took up the matter of Franklin's honor and virtue as their own. The *Boston Gazette* paraphrased Franklin's defense: "The truth is the Doctor came by the letters *honorably*; his intention in sending them was *virtuous*; to lessen the breach between Britain and the Colonies, by showing that the injuries complained of by *one* of them did not proceed from *the other*, but from *Traitors among themselves*."[104] By the traditional tenets of British honor, largely centered on reputation and status, Franklin was wrong. But his ethical thinking and support in America illustrated a changed understanding of the ideal.

In his heart, Franklin believed that he had behaved properly and virtuously in trying to bring about the greater good. However, he was clearly conscious of the fact that Hutchinson and Oliver may not be as guilty as the letters (taken out of context) implied, and that he was using them to a degree. In this respect, it does seem that, for the time period, Franklin's actions were properly censured as being dishonorable by eighteenth-century British standards. However, Franklin's position illustrates that he possessed a different idea of honor, quite unique from those in London. By his terms, Franklin had acted in the best interests of America and was therefore behaving in accordance with honor. Franklin's steadfast resolve in his plan shows that he still considered the greater good to be the final justification of honor. Despite these events, Franklin remained loyal to King George III, but he came to regard the Parliament and counselors as the villains.

This dichotomy between the king and Parliament came to dominate a great portion of the discussion regarding the role of honor and virtue for both Franklin and the colonies until the signing of the Declaration of Independence in 1776. Likewise, the question of where America fit within the wider empire was also a concern. John Adams expressed such a sentiment to his wife, Abigail, in 1774: "And the Question seems to me to be, whether the american [*sic*] Colonies are to be considered, as a distinct Community...?... Or Whether they are to be considered as a Part of the whole British Empire, the whole English Nation, so far as to be bound in Honour, Conscience or Interest by the general Sense of the whole Nation?"[105] At first many colonists arrived at conclusions similar to Franklin's in regard to the British government.

Individual ministers, officials, and officers were singled out for behaving dishonorably. Laurens, running afoul of the authorities—over the seizure and sale of his schooner the *Wambaw* on a usually neglected technicality and again over fines due to petty discrepancies with his cargo aboard his ship *Ann*—stated that the court of vice admiralty, which regulated merchant shipping, was only concerned with "amassing and acquiring fortunes, at the Expence of their Honor, Conscience, and almost ruined Country." Laurens warned that his personal slight "concerns every Merchant on the Continent" and should be viewed as an offense to the collective honor of their trade and country.[106] Another wealthy merchant named John Hancock would not disagree, as his ship the *Liberty* was seized on questionable charges of smuggling, which sparked a dockside riot of a collection of gentlemen, "sturdy boys[,] and Negroes" against British sailors.[107]

Americans were led to think that their plights were shielded from the British people. As Hannah Winthrop said, "The people of England are made to believe we are perfectly acquiescent under the new model of Government, & other Cruel acts."[108] Lee took a more cynical approach and also accused the British people (whom he was quite familiar with due to his London education) of being blind to honor in allowing the continued behavior toward the colonists.[109] While a great deal of the early resentment aimed at Britain was directed only at Parliament, the continuation of slights led this hostility to evolve into animosity toward George III as well.

Many colonists felt bound by their oath of loyalty to the king. How could the Americans maintain their honor while separating themselves from the Crown and breaking their oath? The answer to this predicament came from literature, more specifically from the popularity of Montesquieu's *Spirit of the Laws*. This influential treatise was written in 1748 (and translated into English in 1750). His ideas had been widespread in the American consciousness since the midcentury and had been a crucial element of the education and reading of many of the key founders. As the American perception of British liberty descended more into tyranny, these ideas began to seem more and more appropriate to America's present predicament.

Montesquieu's treatment of government continued to support the close connections between (perhaps even the interchangeable nature of) honor and virtue. He describes a republic as being based on virtue, and a monarchy as founded by honor. Still, there was a fair amount of differentiation when it came to defining these terms. Montesquieu writes, "In a word, honour is found in a republic, though its spring be political virtue; and political virtue is found in a monarchical government, though it be actuated by honour." One seems to have been dependent on the other. You could not have honor without virtue, and vice versa. However, Montesquieu equates the honor of a monarchy with "false honour," sought only for individual glory rather than for the betterment of society. Furthermore, he posits that a despotic government is devoid of all honor. He asks, ".How can honour . . . bear with despotism?" Montesquieu finds that the two are incompatible.[110]

These ideas resonated with the American colonists, who had been arguing that Britain was a nation without honor and virtue. Montesquieu contended that "the prince never ought to command a dishonourable action; because this would render us uncapable of serving him."[111] It did not take much for the patriots to look on British legislation they already considered dishonorable as a sound and principled justification for opposition to the Crown. As political scientist Sharon Krause states, Montesquieu "thought that spirited resistance to the abuse of power was crucial for individual liberty, and he saw honor as the spring of such resistance."[112] But, as is often the case, the words on the page were taken even further through action. By comparing their own suppositions with the dictates of Montesquieu, Americans had a framework that would allow them to separate from Britain while maintaining their honor. They claimed that Britain was a monarchy driven by "false honour" and had descended into a despotism that was devoid of all notions of honor. Honor and virtue were "extremely dangerous" enemies to despotism. On the contrary, republicanism, virtue, and true honor were based on "love" of one's country and the public's interests. The belief that Britain had lost its honor and virtue became the justification for revolution.

In *Two Treatises of Government*, written much earlier, in 1689, philosopher John Locke proposes similar ideas, suggesting that people could take power from a king through a "miscarriage" of his position if "he divests himself of his crown and dignity." Locke meant such actions more for a Nero than a George III, but he still insists that if there was a "breach of trust" between the king and his people because the ruler did "not [preserve] the form of government agreed upon," then such actions against the king were necessary. As Locke explains, "When a king has dethroned himself, and put himself in a state of war with his people, what shall hinder them from prosecuting him who is no king."[113] These ideas resonated with American patriots, as British legislation became more and more oppressive. Coinciding with the thoughts of Enlightenment writers were new religious ideals that helped separate the bonds between a corrupt king and a virtuous people—failing morals could cut religious ties, just as tyrannical laws could break civil obligations.[114] As Boston began to feel the brunt of British military might, the sense that the mother country had turned on its children became an everyday reality.

Since the passage of the Boston Port Bill, which effectively closed Boston Harbor until the destroyed tea from the Tea Party was paid for, the colonies had formed committees of correspondence and created a united communication network. In the fall of 1774, as British troops garrisoned Boston, each colony sent delegates to Philadelphia to compose the Continental Congress, a legislative representative body deeply concerned with maintaining elevated ideals. While some of the congressmen had prior existing relationships, corresponded with each other, or at least had some awareness of their fellow delegates, the Congress was the first time many of America's pivotal founders actually met. Each came with personal and regional variants of honor. But face-to-face interaction and debate among these men helped expedite the advancement of an American notion of honor.

Southern and Northern concepts of honor began to blend into a singular definition. As John Adams recalled, "It is certainly true that some of our Southern Brethren have not annexed the Same Ideas to the Words Liberty, Honour and Politeness that we have; but I have the Pleasure to observe every day that We learn to think and feel alike more and more."[115] Honor and proper conduct were always at the forefront of the thought process of the Congress, and as their conception of the terms became a commonality, their bonds strengthened. They considered themselves bound in honor to each other, their constituents, and their colonies.[116]

Despite this display of union, the colonies were still under British rule, and the Congress technically had no authority. However, on the floor of the Congress, South Carolina delegate John Rutledge recognized that the colonists they represented would be "bound only in Honour, to observe our Determinations."[117] And so it was, as congressional chaplain Jacob Duché marveled at America's "unshaken UNANIMITY" and the "most striking example" of "three millions of people, or a vast majority of them, bound by no other ties than those of honour and public virtue."[118] The fact that the Congress was particularly successful says a great deal about the faith the American people placed in the notion of honor. At such a precarious stage, wavering from this principle could have crippled the Congress. But both the delegates and the people believed, as voiced by John Adams, that "Our Country is the Post of Honour . . . and she behaves in Character."[119] By remaining true to the Congress and each other, the colonists proved that they possessed the character and honor on which the delegates rested their hopes of survival.

Despite these vocal claims of colonial unity, it would take the shots fired at Lexington and Concord the following spring in 1775 to fully join the colonies together and convince them that Britain was lost to all sense of honor. Before this event, there had been more than a slight hope for reconciliation and reasonable compromise, but, as Thomas Jefferson lamented, "this was before blood was spilt."[120] The emphasis placed on the spilling of blood was crucial, as was the question of who fired the first shot. The controversy surrounding the first shot was of central importance to American honor. Diplomatic theorist Emer de Vattel's *Law of Nations*, released in 1759, advanced the principle, "All the right of a power to make war is derived from the justice of his cause," and Richard Lambert, Earl of Cavan and author of *A New System of Military Discipline Founded upon Principle*, claimed, "In all quarrels only one party can be culpable, and that is the aggressor."[121] If the British fired first, any reaction by the Americans could justly be regarded as a defense of honor. Confusion still remains today as to who fired first, but the patriots gathered on Lexington Common leveled the blame on a British officer on horseback armed with a pistol.[122] America had been wrestling with the ethics of violent resistance in the name of honor since the Stamp Act. The more moderate restraint against the avenging principles of primal honor finally gave way after the first battles of the American Revolution. British words, legislation, and rebuffs had been slights to America's honor; this point was never in contention, but the methods to respond to these insults had lacked unanimity. British gunshots now proved to the people that their mother country had fallen beyond repair—and American honor needed to be asserted through war. Jefferson considered the battles in Massachusetts to be nothing less than "unprovoked" "murder" that was "in open violation of plighted faith & honor, in defiance of the sacred obligations of treaty which even savage nations observe."[123]

All patriots throughout the colonies shared Jefferson's opinion. Almost immediately after the battles, Mercy Otis Warren wrote that Britain was "lost to that honour and compassionate dignity which has long been the boast of Britons. Indeed the unparalleled barbarity in the late action of Lexington evinces that they had forgotten the laws and usages of civilized nations."[124] Dickinson and the Congress agreed in virtually identical terms with Jefferson and Warren that the affair was an "open violation of Honor."[125] The Americans believed that they had "appealed to the native honour and justice of the British nation; their efforts in our favour have been hitherto ineffectual."[126] Only a justifiable, defensive war could reclaim America's honor, as Britain had abandoned its own principles.

The Battles of Lexington and Concord brought the colonies to a new level of unity, as there was an understanding that "we consider ourselves as bound in Honor as well as Interest to share one general Fate with our Sister Colonies, and should hold ourselves base Deserters of that Union, to which we have acceded, were we to agree on any Measures distinct and apart from them."[127] While prior collective endeavors, such as boycotts, committees of correspondence, and even the Congress, had helped link the colonies, it was this bloody and brazen insult to their honor that cemented them. Despite a variety of opinions as to how to proceed, all patriots shared one conviction: there could be no peace without honor.[128]

The echo of gunshots triggered the clack of carriage wheels and horse hooves as the delegates of the Second Continental Congress sped from their homes to Philadelphia a few weeks after the conflicts. Samuel Adams and Hancock, who had both escaped the scene at Lexington thanks to Paul Revere, sat together in an open carriage, trailed by John Adams in a less grand two-wheeler. They were a part of the procession of over one hundred carriages that carried the future founding fathers to what would become Independence Hall. This Congress was designed to discuss the major issues affecting America and institute new policies. Within months the members of Congress jointly declared, "Our cause is just. Our union is perfect."[129] But before long there was only one question left to answer: Should America be independent from Britain?

This final hurdle was invariably linked to the matter of retaining honor while separating from the king. Independence and loyalty to the Crown remained a central point of contention throughout the Congress, but one that was moving toward a definite separation from Britain. Echoing Locke and Montesquieu, Vattel advanced that when a "prince" "attacks the constitution of the state," he "breaks the contract which bound the people to him." The former subjects are then "free by the act of the sovereign."[130] For the patriots, theoretical support for such action was conspicuous. Enlightenment thought helped pave the way for a secular split from their sovereign, while religious revivalism also contributed to spiritual separation from the head of Anglicanism. According to evangelical preacher and patriot John Cleveland, God was on America's side. He concluded that since the king had "breach[ed] his sacred covenant," America's only response was to "no longer . . . honor you as our mother . . . King George the third adieu!"[131]

Against the backdrop of the questioning of traditional bonds of fealty, the popular debate was swung largely in favor of independence because of the 1776 publication of Thomas Paine's *Common Sense*. This Philadelphia-published pamphlet was widely read and circulated, and it used the growing understanding of inclusive honor to support American independence. Paine was a self-taught Englishman who lacked social distinctions, and his work reflects a disdain for hereditary rule while appealing to those who viewed honor as both secular and an offshoot of virtue linked to religion. Appealing to the religious sentiments of the Americans, he considers the "the idolatrous homage which is paid to the persons of Kings" as a slight on the "Almighty," who was "ever jealous of his honor," and he argues that Americans thus "should disapprove of a form of government which so impiously invades the prerogatives of heaven."[132]

In a more "eye for an eye" manner, he also presents Britain as lost to all honor after bringing the sword to America. Paine asserts that this severed any ties between America and Britain and labeled the British as inherently dishonorable: "But Britain is the parent country, say some. Then the more shame upon her conduct. Even brutes do not devour their young, nor savages make war upon their families."[133] Since Britain was dishonorable, it was beyond saving, and reconciliation thus could not be counted on or trusted because of Britain's faulty character. *Common Sense* suggests that any such accord would be only temporary and ill fated: "Your future connection with Britain, whom you can neither love nor honour, will be forced and unnatural, and being formed only on the plan of present convenience, will in a little time fall into a relapse more wretched than the first."[134]

Samuel Adams, a vocal proponent for American independence, agreed with Paine on his argument for freedom based on notions of honor. Adams argued that once a state of war existed between America and Britain, independence was a nonnegotiable necessity. As nations in war could not be dependent on one another, independence was the only manner to maintain honor, as dependence inherently suggests a degree of subordination and dishonor. There was a counterargument that such a bold step would prevent any form of truce or reconciliation. Adams dismissed this point as irrelevant, asking, "Upon what Terms will Britain be reconciled with America? . . . Will this redound to the Honor and Safety of America? Surely no."[135]

Paine concluded that American independence was in and of itself a matter of honor. Like Adams, Paine reduced the matter to one of dependence versus independence. America no longer had any tangible ties, oaths, or debts to Britain. As *Common Sense* pronounces,

Debts we have none; and whatever we may contract on this account will serve as a glorious memento of our virtue. Can we but leave posterity with a settled form of government, an independent constitution of its own, the purchase at any price will be cheap. But to expend millions for the sake of getting a few vile acts repealed, and routing the present ministry only, is unworthy the charge, and is using the posterity with the utmost cruelty; because it is leaving the great work to do, and a debt upon their backs, from which they derive no advantage. Such a thought is unworthy a man of honor, and is the true characteristic of a narrow heart and a pedaling politician.[136]

It was common sense to declare independence and worth the price of a war to obtain it.

Though *Common Sense* was readily accepted, opposition still remained. Pennsylvania delegate Robert Morris was opposed to independence because he claimed it would not "redound to the honor of America" but would instead "[cause] division when we wanted Union" because the matter was not unanimously supported.[137] Dickinson, another Pennsylvania delegate, remained unconvinced of the necessity of declaring independence. Dickinson believed that America's defensive war was honorable when compared to the dishonor of British aggression (the crucial fact that kept him from being an official Quaker), but he still refused to embrace separation.[138] He combated the notion of independence as a matter of honor by arguing from a position of virtue. Since the 1760s, Dickinson had been adamant that the colonists must remain loyal to Britain at all costs and that bonds did not simply dissolve due to a mistake by one party. Quakers generally had a strong sense of devotion and "indebted[ness]" to the king "for the continued Favor of enjoying our religious Liberties." Their beliefs were integral to making sure that they fulfilled their debts. For their religious freedom, the Quakers believed that they were "under deep Obligations to manifest our Loyalty & Fidelity, & that we should discourage every attempt which may be made by any to execute disaffection or disrespect."[139] Thus, for Dickinson, independence went too far and would "injure the reputation of a people, as to wisdom, valour and virtue."[140]

Dickinson recognized that arguing against independence would draw "resentment," but it would be the "proof of [his] Virtue." He would do what he felt to be right, and he stated that his resistance was based on his "duty," a powerful Quaker concept, to oppose any matter that could bring more harm to the colonies. He believed he was acting selflessly. He knew his position would cost him his long-held popularity and the public perception of his "Integrity," but he was willing to make the sacrifice because he "fear[ed]" that a strict attempt to regain honor caused by "Resentment of the Injuries offered to their Country, may irritate them to Counsels & to Actions that may be detrimental to the Cause they would dye to advance."[141] Before the Congress, Dickinson advanced that independence could only bring an escalation of war and death, and that Americans must preserve their virtue and cool their emotions to bring about reconciliation.

This plea, though passionate and framed as a defense of virtue, fell on deaf ears, and, in the words of Rev. Ezra Stiles, Dickinson gained only a "dishonorable Reminiscence with Posterity."[142] Dickinson later attempted to rehabilitate his reputation by serving in the Pennsylvania militia in order to prove he acted "solely" for "the good of [his] country."[143] Regardless, five months after *Common Sense's* publication, a committee of Jefferson, John Adams, Sherman, Robert Livingston, and Franklin began drafting what would become the Declaration of Independence. This famed document seized on the arguments advanced by Paine, Montesquieu, and Locke. It formally charged the king with descending into despotism and ravaging his citizens. Also, as argued years earlier by Lee, the declaration indicted the British people for ignoring "native justice and magnanimity." As a result, their British "brethren" deserved no special regard: "We must, therefore, acquiesce in the necessity, which denounces our Separation, and hold them, as we hold the rest of mankind, Enemies in War, in Peace Friends." The colonies were honor bound to throw off the shackles of Britain and claim their independence through war. And in July 1776, the Congress adopted the measure and the United States of America was born. On July 4, the members of the Continental Congress, restating their words from years earlier, swore an oath to maintain the declaration's principles and the interests of the nation by declaring that they "mutually pledge to each other our Lives, our Fortunes and our sacred Honor."[144]

As Warren argued years later, independence was not just a political choice; it was also an ethical one. The declaration illustrated that Americans "considered themselves no longer bound by any moral tie, to render fealty to a sovereign thus disposed to encrouch on their civil freedom."[145] In essence, the American Revolution was spurred by matters of honor, but not in the sense of the traditional perception of a slight. Instead, British policy enabled Americans to view themselves as being in a position of moral superiority, and their understandings of honor and virtue reflected this ethical dimension. Through shared ethical sentiments and belief in the common good, the formerly exclusive conception of honor began to be opened up to all who served this righteous cause.

CHAPTER FOUR

Maintaining Moral Superiority
How Ethics Defined the Early War Years

Shortly after the Battles of Lexington and Concord, but before the signing of the Declaration of Independence, the women of New England were very clear on how the war would manifest itself. Mercy Otis Warren wrote a poignant letter to a friend in which she prophesied that the American Revolution would be "a test" against the British "shackles" that "Their Honour" despises.[1] Likewise, Abigail Adams concluded that only America's "own virtue" could produce a favorable outcome to the war.[2] In both epistolary instances, John Adams was the intended recipient of these views, but this idea of the American Revolution as a test of virtue and honor spread far beyond the Adamses and Warrens' social circle.

The ideologies of honor and virtue that shaped the path to war also became the guiding principles behind fighting it. America's founders wanted a war fought based on lofty principles, which would demonstrate the true worth of their cause to the whole world. Honor and virtue therefore factored into the core foundation of wartime legislation, strategy, and governance. In *The Law of Nations*, a text Washington specifically would have been familiar with, as he had previously ordered it for his stepson Jacky Custis, Emer de Vattel wrote, "True glory consists in the favourable opinion of wisdom and discernment; it is acquired by virtue, or the qualities of the mind and the affections, and by the great actions that are fruit of these virtue."[3] Honor could only come by behaving virtuously in war. Members of both civilian and martial society were expected to contribute to the cause through honorable and virtuous behavior that reflected their status. Thus, the ideological became inherently connected to the practical needs of the war effort. Americans were facing a war on their own soil, one that required the mobilization of the population at large. Through this societal upheaval, honor was democratized, in large part due to the necessity of protecting America. But for the founders, it was not enough to simply win the war—they wanted to win well.

The American patriots had set high ideals for themselves as a people and a new nation. The Continental Congress was actively vocal in encouraging the country's preservation of honor and virtue as vital to the success of the United States in war and peace. As John Adams recognized, "More Virtue is expected from our People, than any People ever had."[4] Americans had to make a conscious effort to prove to the world and themselves that they were truly the paragons of virtue and honor they claimed to be. In doing so, they would also justify their admonishments of Britain for having lost these same ideals. Maryland delegate Samuel Chase proclaimed that the British "openly traffic their Integrety & Honor" and that "they no longer regard even the Appearance of Virtue."[5] This vilification of British morality helped distance America from its former ruler, but it also tentatively placed America on a pedestal. This criticism of Britain therefore became the same measure by which Americans and the world would judge the Revolution.

Consequently, there was also a heightened sense of importance of the notion of collective honor and virtue that had been developing since the 1760s. It made the actions of individuals crucial to the maintenance of national principle. For George Washington, decisions were to be made in accordance with "your own Virtue and good sense" and "without relinquishing in some degree that Character For publick Virtue and Honor which you have hitherto supported."[6] If you dishonored yourself, you also dishonored the country.[7] The honor of each state and the nation was at stake, to be determined by the personal actions of its citizens.[8] The failure of a few could doom the many.

While preserving this concept would lead to happiness, the lack of it would have far more ominous repercussions. William Hooper, a delegate from North Carolina, recognized that if the people failed, "we must be satisfied to sit down the Spectators of the Triumphs of our Enemies over our dearest rights & privileges, condemned to abject Slavery, as the reward of our successless virtue."[9] Slavery had long been considered to be the absence of honor, and the linkage between a loss of virtue and enslavement continued to show the ambiguous separation between the two concepts. The two terms blur consistently over the period, but there was a mutual understanding that they represented the same (or at least a fairly similar) ideal.

One of the most pressing concerns after the bloodshed at Lexington and Concord was to form a proper army, but in a war based on honor and virtue, such an army had to be held to comparably high standards. Rhode Island delegate Samuel Ward regarded the recruitment of such a force as consistent with "the true Interest Honor & Happiness of the Colo[n]y."[10] Ideological fervor and the *rage militaire* inspired men from all walks of life to volunteer for service to the cause.[11] In 1776, Thomas Simes intimated in his Philadelphia-published text, *The Military Guide for Young Officers*, that the principal motivation for all volunteers was "to gain honour and preferment, by exposing themselves in the service."[12] There was agreement among the people that honor and virtue were at stake and needed to be defended.

Through a combination of personal experience, education, and literature, wide cross sections of the American population came to similar conclusions. Booksellers, such as Henry Knox and Benedict Arnold, had been digesting the very texts they supplied to the public, and they leapt into the fray. Bostonian Knox had experienced the harshest of the British slights firsthand and became convinced that he must display self-sacrifice for his "distressed & devoted Country."[13] Arnold too enlisted to avenge the nation's honor, but his personality, sensitive over his reputation and the opinion of others, already hinted at a quest for glory.[14] Similarly, college students—long inundated with both tangible and theoretical models of honor and virtue—were quick to adopt the martial spirit. The Athenian Society of Queen's College (now Rutgers University), which was founded in order to "polish our Minds and beautify our manners" and admired "all the polite Nations and Ages of the World," took up arms against the British, who had strayed from this path.[15] They marched together in step as students, club members, soldiers, and Americans.

The choice of commander of the Continental army was a crucial decision, as the position required someone with significant military skill who also reflected the ideological convictions of the founders. Washington did not openly solicit the post, nor was he the unanimous choice, but he was elevated to the rank of general and given command over the army. Ever the reluctant officer, Washington lamented to his wife, Martha, "Far from seeking this appointment, I have used every endeavor in my power to avoid it."[16] However, he felt compelled to accept: "It was utterly out of my power to refuse this appointment, without exposing my character to such censures, as would have reflected dishonor upon myself, and given pain to my friends."[17] But in order to distance himself from his youthful outrages over pay and show his internal merit, he refused to accept the commission with the burden of payment; a gentleman of honor was beyond the dependence of such a salary.[18] He had taken up the mantel of Stoic duty to country, and—unlike in the previous war—personal honor would not overcome national honor. By accepting the commission to avoid "dishonor" and forgoing pay to remain financially disinterested, Washington brought virtue to himself and the "sacred Cause of [his] Country, of Liberty, and human Nature."[19] Liberty as freedom was a larger reflection of a gentleman's need for personal independence. For Washington, the absence of liberty robbed the individual of his independence, thereby preventing him from acquiring rank and honor. Liberty was the polar opposite of slavery; to be reduced to such a status is nothing other than "dishonourable."[20]

Washington was "a compleat gentleman" whose honor became tied to that of his country.[21] He united his Stoic honor with his genteel conduct to create a practice of military deference to civilian authority. There had been a fear of armies in the Anglo-American mind-set since the time of Oliver Cromwell, and the issue reemerged numerous times throughout the coming of the Revolution. In 1774, Virginian statesman Richard Henry Lee labeled such an army as "inconsistent with the honor and safety of a free people to live within the Controul and exposed to the injuries of a Military force not under government of the Civil."[22] Washington made it evident that his powers were drawn from civil government and that it was his duty to uphold their legislation, even against his personal honor.[23] During the French and Indian War, Washington had prioritized his "own Honor and Country's welfare."[24] But in a complete reversal, he now viewed it as his responsibility to support his "Country's Honour" and his "own Character," in that order.[25] Washington's term "Country's Honour" and his later phrasing of "national honor" are interchangeable and represent the same ideal: a form of honor or duty to country.[26] In speaking of being American and speaking of his country, he had taken the codes of honor and applied them to something loftier.

National honor became the impetus behind Washington's formation of the army, but social status was still used to support military rank.[27] Washington applied his European-based rules of genteel behavior and honorable conduct to the formation of the officer corps.[28] Still resistant to patronage, Washington was conscious of the possibility of unmerited individuals filling the ranks of the American officer corps and thought that only "Gentlemen, and Men of Character," should gain commissions.[29] Officers should be examples of gentility on and off the battlefield. As he clarified, "The Degrees of Rank are frequently transferred from civil Life into the Departments of the Army—the true Criterion to judge by . . . is, to consider whether the Candidate for Office has a just pretention to the character of a Gentleman, a proper sense of Honor, & some reputation to loo[s]e."[30]

While most Americans possessed some conception of honor and virtue within civil society, fewer had any tangible experience with these ideas from formal military training. But men like Washington—veterans of the French and Indian War and participants in local native conflicts—did have martial backgrounds, but ones that lacked the rigidity of a European military education. It also may explain why the Continental army came to be more inclusive and less rigid in individual advancement. The civilian conceptions of honor and virtue, as linked to liberty and equality, carried over into the military during the recruitment of the army, and they came to influence its ranks in ways quite foreign to European armies. This does not mean that Americans shunned the traditional trappings of European martial honor, discipline, and hierarchy; in fact, in many ways, they embraced them. But they came in with a preconceived notion of what they hoped the army would be.

To make up for their lack of military experience and martial ethic, many American officers and soldiers turned to books to cultivate their own conception of honor, much as Washington and Benjamin Franklin had. This was not a habit exclusive to Americans, as British officers also "believed that books were essential for mastering the art of war," but reading such texts was the most prevalent means of military education available to the Continental army.[31] As America lacked any formalized military tradition outside of minimally trained local militias, their sources for study were predominately European in nature. While more philosophical and intellectual print sources tended to wax poetically about the connection between honor and virtue, without actually offering a firm definition, military texts tended to be more forthright in their summary of these core ideals. Some texts, such as Edward Waterhouse's *Discourse and Defence of Arms and Armory, Shewing the Nature and Rises of Arms and Honour in England,* placed the soul of honor firmly within the military: "Honour sprang originally from the Field, for it being the effect of Power, and Power creating right of Empire, Honour must be concluded to be purchased by venture and a high mettled Courage."[32] Such definitions of honor were commonplace and offered a notion of honor only as valor. Some Americans would base their ethic on such ideas, usually to their detriment.

Other military studies acknowledged the various meanings of these terms. But these varying definitions still remained clear-cut and capable of adoption by the Continental army. Again, the sources displayed a close connection between honor, virtue, and religion. This linkage shows the continued confusion that existed regarding these terms. However, the military texts were quite adamant in their terminology, and these ideas seem again to be joined either consciously or unconsciously in the minds of their readers. Published in Philadelphia, Roger Stevenson's *Military Instructions for Officers* noted that religion is the principle "upon which alone true honour is founded."[33] As defined in J. Watson's *Military Dictionary,* "Honour consists in the constant Practice of Virtue; and the Duty of a Soldier is honourable and honest, where properly performed." In simple terms, acting virtuously (often regarded as a religious ethic) was honorable—thus, for the purposes of the military, honor and virtue were essentially indistinguishable. Watson did not spend any lines discussing nuanced differences; for the soldier, it was enough that the two were linked. Honor, and thus the military, "abhors" any "who make their Valour consist in doing Actions of Violence and Brutality." This refuted Waterhouse's interpretation; Watson stated that honor is not gained by vanquishing a foe on the field if the motives behind it are not just. The definition stated that "none are distinguished, none honoured, none recompenced but the Man of Worth, who regulates his Duty by Religion, Humanity, and Justice."[34] Only those who behaved ethically could possess honor.

Justice was related to honor in that actions had to be righteous and proper; a war could not bring honor if it was unjust. Waterhouse also recognized this, arguing that "the Souldiers then that fight for honour, must fight according to the Lawes, and for the well-being of Honour."[35] His insistence on a set of laws speaks to the conception of the rules of war. The Americans believed they were fighting a defensive war to reclaim their liberty from British injury. And, based on the concepts offered by military treatises, they were in the right. The seventeenth-century book *Honor: Military and Civil* maintained "Militarie Iustice [military justice] generally is a Law made by consent of all Nations, the propertie whereof is to repulse force, and to redresse iniurie [injury]. For who so in defence of his owne person doth resist force with force, shall be thought to haue [have] so do iustly [justly]."[36] Likewise, eighteenth-century thought maintained a comparable principle that connected the concepts of resisting injury and supporting liberty. *The Antient Policy of War* defined just war as "just by reason, by the instinct of Nature, and by Custom of all Nations, and by Religion, it self, is that which is undertaken in defence of our Country, Religion, Liberty, and State."[37] British general James Wolfe's *Instructions to Young Officers* supported the acceptable nature of defensive war but added that this alone was not enough to make a war honorable—it required the right conduct of the nation's army to maintain its exalted nature. He wrote, "The men should consider that they are upon the point of entering into a war for the defence of their country against an enemy who has long mediated the destruction of it: that a drunken, vicious, irregular army is but a poor defence to a state; but that virtue, courage, and obedience in the troops are a sure guard against all assaults . . . to execute their part with honour and spirit."[38] Just as there was a proper way to fight a war, there was a proper way for soldiers and officers to behave and thereby influence the conduct of the fighting itself.

Like those administered by America's colleges, codes of discipline and rank hierarchy became the core foundation of this ethic of honor within the military. Military texts reflected their essential nature in instilling honor. As Stevenson wrote, "To support the honour of this corps upon a solid and respectable footing, the strictest subordination must extend from the chief to all the officers, and the most rigid discipline inspire vigilance, patience, bravery, and love of glory to the whole corps."[39] Codes of conduct in regard to everything from dress to morality were viewed as a crucial step toward enforcing military discipline. The army's officers were considered to be the linchpins in the instillation of these codes. Following orders and the chain of command reinforced hierarchy and the importance of honor. British general Humphrey Bland's *Treatise of Military Discipline*, perhaps the most popular book of its kind, insisted, "Men must be taught to rely entirely on the Conduct of their Officers, and to wait with Patience for their Orders, before they perform any Motion; the due Performance of which, both their Safety and Honour depend on."[40] Thus, the success and safety of the cause depended on the character, quality, virtue, and honor of the Continental army's officers. Because of this perception, great lengths were taken to ensure that an ethos of honor and virtue dominated the officer corps.

While the Continental army embraced a great deal of the wisdom of European military texts, it also resisted conceptions that disagreed with the fundamental principles of the Revolution. Social hierarchy may have supported military rank, but that did not mean it precluded advancement based on proper conduct. A long-held perception among European militaries was that soldiers represented the "dregs" of society, had to be "dragooned or hired" into service, and "felt neither moral commitment . . . nor loyalty to their nation." Furthermore, it was assumed that common soldiers came "entirely from the impoverished classes" and were "incapable of honor."[41] This view was supported by various military texts. *The Military Guide for Young Officers* labeled common soldiers as possessing the "frailty of the human heart" due to a "want of that principle of honour to support them, inherent in the officer as a Gentleman."[42]

As in all armies, there certainly was hierarchy within the ranks. But with the Continental army and the various militias, there was a deliberate attempt to grant honor to any who served the cause.[43] Just like officers, soldiers should be viewed as men of honor. *The Soldier's Faithful Friend*, another military text, concurred that "a *good man*" will "fight *manfully*; and you may be sure of his fidelity upon this motive," for "the lower classes of men" were just as influenced by ideals as those of loftier social standing.[44] Through service, honor became democratized, regardless of birth or local origins. This belief was particularly instilled in members of Colonel Nathaniel Heard's brigade, who were lectured that "all Distinctions Sunk in the Name of an American to make this honourable and preserve the Liberty of our Country ought to be our only Emulation and he will be the best Soldier and best Patriot who Contributes to the Glorious work, what so ever his Station or from whatsoever part of the Continent he came."[45] By 1775, common soldiers could also be regarded as "Gentlemen Soldiers." The use of the title "gentleman" in an eighteenth-century context was not an empty matter of ceremony. It conveyed a great deal about perceived status and morality, and, in a British military context, the use of the terms together would have been an inherent contradiction. Traditionally, gentlemen were officers, not soldiers. Gentlemen were expected to be men of honor. In this fundamental alteration, these "Gentlemen Soldiers" had acquired honor through their "good conduct" and "noble character" while "in the service of [their] country."[46] Comparable expectations were noticeable throughout the country. The men of Colonel Elias Dayton's Third Battalion of New Jersey were reminded that "every Soldier should be a gentleman."[47] In Virginia, Captain George Stubblefield recorded similar recognitions in his orderly book, noting that all soldiers needed to "pay the Strictest attention to their Duty," for it was "necessary to their own Honour."[48] Such thinking showed that honor was accessible to all ranks, and it illustrated a tremendous change from the traditional European perception of common soldiers. A soldier's own conduct, based on merit and service to the country, was his path to honor. General Anthony Wayne similarly noted that honor could be "conferred on every Officer & Soldier," while reminding his men that Washington "receives the greatest pleasure in rewarding merit."[49] As echoed in the Philadelphia-published *Treatise on the Military Service, of Light Horse, and Light Infantry*, when "merit is preferred," the army advances "men of reputation, experience, and conduct."[50] Because of this expanded capacity to gain honor, it was equally important in the eyes of the nation that each individual behave honorably.

The manner in which the war was fought was of crucial importance to the founders. The patriots made a conscious effort to frame their behavior as honorable and virtuous, especially in relation to the British. It was important for the Continental army to behave well as individuals, but it was even more crucial to the collective honor for them to perform properly together in the field. This performance did not mean that they displayed outstanding examples of military skill. Nearly all participants in the war recognized the vast superiority of the British army in training and techniques. America's chief weapon became its ideals.

General Nathanael Greene, a fighting Quaker from Rhode Island who expressed a belief that religion was secondary to morals, understood this fact when he wrote to Rhode Island deputy governor Nicholas Cooke, "I lament the want of knowledge in Generalship. But as we have been cultivating the arts of Peace, its [*sic*] no wonder that we are deficient in the Art of War. I am confident the opposition will be crowned with success finally, but when or how lies in the womb of futurity. My confidence don't arise from our discipline and military knowledge, but from the Justice of the cause and the virtue of America."[51] Honor and virtue would be America's defense against Britain. The founders deeply believed that their internal ethics would sway the war in their favor. Obviously, traditional victory could bring honor, but, for the founders, the manner in which the battles were fought was equally, if not more, important.

Proper conduct as a manifestation of honor was always at the forefront of the founders' minds throughout the war. Greene believed that even the smallest regulation of personal behavior could influence the character of an army. His orders reveal a deep-seated concern with such regulations: "The officers are Desired to Supres[s] as m[u]ch as Posable all Debauchery and Vulger Language Inconsistent with the Character of Soldiers."[52] Just like for college students at the time, soldiers' characters reflected the army as a whole, and Greene felt that proper behavior would translate onto the field. This theme remained true for Greene and the Continental army throughout the war. Generals mandated such behavior as necessary; officers were expected to both follow and regulate it, and the army chaplains' sermons reinforced the gravity of the message.[53] For example, chaplain Enos Hitchcock preached, "To the distinguished character of a patriot & a soldier it should be your highest glory to add the more distinguished character of a virtuous, good man—then you can quit this stage in the full blaze of honor."[54] These were not hollow words but rather careful instructions that specified that honor and virtue were acquired through ethical action. John Eager Howard, a Continental officer from Maryland, reflected the collectivization of this ideal when he wished his "Conduct may be such as will reflect Honour upon my Colonel, merit it for myself, and do Good to my Country's Cause."[55]

Traditional martial notions of honor through victory were not absent from the Continental army. The officers and soldiers were familiar with the basic European martial values that had been cultivated through shared experience with British soldiers during the French and Indian War and from the military manuals that were widely digested by American officers.

The Continental army soon learned that honor could be acquired without necessarily winning a battle. However, this resulted in contention among those who still identified with the more antiquated model of honor through victory. In many respects, the Revolution led the Continental army, especially its leaders, into a war against their own understanding. It was this inner conflict, combined with the ethics of the Revolution, that advanced the change and progression of honor in the American military.

Early successes in the war helped give some credence to this cult of honor through victory. The heroic minutemen were lauded for forcing the British regulars back to Boston after the Battles of Lexington and Concord. So too were the men who repulsed several British advances atop Bunker Hill, leaving the field only when their ammunition supplies undermined their resolve and courage. The capture of Fort Ticonderoga by forces under Ethan Allen and Arnold proved the American resolve. The pounding of cannons (captured and transported by Knox from Fort Ticonderoga) from Cambridge Heights on the British-garrisoned city of Boston and the eventual evacuation of the redcoats gave the Americans their first true taste of victory. These early days supplied large doses of optimism that were a fine boon to those who cherished honor through victory.

Following these celebrated victories, the American resolve to defend New York in large part was based on an idea of honor, in that the army was duty bound to protect its states. The ultimate American defeat called into question the strength and honor of the army. Though the army was able to retreat in good order, some still lamented that without victory there was no honor. Although North Carolina congressional delegate William Hooper recognized that Washington had no choice but to retreat, he still bemoaned the decision: "Our General wisely ordered a retreat, which was conducted without any loss but that of our honor."[56] New interpretations of honor were not always universal or immediate, as Hooper's comments illustrate a continued belief in an older tradition.

Facing the British on the field as equals was considered by many to be the epitome of honorable behavior and proof of America's virtue. After the outbreak of the war, Americans already considered themselves to have bested the British in honor and virtue. Meeting the British as equals on the battlefield would be an outward display to prove these sentiments true to the world. Offensives inherently possessed a greater potential for gaining honor—they were romanticized and regarded as the principal means to acquire prominent martial valor. Washington himself initially embraced such modes of thinking; his staff once even had to restrain him from ordering an assault on Boston. But throughout the Revolution, Washington and the Americans came to understand that there were paths to honor independent of military victory. Especially after they lost the battles of New York in the summer and fall of 1776, a concerted effort was made to show that victory alone did not ensure honor, just as defeat did not necessarily cast dishonor. This point was supported by Bland's *Treatise of Military Discipline*, which alluded to the fact that so long as the officers and the soldiers behaved well in an engagement, there could be no dishonor cast on them, regardless of the outcome. As Bland wrote, "When an Officer has had the Misfortune of being Beat, his Honour won't suffer by it, provided he has done his Duty, and acted like a Soldier." An officer could only be censured if he were "neglecting the common Methods used to prevent" defeat; if that was the case, Bland warned that his "Character is hardly Retrievable, unless it proceeds from his Want of Experience, and even in that Case he will find it very difficult."[57] Likewise, officers' and soldiers' characters could not be called into question if they had fought well and followed orders but the battle did not receive a favorable conclusion. Bland continued, "We shall gain Honour and Reputation enough, if we adhere strictly to our Orders; but Disgrace may attend the exceeding of them, as well as the falling short."[58] The American civilian government wholeheartedly accepted Bland's reasoning.

The North Carolina delegates of the Congress agreed with the assessment Bland offered in his military text. They pronounced, "The Check which the American Arms have lately received on Long Island reflects no dishonor upon those who bore them." Since it was concluded that "the Struggle was bravely maintained by our young Soldiery," no aspersions should be cast on the dishonor of the army. However, the delegates did notice "a want of Generalship in some of our inferiour Officers" and implied that a lack of experience was the culprit.[59] While Bland stated that even a lack of experience could not prevent the loss of reputation, many civilians still supported the idea that as long as the army behaved well, there should be no stigma attached. Benjamin Rush, writing on the failed assault on Canada, said of Arnold that in defeat "he has lost all save honor and the honor of the States."[60]

General Washington would describe the Revolution to Congress as a "war of posts" (combat intent on preserving the army). His ability to embrace a more pragmatic style of war and avoid defeat showed a marked change from the youthful, impulsive, and impatient Virginia militia officer he once was. The ability to both control his emotions and submit to what he perceived as the good of the nation clearly shows the elevation of national honor over personal honor. Keeping the army and its soldiers in a position to fight was viewed as essential to long-term success.

Frederick the Great wrote in *Instructions to His Generals*, a text that was widely read by the Continentals, that "numbers are an essential point of war, and a general who loves his honor and his reputation will always take extreme care to conserve and recruit his troops."[61] Maintaining an army in the field became regarded as honorable in and of itself. Washington would later say to the Marquis de Lafayette, "*No rational person* will condemn you for *not fighting* with the odds against [you] and while so much is depending on it, but all will censure a rash step if it is not attended with success."[62] The importance of maintaining the army and conserving troops was not just a practical lesson; it was one that also illustrated the value placed on individual soldiers, which was indicative of a shifting status.

The innate differences between the Revolution's egalitarian ideals and socio-military hierarchy reflected an internal struggle between new and old ideas of honor. To facilitate a greater sense of rank distinction, Washington sought to rectify the matters that had grieved him as an officer in the Virginia regiment by making sure that his officers were paid in accordance with their status: "Besides, something is due to the Man who puts his life in his hands, hazards his health, and forsakes the Sweets of domestic enjoyments."[63] Honor was not inherently tied to wealth, but a gentleman was expected to present his internal character externally. Military wages were not a way to get rich but were merely to allow one to act morally by escaping dependence—essentially, the system was designed to allow them to possess honor. The junior officers of the artillery corps wrote, "We wish Sir but for a Sufficiency to support genteely the Character of Officers in[?] the Continental Army, we are not mercenary—we desire not to hoard up, but had we Millions would with Pleasure spend them in our Country's Cause—but your Honour is undoubtedly sensible that this is not the Case—that most of us depend solely on our Wages for Support—that we've nothing to offer our Country but our Lives, which we'll hazard, or even sacrifice, for its Honour & Defence."[64] Officers and soldiers were willing to risk their lives for the country's honor, so long as they would be allowed the privilege of an honorable existence while employed in military service.

At the same time, there was a widely held perception that the highest reward for service in the Continental army was the privilege of serving the cause. Washington reflected this dualism, as he combined personal honor with the honor of the country. Although he continued to support hierarchy, as he was personally serving as a volunteer, he used the same language of selflessness to appeal to Continental army officers. Washington expected honorable duty to country to be the ultimate reward for service: "I should hope every Post would be deemed honourable which gave a Man Opportunity to serve his Country."[65] Any action that contributed to the war effort was thus honorable. And Washington wanted officers who understood his expansive conception of honor and his devotion to virtue. General Greene's thinking was consistent with his superior's, as he stated, "My task is hard and fatigue great. . . . But hard as it is if I can discharge my Duty to my own Honor and to my country['s] satisfaction, I shall go through the Toil with Chearfulness."[66] Likewise, Knox, who would become Greene's close friend, wrote to his wife, Lucy, "I long to see you which nothing should prevent but tho the flattering hope I being able to do some little service to my distressed & devoted Country."[67] But even more than that, Continental officers wanted to be great; as Knox's subordinates declared, "In what ever Station we shall be placed, we flatter ourselves, we shall behave as Men—as *Great Men*, fighting for every thing dear & Valuable—We wish so to do & we wish likewise to appear as Gentlemen."[68] For Washington, Greene, and Knox, this was a war for independence and posterity.

In line with this notion of duty were the methods employed for advancement and promotion within the Continental army. Many have asserted that the army became essentially Anglicized over the course of the Revolutionary War.[69] While it is certainly true that some European trappings, strategies, and techniques were readily borrowed, the fundamental structure of the army reflected the same ideas of honor and virtue that dominated civilian ideals. Toward the end of the French and Indian War, Washington slowly abandoned the practice of promotion through patronage, which accounted for a great deal of his own rise in Virginia, in favor of one based on merit. From the start of the Revolution, Washington sought to employ this open concept of advancement. It did not mean that hierarchy was abandoned, but rather that more people were eligible for participation, in contrast to the old British model centered on birth and status. Continental army commissions were not bestowed because of birth, lineage, status, or wealth, and the British practice of purchasing officers' commissions was forbidden in America.

This policy meshed well with and was also reflected in America's civilian government. John Adams shared Washington's support of merit, as it was a continuation of the basic Revolutionary ideal of equality.[70] Like his cousin, Samuel Adams believed that jealously guarding official appointments and being suspicious of those who aspire to the positions was not an insult but a "political Virtue." He wrote to Elbridge Gerry, a delegate in the Congress, "Bad Men may be kept out of places of publick Trust. The utmost Circumspection I hope will be used in the Choice of Men for publick officers." Adams recognized that there were unscrupulous people in America who cared only about personal advancement and not the cause. Such behavior was considered dishonorable, as it did not conform to the concept of the greater good. Adams lamented, "It is to be expected that some who are void of the least Regard to the publick, will put on the Appearance & even speak boldly in the Language of Patriots, with the sole purpose of getting the Confidence of the publick & securing the Loaves and Fishes for themselves or their Sons." Thus, it was essential that "Men who Stand Candidates for publick posts should be critically traced in their Views and Pretensions."[71] By 1779, Thomas Jefferson had laid the foundation of what would come to be called a natural aristocracy, which placed people "whom nature hath endowed with genius and virtue" in positions "to guard the sacred deposit of the rights and liberties of their fellow citizens, and . . . they should be called to that charge without regard to wealth, birth, or other accidental condition."[72] It was an assertion that an individual's own conduct was the sole judge of his character. Jefferson and both Adamses agreed that unmerited patronage had to be eliminated to preserve the country's honor.

Despite the high level of approval of these policies, they were not always readily welcomed by all; some in the Continental army viewed the military in more traditional British terms or sought civilian recognition for their wartime deeds. While John Adams acknowledged this possibility, he still disapproved of it and regarded it as a minority opinion: "That the Promotion of extraordinary Merit may give disgust to those officers is true, over whome the advancement is made, but I think it ought not."[73] Artillery officer Knox, although raised in Boston, the epicenter of the Revolutionary idealism, still harbored ideas of the old style of patronage, as he attempted to gain his brother William an officer's commission in the artillery corps. Continental army general Charles Lee, British by birth and training, felt there would "be no difficulty" in giving him a commission and saw no conflict with Revolutionary ideals. Such sentiments from Lee were not surprising, as he had spent a great portion of the decade since his service in the French and Indian War bouncing around Europe in search of higher rank.[74] Similarly, Knox continued to "endeavor to effect" his brother's commission through General Horatio Gates (like Lee another British-born and British-trained officer), before appealing to General Washington.[75] Needless to say, after Knox apprised Washington of the situation, the matter was dropped, and William Knox remained a civilian throughout the war. But as the war progressed, Henry Knox came around to Washington's manner of thinking and began to view patronage as only for those who had earned it by merit.[76]

A year after Knox's attempt, Cecelia Shee, a married Philadelphia woman of Delaware extraction, tried to use patronage and nepotism to her family's advantage and secure her brother, Lieutenant John Parke, a promotion. She instructed her brother to appeal to General Washington and attempt to gain his promotion through a rather loose familial connection (Martha Washington's

first husband was their second cousin). Instructing her brother to feign igno-
rance of the connection, she hoped that Washington would realize this relationship and reward him. As she planned, "I think if for some time you was in
the company of the General—you would modestly drop a hint that your father
had an uncle who did live in Virginia—and ask if he left any descendants there
you can do it without letting him [know] that you know that they are related
to him." Unlike Knox, Shee was clearly conscious of the new exaltation of
merit and aversion to patronage, as she warned her brother, "Burn this letter
as soon as you read it." The Shees still hoped to bypass merit with cunning.
The ruse ultimately failed and Parke, again due to the prodding of his sister,
sought out other patrons.[77] While such attempts did certainly occur, there
was a conscious effort to promote based on merit, and these ideas were broadly
reflected in official protocol. In 1779, under the guidance of Baron Friedrich
Wilhelm von Steuben, these ideals were institutionalized through the publication of *Regulations for the Order and Discipline of the Troops of the United
States*. The *Regulations* recognized that "the order and discipline of a regiment
depends so much upon *their* [officers'] behaviour, that too much care cannot
be taken in preferring none to th[a]t trust but those who by their merit and
good conduct are entitled to it."[78]

These ideas of rank distinction and merit exhibited themselves not only
within the highest levels of military society but also within the lowest. When
speaking to his soldiers, Washington used enslavement as the ultimate horror
that could befall Americans.[79] He was a slaveholder and recognized an inherent
social hierarchy—one that subordinated whites as well as blacks.[80] But slaves,
as property, were absent from this hierarchy. This stratification resulted in a
hesitancy to allow African Americans to enlist in the army, though he was not
opposed to allowing them to serve the army in noncombat capacities.[81] Most
likely, Washington's background as a planter contributed to his resistance to
African American enlistment. Slave rebellion was a fear in the South, and the
arming of African Americans had the potential for disaster.[82]

The role of slaves in the Continental army was precarious at first. As historians Philip D. Morgan and Andrew O'Shaughnessy contend, "Soldiers supposedly possessed the qualities of honor and courage, and slaves were the
dishonored par excellence. Making soldiers of slaves seemed an inherent contradiction."[83] At the outbreak of war, Washington likely held the common belief that "slavery was a condition of dishonor and the presence of slaves would
dishonor an army."[84] But as the view of honor expanded, so did the nature of
service.

As early as 1773, Boston slaves, building on the patriot concept of liberty, petitioned the government for their freedom based on the ethical reasoning that they were "virtuous," despite the fact that "their Condition is in itself so unfriendly to . . . every moral Virtue except Patience." The petitioners asserted that many slaves deserved freedom because they were moral equals and could in turn "be able as well as willing to bear a Part in the Public Charge."[85] They were offering their service to their country on the same terms as white patriots. Another appeal, issued by the self-titled Sons of Africa, used the language of honor combined with the principles of "Humanity" to compel slaveholders to grant their emancipation. They claimed, "The word of God commands us to give Honor to whom Honor is due, and surely it is not due to any more than to those who relieve the oppressed, and give Liberty to them who are in *Bondage*."[86] Thus, a person relieving the plight of slaves could claim greatness. Similarly, abolitionist Robert Pleasants agreed that ending slavery "would redound to the honor as well as advantage of America."[87] In both of the aforementioned instances, slaves recognized and applied honor and virtue as ethical terms. But the leaders of the Continental army had not necessarily recognized that slaves were capable of honor.

During the Revolution, Washington first came in contact with African American troops in Cambridge, Massachusetts, during the Siege of Boston. In May 1775, the Massachusetts Committee of Safety had announced "the admission of any person as Soldiers into the Army now raising, but only such as are Freemen," and specified "that no slaves be admitted into this Army upon any consideration whatever."[88] This enactment meant that free blacks, such as Lemuel Haynes and Salem Poor, could be found within Massachusetts regiments.[89] Free black soldiers served admirably during the Battles of Lexington, Concord, and Bunker Hill. The Massachusetts government did not go so far as to arm slaves, for fear that it would "reflect Dishonor on this Colony," but Southerners and high-ranking officers and officials viewed the inclusion of black soldiers as a threat to the social order.[90] Highly suggestive of a broad opening of society, Henry Wiencek explains, "the common white New England soldier seems to have accepted blacks. The objections . . . came not from the rank and file but from the highest levels."[91]

After taking command of the Continental army in July 1775, Washington showed disdain for the recruitment of African Americans as soldiers, based on a desire to preserve the social hierarchy.[92] He was critical of Massachusetts troops in general, whom he called "an exceeding dirty & nasty people," based on what he viewed as an inferior class status and a lack of cultivation, complaining that they suffered from "a kind of stupidity in the lower class of these people, which . . . prevails but too generally among the Officers."[93] Washington did not resent the presence of African Americans in the army in an unarmed capacity; he had employed "Mulatto's and Negroes" as "Pioneers or Hatchetmen" during the French and Indian War.[94] Such positions, according to standard military texts, "do not pass for Duties of Honour, but only those of Fatigue."[95] But Washington strictly forbade them from being enlisted and bearing arms as soldiers.[96] Despite the army's desperate need for troops, Washington maintained the traditional Southern planter fear of insurrection, an anxiety not experienced by New Englanders, and the trepidation that slaves free from bondage could infringe on the personal independence and honor of the white gentry.[97] Washington was not alone in this thinking; his council of officers "agreed unanimously, to reject all Slaves, & by a great Majority to reject Negroes altogether."[98]

Despite this precarious start, the fate of the African American soldier changed due in part to a mixture of fear, pragmatism, and a recognition of personal honor. On November 7, 1775, Lord Dunmore, the British governor-general of Virginia, issued a proclamation that "declare[d] all indented servants, Negroes, or others (appertaining to Rebels) free, that are able and willing to bear arms, they joining His Majesty's Troops."[99] As a result, the British formed the Ethiopian Regiment, composed of approximately three hundred slaves who were granted their freedom under Dunmore's proclamation.[100] This act aroused great anxiety among the Southern gentry.[101] The British had offered freedom to slaves in exchange for fighting against their former masters. This was insurrection on a scale that exceeded even the planters' worst fears.[102]

Dunmore's tactics were viewed as unethical. David Ramsay recalled that the proclamation "produced a predatory war, from which neither honour nor benefit could be acquired."[103] Washington recognized the gravity of Dunmore's actions and echoed the worries of the Virginia gentry: "If the Virginians are wise, that Arch Traitor to the Rights of Humanity, Lord Dunmore, should be instantly crushed, if it takes the force of the whole colony to do it. [O]therwise, like a snow Ball in rolling, his army will get size—some through Fear—some through promises—and some from Inclination joining his Standard—But that which renders the measure indispensably necessary, is, the Negroes. For if he gets formidable, numbers will be tempted to join, who will be afraid to do it without."[104] Washington called Dunmore "the most formidable Enemy America has" and altered his own decision regarding the enlistment of African Americans in order to combat the threat of their joining the British.[105] He wrote to John Hancock, the president of the Continental Congress, "The free negroes who have Served in this Army, are very much dissatisfied at being discarded—as it is to be apprehended, that they may Seek employ in the ministerial Army—I have presumed to depart from the Resolution respecting them, & have given license for their being enlisted."[106]

There are several reasons for this reversal. The first is an obvious reaction to Lord Dunmore, combined with military necessity.[107] The second lies in the fact that the black soldiers had acquitted themselves well during the engagements around Boston. During the Siege of Boston, General John Thomas regarded his African American troops as "Equally Servicable with other men" and commended them for "hav[ing] Proved themselves brave" in combat.[108] Haynes, who had served as a minuteman since 1774, was described in his later years as being "imbided" with "principles respecting 'the rights of men.'"[109] Shortly after Bunker Hill, six officers (including the battle's famed hero Colonel William Prescott) signed a formal petition acknowledging the "character of so Brave a Man" as Poor, who "behaved like an Experienced officer, as well as an excellent soldier."[110] This recognition of Poor's conduct as being on par with that of not only an average soldier but also an officer was significant praise from high-ranking individuals, making it difficult to ignore. Due to his knowledge of the service of these soldiers, Washington could not deny that they had gained honor through valor, and "the General may well have been impressed and moved by the courage and dedication of black troops in the American army."[111] Historian Walter Mazyck hypothesizes, "One may pity a helpless individual or group but never respect such persons. However, when they first show signs of independent thought and action, at that moment respect is born."[112]

The third possible reason for the transformed thought process was more personal and centered on a respect of intellect and culture. In December 1775, Washington received a poem from Phillis Wheatley, a slave. Wheatley's poem exalted the general: "A crown, a mansion, and a throne that shine, With gold unfading, WASHINGTON! Be thine."[113] Wheatley's tone was conspicuously reminiscent of *Cato*, Washington's favorite play, and as he could not deny her talent or skill, it "might have jolted Washington into a deeper understanding of the humanity of the black people."[114] Perhaps this, coupled with the soldiers' displays on the battlefield, helped him recognize that blacks were more than mere laborers; they also possessed a capacity for intelligence and honor. The general was so moved by Wheatley's words that he invited her to his headquarters in Cambridge, where "she received marked attention" for half an hour; he even addressed her by a title, referring to her as "Mrs Phillis (a substantial recognition of her status in society)."[115] During the winter of

1775–76, Washington was presented with an opportunity to confront the honor and humanity of African Americans, and it seems to have altered his perception.

Ultimately, Washington would come to match Dunmore's offer of freedom to slaves in exchange for military service.[116] In fact, the general supported the formation of black regiments, such as Colonel Christopher Greene's Rhode Island regiment and Lieutenant Colonel John Laurens's failed South Carolina regiment.[117] Black soldiers served valiantly throughout the Revolutionary War, and Washington's offer of freedom released many slaves from a life of servitude. Before the war was concluded, over eight thousand free and enslaved African Americans had fought in Northern and Southern forces.[118] As a result, Washington came to view blacks with a greater sense of humanity, and their courage on the battlefield earned them honor.[119] This view was also reflected in General Nathanael Greene's recommendation that "Negros be allowed the same wages granted by Congress to the Soldiers of the Continental Army."[120] Equal wages would represent a tangible recognition of honor. Another Virginian slaveholder, Continental Congress delegate James Madison, believed that making "soldiers at once of the blacks" would "certainly be more consonant to the principles of liberty which ought never be lost sight of."[121] For Madison, creating African American soldiers maintained the ethical principles of the Revolution.

Washington saw African American soldiers as men of honor, and, even decades after the war, this idea remained. The House Committee on Revolutionary Pensions, speaking in this instance about black soldier Primus Hall but echoing additional statements it made about African American service in general, said his "bravery and good conduct are proved to have been such as would have done honor to any man."[122] By acquiring honor, African Americans were elevated into a newly expanded social hierarchy—not as equals but as participants in the hierarchy nonetheless. According to Madison, military service in essence created a new class of men, "experience having shown that a freedman immediately loses all attachment & sympathy with his fellow former slaves."[123] A similar perception may have contributed to Washington's dramatic shift to a personal sense of abolitionism, as he now "wish[ed] to get quit of Negroes."[124] When an attempt to construct an all-black unit in South Carolina failed, Washington was discouraged by the lack of personal sacrifice of whites to embrace these troops for the sake of national honor: "That spirit of Freedom which at the commencement of this contest would have gladly sacrificed everything to the attainment of its object has long since subsided, and every selfish Passion has taken its place."[125] By failing to heed the needs of the cause, those who opposed the unit were in essence attacking the nation's honor. Washington continued to uphold the supremacy of national honor over his personal honor.

As merit could not be denied and service to the cause was regarded as the pinnacle of honorable behavior (and a national necessity), women, like African Americans, were admitted into the discussion of honor. As previously shown, the early days of anti-British sentiment represented the first moment in which women gained honor that was regarded as equal to men's through their participation in boycotts and nonimportation agreements. Before the war, women had already shown that they were as capable of patriotism as any men, thereby forcing themselves into honor culture.

Despite common misconceptions, women had a concept of honor that was equally as rigid as any found in the masculine world. In addition, female honor had the same confusion over definitions that existed for honor more generally. This is unsurprising, since American ladies had been schooled in honor culture from sources that were almost identical to those men learned from—largely classical and contemporary literature. A passage written by Philadelphia poet Hannah Griffitts, copied down by Milch Martha Moore into her commonplace book, shows the dual importance of literature:

> Maternal love can glow upon the Page
> And all the Wisdom of experience'd Age,
> Honour, Religion, & each sov'reign Truth,
> Advice & Caution, to each unguarded Youth
> All this & more, can pow'rful Letters give,
> And Paper may be almost said to live.[126]

Griffitts is saying that honor could be learned through individual study and, in the absence of parental guidance, literature could become a successful substitute. Classical, biblical, and historical feminine figures such as Portia (a nickname assumed by Abigail Adams), Volumina, Judith, Deborah, and Esther became models to which to aspire.[127] While most women lacked experience with the institutionalized codes of conduct that taught honor in schools, they possessed an ingrained sense of right conduct that was instilled from birth. Virtue and honor were linked together, and again they were often indistinguishable from each other. Griffitts charged her fellow women to maintain this principle when she asked, "Is Virtue now a Fiction of the Brain? Is Female Honour but an empty Name?" Her questioning was designed to make women look at themselves and recognize that only proper action could defend their honor. Thus, female conceptions were interchangeable with the male.

> Not Birth nor Beauty, Wit nor Wealth can claim
> The fair Distinction of unsullied Fame,
> Be this yr. glorious Badge, yr. Boast
> And thus retrieve the female Honour lost,
> Virtues immortal Flame inspire yr. Breast.[128]

Fundamentally mirroring the charges of the Congress and the army, women were aware that only through virtuous conduct could there be any hope of remaining honorable. But as women were not ensconced in the halls of political or military power, their embrace of this idea shows an in-depth understanding of the greater good. From the start, women's conceptions of honor stressed behavior and disinterestedness in ways that were often ignored by men.

While it was a common masculine tool to denounce all the weaknesses of the body and spirit as effeminate, it was not uncommon for Revolutionary-era women to dismiss gentility and material culture—long external displays of male honor—as nothing but vanity, immorality, and false honor.[129] Women, particularly readers of *Clarissa* or those spurned by dishonest suitors, believed that the external could hide flaws of character.[130] Mercy Otis Warren was the most vocal protester against the trappings of honor without the substance. She described a gentleman whose "manners are smoothed" and who has "studied the belles lettres sufficiently to converse with ease, whether the subject is business, politics, or pleasure," as often ruled by a "prostituted name of *honour*."[131] Likewise, she denounced works that stressed appearance over substance, especially taking issue with Lord Chesterfield, whose writings had "enraptured" her own son. She accused Chesterfield of "sacrific[ing] truth to convenience, probity to pleasure, virtue to the graces, generosity, gratitude and all the moral feelings to a momentary gratification." She viewed his work as nothing more than the "pretended blandishments of honour."[132] Her friend and frequent correspondent Hannah Winthrop agreed: "I think myself happy in a similarity of sentiments with you respecting the trifling satisfaction of an acquaintance with the gay and unthinking, compared with the sincere and virtuous Friend."[133] Abigail Adams also denounced Chesterfield, saying he was spreading "pernicious and Libertine principals into the mind of a youth whose natural Guardian he was, and at the same time calling upon him to wear the outward Garb of virtue."[134] For women, honor was solely ideological, based on proper ethical actions, deeds, and beliefs.

As daughters, sisters, wives, and mothers, women instinctively understood the nature of self-sacrifice and devotion, and these ideas translated themselves fairly smoothly into support of the war effort. Women, like men, viewed the

Revolution as a matter of honor and felt that Britain had lost its honor and virtue.[135] Since the 1760s, there had been recognition that by joining the cause women could elevate their status and reputation.[136] Moreover, many women held a sincere devotion to the American cause. Self-sacrifice was prized as the most honorable type of conduct, as it showed true devotion to the ideals of the Revolution. Virtue and honor could be gained through such commitment.[137]

For some, women were the only group in America that could claim to possess totally disinterested honor and virtue. Esther Reed, wife of the Pennsylvania governor, publicly acknowledged the female devotion to disinterestedness and virtue. In a published broadside, "The Sentiments of an American Woman," Reed—speaking from an assumed representative position—proclaimed, "I can answer in the name of all my sex. Brave Americans, your disinterestedness, your courage, and your constancy will always be dear to America as long as she shall preserve her virtue."[138] Abigail Adams would agree, stating, "Patriotism in the Female Sex is the most disinterested of all virtues. . . . All History and every age exhibits Instances of patriotic virtue in the female Sex; which considering our situation equals the most Heroick."[139] Women believed they were just as selfless as any man in service of the nation, if not more so.

As early as 1774, Warren had concluded that every American, and more specifically every woman, would be an active participant in the Revolution. She wrote to Hannah Quincy Lincoln, "But as every domestic enjoyment depends on the decision of the might contest, who can be an unconcerned silent spectator?—not surely the fond mother or the affectionate wife."[140] After the outbreak of war, women performed a variety of roles that helped advance the cause. Though their actions were quite varied, and often far removed from the traditional trappings of martial valor, they managed to gain honor for their gender.

There was a wide recognition among the female population that they were capable of acquiring honor through any service they could perform to aid the war. Women frequently used the language of honor (and conversely dishonor) and praised examples of duty and self-sacrifice.[141] For many, the most basic sacrifice was encouraging the honorable service of their fathers, husbands, brothers, sons, and friends. Reed likened it to "the fortitude of the mother of the Maccabees in giving up her sons to die before her eyes."[142] Women were instrumental in not only instilling principles of honor in young children but also enforcing them in grown men through a combination of exaltation and the threat of shaming. For example, in New Jersey, a wife offered her husband the parting words, "Remember to do your duty! I would rather hear that you were left a corpse on the field than that you had played the part of a coward."

Nearby, a grandmother instructed her children and grandchildren, "Let me beg of you . . . that if you fall, it may be like men." Not only were they hoping to motivate honorable behavior purely for the sake of the men, women consciously realized that the conduct of their relations would reflect on them. Upon sending her brother off to war, a woman in Philadelphia remarked, "I hope he will not disgrace me; I am confident he will behave with honour and emulate the great examples he has before him."[143] After the fall of Charleston, South Carolinian legislator and militia volunteer David Ramsay remembered, "When poverty and ruin seemed the unavoidable portion of every adherent to the independence of America, the ladies in general discovered more firmness than the men. Many of them, like guardian Angels, preserved their husbands from falling in the hour of temptation, when interest and convenience had almost gotten the better of honour and patriotism."[144] Women were equal parts practitioners and enforcers of the honor code. By embracing these concepts of honor, it is clear that the ideal was not gender exclusive but rather permeated diversely throughout society.

While women championed honor through participation in the cause, there were relatively few services they could perform officially. Instead, they volunteered for a host of duties that benefited the patriots in an unofficial capacity—most of which conformed to traditional gender roles. Even this was reminiscent of a classical understanding of female honor and the exaltation of the Roman matron. Connecticut delegate to the Congress Oliver Wolcott Sr. wrote to his wife, who was tending their home and family in his absence, "The Roman and Grecian matrons not only bore with magnanimity the Suspensions of Fortune, but Various kinds of adversity, with amazing Constancy, an American Lady instructed in sublimer Principles I hope will never be outdone by any of these illustrious Examples if she should be called to the Exercise of the greatest female Heroism."[145] Simply behaving well within the traditional constraints of society and maintaining the home front during the war was recognized as honorable behavior. In fact, this allusion to the classical age demonstrates that American women possessed the greatest degree of honor and virtue of all time—an exact representation of the general feelings by Americans toward their country as a whole.

However, there were other ways to participate outside the domestic realms. Women could be more than just matrons; they could be the heroic women of ancient Rome who were "forgetting the weakness of their sex, building new walls, digging trenches with their feeble hands, furnishing arms to their defenders, they themselves darting the missile weapons on the enemy, resigning the ornaments of their apparel."[146] It was through more elaborate, less traditional means that women became recognized for their merit and their possession of honor. Such women fully embodied Washington's declaration that all posts in service of the nation were honorable.

Following the example first demonstrated in the pre-Revolutionary boycotts, women often banded together to collectively support the cause. One of the most public displays of female devotion occurred in Philadelphia when Sarah Franklin Bache (Benjamin Franklin's daughter) and Reed led a campaign to collect money for the Continental army.[147] Reed, under the pseudonym "an American Woman," authored "The Sentiments of an American Woman" claiming "the Women of America manifested a firm resolution to contribute as much as could depend on them, to the deliverance of their country. Animated by the purest patriotism, they are sensible of sorrow at this day, in not offering more than barren wishes for the success of so glorious a Revolution."[148] Women went door to door collecting funds for the war effort that ultimately went to providing clothing for the soldiers. Participants and observers alike commended this honorable action by "the best ladies." Mary Morris regarded herself as being "Honourd" by her contribution.[149] Rhode Island onlooker Jane Mecom (Franklin's sister) wrote to her niece, Sarah Bache, to commend her on her devotion to the Revolution, stating, "I have as you suppose heard of yr Ladies Noble & Generous subscription for the Army and honour them for it."[150]

The ladies' "noble Example," as termed by Ezra Stiles, spurred other women, including Mary Dagworthy in New Jersey, Mary Lee in Maryland, and even Martha Washington and Martha Jefferson in Virginia, to similar fund-raising efforts for the soldiers.[151] Thereby proving Reed's boast that female patriotism "is universal from the north to the south of the Thirteen United States."[152] Dr. Benjamin Rush, a physician, writer, and founding father, remarked that such conduct elevated the status of women: "The women of America have at last become principals in the glorious American controversy."[153]

Although there were few official positions for women available in the war effort, by far the most commonly held was that of nurse. Nurses' duties, remarkably less glamorous than even their nineteenth-century counterparts', were to dispense medicine, distribute food, and maintain cleanliness. Women provided this necessary and important service, which both aided the sick and wounded and freed more men to serve in the field.[154] Nursing not only provided an avenue for women to assist the army, it also granted them honor. Hearing "every Cough, Sigh, and Groan" of a neighboring "violently ill" man, John Adams wrote to his wife lauding the medical attention given by a nurse.

Adams marveled at "Miss Quincy...very humanely employed in nursing him." He recognized her value, noting, "This Goodness does her Honour."[155] Similarly, Dr. Rush was so taken with Irish nurse Mary Waters's duty to her patients during the Revolution that he declared, "Her profession is a noble one," and he even began to compile notes on her for a biography. This prominent recognition of women's service was in relation to not simply their traditional duties but also their status as active honorable participants in the Revolution. Their service elevated them in status and reputation; indeed, as Rush said of his planned Waters biography, "Only a few man can be Kings—& yet Biography for a while had few other subjects."[156]

Although it was exceedingly rare, a woodcut by a "Daughter of Liberty" entitled *A New Touch on the Times* depicting a gowned woman firmly holding a musket and powder horn alludes to the fact that women did possess a martial tradition.[157] Just as it did for men, literature again provided the gateway. Images of Joan of Arc glittering in armor under a fleur-de-lis banner leading the French armies (conveniently against the British) spoke to the heights a woman could reach. In *The American Crisis*, Thomas Paine wished for a similar savior to rescue the Continental army after failures in New York and New Jersey. He dreamed of a "Joan of Arc" arising from "some Jersey maid to spirit up her countrymen."[158] American women also were aware of the long literary tradition pertaining to female warriors known as the Amazons. In fact, Abigail Adams claimed that, should the need arise, "you would find a Race of Amazons in America."[159]

In addition to these grandiose female examples, American women had one figure more relatable—and again it came from literature. In 1750, the story of Englishwoman Hannah Snell, who disguised herself as a man and served as a Royal Marine, was published as *The Female Soldier*. This book was readily available throughout America during the Revolutionary era. In fact, the image of Snell, complete with musket and powder horn, that accompanied the book would be adapted into the woodcut *A New Touch on the Times*. The book championed Snell as a shining example of female virtue and (the traditionally masculine) martial honor. She was a woman who both understood traditional womanly expectations of virginity and wanted to claim her share of a form of honor that was normally reserved for men. Snell was described as joining the military "to acquire some Honour, in the Expedition; and so distinguish herself by her intrepid Behaviour." It would not be long before she would prove herself in battle: "And our *Hannah*, tho' then but a raw Marine, exerted herself so far, that she procur'd the Love, and Esteem of all her Fellow Soldiers." Snell was able to gain honor through valor, and, even more than that, her fellow soldiers (all men) recognized her conduct as worthy of honor. While the author went to great lengths to prove that Snell retained her "virtue" (in this case referring to chastity), it is specifically differentiated from her "preservation of Honour," both of which she was said to have regarded as worth "more than Life itself." Snell became a symbol of heroism and was heralded a modern-day Amazon. Her conduct spoke "to the Honour of her Sex and Country," and her behavior on the field was lauded as a symbol that "Her Fortitude, to no Man's second. To Woman's Honour must be reeckon'd."[160]

Because female military service was so rare, it made the acknowledgment of a woman's honorable behavior and merit conspicuous. As seen with African American soldiers, honor gained through combat was difficult, though not impossible, to dismiss or disparage. Only two short years after Reed's cry for women to assume the model of Deborah, a woman (with an appropriate name) emerged as the most complete fulfillment of this idea. In 1782, a twentysomething woman from Massachusetts named Deborah Sampson disguised herself as a man and enlisted in the army for a three-year term under the name of Robert Shurtliff. Sampson represents a perfect amalgamation of the motivation and background of the female patriot. She was born to a poor family of farm laborers, orphaned shortly thereafter, and forced to work as a servant. Still, she was already literate and quite precocious, devouring any books that she came across, usually her employer's sons'. While she did not have any formal education, Sampson was taught "lessons of morality and virtue."[161] These values remained evident throughout her life.

On the eve of Revolution, Sampson became a weaver—and thus a member of a group of women valuable to the British boycotts. Whether she acquired a patriotic fervor from her occupation or chose that profession as a result is unknown. But she was certainly aware of this collectivized sense of honor that was building in Massachusetts, especially through women's boycotts. Before long, her literary indulgences transitioned her into a career as a schoolteacher, where she was famed for her strict discipline—evidently imparting lessons of proper conduct to her students. Sampson's biblical namesakes, Deborah (a favorite of Reed whose military advice led to a great victory for Israel) and Samson (famed judge and strongman, and also the early spelling of her family name), also gave her inherent models for emulation. As her height (approximately five feet seven, larger than average for even a man at the time) made her look the part of an Amazon, "the general muster-master, was, doubtless, glad to enroll the name of a youth, whose looks and mien promised to do honor to the cause, in which she was then engaged."[162]

Sampson served for seventeen months as a member of the Fourth Massachusetts Regiment's light infantry (a corps whose members were specially selected based on physical and intellectual prowess) and saw action in combat multiple times, during which she supposedly wished that she "never might be so lost to all sense of virtue and decorum, as to act a part unworthy her *being*, thereby not only bring infamy on herself, but leave a blemish and stigma on the female world."[163] She was a woman who had her own personal sense of honor, and her awareness that her conduct (if she was discovered) could impact all women showed a clear understanding of collective honor as well. During her tour she suffered two musket wounds, but her identity was ultimately discovered during a bout of sickness. Her unveiling was met not with hostility but with an honorable discharge at West Point by General Henry Knox. Sampson not only fought and was wounded for her country, she was a member of a specialized unit—these facts could not be overlooked. The mere fact that Sampson was given an honorable discharge speaks to the approval of her superior officers and shows in the most clear-cut way imaginable that they did in fact accord her honor. Sampson's service was commended by her officers and the *New York Gazette* as "an extraordinary instance of virtue in a *female soldier*" that "redounds to her honor."[164] Historian Alfred Young speculates that the author of the *Gazette* article was General John Paterson, which gives the praise even more weight.[165] Her memoirist Herman Mann, who penned her story as *The Female Review*, used it as a platform to attempt to elevate the status of women, lamenting, "Ah, females—we have too long estimated your abilities and worth at too mean a price!"[166] She had risen from being an orphan of laborers to receiving accolades from a general and her country. The case of Sampson shows how merit and valor on the battlefield could bestow honor on those of even the humblest origins and elevate them to positions of reputation.

Sampson's gain of honor through combat is consistent with similar stories surrounding the near-mythical Margaret Corbin and Mary Ludwig Hays McCauley (both commonly identified as "Molly Pitcher"). The two women received equal honor and formal recognition for "heroically" manning their fallen husbands' places on the artillery line. When a woman was at the helm of the raw destructive power of a cannon, it was difficult to cheapen her contribution in comparison to a man's. The reaction to the women's valor seems to have been general acceptance as soldiers of equal standing and honor. McCauley was heralded as "Major [or Captain] Moll" by the grateful troops, given a pension, and, according to legend, personally acknowledged or even promoted to sergeant by General Washington. Like McCauley, Corbin would also receive a war pension and ultimately a formal military burial at West Point.[167] The less documented case of Anna Maria Lane, who served as a "common soldier" alongside her husband and was wounded at Germantown, follows the same pattern, with her ultimately receiving accolades and a pension for her service.[168] Such recognition illustrates that honor was accessible to anyone through service to the cause.

Much like for African Americans, honor for women through military service was not a given, and reception often varied. At least three other women enlisted in the military disguised as men, but their reception was quite different from Sampson's. Boston "spinster" Ann Bailey was arrested, fined, and sentenced to two months in prison for her impersonation. Anne Smith of Springfield, Massachusetts, was similarly imprisoned, while an unnamed New Jersey woman was publicly shamed by her commanding officer, who "ordered the drums to beat her Threw the town with the whores march." This behavior is not unsurprising given the male-dominated culture of the eighteenth century, but that does not make it the rule. A constant theme was that all three women's true identities were discovered fairly early on in their service; perhaps the fact that these female soldiers had not yet proved themselves sufficiently in the field heavily influenced the reaction.[169]

Despite the mixed response from the male world, women believed that their support of the Revolution elevated them in society. Their participation in the run-up to the war had taught them to disregard the old rigidity of hierarchy. Griffitts, commenting on the death of Thomas Penn, had taken aim at unmerited offices and titles:

> Now let the thirst of eastern Pomp attend
> And on this striking Lesson spare an Hour,
> Of envy'd Greatness, here behold the End,
> And wild Ambition, mad with reach of Pow'r.
> Aiming at Titles—& with Titles crown'd,
> Grasping at Wealth, & swell'd with Riches Boast,
> Where was the Balance of the Bliss he found?
> "A Tortur'd Conscience, & his Honour Lost."
> Ah wretched grandeur, now unenv'd lye.[170]

Griffitts highlighted the inclusive understanding that merit and virtuous conduct were the only way to acquire honor. Even before the outbreak of war, women had realized that the only true way to judge one's actions was based on the sense of proper action dictated by one's conscience. Warren wrote to Winthrop that when one acted "faithfully and fulfilled the duties of life, the distinctions made between the master and the servant, the prince and the peasant may be in favour of the latter." Women who devoted themselves to the war could not be denied their just share of honor, especially when compared to the "inferior votaries of ambition who daily prostitute conscience and all the sacred ties of humanity, for the pageantry of the day."[171] Interestingly enough, even some men joined in this thinking—including Winthrop's husband, John Winthrop. Both Winthrops supported both men and women who were "disinterested by noble principles" and as a result "may be the ground work of the proposed reform and [ensure] that the mighty fabrick may endure to the latest generation."[172]

The Revolution was viewed as a test of honor and virtue in which America had to prove the righteousness of its cause. Seizing the moral high ground acquired from the Battles of Lexington and Concord, the United States and Continental army were charged with maintaining their ideals by conducting a war on ethical principles. The overwhelming nature of the task of facing the British army also mandated support from broad sections of society. In this respect, those previously excluded from positions of honor were admitted, as service to the nation was cast as the highest good. Because of this, all people could claim their share of honor and virtue through proper conduct, duty to the nation, and, above all, ethical behavior.

CHAPTER FIVE

From Tension to Victory

Overcoming Civilian and Martial Differences
on Honor and Virtue during the Later War Years

Although honor and virtue continued to be the guiding principles for America during the early years of the war, the patriot record on the battlefield was less than encouraging. By the fall of 1777, the American cause had been dealt crushing blows, resulting most prominently in the British occupation of New York and the U.S. capital of Philadelphia. Despite numerous losses, the Continental army was spurred on by a continued belief that proper conduct could maintain honor in defeat. This varied rate of success kept America's diplomats, led by Benjamin Franklin, from being able to entice other European powers to join in the war. The assistance of the French was much sought after, and many correctly believed it to be of vital importance to any hope for American victory. In September, while Philadelphia was falling, America's Northern army, under General Horatio Gates, met the British army, under General John Burgoyne, in Saratoga, New York, and began a clash that fundamentally changed the direction of the war—and altered the American perception of honor and virtue.

On the morning of September 19, 1777, Burgoyne's undersupplied army, still recovering from an arduous two-hundred-mile wilderness march from Quebec to upstate New York, faced an American force entrenched behind breastworks and redoubts on Bemis Heights, just outside Saratoga. Scattered fighting continued into early October as the Americans encircled the British, at which point Burgoyne was all too aware that his battle-weary troops were essentially cut off from retreat. On October 7, he attempted to break out from his position, but a series of valiant charges led by headstrong Connecticut-born general Benedict Arnold pushed the British back. On October 17, Burgoyne finally surrendered his army to Gates; this victory has typically been credited as the spark that would draw the French into the American Revolution—thereby making it a global conflict.[1]

The victory at Saratoga, and the later entry of the French into the war, was a moment of unparalleled rejoicing for the Americans. But amid this elation, tensions over personal and collective honor and virtue festered within

American civilian and martial society. Beneath a veneer of victory, Americans were battling with each other over who possessed these ethical qualities.

Publicly, national honor and virtue continued to be regarded as the pinnacle of the American Revolutionary ideal. But as early as 1776, cracks in the unified stance of collective honor and virtue began to appear in American society, as soldiers and civilians questioned each other's ethics. Tension between the old British and new American styles of honor became common among both soldiers and citizens and threatened to undermine America's moral high ground. From the start of the war, Americans believed that they could only win by maintaining a firm grasp on their honor and virtue. In 1777, General George Washington knew that a collective loss of these ideals could cripple the cause. In his general orders, he implored, "Will no motives of humanity, of zeal, interest and of honor, restrain the violence of the soldiers, or induce officers to keep so strict a watch over the ill-disposed, as court-martial effectually to prevent the execution of their evil designs, and the gratification of their savage inclinations?"[2] He believed that Americans had to remain devoted to the nation and not spurn it for personal motivations or self-gratification. Despite Washington's pleas, the coming years would be rife with what the general feared was the fall of American honor and virtue.

After the initial American successes against the British in 1775, the war took a more ominous turn. The British occupation of New York City and Washington's subsequent adoption of a defensive war of posts, or defensive positioning, placed a damper on America's ability to claim honor through victory. As mentioned in the previous chapter, there was a widespread adoption of the principle that there could be honor in defeat, as long as the army performed well. However, this was not a universal belief.[3] Civilian government and society began equating the losses with the army's falling level of honor and virtue. In Williamsburg, Virginia House of Delegates member (and future Continental congressman) John Banister wrote, "It is not a glorious Retreat or the Heroism of saving a Country on the Brink of destruction by the finest dispositions of defensive war, but the Eclat [shine or luster (French)] of Victories, that strikes the gross of Mankind."[4] He relayed the sentiments of the common people: they wanted victory, not honor in defeat. The government and the people began to look at the army as losing its honor and virtue. They saw orderly retreat, yes, but no victories—and a collection of soldiers that seemed more concerned with their personal status than with the cause. From this difference of opinion stemmed civil-martial hostility.

Americans, as former British subjects, possessed an innate fear of standing armies and the dictatorial powers of an Oliver Cromwell. Soldiers and officers were quick to assert their personal claims to rank, pay, and prestige, which many civilians saw as a grab for greater power. Lawyer and prominent Bostonian William Tudor questioned the morality of the army: "So many of our Officers want Honour, and so many of our Soldiers want Virtue civil, social and military."[5] As John Adams anxiously observed, "Congress seems to be forgotten by the Armies." And he deduced the cause: "Unfaithfullness in public Stations, is deeply criminal. But there is no Encouragement to be faithfull. Neither Profit, nor Honour, nor Applause is acquired by faithfullness. . . . There is too much Corruption. . . . Virtue is not in Fashion. Vice is not infamous."[6] Adams believed that the army was moving away from its core ideals of national honor and virtue.

By far, the most common disconnect between personal and collective honor was the Continental army officers' sensitivity toward their rank, pay, and reputation. Despite the urging of senior officers, such as General Israel Putnam, that "True Honor Results not so Much from Elevation of Rank & Place, as from sublimity of soul & Great Military Exploits," many members of the Continental army became consumed with the "Trifling Considerations Respecting Precedence & Rank."[7] Much like Washington during the French and Indian War, young men newly thrust into positions of command and authority sought to mirror the behavior and prestige of their British counterparts, and they viewed their military rank as the most practical way to elevate their reputations. However, unlike the young Washington, there was in many cases a considerable gray area between personal and collective honor. Recently developed sentiments that the reputation of the individual reflects on the honor of the country as a whole often confused the issue of what was purely self-interest.

Unsurprisingly, Henry Knox's artillery regiment was particularly active in such confused quests for personal reputation linked with collective honor. Knox himself had shown previous sympathy for older sentiments of honor culture, including patronage, so it is not so far-fetched to assume that some of his ideas rubbed off on his men.[8] Early in the war, Continental army officer John Eager Howard groused that the conflict had dragged on longer than he expected. Howard, like many Americans who rushed to the cause, expected a relatively brief engagement that would not deprive him of his personal independence and financial security for very long. Howard resented the strain the war began to place on his wallet and reputation. He lamented to Knox of his escalating misfortune, "Were I stripped by the Misfortunes of War, in which I had bravely acted my part, my Poverty would be to my Honor but here, 'tis low—'tis mean—who can bear it?"[9]

As already stated, honor was not directly related to wealth, but finances did play a role in one's ability to assume the outward trappings of respectability. Howard continued, "Neatness & Uniformity of Dress, adds Beauty to the Appearance, Honor to the Employment, and solicits with irrefutable force, numbers to engage in the character of soldiers. But these things are attended with expense." Though he wanted to improve his personal situation, he still continued to frame it in reference to collective honor, stating that his behavior would "reflect Honour" on the army, his superiors, and the country.[10] Indeed, many officers continued to advance the notion that the actions or reputation of a single man could influence the country's honor. While the rhetoric was clearly in line with these collective sentiments, it featured an obvious personal hue—but one that could not be immediately labeled as placing the self over the cause.

Likewise, eight of Knox's junior officers (all captains and lieutenants) expressed similar concerns over how their wages reflected their reputation and honor. These artillery officers began their service with ranks and pay commensurate with those of their infantry counterparts, but before long they fell behind in both categories. The artillery officers complained that they could not "recollect any one Instance where the Captains in the Infantry have merited this Superiority which their Wages entitle them too [sic]." Furthermore, they proclaimed, "Our Commissions are equally Honourable—we've universally suppos'd to hold the same Rank." They felt that the artillery was not held in the same regard as the infantry, which claimed more fame from victory in battle. The officers petitioned Knox, "We wish Sir but for a Sufficiency to support genteely the Character of Officers in the Continental Army, we are not mercenary—we desire not to hoard up, but had we Millions [we] would with Pleasure spend them in our Country's Cause."[11] Again, complaints were carefully framed within the context of collective honor, thereby making any accusation of personal interest hazy at best. Contrary to such protests, most Continental officers would ultimately come to embrace national honor over the personal.

The democratization of honor opened up the chance for advancement to large sections of society based on merit, but this growing sense of equality also created complexities regarding issues of fairness, military hierarchy, and civilian control. Slights of rank, particularly among the upper echelons of military leadership, and disputes with civilian authorities created a great deal of discord for the American cause. The three-year period from 1777 to 1780 marks a moment in time when definitions and understandings of honor and virtue became even more complicated. For the first year and a half of the war, the lofty notions of collective honor and virtue had dominated Revolutionary ideals, but by the second year the quest for personal interest and glory remerged.[12]

Questions of rank, personal and professional animosity, and simple location brought together two generals who would come to personify two distinct forms of dishonor. The men first encountered each other in the summer of 1776 in upstate New York. Brigadier General Arnold arrived amid a conflict of rank between Major Generals Philip Schuyler (whom he had previously served under) and Gates. Gates, a freshly minted major general, challenged Schuyler's supremacy of command immediately upon his promotion and reassignment, based on wordplay, semantics, and his interpretation of congressional orders to command the army in Canada (which no longer existed). Despite Gates's lack of seniority, the politically minded general took his complaints before Congress. Though Schuyler prevailed, as historian Willard Sterne Randall commented, it began a "power struggle" that "would disturb the army for years."[13] With such an auspicious introduction, it is no wonder that a heightened awareness of personal honor was always present between the two men.

Despite the infamy attached to his name today, Arnold always followed his own sense of honor. But from his days as a merchant-smuggler in Connecticut (seeking personal retribution in the mass hysteria surrounding the Stamp Act) to his time as a commander in the Continental army, Arnold always seemed different, a bit more extreme. Even before the Revolution, honor had been a significant principle in his life. His devotion to honor could not be disputed (and he would not hesitate to correct someone who insinuated otherwise), and his quickness to rectify any slight either by pistol or by lash was plainly evident. Honor mattered to him. But could his personal honor remain subordinate to the greater good of America? Therein lay the problem. Arnold existed throughout the war as an anachronism, a medieval knight at tournament out for personal glory and valor.

Almost immediately after his initial meeting with Gates, Arnold became embroiled in one of the first of his many attempts to vindicate his personal honor. Regardless of his faults, no one could call Arnold a coward. General Nathanael Greene wrote to John Adams, "The Enemy gives General Arnold the character of a devilish fighting fellow."[14] By 1776, Arnold had proved his bravery on the battlefield with victory at Ticonderoga and even defeat in Canada—and it had won him valor and public recognition.[15] Even in accepting accolades, Arnold was unique among his contemporaries. While it had become commonly recognized in America that there could be honor in defeat, Arnold rejected the thought. He complained to Gates that his retreat from Montreal gained him nothing but a "reputation lost." He hoped to reclaim the "honour of America" but believed it could only be done through battle—which would also naturally do a great deal to restore what he felt was his lost personal reputation.[16]

During the war, the manner in which Arnold executed his duties often left something to be desired. Militarily, Arnold was as competent a commander as any in the American service, but he became accused of not maintaining the ethical standards that the Revolution was based on. From late July through early August 1776, Arnold's conduct was formally questioned before a court-martial (the first of three he would face during his career) at Fort Ticonderoga, the site of his former glory. Clouding the perception of his previous valiant service, Arnold was charged with looting Montreal as his army retreated. Facing a hostile court, Arnold's crucial witness was dismissed for a lack of disinterestedness, causing Arnold to rage against the court because it failed to simply accept his word of honor. The court called Arnold's behavior "illegal, illiberal, and ungentlemanlike" and expected an apology. Instead of asking for pardon, Arnold offered a duel. Despite the pervasiveness of the negative connotations surrounding dueling in New England, the Connecticut general was no stranger to the practice, as he had previously fought in the West Indies over an allegation that he contracted a venereal disease from a prostitute.[17] At the court-martial Arnold declared, "I shall ever, in public or private, be ready to support the character of a man of honor.... As your very nice and delicate honor, in your apprehension, is injured ... I will by no means withhold from any gentleman of the court the satisfaction his nice honor may require." The court immediately ordered Arnold's arrest, but Gates refused and negated its judgment on the grounds that its members held "too much acrimony."[18] While the event came to nothing, the charges against Arnold, his reaction, and Gates involvement reveal a great deal about both generals' conceptions of honor. Arnold's ferocity and Gates's support for his subordinate officer show that both men had highly developed senses of personal honor—and were unwilling to allow their reputations to be infringed on, even by governmental procedures.

Arnold's fame continued to rise after his command at the Battle of Valcour Island in Lake Champlain. But his estimation in the minds of the Continental Congress did not, and Brigadier General Arnold was passed over for promotion to major general in favor of William Alexander, Thomas Mifflin, Arthur St. Clair, Adam Stephen, and Benjamin Lincoln, all men he deemed less worthy than himself. He had already hinted at a mistrust of Congress, having previously complained to Schuyler's aide, Lieutenant Colonel Richard Varick, "I heartily wish they were more carefull in rewarding Merit, & Merit only."[19] He may have claimed it was a matter of merit, but being denied a rank he viewed as commensurate with his ability was regarded as nothing less than a slight on his personal honor. Arnold hastily complained to Washington, "The Person who void Of the nice feelings of honour will tamely Condecend to give up his right, & hold a Commission at the Expence of his reputation, I hold as a disgrace to the Army & unworthy of the Glorious Cause in which we are engaged." The slighted brigadier general was perfectly clear: he believed that his personal honor had been insulted and that no man conscious of such an offense could stand idly by and bear the shame. He still sought to maintain an appearance of favoring the collective honor of the cause when he concluded, "I sensibly feel the Ingratitude of my Countrymen, every Personal Injury shall be buried in my zeal for the safety & happyness of my Country."[20] However, the pent-up rage that exuded from his cries of dishonor (and continuing lamentations) illustrates that his own reputation was still his chief concern.

The brooding Arnold was not alone in his assessment of the situation. A shocked General Knox wrote to his wife, "Would you have thought it they have skipped over Genl. Arnold who was the eldest Brigadier and made five Younger Brigadiers over him. This most [certainly] pushes him out of the Service." Knox, a man not devoid of sentiments of personal honor, recognized Congress's affront and made it seem that Arnold's resignation would be entirely justified, perhaps even necessary to maintain his honor. The loss of a valued commander, as well as the potential repercussions such congressional intervention could have on subsequent promotions within the army, led Knox to write, "I hope the affair will be remedied."[21] By May 1777, it was—to a degree. Arnold was elevated to major general, and, in the words of his new commission, was granted "especial Trust and Confidence in [his] patriotism, Valour, Conduct, and Fidelity," but the date of his promotion made his rank inferior to that of the men elevated before him, based on the seniority of their appointment.[22] Thus, it was an insult that continued to sting, as Arnold had to subordinate himself under the younger, less experienced General Lincoln. Arnold continued to plead and petition for redress, but none came. This omission led him to attempt to resign his commission, writing to Congress, "Honor is a sacrifice no man ought to make," but it took the threat of Burgoyne's force and a personal intervention by Washington to keep him in the service.[23]

Before long, Gates, under congressional orders, replaced Schuyler after the fall of Fort Ticonderoga and assumed command of the Northern army. This promotion created two distinct problems in untangling matters of rank.

Before this promotion, Washington had refrained from personally giving Gates command, out of a desire to show his submission to the supremacy of civilian government. However, this would have a tremendous backlash, as it convinced Gates that his authority was independent from Washington's. Second, one of Gates's initial duties after his elevation required him to make Lincoln his second-in-command (based solely on the seniority of his promotion). Already enraged by this continuous slight, Arnold began to quarrel with Gates over strategy, the assignment of soldiers, and most of all his rank and reputation. Matters were not helped by the fact that Arnold refused to dismiss his advisers (Lieutenant Colonel Varick and Colonel Henry Livingston), both fervent Schuyler supporters who repeatedly questioned Gates's ability. Gates and Arnold each came to conclude that the other possessed malevolent designs.[24]

It was against this backdrop that the Battle of Saratoga was waged. From the start of the battle, Arnold urged the attack; valor would win him honor and reputation, and he had no time for Gates's caution. Under his personal command, Arnold's division excelled at the Battle of Freeman's Farm, but he still felt stifled, although it didn't stop him from congratulating his men's "Brave Spirited Conduct in withstanding . . . the force of the Whole British Army"— thereby also commending himself.[25] Although most other commanders had remained ensconced behind their defensive breastworks, Gates excluded any mention of Arnold in his communications with Congress, designed to grant a "Publick Mark of honour and Applause to the Brave Men whose Valor has so Eminently secured their Country."[26] For a man desperate for praise and reputation, silence was almost as bad as a direct insult.

Arnold was livid, and harsh words were spoken; he knew the omission represented a clear message: Gates wanted the honor of victory for himself. Lieutenant Colonel Varick, Arnold's adviser, commented, "Gates seemed to be piqued that Arnold's division had the honor of beating the enemy on the 19th. This I am certain of: Arnold has all the credit for the action. . . . Had Gates complied with Arnold's repeated desires, he would have obtained a general and complete victory."[27] Varick's words were bold; not only was he stating that Gates wanted to rob Arnold of any valor, he was also indirectly insinuating that Gates's prejudice had harmed the nation. Speculation abounded that this affront may force Arnold from the service or, even more dramatically, result in a duel.[28] But he did not leave, nor did he make a challenge, and his supporters used this as a reason to praise his devotion to the cause.[29] But Arnold was not satisfied, and disharmony persisted; he accused Gates of envy, saying, "Your treatment proceeds from a Spirit of Jealousy."[30] Gates responded by stripping Arnold of command and replacing him with Lincoln; for Arnold, a more direct insult could not have been chosen.

As fighting began on October 7, 1777, Arnold defied Gates's orders and his loss of command, shouting, "Victory or death," as he led a charge that split the British lines. Arnold rode into harm's way, waving his sword against continued volleys of enemy musket and cannon fire. Almost single-handedly, he rushed at the enemy; this was his moment of glory. As his men followed, Arnold's horse was felled and he took a Hessian bullet in his leg. Pinned on his back by the weight of his horse's body, he had a moment for self-assessment amid the pain. As his men freed his body and carried him from the battlefield on a litter, like a Spartan warrior of old returning on his shield, he thought there could be no higher honor, prompting him to say of his wound, "I wish it had been my heart."[31]

The Americans would go on to defeat the British under Burgoyne, and the Northern army gained considerable glory from the surrender of so large and dangerous a host. In its far-reaching repercussions, the Battle of Saratoga was probably the most important victory of the war. It proved the Americans' worth on a worldwide stage, and it was directly responsible for drawing the French into the war, as it illustrated that the British could be defeated. But at the same time, Saratoga also accentuated a reemergence of personal honor. Gates and Arnold (despite the latter's defiance of orders) both emerged to unparalleled heights of fame. As the accolades rained downed on two men who were already more than skirting the line in favor of personal over collective honor, the scales tipped.

Fate conspired to make Gates's victory at Saratoga seem even more impressive. At nearly the same time as the Battles of Freeman's Farm and Bemis Heights, General Washington had suffered two defeats at Brandywine and Germantown, both in the shadow of the capital of Philadelphia, directly contributing to the city's fall. Some felt that the loss of Philadelphia meant the end of the war, which heightened the growing sense that America had lost its virtue.[32] But it was not the loss of Philadelphia that led to the perception that America had lost its virtue—it was the exact opposite. Had America been preserving its virtue, this defeat would have been impossible.

As news of the September and October battles spread, Gates gained acclaim, while Washington drew criticism. Continental congressman John Harvie wrote to Virginia governor Thomas Jefferson, "Gates's Rapid Successes to the Northward does him honour as a Great and deserving Officer."[33] The news of the victory at Saratoga came as a shock to Washington, as Gates had failed to notify his commander in chief, preferring instead to extol his accomplishments in a letter to Congress.[34] While Washington praised Gates for "an Event that does the highest honor to the American Arms," he also quite understandably criticized him: "I cannot but regret, that a matter of such magnitude and so interesting to our General Operations, should have reached me by report only" and not from a directly addressed letter.[35] Washington felt insulted, but he was also not ignorant of the political ramifications of his defeat and Gates's simultaneous victory. It did not take much for the Saratoga success to go to Gates's head. Always driven by self-advancement, he saw his newfound fame as an opportunity to advance to higher stations—perhaps even one currently occupied by Washington.

The victory at Saratoga and the loss of Philadelphia had emboldened members of the military and government to think that Washington needed to be replaced with a more able general. An anonymous pamphlet entitled *The Thoughts of a Freeman* summed up these grievances and began to make the rounds through Congress. The author charged "that the proper methods of attacking beating and conquering the Enemy has never as yet been adapted by the Commander in C—f." In essence, the pamphlet claimed that Washington was unable or unwilling to win; it took issue with force-preserving retreats and a defensive war, and instead yearned for the valor and glory provided by offense. He chided "that it is better to dye honourably in the field then [*sic*] in a stinking Hospital." Congress was "Honourable" (indirectly implying that perhaps others were not), the war could be won under Gates, and Washington had to be removed, for otherwise it would be "a very great reproach to America, to say there is only one General in it."[36]

Based on civilians' favoritism for offensive war, the estimation of Gates by himself and by others grew exponentially. And unfortunately for Washington, Gates's meteoric rise coincided chronologically with the darkest period of the war for the Continental army: the winter at Valley Forge. As Congress pushed for victory, Washington and other high-ranking officers viewed such an offensive as foolhardy, as they believed that "under These circumstances a winters Campaign [would] Dissolve the Army."[37] Knox spoke in the language of honor and also concluded it was not worth the risk "of sacrificing the happiness of posterity to what is called the reputation of our arms."[38] They believed national honor was of the utmost importance.

The vigor with which fortune had smiled on Gates in the North caused Washington to begin to question the devotion of civilians. About twelve thousand New Yorkers took up arms as militiamen to reinforce Gates's army, but Washington's force did not receive such ardent support in Pennsylvania. The vast discrepancy in public support indicated to Washington that there might be a waning sense of virtue in different regions of the nation. He professed his concern: "How different our case! [T]he disaffection of great part of the Inhabitants of this State—the langour of others, & internal distraction of the whole, have been among the great and insuperable difficulties I have met with, and have contributed not a little to my embarrassments this Campaign."[39] Washington was not alone; the aftermath of Saratoga caused a great deal of reevaluation in American society.

Brigadier General Thomas Conway was an Irish officer in the French army, serving with the Continentals in search of wealth and glory. His thoughts on the state of the war led to a direct conflict in martial and civilian interrelations. Conway placed all the blame for American failure squarely on Washington. He wrote to Gates of Washington's force, "The more I see of this army, the less I think it fit for general action. . . . I speak to you sincerely and freely, and wish to serve under you."[40] Conway, clearly situating himself as an outsider, continued, "Heaven has been determind to save your Country; or a weak General and bad Councellors would have ruind it."[41] Conway believed that Gates, not Washington, would be the savior of America. This shows a further shift from a collective ideal to one that was more individualistic. In this new vision, one man (Gates) could make the difference, rather than depending on the virtue and honor of society as a whole.

This letter sparked what became known as the Conway Cabal, a supposed conspiracy between military leaders and politicians to remove Washington from command. As many historians have correctly surmised, this alleged conspiracy was much less organized than it was given credit for. In actuality, it was at best an unregimented confederacy of those whose ambitions and thoughts were hindered by Washington's presence. Washington had foes who worked against him, but it was far from the villainous plot that has become legend. However, Washington and his supporters believed the cabal to be a very real threat, and they reacted in turn. Thus, the mere fact that Washington was convinced of its existence makes it an intrigue of particular note, as it upset civil-martial relations.

Conway's letter quickly became public, due to the drunken boasting of Gates's aide James Wilkinson, who was traveling under orders to praise his general's victory before Congress.[42] Washington wasted little time in confronting both Gates and Conway. Conway, extremely aware that the commander in chief had taken the matter as a slight to his personal honor, haughtily declared, "I Defy the most Keen and inveterate Detractors to make it appear that i [*sic*] levell'd at your Bravery honesty, honour, patriotism or judgment."[43]

The situation was also escalated by Conway's petition for a promotion to major general. Washington attempted to block this elevation because of his own distrust of the Irishman's soldierly virtues and because such a promotion would elevate him above many more-deserving brigadier generals. But a congressional conversion of the formerly legislative Board of War into one that had supervisory powers over the army gave Washington's critics a chance to injure him. From his winter quarters at Valley Forge, Washington could only watch with horror as Gates, Mifflin, and Conway (all hostile to him) were made members of the Board of War. Washington took these appointments as a slight, and they convinced him of the reality and severity of a conspiracy leveled against him. But unlike the young Washington of the French and Indian War, he did not resign his commission, cry out against a personal affront, or even waver in his belief in civilian supremacy; instead he vowed to "always afford every Countenance & due respect to those appointed by Congress."[44]

Washington showed continued concern over the interests of the nation and his officers, and in turn his officers rallied to support him. He declared, "I have no other view than to promote the public good, & am unambitious of honours not founded in the approbation of my Country."[45] In contrast, the evasiveness, denials, and subterfuge of his accusers identified them as not having the nation's best interests at heart. Washington retained his command, and the personal motives of his detractors became self-evident. Knox accused Gates and his cronies of losing sight of the tenets of national honor and of being "people who have never given any unequivocal evidence of their attachment to our rights, or whose boundless ambition has been checked by . . . patriotism." He wrote to Washington, "We set out in the contest with notions and sentiments very different from these. We then considered we were contending for our *all*. . . . But it now seems otherwise with many persons, whose anxiety for military fame seems to absorb every other consideration." Knox further retorted that the entire nation knew Washington's true character and it was only a small group of self-interested parties who sought to slander him. The artillery general assured his commander that he, the army, and the country praised him: "I am not of opinion that your Excellency's character suffers in the least with the well affected part of the People of America. I know to the contrary, the people of America look up to you as their Father, and into your hand they entrust their *all*, fully confident of every exertion on your part for their Security and happiness;—and I do not believe there is any man on earth for whose welfare there are more solicitations at the Court of Heaven than for yours."[46] Likewise, Greene asserted that the members of the cabal were "universally condemned." He also charged the conspirators with "boundless"

"Ambition" and with one of the worst crimes that could possibly be leveled at a gentleman: "Ingratitude."[47]

As the scheming came to public light, the intriguers faced backlash. Gates attempted to shift the blame and dishonor by accusing Washington's aide, Lieutenant Colonel Alexander Hamilton, of having "stealingly copied" his private correspondence.[48] Despite these denials and childish cover-up attempts, it became blatantly obvious that Gates had been involved in the affair, and Washington made sure that Gates learned via Congress that Wilkinson, Gates's own aide, had been the leak. Out of a sense of embarrassment, Gates publicly stripped Wilkinson of his rank in front of the rest of the general's staff. The shamed and dishonored Wilkinson promptly challenged his superior to a duel to rectify the disgrace. No duel was fought, as Gates conveniently delivered the controversial letter to Congress. However, the mere fact that Wilkinson, an inferior officer, challenged a major general to a duel shows that there was a growing democratization of honor. It would have been unthinkable for an inferior officer to challenge his superior under the traditional European notions of honor. In addition, the escalation of the event to a duel shows a clear elevation of personal honor in the minds of these officers. The exposure of the gravity of the accusation against Washington, which according to Henry Laurens was "ten times worse in every way," effectively lost the cabalists any remaining hope of increasing their prestige.[49]

It was not only anti-Washington officers who became immersed in this flare-up of personal honor. Since the outset of the war, dueling was punishable by court-martial, as dictated by the Continental Congress–issued *Rules and Articles for the Better Government of the Troops*.[50] But as historian Charles Royster has shown, there was a noticeable rise in instances of the Continental army's officers' engaging in duels, beginning with the winter spent at Valley Forge. Due to a combination of factors, including physical hardship, insult of rank and status, the professionalization of the army, and emulation of European officers, dueling became fashionable.[51]

The interaction with and attempts to conform to the European model of honor began to alarm the American government. A revised version of Congress's *Rules and Articles* continued to outlaw issuing a challenge or fighting a duel. But realizing the link between the duel and personal honor, Congress now attempted to combat it by continuing its appeal to national honor. It ordered that "all officers and soldiers are hereby discharged of any disgrace or opinion of disadvantage, which might arise from their having refused to accept of challenges, as they will only have acted in obedience to the order of Congress, and done their duty as good soldiers."[52] The civilian government advanced the notion that not engaging in a duel could be honorable, as it showed a devotion to civilian supremacy and the greater good. Major General John Sullivan, showing a clear regard for personal honor, complained, "I am by no means an Enemy to Duels & most Sincerely wish that Congress had Incouraged Instead of prohibiting them."[53]

Illustrating the direct opposition to the congressional statues, the *New Jersey Gazette* alerted the public that the duel had "of late become so much in vogue among the Gentlemen of the Army."[54] Royster suggests, "These pretensions made the officers' growing professional self-consciousness look very sinister to many of their fellow [civilian] revolutionaries."[55] If the officers defied civilian authority in this respect, what else were they capable of? Dueling was associated with personal honor, and the rise in its practice was a clear indication of the elevation of this individualized concept of honor. More importantly, it called civilian attention to this change within the military.

With dueling now considered by many to be a viable solution and Conway continuing to voice his opposition to Washington, General John Cadwalader decided he had had enough and challenged Conway. The resulting battle of pistols left Conway seriously injured (ironically with a bullet to the mouth). Washington vigorously opposed dueling as dishonorable, but many ignored these sentiments. General Greene, though also an opponent of dueling, still congratulated Cadwalader on his victory and proclaimed, "Most People rejoiced at Mr. Conway's fate."[56] Cadwalader had been a bit tentative about embracing such a visible position of personal honor, but Greene's words relieved him of any doubts that he had dishonored himself. A weight was lifted from his shoulders as he sighed, "It gives me great pleasure to hear my friends approve my conduct, as it would have added greatly to my uneasiness if it had been thought that my conduct proceeded from a turbulent Disposition."[57] Because Cadwalader was defending Washington's honor (and indirectly the honor of the army and the nation), rather than his own personal honor, it was in a way a matter of collective honor. Still, the fact that his action—participation in a duel, which usually was over personal honor—was so well received illustrates the revival of personal honor during the middle years of the war.

Although the Conway Cabal amounted to very little in the broader narrative of the war, it illustrates a larger, growing separation between civilian society and the military.[58] Matters of rank, personal honor, merit, and patriotism continually intersected during this period. And the resulting confusion kept many Americans on edge. Throughout the affair, Conway's promotion to major general was a principal cause for concern, due to the fact that it placed him above roughly twenty more-deserving officers. The outrage was similar to that felt by Arnold when (he believed) less skilled officers were granted seniority over him. Washington wrote to Conway, "You may judge what must be the Sensations of those Brigadiers, who by your Promotion are Superceded. I am told they are determin'd to Remonstrate against it."[59] Greene concurred and became resentful of Congress's constant interference in military matters. This time taking aim at Wilkinson, another Gates supporter who had also gained a generalship at only age twenty, Greene wrote, "Military rank being conferred upon people of all orders so lavishly has rendered its value of much less importance than formerly. It was once considered a jewel of great value, but now begins to be held in light esteem."[60]

Such complaints became far too common, as they bogged down the minds of officers who either neglected or were required to deal with those who felt passed over. Lieutenant Colonel Aaron Burr, whose most famous conflict over honor was still decades away, viewed his unreceived promotion as nothing less than a matter of personal honor. He wrote to Washington, "I would wish equally to avoid the Character of turbulent or passive, & am unhappy to have troubled your Excellency with a Matter which concerns only myself, but as a decent Attention to Rank is both proper & necessary, I hope it will be excused in one who regards his Honour." Burr was following the standard pattern: personal honor needed to be defended; he recognized and acknowledged that this was a personal matter, but one that was of the highest importance nonetheless. Clearly aware of the new openness afforded to the honor system based on democratization, the colonel also "beg[ged] to know, whether it was any Misconduct in me or extraordinary Merit or Services in them."[61] Burr recognized that merit could advance a man, even if he didn't believe in it, but his statement still shows that officers were cautious of this new openness when it was to their detriment.[62]

From their winter quarters in Valley Forge, Pennsylvania, eight Continental officers jointly asserted, "Our knowledge of mankind hath taught us that Interest, tho' inferior in point of Honor or others, is yet the most general motive to action." Their use of the word "Interest" suggests a meaning of personal honor, and the word "Honor" seems indicative of the more collective sense. They were all in agreement and could not "help complaining of eccentric promotions, promotions not calculated to reward the meritorious, but which only prefer the favorite, and tend to disgust the Army. Our honour as Soldiers obliges us to dwell on this Article." By "merit" they meant that men of "Bravery, Enterprize, or Accident, will sometimes make an Officer ostensible and render him famous." They believed such promotions to be "necessary to keep this incitement to Gallantry and Valour." But they were strictly opposed to men like Wilkinson and Conway, "whom even good fortune hath not favor'd with an appearance of superior military abilities; It must argue great demerit in those to whom he is preferr'd and is an Affront which they must highly resent."[63]

General Sullivan feared that this slight to the officers' personal honor could lead to a mass resignation of commission—thereby leaving the army weakened during a time of great need. He warned Washington, "This is not the Language of a few officers of Inferiour Rank but of high & Low Such." This growing usage of the language of personal honor was not the work of a few social climbers out to exploit the military to raise their status; it was instead indicative of a major ideological shift within the army itself. Although the officers' argument seemed to be very much a concern over personal honor, Sullivan suggested that it was actually the exact opposite. He stated that collective honor was of the greatest importance and that "in Instances of Rank which give universal Dissatisfaction the Honor of a few individuals Should be Sacrificed to the good of the whole."[64]

Sullivan's suggestion, though practical and in many ways consistent with the principles of national honor, could not be easily adopted. Tension over rank continued to create "uneasiness, discord and perplexity in this army." Officers who were promoted erroneously over others were equally protective of their newfound honor, if not more so, regardless of whether it was justly earned. As Washington explained to the Continental Congress,

> We find, that however injuriously to the rights of others, an officer obtains irregular promotion, he is not the less tenacious of it; but it is with the utmost difficulty, if at all, he can be convinced of the propriety of doing an act of justice by abandoning his claim; though he will confess there was no just cause, in the first instance, for giving him the preference. But as it did happen, he pretends his honor would be wounded, by suffering another, who is, *in fact*, his inferior, to come over him; not considering how much that other was injured by the act, which gave him the superiority.[65]

Washington was adamant that promotions needed to follow a standard protocol—rank should only be based on merit or demerit. Doing so would inspire the men to better themselves and "would teach the good officer to aspire to an excellence, that should intitle him to more rapid preferment." Conversely, a failure to behave well would instill the "fear of being superseded, with dishonor," and "would teach indifferent ones to exert more activity, diligence and attention, than they otherwise would."[66]

Meanwhile, complaints over rank continued to thrive throughout the middle years of the war. Lieutenant Colonel John Brooks petitioned Washington, recognizing that "the great Concerns must engross" the commander's time but still feeling compelled to "trouble" him with "a Matter of a more private Nature." He had served in the army since November 1776 under Colonel Michael Jackson, whose wounding had caused Brooks to take up the regimental command without the benefit of an elevation in rank. If Brooks was to assume Jackson's command, he felt that he also deserved Jackson's rank. He claimed, "It would be incompatible with my Honor as an Officer to open a second Campaign as Lieutt Colonel commanding a Regiment"; such a duty demanded a higher rank. If he did not receive his new commission, he warned, "it would give me the greatest Uneasiness to take the Field under my present Circumstances," essentially threatening a resignation.[67] Washington responded that waiting for an officer's "personal honor cannot therefore be affected" by waiting for promotion. Furthermore, Washington suggested that simply promoting Brooks to replace the injured colonel Jackson "would lessen the incitements to bravery, and prove most injurious to the service."[68]

Washington and many of his subordinates clearly had different interpretations of personal honor. The general continued to espouse duty to the nation as the highest honor. Regardless, officers continued to resign their commissions over such perceived slights. In most cases, Washington, who was conscious of the power of personal honor, did not stand in their way if their rationale was even moderately justifiable.[69] However, the situation became so extreme that some officers sought to leave service because they felt dishonored by having to march with units to which they were not assigned. Washington was equally perplexed and frustrated by this, and he sorrowfully acknowledged, "I am sorry that any officers should be so far lost to all sense of honor and duty," but at the same time he refused to "indulge" them and threatened to level the most severe punishments available under martial law.[70]

In addition, the physical hardships endured by the Continental army during the winter at Valley Forge made slights to honor that much more difficult to bear and also created a further ideological divide between soldiers and civilians. As the underfed members of the Continental army waited with worn-out cloths and shoes in ankle-deep snow for a spring campaign that seemed it may never come, many of them began to ponder what the rest of the nation was sacrificing for this war.

Writing to Washington, Generals Sullivan and Enoch Poor created an image of American soldiers maintaining the ideological cause of the Revolution.

They argued, "Previous to our appointments we had considered ourselves, as Citizens of America, bound to espouse the common cause, and to make every sacrifice our country could require, to defend its Liberties—But after we were called to the field, not only the obligations of Citizens, but our duty as soldiers, bound us to risque our Lives and Fortunes to support the violated rights of America."[71] They saw themselves as citizen-soldiers, but there was a growing sentiment that if there was any remaining honor and virtue in America, it rested exclusively with the soldiers, not the citizens.

As the bitter cold of winter gave way to the campaigning season, the spring weather did not thaw the still-frigid relations between personal and collective honor—but the summer months certainly inflamed tempers. On June 27, 1778, the American and British armies met in New Jersey at the Battle of Monmouth Court House, an engagement that had far-reaching implications for the war, civil-military relations, and the understanding of honor. Before the battle even began, there was disharmony among the army's top commanders, caused by concerns over personal honor by Major General Charles Lee.

Newly released from his term as a British prisoner of war, Lee had recently rejoined the Continental army after an absence dating back to 1776. In many ways, the resulting tension between Lee and Washington occasioned by this less-than-happy reunion was not shocking, as both possessed fundamentally different ideals and, evidently, conceptions of honor. Leaving aside the question of Lee's (then unknown) alleged treason while a prisoner, the British-born general's years in captivity may have left him simply out of touch with the war, the army, and his own sense of importance. These issues, combined with a certain lack of decorum, and set against the aftermath of the Conway Cabal, were all contributing factors.[72]

Nevertheless, as Lee was the second-highest-ranking officer present, Washington offered him the prestigious position of leading the vanguard in battle. Lee refused the post, saying it was not honorable enough for a person of his status and fit only for a more junior officer. Washington gave the command to the Marquis de Lafayette instead. Almost immediately, Lee had a change of heart, realizing that allowing the younger, lower-ranking Frenchman to take command would reflect poorly on his own reputation, so he consented to accept the post. After his reevaluation, Lee concluded that the vanguard, "a Corps consisting of six thoushand [*sic*] Men[,] . . . is undoubtedly the most honourable command next to the Commander in Chief." Lee's own words reveal that his decision was made based only on his personal motivation to achieve glory and honor. He wanted to be viewed as being on par with Washington; thus, he needed his command to reflect his importance. After initially passing on Washington's request, Lee asserted, "My ceding it woud of course have an odd appearance," stating that he realized that his first course of action would hurt his reputation and infringe on his personal honor, and that he should lead the troops.[73]

Under the sweltering heat of the June sun, Lee, with firm instructions from Washington to attack the British, led the American advance. The rationale and justification for what transpired next was hotly debated among the American military and public—and is still very much contested by historians today.[74] During the battle, Lee disobeyed Washington's orders and retreated. Historical analysis has proved Lee's decision to be the correct choice, as the British grenadiers would have overwhelmed the Americans in numbers and skill. But though hindsight exonerates Lee, it has the benefit of facts of which he was completely ignorant. He lacked the information to correctly call for a retreat. Other American generals on the front line were both confused and openly opposed to Lee's strategy, which directly countered Washington's plan of attack. There was a very real sense among the American officers on the field that an attack could have delivered a resounding victory, and that Lee had robbed them of it. Regardless, the major general disobeyed his orders and his force retreated—right into a mounted and onrushing Washington.

An incredulous Washington came face to face with the fleeing troops, and it fell on a terrified young fifer to break the bad news to the commander in chief that Lee had ordered a retreat. Still refusing to accept the young man's tale, Washington advanced as more and more soldiers ran from the battle in "disorder." As Washington encountered a "confus[ed]," retreating Lee, disbelief gave way to unbridled fury. Washington shouted at Lee, "What is the meaning of this, sir?" Lee only feebly muttered, "Sir? Sir?" in reply. Washington continued to batter the now embarrassed Lee, who justified his retreat by denouncing the valor of his soldiers. Lee sheepishly claimed, "The American troops would not stand the British bayonets." Lee even blamed Washington by asserting that he had previously been apprised of this point. Lee then criticized the collective and personal honor and bravery of the militia, the same force he had praised earlier in the war, saying that the "American militia could not look British grenadiers in the face." Legend (and an elder Lafayette) has controversially held that an incensed Washington screamed, "You damned poltroon [coward]," before charging Lee with failing to make a valid attempt at an attack. Disgusted, the commander angrily affirmed, "I should not have entrusted you with the command." The accuracy of this exchange has been debated, but clearly something was said that caused Lee to believe that Washington was challenging his "courage." After his very public rebuking, Lee was ordered to the rear of the troops and would never see another command.[75]

After Lee's failure, the legend of Washington would rise to unimaginable heights. As Lee's soldiers left the field, Washington raced around them and personally stopped the retreat. From atop his galloping charger, he willed the soldiers to fight and personally led the charge against the British lines. Neither bayonet nor grenadier deterred the men following Washington's pointed sword. A stunned Lafayette remarked, "His presence stopped the retreat.... His graceful bearing on horseback, his calm and deportment which still retained a trace of displeasure ... were all calculated to inspire the highest degree of enthusiasm.... I thought then as now that I had never beheld so superb a man."[76] Though the end result of the battle was technically a draw, Washington had saved the army from the brink of disaster. His personal heroism and that of his soldiers prompted the British to withdraw from the field under the cover of night, rather than risk a subsequent engagement. Arnold had Saratoga, and now Washington had Monmouth. But where did this leave Lee?

After the battle, Lee took up the mantle of the aggrieved, misunderstood hero. He fully admitted his part in the retreat and was convinced of the validity of his actions. Lee was undoubtedly aware of the prevalence of the notion that honor could come from defeat, if the soldiers behaved well. Unlike Arnold, Lee was willing to embrace these principles. Writing to Richard Henry Lee, he praised his own battlefield command, saying, "The retreat did us, I will venture to say, great honour. It was performed with all the order and coolness which can be seen on a common field day." Never one to support the virtue of modesty, Lee even avowed, "Had I not acted as I did, this army, and perhaps America, would have been ruined."[77] Lee claimed he saved the nation with his retreat.

He argued that his strategy had "entirely" won the day, and he stated that he was insulted by Washington's admonishments, which he regarded as "an act of cruel injustice." It takes a very special type of officer to have his courage questioned by the commander in chief and then expect an apology, but that was Lee. When no remorseful words arrived, Lee pressed the issue and demanded that Washington explain himself. After giving Washington backhanded compliments concerning his character, Lee launched into what for him was the heart of the problem: the insults he received. Lee felt disgraced that Washington's words "implied that [Lee] was guilty either of disobedience of orders, of want of conduct, or want of courage." On the grounds of preserving his personal honor and reputation, he insisted that Washington let "me know on which of these three articles you ground your charge—that I may prepare for my justification which I have the happiness to be confident I can do to the army, to the Congress, to America, and to the world in general." Further escalating the language of personal honor, Lee stated, "And I think Sir, I have a right to demand some reparation for the injury committed."[78]

Instead of eliciting a favorable response, Lee's letter provoked Washington to the point that he too now felt personally insulted. Washington's response was terse: Lee's words were "in terms highly improper." The commander reiterated that his battlefield critique was "warranted" and again charged Lee with being "guilty of a breach of orders and of misbehaviour before the enemy . . . and in making an unnecessary, disorderly, and shameful retreat."[79] Surprised and shocked, Lee demanded a court-martial to clear his name; Washington assented and had the malcontent general promptly arrested.[80]

Lee's trial began on July 4, 1778, under the watch of Major General Lord Stirling and twelve other senior officers. In addition to the charges leveled against Lee on the battlefield, the tribunal added "disrespect of the Commander in Chief" to his list of crimes. During the six-week trial, Lee asserted his innocence and maintained that he was "more solicitous of the safety and honor of the troops than [his] own person."[81] But privately, he railed against what he viewed as a "hellish plan" designed "to destroy forever" his "honour and reputation."[82] He continued to make it clear he was concerned first and foremost with his personal honor. In light of such statements, his cries of collective honor fell on deaf ears; Lee was convicted of all three charges and suspended from service for twelve months—a sentence that effectively ended his military career.[83] However, Lee refused to go silently.

He believed that Congress would exonerate him of the verdict. Lee bragged to Burr, "The affair redounds more to my honour, and the disgrace of my persecutors."[84] When Congress ultimately affirmed the sentence, four long months later, he took his grievances to the people through a letter in the *Pennsylvania Packet* newspaper, entitled "General Lee's Vindication to the Public."[85] The false assertions made by Lee bothered Washington, who feared that "not to attempt a refutation is a tacit acknowledgement of the justice of his assertions"; after all, honor demanded defense.[86] However, showing great restraint, Washington viewed his duties as more pressing than engaging in a battle of words with the disgraced Lee.

This did not stop others from attempting to settle the matter in Washington's place. After narrowly avoiding a duel with General Baron von Steuben, Lee mocked the situation by offering a faux challenge to a woman. Making sport of a trivial comment (that Lee's pants were the wrong color) by Rebecca Franks, a Philadelphia Tory, Lee incredulously blustered, "But, Madam!

Madam! Reputation . . . is a serious thing. You have already injured me in the tenderest part. . . . I demand satisfaction; and as you cannot be ignorant of the laws of dueling . . . I insist on the privilege of the injured party." In challenging a woman, Lee was poking fun at those who had viewed his failure to take the field against Steuben as a dishonorable act. He playfully swore to Franks, "The world shall never accuse General Lee with having turned his back upon you."[87] Any laughter Lee had at the expense of Franks or his other persecutors was short lived, as only three days later he stared down the barrel of a pistol.

Although no British soldiers were present, the guns of two prominent American officers fired on the afternoon of December 23, 1778, just outside Philadelphia. Colonel John Laurens, Washington's aide-de-camp, had grown tired of the aspersions that Lee had leveled against Washington's personal honor and character and challenged him to a duel. Seconded by Colonel Hamilton, the challenge was a bold assertion of the new democratization of honor that had been felt during the Revolution. As Brigadier General Wilkinson did in his offer to Major General Gates, Laurens (contrary to the traditional rules of dueling and honor-based hierarchy) challenged a higher-ranking officer. However, this duel was even more novel in its conception, as Laurens did not claim a grieved status but rather wished to serve as a proxy for Washington. Washington, who abhorred dueling and never failed to decry its evils, had chosen to ignore Lee's abusive conduct out of a sense of duty to the Revolutionary cause. But Laurens was not willing to let his commander's name and honor be sullied. Thus, the duel represents a highly original moment in the evolution of American honor. A duel, always a matter of personal honor, was being fought not by a principal but by an outsider; it was instigated in order to protect both personal honor and the collective honor of the army and the nation. Despite this, the rise in dueling continued; as General Greene would complain, "The spirit of dueling . . . goes on here as much as ever."[88] It continued to serve as a direct indicator of the reemergence of personal honor.

As Laurens and Lee advanced on each other while firing their pistols, a bullet struck the general in his right side. After some deliberation, the duel was halted when Lee declared that he meant no personal insult to Washington but only questioned his military skill and felt that the verbal "abuse" he sustained at Monmouth "would be incompatible with the character, he would ever wish to sustain as a Gentleman." With these words, the matter was resolved, and each man's second (Hamilton and Major Evan Edwards) affirmed the duel and its conclusion as a "piece of justice to the two Gentlemen."[89] With the firing of these shots, both Lee and Laurens were acquitted with honor (though some would not agree that this one act cleared Lee's name, and they continued to regard him as a dishonorable coward).[90] But the simple fact that part of the population could now overlook Lee's prior conduct was a clear indication that within certain circles personal honor was more highly regarded than previously.

The shadow of Monmouth continued to define the fall of Lee against a backdrop of differing interpretations of honor. Lee's clear regard for his own "personal Honour" seems to have irreparably altered (or at least revealed) his thinking to a point that he could protest to General Anthony Wayne that he was "too much persecuted for the honour of this country," while also speaking fondly of "the Empire of Great Britain" as "my Country" to his sister. Within a year, his lack of tact and aggrieved claims of personal suffering ran afoul of Congress, thereby prompting his permanent dismissal from service—despite his retort that he was intending to resign anyway, as he "could not have served with safety and dignity." He died two years later, financially and emotionally broken and undermined by his devotion to personal honor.[91] With implications beyond the end of his career and legacy, Lee's varied thinking on honor was indicative of broader internal tensions challenging the nation.

As the war dragged on, civilian-military relations became more strained, and by 1779 each side had accused the other of losing all sense of virtue. As indicated previously in this chapter, the middle years of the war were already marked by a drastic rise in the importance placed on personal honor in both civilian and martial society. As earlier discussed, this does not mean that a dedication to national honor vanished, but that the more individualized elements that had been overwhelmed by the Revolutionary ideals and had lain dormant finally awoke. But the reemergence of personal honor is a sign or symptom of this loss of virtue. Virtue had always denoted a sense of disinterestedness and selflessness that was in many ways incompatible with personal honor.

Not far from the scene of the Laurens-Lee duel, and only a month earlier, the recently named military governor of Philadelphia, Arnold, who was still recovering from the wound he suffered at Saratoga, confirmed America's waning virtue. He noted, "Our affairs both at home and abroad are in so deplorable a situation as forms a Picture too horrid to dwell upon, and must give pain to every Man who is interested in the safety of his Country; which in my Opinion was never in a more Critical Situation than at present." Who was to blame? Being situated in close proximity to the Congress in the newly reclaimed, formerly British-occupied capital, Arnold was quick to point his finger at "the great Council of the Nation [Congress] Distracted and torn with Party and faction." Arnold further argued that the congressmen had "lost the Confidence of the Army" because they had "abused or neglected their most faithful Servants."[92] These words were certainly tinged with feelings of personal resentment toward Congress for overlooking him for promotion throughout his career. Similar personal experiences came to form the officers' collective thought. These views were far from just the ravings of a sensitive soon-to-be traitor.

Soldiers who had suffered the horrors of war and the hardships of Valley Forge resented civilians, whom they viewed as sacrificing nothing for the cause while at the same time meddling in military affairs. Even earlier, General Cadwalader resented the "great number of men, equally able to bear arms," who "remain at home with their families enjoying peace, at a distance from the enemy." He concluded that their absences and prosperity were only possible because of the army and "the Virtuous efforts of those who have ventured their lives in the defence of liberty and their country."[93] Officers up and down the rank hierarchy could all point to slights suffered due to the promotion of less qualified men over them. Meanwhile, Congress's members were constantly bombarded with anger from the military over what seemed to them to be nothing more than trivial personal interests. The civilian government had witnessed fighting, scheming, and arguing in attempts to rise in rank and reputation. The upsurge in dueling within the military did nothing to discourage the civilian perception that the army personnel were just out for their own individual glory. Civilians contended that the home front had been mobilized in support of the war effort since the first shots at Lexington and Concord, and they resented being cast as villains.

For soldiers and officers, Congress was the source of this fall of virtue. Washington was constantly petitioning it for the clothing, food, and supplies that the soldiers badly needed. Other soldiers argued over pay; as Knox complained to John Adams, "They are not vastly riveted to the honor of starving their families for the sake of being in the army."[94] But most arguments centered on rank and personal honor. Generals Knox, Greene, and Sullivan all threatened Congress with their resignations when word spread that it planned to promote a Frenchman over them.[95] Again, Greene would run afoul of Congress. Taking the position of quartermaster general at the behest of Washington, Greene was tasked with the unenviable position of supplying the army. The post was not glamorous or tangibly rewarding, but Greene did his duty for the honor of the cause. But running any army costs money, and Congress began questioning Greene about the nature and amount of his spending. Greene viewed this as not only calling into question his own honor but also an indication that Congress was hampering the cause. Greene lamented, "My Enemies will take great pains to perplex and embarrass my affairs; and without some little share of fortune we must inevitably sink into contempt."[96] He further accused Congress of ulterior motives, saying, "Nothing is viewed in Congress respecting the Staff departments but through the dark medium of prejudice."[97] The general lashed out and insultingly referred to the Congress as the "Administration," a term reserved for the British Parliament. For Greene, Congress was lost to both honor and virtue—its members were no different from the British.[98] His opinion of Congress sank so low that he crestfallenly wrote to his wife, "There is so much wickedness and villainy in the World and so little regard paid to truth, honor, and justice, that I am almost sick of life."[99] But still he maintained his role and his duty to the cause.

Despite the preference of some of the military to credit Congress with inspiring the loss of civil virtue, cries against the general population for selfishness and a lack of ethics were just as common. General Alexander McDougall wondered, "Can the Country expect Spartan Virtue in her Army, while the people are wallowing in all the luxury of Rome in her declining state?"[100] Months later he would answer his own question: "I think the American cause is at deaths door and every Man is pushing forward after wealth, regardless of the common cause. If we are to be saved it must be by simplifying the Governments; and receiving Aid from the Court of France. The virtue of the people is not equal to the sacrifices necessary."[101]

When not chastising Congress, General Greene worried, "There is a terrible falling off in public virtue since the commencement of the present contest. The loss of Morals and the want of public spirit leaves us almost like a Rope of Sand."[102] Every penny the army had to pay to merchants and tradesmen was taken as a sign that civilians were only concerned about their own welfare. Colonel Henry Hollingsworth was "so perplex'd that [he knew] not how to act" due to "the want of Virtue in the Farmers, misbehavior in Shallopmen, Waggoners, and WM [wagon masters]."[103] Washington admonished civilians who profited and profiteered from the dire needs of the army as the "pests of Society, & the greatest enemies we have, to the happiness of America."[104] By 1780, the military held a resounding perception that "public spirit & public virtue seem . . . to exist, now, only in the Army."[105]

Congress and the citizenry fought back against the martial perception that they had lost their virtue. After all, had they not persevered when faced with the bayonets of the British army, such as in South Carolina, where "several of the richest men in the state suffered their fortunes to remain in the power and possession of the conquerors rather than stain their honor, by joining the enemies of their country"? They and many others had "ris[ked] life and fortune" for the cause in the name of "a high sense of honor and the love of their country."[106] The citizenry continued to believe that they were the ones championing the ideals of the Revolution. The fear of Cromwellian rule remained, and Joseph Reed wrote, "The Changes of Sentiment which have taken place in the Army with Respect to civil government have for the first Time given me Apprehensions."[107] As Reed questioned the honor and virtue of the army, no one had to ask Arnold his opinion—he gave it willingly.

Although the British occupation of Philadelphia had ended, Arnold was still at war in the American capital as the city's military commander. Requiring any military officer to head a post that required him to juggle Congress, the Pennsylvania state government, neutral Quakers, and British-sympathizing Tories so soon after enemy occupation was a tall order. Expecting the volatile and still bitter Arnold to effectively perform his duty while also pacifying the government and civilian population should have been viewed as a virtual impossibility. Aware of this complex situation, Washington still offered the post and Arnold still accepted—the prestige of such an important command would grant Arnold a large portion of the personal honor he had been expecting since the start of the war. Almost immediately, Congress and Arnold renewed their long-standing hostilities when Congress forced the war hero general to swear an oath of loyalty. Although loyalty oaths were common (for civilians, soldiers, and officers), Arnold took this to be a congressional insult to his history of valor and military service. Who was Congress to question his loyalty? Arnold did take the oath, but he delayed the process for as long as possible and would only swear it to his friend and fellow officer Knox.[108]

Arnold's military governorship proved to be a powder keg waiting to erupt. After the tension surrounding the loyalty oath, both Congress and Arnold took exception to almost any move the other made. As Arnold mixed with Philadelphia society, his actions immediately drew speculation, both real and imagined. Upon his arrival, Arnold, in a sign of his growing disillusionment, hosted a ball for the citizens of Philadelphia to which he managed to not invite any Continental army officers. Curious onlooker and former Rhode Island attorney general Henry Marchant noted that Arnold "has rendered himself not a little unpopular with the officers of the army in Philadelphia." Furthermore, Marchant predicted that such an insult would invite reprisal: "I am very sorry for his circumstance, as it will render his situation disagreeable, owning to the clamor and cabal of those who conceive themselves injured."[109]

Arnold also did not discriminate against Tory families, even becoming a member of one through his marriage to Peggy Shippen, which drew the ire of his patriot neighbors.[110] General Cadwalader noted this animosity almost immediately: "Gen. Arnold is become very unpopular [among the] men in power in Congress, and among those of this state in general." But he dismissed any anti-Arnold sentiment as nothing but "the purposes of Party or Faction." Arnold was the hero of Saratoga, and such petty issues could "never injure the character of a man to whom his Country is so much indebted."[111] The pervasiveness of such thinking caused many to avoid deceased Cambridge professor Thomas Rutherford's warning in the *Institutes of Natural Law*, "The same partial application of the standard of honour, which misleads us in judging of actions, misleads us likewise in judging of the characters of men. We attend so much to some striking part of their conduct, as not to observe the rest of it."[112]

While many dismissed the negativity aimed at the Connecticut general, Arnold chose to treat his critics with "the Contempt which I think they deserve by taking no Notice of them." (He was never one to accept censure well.) But inside, Arnold did take them to heart. He believed he had sacrificed so much for the Revolution, and years of neglect by Congress now caused him to charge its members with ingratitude.[113]

At the start of the war, Arnold had been a wealthy man, and he had used a considerable portion of this wealth to finance the assault of Quebec. However, the duration of the war had taken its toll on his personal finances. Arnold would have agreed with Cadwalader that America owed him for his physical and financial sacrifices. He took the forced absence from the battlefield as a chance to help replenish his wealth. Arnold embarked on a series of suspicious business ventures that, while ethically questionable, were not technically illegal, including investing with a known Tory shipping merchant, using government wagons to transport private goods, and taking advantage of insider trading (although the last would only be discovered years later). Soon Arnold was called before his second court-martial in as many years. The charges only incited his malevolence further; the general, "tho' deprived of the Use of either Leg, and in constant pain, feells so much more sensibly, the Wounds his Character has received." Still, supporters came to his aid; former Continental Congress delegate Silas Deane called the accusers men "who while they pretend . . . to Virtue, and Patriotism are employed solely to gratify their private resentment."[114]

Arnold went to trial convinced of America's "ingratitude and punie faith."[115] He addressed the court under Major General Robert Howe, expecting that its members' personal honor would enable them to recognize the insult that such a proceeding leveled against him. He publicly declared, "I feel it a great source of consolation, to have an opportunity of being tried by gentlemen whose delicate and refined sensations of honour, will lead them to entertain similar sentiments concerning those who accuse unjustly." But at the same time Arnold was conscious that he must be "the guardian of [his] own honour." While he was acquitted of several of the charges, the court determined that his behavior was "imprudent and improper" and convicted him on two counts based on his dealings with Tory shipping and the use of government wagons.[116]

The court sentenced Arnold to be publicly reprimanded in general orders by Washington, who reluctantly complied, writing that he "would have been much happier in an occasion of bestowing commendations on an officer who has rendered such distinguished services to his Country as Major General Arnold." Still, out of "a sense of duty," Washington labeled Arnold's behavior "as peculiarly reprehensible, both in a civil and military view," and agreed with the court that it was also "Imprudent and improper."[117] Given the tense civil-military relations, Washington made it clear that the court's findings were consistent with all manners of justice. The verdict floored Arnold, who expected exoneration based on his prior service. This expectation was not entirely unfounded, considering the presence of similar views among other prominent Americans who believed that even if Arnold was "blamable in some little matters, his services and sufferings have been sufficient to wipe away a multitude of errors."[118] Even the commander in chief's scolding was purposely mild, but the incident had fully convinced Arnold beyond all doubt that America had sacrificed its and his honor.

Because of continued slights to his personal honor, Arnold now viewed Congress, his long-time supporter Washington, and America as lost to virtue. Through his new wife, Peggy, Arnold gained an introduction to Major John André, aide-de-camp to General Sir Henry Clinton and the British agent behind his eventual treason and defection, with designs to betray the cause. In an attempt at reconciliation, Washington, knowing Arnold's fondness for valor, offered him a choice command, but Arnold uncharacteristically refused and began angling to be given control over the New York military garrison at West Point for the secret purpose of turning it over to the British.

Either through coincidence or fate, the rise and fall of both Arnold and Gates occurred virtually simultaneously. Since the aftermath of the Conway Cabal, Gates, for fairly obvious reasons, had been attempting to secure a command independent from Washington. The Battle of Monmouth had caused the British to rethink their strategy in America; they were convinced that holding Northern cities and towns was not the answer. Instead, the British, under Lord General Charles Cornwallis, hoped to exploit the perceived loyalist sentiment in the South to achieve victory. The fall of Charleston, South Carolina, under General Lincoln (whom Arnold had singled out as an inferior officer) created the need for a new Southern command. Washington pushed for Greene, but, again showing the civil-military divide, Congress gave Gates the position. Despite this new appointment, old hostilities toward Gates from Washington's numerous supporters remained. General McDougall mockingly referred to Gates as the "Northern Hero" who showed continued "acts of disrespect. But they will ultimately reflect no Honor on himself."[119]

McDougall's words were prophetic, as Gates's Southern campaign would spell the end of his career and universally dishonor him. On August 16, 1780, at the Battle of Camden in South Carolina, Gates led a force largely composed of militiamen against General Cornwallis's regulars. Through a combination of personal blunders, highlighted by placing the untested militia at the center and left of the battle lines, Gates ensured that Camden was a resounding victory for the British. As the American lines broke, Gates fled the battle, leaving the rest of his army far behind him, riding hard and not stopping for breath until he reached Charlotte, North Carolina.

While the military loss was traumatic to the American cause, it was Gates's craven retreat that was the source of his dishonor. The outcome of the battle was not regarded as Gates's "defeat," but rather as his "flight."[120] General Greene, Washington's choice for command, labeled Gates a coward and was disgusted that he "was obliged to retreat 180 miles before he thought himself safe from the pursuit, so as to set down to gain an account of the action."[121] Alexander Hamilton satirically claimed he was shocked not by the fleeing but by the fact that Gates was physically capable of such a feat, as "he showed that age and the long labors and fatigues of a military life had not in the least impaired his activity; for in three days and a half, he reached Hills borough, one hundred and eighty miles . . . leaving all his troops to take care of themselves."[122] Although the retreat was in reality only sixty miles, the point was clear: Gates was more concerned with his personal safety than his own honor. Even in the midst of his treasonous scheming, Arnold, an old adversary of Gates, took the time to twist the knife and cast dishonor. He wrote, "It is an unfortunate piece of Business to that Hero [Gates] and may possibly blot his Escutcheon with indelible Infamy." The conspicuously brave Arnold sought his own vindication and flippantly remarked, "It may not be right to censure Characters at a Distance, but I cannot avoid remarking that his Conduct on this Occasion, has in no wise disappointed my Expectations, or Predictions on frequent Occasions."[123] This opinion was far from just personal prejudice, as Hamilton also mentioned that Gates "has confirmed in this instance the opinion I always had of him."[124] The dishonor proved so great that Gates would never hold another command, leaving Knox to mockingly conclude, "The heat of the southern climate has blasted the laurels which were thought from their splendor to be evergreens."[125] But his behavior was about to become overshadowed.

Throughout the country, the army's failures in the South caused a sharp decline in morale. Civilians blamed the military, and the military blamed civilians. Lieutenant Colonel Ebenezer Huntington lambasted his brother, Andrew, "Why don't you reinforce your army, feed them, clothe and pay them?" He continued, "Why do you suffer the enemy to have a foothold on the continent? You can prevent it. . . . You don't deserve to be freemen. . . . I despise my countrymen." The colonel didn't hide his disgust over the nation's civilian citizens, stating, "I wish I could say I was not born in America. . . . The insults and neglects which the army have met with from the country beggars all description."[126] Even Hamilton began to consider his options if America lost the war, but he still refused to sacrifice his honor: "I was once determined to let my existence and American liberty end together. My Betsey [his future wife Elizabeth Schuyler] has given me a motive to outlive my pride, I had almost said my honor; but America must not be witness to my disgrace."[127] But America would soon be revitalized by one of the darkest moments of the war.

After months of negotiation, Arnold and the British had finally come to terms on the price of his treason. Although Arnold was to receive a staggering sum of £20,000, the money was far from the chief issue—his personal honor was. As biographer Clare Brandt illustrates, "Arnold desired money not so much for itself as for the respect it implied, and the prestige it conferred. A man's salary bespoke his worth."[128] The betrayal was the direct result of years of perceived insults at the hands of America. The American Revolution had started as a matter of honor; this was Arnold's own personal revolution. To illustrate this point even further, Arnold agreed to accept the British rank of brigadier general, a downgrade from his American title—this was not about advancement; it was about principle, about honor.

Despite careful planning, on September 25, 1780, Arnold's plot to hand West Point over to the British was discovered after Major André was captured by a group of American militiamen. Arnold was forced to flee West Point with Washington fast on his heels and boarded the British warship *Vulture*, on which he sailed off into infamy. While the treason was shocking, the scale of it was consistent with Arnold's character. As acquaintance Colonel Charles

Petit reminisced, "He seems to have been determined not to be a little villain. Nothing short of the highest rate could satisfy him."[129]

In just over a month, two of America's greatest champions, the heroes of Saratoga, had fallen from honor. While Arnold's betrayal dwarfed any of Gates's faults, these two events must be examined jointly in order to understand the American perception of dishonor at the time. As personal honor began to grow in exaltation during the middle years of the war, the fall of Gates and Arnold served as a lesson about the dangers of forsaking the national cause. Their examples galvanized the population to once again champion national honor as the highest goal, while labeling personal interest as selfishness that could lead to treachery and dishonor. Such a transformation is not uncommon, as moments of extreme crisis throughout American history, from the Revolution to the bombing of Pearl Harbor to the September 11 terrorist attacks, have continually resulted in an aftermath of extreme patriotism and national unity.

"Treason of the blackest dye," proclaimed Washington in his post-Arnold general orders. Of all the accusations and insults hurled at Arnold, the first among them came from Washington, who said he was "lost to every sentiment of honor."[130] Hamilton stated that this treason was nothing less than Arnold's "sacrificing his honor reputation and duty."[131] But Arnold would have disagreed; he would have contended that his defection was based entirely on honor—albeit personal honor. He had a duty to defend his honor from American "ingratitude," just as he felt it necessary to clear the honor of his intimates who took no part in his crime.[132] Arnold's treason and its aftermath became a moment of drastic change for America. It was a moment in which the rise of personal honor was not only halted but fundamentally reversed, returning it to its status in the early days of the Revolution, when national honor was the greatest good. Colonel Alexander Scammell explained the process: "We were all astonishment, peeping at his next neighbor to see if any treason was hanging about him: nay, we even descended into a critical examination of ourselves."[133] Arnold's infamy shocked the nation back into agreement.

Washington seized on this astonishing treachery and was the first to use it to champion American honor and virtue. Washington said of the dichotomy created by Arnold's treason, "Great honor is due to the American Army that this is the first instance of Treason of the kind where many were to be expected from the nature of the dispute—and nothing is so bright an ornament in the character of the American soldiers as their having been proof against all the arts and seduction of an insidious enemy." Out of a period of civil-military tension, during which countless officers threatened to and did resign over personal slights, there had been no crime to match Arnold's. Washington made sure to highlight this point and use it as a beacon for the resurrection of national honor.

Furthermore, the treason showed how far the British had fallen from any sense of honor: "Our Enemies despairing of carrying their point by force are practising every base art to effect by bribery and Corruption what they cannot accomplish in a manly way."[134] From his diplomatic mission in Amsterdam, John Adams seconded Washington in a letter he wrote to Congress: "We have one Enemy more pernicious to Us than all their Army and that is an opinion, which Still prevails in too many American Minds that there is still Some Justice, Some Honour, Some Humanity and Some Reason in Great Britain."[135] By resorting to such cowardice, such trickery, the British had again affirmed the moral superiority of the American cause.

As Abigail Adams correctly foresaw, virtue would again reign—after a temporary succession by vice. She wrote her husband, "Pride, vanity, Envy, Ambition and malice, are the ungratefull foes that combat merrit and Integrity. Tho for a while they may triumph to the injury of the just and good, the steady, unwearied perseverance of Virtue and Honour will finally prevail over them."[136] True honor would prevail.

The people reverted to the previous tradition of championing collective honor. Arnold became a man whose treason was evident from his earlier behavior—his greatest sin was viewed as a foregone conclusion. He had the "pride of an ambitious man" and "the pretension to [honor] which every man of station thinks himself bound to wear the appearance of, whether he really feels it or not." Though it was reluctantly admitted that there was courage in the gravity of Arnold's plan, bravery alone did not denote honor.[137] While Arnold had rallied behind the cry of personal honor, such ideas now became dismissed as nothing but false honor. Arnold caused America to resurrect the mind-set that the Revolution was a test of virtue. As General George Weedon wrote, "If we have not Virtue enough among ourselves to Check Mr. Arnold without loosing [*sic*] sights of the Grand Object we Ought to Suffer."[138] Ultimately, as reported by the *Continental Journal and Weekly Advertiser*, "the highest offense" Arnold "committed was against himself," as his treason against America had robbed him of the one thing he coveted most: "immortality."[139]

Merit and morality were again championed as the path to true honor.[140] Congress was again regarded as "possessed of some of the most estimable & virtuous Characters this or any other Country can boast & . . . few publick

Bodies could have displayed more Ability & Honesty in their arduous Work."[141] Self-interest became nothing more than dishonor.[142] Even Greene, one of Congress's most vocal detractors, seconded this point: "I will never sacrifice the public good from false delicacy or court popularity at the expense of truth."[143]

While there is an abundance of evidence that suggests an ideological revitalization, the case can certainly be made that the vocal professions in favor of national over personal honor were simply a means to distance oneself from Arnold. Lieutenant Colonel Varick, one of Arnold's subordinates, even demanded a court of inquiry in order to be "acquitted with Honor" and prevent his reputation from being tarnished by association or accusations of treason.[144] For some perhaps, the assumption of the rhetoric of national honor was a means to prove their own loyalty. For others, Arnold's treason could have been a harsh reminder of what could result from a quest simply for personal honor. In any event, regardless of the motivation, national honor once again became one of the unifying principles behind the American Revolution.

Although Arnold's infamy was directly responsible for the nation's ideological revival, America's collective rage was still aimed directly at the fallen general, who was cast as something between the devil incarnate and Judas reborn. The country demanded justice, but unfortunately Arnold had escaped. However, the army did hold his accomplice prisoner. The case of Major André provided an opportunity to advance this reasserted devotion to national honor. It became an opportunity for the army, in particular, to publicly prove and reaffirm its devotion to the cause.

While on his way to meet Arnold and arrange for the surrender of West Point, André was captured in civilian clothing with incriminating papers, and thus was held as a spy.[145] But André was every part the ideal gentleman, and he tried to appeal to Washington's sense of gentility and honor by using a deferential tone to address the man of a "superior station" and attempting to justify his actions by noting that he was "branded with nothing dishonorable as no motive could be mine but the service of my King and as I was involuntarily an imposter."[146] It was a deliberate attempt to try to overwhelm duty for the sake of personal conviction. Throughout the war, Washington often faced this conflict between his personal and national honor.

But Washington was not alone in experiencing this inner turmoil. Hamilton claimed it was Arnold who "insisted" on disguising André, who was then "undesignedly brought within our posts." The British major should not be faulted; he was simply collateral damage of Arnold's treachery. Hamilton, a frequent visitor to the prisoner, was more than a little sympathetic to André and seemed convinced that he was "a person who though unfortunate" was "guilty of nothing dishonorable."[147] But his thinking was not all for the sake of André; Hamilton also showed great concern that any severe measures taken against the spy could infringe on America's moral high ground and potentially Washington's character.[148]

For Washington, this incident served as a flashback to his service during the French and Indian War and the Jumonville affair. According to conventional military tradition, "spies were venial characters who had to be paid for their work. They were grubby, untrustworthy, plebian men."[149] André did not look the part of a spy and therein laid the dilemma.[150]

(It is interesting to note that only four months earlier, British general John Vaughn lambasted Katharine Farnham Hay, an acquaintance of Lucy Knox who was on her way to New York and carrying personal papers. He mistakenly took her for a spy, saying "he would have no damned smuggling work if the Damned Rebels wanted to get Intelligence it should not be by Ladies."[151] Vaughn was visibly upset by the prospect of a person engaging in espionage who did not have the look to match. While he seemed to accuse the patriots of moral failing, his own army would soon employ a similar tactic.)

The Jumonville affair exhibited how genteel manners and appearance, or the lack thereof, clouded Washington's judgment.[152] This time, the visible façade seemed in André's favor. Washington refrained from meeting or corresponding with André, possibly because he sensed that he may be swayed by the major's charm and gentility.[153] Notably, however, Washington ordered that André "be treated with civility," allowed him to don his uniform, and even sent him breakfast from his own table.[154]

While Washington did not want the British major "to be treated with insult," he recognized that due to André's involvement in espionage, the case could not be granted any leniency: "He does not appear to stand upon the footing of a common prisoner of War and therefore he is not intitled to the usual indulgencies they receive."[155] Washington had learned from Jumonville, and he did not take any chances with André. In appearance, André fit the model of gentility. But by disguising himself, André, in Washington's view, had forfeited his honor. He could no longer be regarded as the genteel archetype, and this reconciled any tension between Washington's duty to his nation and his own personal honor. He had an obligation to his country, and André's status as a gentleman could not infringe on that duty.

Washington called a military tribunal of generals to judge the affair. André "confessed with the greatest candor," was found guilty of espionage, and was sentenced to death.[156] The tribunal members echoed Washington's sentiment that the preservation of national honor was their highest duty. Washington's hands were tied in the matter: to exchange André for anyone less than Arnold was unacceptable, and to spare his life was not only to invite mutiny from the common soldiers but to forsake the nation's honor.[157]

Hamilton remarked, "There was in truth no way of saving him. Arnold or he must have been the victim; the former was out of our power." But he still wished for the execution to be carried out by "under actors . . . and let the authority by which it is done be walled in obscurity and doubt" in order to shield Washington from personal smears.[158]

André was sentenced to hang, but he requested a proper death by firing squad, which befitted "a man of honour."[159] This was highly controversial, infringing on the assertions in *The Law of Nations* that "a man of honour, who would not expose himself to die by the hand of a common executioner, ever declines serving as a spy: he counts it beneath him, as it can scarce be done without some kind of treachery."[160] It appeared that André's own conduct had placed him in this predicament, as he had forsaken the traditional rules of honor. Still, General Greene "wish[ed] to heaven it was Arnold instead of him that was to suffer," and he even suggested that the major's blood was also on Arnold's hands—another loss of honor.[161] But to Washington, André had sacrificed his honor, and as a result he was dispatched with the noose, in a manner befitting a spy.[162] Revolutionary ideologist Thomas Paine, author of *Common Sense*, agreed with this perception of dishonor, since André "suffer[ed] himself to be taken as a coward."[163]

National honor needed to be pacified, but, as Hamilton would lament, "never perhaps did any man suffer death with more justice, or deserve it less."[164] This sorrow was far from one of military camaraderie, as Mercy Otis Warren, far from the gallows, shared a similar view: "While Every tongue acceded to the justice of his sentence, Every Eye droped [*sic*] a tear at the Necessity of His Execution."[165] Years later, Hamilton still agonized that the execution of an "innocent" man would jeopardize America's morality.[166] But it was a chance that needed to be taken. André's death, against personal inclinations, was a pledge of the Continental army officers' and the American people's devotion to national honor. Just as Massachusetts privateer Isaac Sears "lamented" this "ignominious death," he still acknowledged that "[André] deserv'd it by the Laws of Nations, & therefore suffer'd justly."[167]

The revival of national honor renewed the vigor of the Continental army and strengthened civil-military relations, thereby eliminating a great deal of the time-consuming infighting, distracting personal interest, and inter- and intraorganizational squabbles. This return allowed the army and Congress to focus their animosity on their true enemy: the British; and this rebirth thus became a crucial turning point in the American successes on the battlefield.

By the fall of 1781, Washington was engaged in Virginia, besieging Corn-wallis's army on the Yorktown peninsula. Farther south, guerrilla warfare con-tinued in the Carolinas as patriot militia (including a teenage Andrew Jackson) fought loyalists, leading to a simultaneous test of the nation's ethical resolve. With the end of the war in sight and Tories being commonly vilified for up-holding their oaths to Britain, a greater degree of brutality, perhaps even ven-geance, manifested itself in battle.[168] But with Arnold's treason still fresh in recent memory, General Greene continued to advance the notion of proper conduct that he had espoused since the early days of the war. Each man had to be kept in check; otherwise, in the words of Brigadier General William Ir-vine, it "ultimately" could lead to "ruinous consequences [for] the Cause & interest of the United States."[169] America could not sacrifice its principles for the whims of one man and thus jeopardize the cause as a whole. As with Arnold, sometimes the greatest enemy was from within.

At the center of the frontier conflict was Brigadier General Griffith Ruther-ford, a North Carolinian of Irish birth, and his Salisbury District militia. Ruth-erford had served as a militia officer since the French and Indian War, but with a questionable record, owing largely to his involvement in an expedition on the North Carolina frontier against the Cherokee in 1776. While a family his-torian described Rutherford's orders as containing the provision that "the peaceful Indians were not to be interfered with," his command resulted in atrocities ranging from plundered crops to burned native villages.[170] Stories emerged, such as one from his subordinate Captain William Moore, of a lone, outnumbered native "Killed and Scalped" by a force of fifteen militiamen, with other captured Cherokee offered enslavement or death rather than imprisonment.[171] After a brief period as a British prisoner of war himself, Rutherford returned to the field, taking up arms against a second "internal enemy," his loyalist neighbors.

Soon, news began to trickle back to Greene with shocking reports of "c<ruel and barbar>ous [*sic*]" conduct by Rutherford and his men. Tales of attacks on loyalists' "wives and Children" and the "burning [of] their houses and [the] laying waste [of] their plantations" challenged the lofty ideals of the Revolu-tion.[172] Vattel considered such actions as somewhere between a "dreadful ex-tremity" and a "savage and monstrous excess," and Greene was inclined to agree.[173] He raged to Governor Alexander Martin of North Carolina that Tories should be fought only within the bounds of the "laws of humanity," and that any deviation threatened "the honor of our cause[,] the dignity of Government and the safety of the people."[174]

An irate Greene demanded answers directly from Rutherford for the sake of the country's honor. While Greene understood the festering hostility created by the loyalists' "infidelity," he warned the militia officer that "in national concerns as well as private life passion is a bad counselor and resentment an unsafe guide." Barely a year earlier, Arnold had fallen due to a combination of "passions" and "resentment." A failure to curb personal satisfaction had nearly undone the nation, and refusing to heed this warning, even in battle against an enemy, could cause the patriots to descend to the same "barbarities" ascribed to the British.[175] Vindictive reprisals could hurt the morality of the cause more than any loyalist bullet or British bayonet.

Naturally, Rutherford dismissed all of the charges as "groundless." And, nominally, Greene (barring evidence to the contrary) had to accept this explanation. But the tone of his subsequent letter reveals that he probably still questioned Rutherford's conduct, likely due to the killing, scalping, and burning of 1776. The Rhode Island general, who valued morality over religion, was disgusted. And in a letter that could have been as easily written in 1776 as 1781, Greene did not waiver in his recriminations of Rutherford's real or exaggerated conduct. "Cruelty was dishonourable," and this fact needed to be embraced by every officer and soldier to uphold the Revolution. Even enemies needed to be treated with "moderation" and "humanity" and subject to the "rules of common justice." He wrote "not from any regard to the Tories" but because of its necessity for "our own sakes." Despite victory, all could still be lost if the patriots abandoned the ethical foundation of the war.[176]

Greene's advancement of moral conduct and national honor, a rejection of the prioritization of personal satisfaction, was indicative of the more widespread ethical thinking. In just over a year, Arnold's actions had inspired the United States' greatest high. His treason helped reinforce the original ethical ideals of the Revolution. With its joint principles restored, America was able to bring about the virtual conclusion of the war at the Battle of Yorktown in 1781.

But after the British were defeated, Washington had one last battle to fight, and it was against his own men's ambitions. Many of the Continental army's officers and soldiers were embittered by Congress's inability to pay their salaries and provide them with "an honorable and just recompense for several years hard service."[177] The coming peace would dissolve the army, and the officers believed that if they disbanded, they would never be paid. This episode represented a test to gauge whether the army had indeed cast off its flirtation with personal honor in favor of national, collective honor.

In what became known as the Newburgh Conspiracy, senior military officers threatened Congress with a coup if their demands for financial compensation were not met.[178] Washington overruled the conspirators' scheduled strategic meeting, as "his duty as well as the reputation and true interest of the Army require[d] his disapprobation of such disorderly proceedings," but cannily convened a conference of his own in order to illustrate his supremacy of rank.[179]

Washington interceded to preserve the honor of the army and "to rescue them [his officers] from plunging themselves into a gulph [gulf] of Civil horror from which there might be no receding."[180] He was sympathetic to the plight of his officers; he too had experienced the burden of dishonorable pay as a young colonel and had fought for their compensation rights throughout the war.[181] Washington urged Congress, regardless of "however derogatory these ideas are with the dignity, honor, & justice of government," to resolve the grievance, lest matters escalate further.[182] Though Washington likely understood his officers' emotional reaction to the slights suffered by them, he had no intention of condoning any action that could potentially subvert the civilian authority he had subordinated himself to. Washington presented "the classical republican" image of the officer eternally linked with the honor and reputation of his army but not at the expense of his country.[183] When Washington addressed his officers, he appealed to the preservation of their own personal and national honor: "And let me conjure you, in the name of our common Country, as you value your own sacred honor . . . to express your utmost horror and detestation of the Man who wishes, under any specious pretences, to overturn the liberties of our Country."[184] The general defused the situation by espousing the links between personal and national honor, the new ethical principle that he and his officers jointly cherished.[185] The affair "ended as we could wish—to the Honor of the Army—& great Satisfaction of his Exly [Excellency]."[186] The mutiny had been averted, but Washington informed Congress that it was its duty to right his officers' grievances—which it did.[187] As historian Richard Kohn remarks, "Instead of arousing suspicion and distrust by its flirtation with mutiny, the army emerged from the Newburgh affair with enhanced prestige and honor."[188]

As the unity of the war's early years gave way to a rise in personal honor over common interests, the nation seemed on the precipice of a catastrophic deterioration in civil-martial relations. Charges of dishonorable behavior and a failure of virtue on both sides created a period of dissension regarding ethical thinking. But, spurred by the treason of Arnold, national honor and virtue enjoyed a revival, as the horror of the crime forced Americans to reevaluate themselves and each other, leading to a renewed devotion to duty and proper conduct. The aftermath of Newburgh illustrates the preservation of a national ethical identity. Washington's successful management of the conspiracy swayed the public's traditional fears of a standing army and also helped set the stage for another affirmation of national over personal honor.

Even with the war at its end, uncertainty remained. But Washington would again allay all fears. The American Revolution would not end in a failure of its ethical ideals; there would not be a Cromwell or a Caesar. In the late fall and early winter of 1783, Washington staged a three-part, three-location farewell from military service that reinforced the devotion to national honor and civilian supremacy that he had heralded since he took up command. Washington would lay down his sword and say goodbye to his men, his officers, and the nation.

He first bid adieu to his soldiers in his farewell orders issued outside Princeton, New Jersey, reminding them to continue to uphold the values of the Revolution. Washington spoke to his "brave Men" in a reversal of terms he had employed at the start of the war; it was now time "to enable the Soldier to change the Military character into that of the Citizen." He reminded "all the Troops" that based on their "steady and decent tenor of behaivour [*sic*]," they needed to "prove themselves not less virtuous and usefull as Citizens," for the army had advanced based on merit and due to the actions "from every Class—and in every instance."[189] Men of all ranks had proved themselves, and now he urged them all to uphold those same standards as U.S. citizens. In a more intimate affair nearly a month later in New York, which had been recently evacuated by the British, he reminded his officers of their "honorable" service and gave them a tearful goodbye at Fraunces Tavern, filled with emotional embraces.[190] But Washington saved his resignation to Congress for last, for in his mind the nation was and remained most important.

On December 23, 1783, Washington entered the Maryland State House in Annapolis, ready to relinquish the commission he had accepted over eight years earlier. With one of his two aides-de-camp, Lieutenant Colonel Benjamin Walker and Colonel David Humphreys, at each arm, Washington sat in the center of an elegant Georgian-style chamber surrounded by a silent audience of both male and female spectators. To his front were the members of Congress, all seated with their hats still on—a conspicuous and conscious display of etiquette that showcased civilian over military authority. Washington would not be a king. To his rear, a "throng" of gentlemen crowded around the four columns that supported the Ladies Gallery, which was "as full as it would hold."

As Washington rose from his chair, he bowed before the members of Congress, who then doffed their hats but would not bow in reply. All inside understood the magnitude of this "solemn and affecting occasion," and this ceremony, carefully planned by delegates Thomas Jefferson, Elbridge Gerry, and James McHenry, was a public display of Washington's devotion to civilian supremacy. Washington stood ready to "surrender" his commission, "the trust" his nation "had committed" to him, "into [the Congress's] hands." With emotion that overwhelmed the general and the onlookers alike, he praised the war for granting "the opportunity afforded the United States of becoming a respectable Nation." From the very beginning, this was not just a revolution of thought, but one that had to be supported with deeds that reflected its ideals. The Revolution had been one based on ethics, and Washington always had "a confidence in the rectitude of our Cause." It was this common belief in the cause's ethics that had allowed the establishment of and would preserve the new nation. Wishing a blessing on the "Interests of our dearest Country," the general surrendered his commission, and with it "many tears were shed" by nearly all in attendance.

With his resignation, Washington proved again that his devotion to national over personal honor was not rhetoric. He led by example, and the surrender of his commission was a historically unparalleled moment of civic duty, patriotism, and ethical responsibility. In orchestrating a peaceful transition of authority, he had demonstrated through action something that could never fully be conveyed in words alone. This fact was plainly evident. Thomas Mifflin, the president of the Congress, declared that "the glory" of Washington's "virtues . . . will continue to animate remotest ages." While looking down from the gallery, Annapolis resident and eyewitness Mary Ridout no less profoundly proclaimed, "I think the World never produced a greater man."[191]

Expanding Ethics

*The Democratization of Honor and Virtue
in the New Republic*

The American victory at Yorktown, while technically not the official end of the war, brought the combatants to the peace table. Talks began in April 1782. While it was a time of hope and optimism for the Americans, there was still apprehension over the manner in which the war would be concluded. In Paris, the United States' peace commission, comprising Benjamin Franklin, John Adams, Henry Laurens, and John Jay, would be open to negotiation on all but one point: there could be no peace without honor.[1]

Even before the start of the Revolution, the phrase "no peace without honor" (or "honorable peace," "peace with honor," and so on) was broadly considered to be the standard by which America could conclude its confrontations with Britain (and it later became the basis for international relations). Faced with the mounting tension imposed by British legislation, Maryland delegate to the Continental Congress Thomas Johnson Jr. wrote to Horatio Gates, speaking of the colonists, "They look towards an honourable peace or successful Opposition."[2] In those early days, an honorable peace could have been initiated with a cessation of punitive British legislation and the establishment of colonial representation in Parliament. But as words turned to bullets, an honorable peace could only come about at a much higher price.

No one was more aware of this American mind-set than Adams, who, along with Jay, took the lead in the peace negotiations. Adams had been inundated with letter after letter from family, friends, and acquaintances demanding nothing less than peace with honor since the outbreak of hostilities.[3] In 1774, Abigail Adams lectured her husband, "There is nothing more desirable, or advantages [*sic*] than peace, when founded in justice and honour."[4] During the early months of the fighting, lawyer William Tudor wrote to his mentor John Adams, "The universal Voice is, if the Continent approve, and assist we will die or be free. The Sword is drawn and the Scabbard thrown away, till it can be sheath'd with Security and Honour."[5] Tudor, citing his opinion as "the universal Voice" and basically equating it with the country's viewpoint, illustrates that American patriots readily accepted this concept. It was embraced by both men and women, as Mercy Otis Warren echoed the words that Adams already knew by heart: "I will breath [*sic*] one wish more ... for the restoration of peace; peace ... on equitable terms. .... I cannot wish to see the sword quietly put up in the scabbard, until justice is done to America: the principles both of honour and humanity forbid it."[6]

The Declaration of Independence fundamentally changed the meaning of an honorable peace. Peace with honor now mandated British recognition of American independence. But a dishonorable peace remained a submission to slavery and tyranny. Americans continued to embrace the idea of no peace without honor as what could be considered an informal slogan of the war. During a formal parlay across enemy lines, Continental army officer Cuthbert Harrison was asked if America would make peace. He replied, "We are like all other just men [and] wish to do it on Honourable terms."[7] Bostonian David MacClure wrote to William Knox that no matter how "dreadful War is, better have that than inglorious peace & submitting to Tyranny."[8] Likewise, Abigail Adams continued to espouse the point to virtually anyone who would listen: "We most sincerely wish for peace upon honorable terms. .... We rejoice not in the Effusion of Blood, nor the Carnage of the Humane Species but having forced us to draw the Sword we are determined never to sheathe it the Slaves of Britains."[9]

John Adams knew that for America to leave the war on favorable terms, Britain would have to forfeit its honor. He wrote the Congress, reminding them, "Great Britain never can obtain a Peace, without a Diminution of her Honor and Dignity." He realized what was at stake. Peace was a matter of "National Honor," and Adams vowed he would "never depart from his Honour, his Duty."[10] Independence was a precondition, not a bargain chip. On September 3, 1783, the Treaty of Paris, which formally "relinquishe[d] all Claims" of George III on America, was signed by the four delegates—America had its peace with honor.[11]

Alexander Hamilton forwarded on his praise that the peace "exceeds in the goodness of its terms the expectations of the most sanguine." It thus "does the highest honor to the men who made it."[12] Franklin would joke, "There never was a good war or a bad peace."[13] But Adams knew the rest of the nation disagreed, "for People cannot bear the Ideas of national Disgrace."[14] With national honor vindicated, Americans became exceptionally protective of this newly won and tenaciously acquired laurel. The policy, politics, and culture of early republican America would be dominated by an obsession with maintaining national honor.

Back in the United States, with peace now formally declared, it was time for the army to disband. But after years of fighting hard and fostering close

relationships, the officers of the Continental army hoped to retain that camaraderie. Largely under the guidance of General Henry Knox, plans for an organization of Revolutionary officers began to take place even before the end of
the war. Years of civil-military tension, broken promises, and a near mutiny
against Congress had left some to think that such a group was needed to watch
over the interests of the former officers. Thus, from the uncertainty of the
Newburgh Conspiracy and the war's conclusion with the Treaty of Paris, the
Society of the Cincinnati was born.[15] It was (and still is today) a hereditary
fraternal organization devoted to the preservation and advancement of the
French and Continental army officer corps.[16] But this group was far from a
revived Newburgh Conspiracy; its initial conception predated the episode,
and the society was founded on the principles of civilian supremacy over the
military.[17] The officers possessed "the highest veneration for the character"
of Roman general Lucius Quintus Cincinnatus, who voluntarily laid down
his sword after his duty was performed, rather than retain power and become
a dictator.[18] Conceived as both a state and national organization, its members
maintained national honor as their highest duty. The society pledged "to promote and cherish between the respective states, that Union and national
honor so essentially necessary to their happiness, and the future dignity of
the American Empire."[19]

On May 13, 1783, in Fishkill, New York, the society held its first official
meeting, chaired by Hamilton and under the eye of their future secretary-
general Knox. At a subsequent meeting, the members elected George
Washington, who was regarded quite fittingly as the American Cincinnatus,
president-general of the society in absentia. This honor-based concept coincided with Washington's beliefs, leaving him "warmly in favor of it."[20] His
devotion to "support my Country's Honor, and my own Character" was the
same sentiment as the society's devotion to "national honor" and to its
members.[21]

More than simply embracing an ideological motto, the Society of the Cincinnati was governed almost exclusively by honor. Like the signers of the
Declaration of Independence in 1776, the members of the Cincinnati took an
oath to "solemnly pledge each other our sacred Honor."[22] There certainly
were elements of personal honor within the society—such ideas had never
gone away—but they remained relegated to the national cause, even in civilian life. Membership was "constituted on the high principles of Friendship
and Honour" and originally composed of former Continental army officers
"who left the Service with Reputation," and later their blood descendants (it was
also expanded to include French officers).[23] Regulations were largely based

on a single principle: that members must possess the "conduct" of "a Gentle-man and a Man of Honour"; to illustrate behavior "inconsistent" with this rule labeled one "unworthy" and led to formal inquiry and possible expulsion.[24] Such infractions were taken very seriously, and committees on conduct (basically courts of honor) were formed to regulate the behavior of the membership—ranging from public drunkenness to "ungentleman like conduct."[25] The Cincinnati institutionalized honor in much the same way that American colleges had been doing for years: through disciplinary codes.

Despite professing to hold to tenets of national honor, the society did not meet with universal favor from the public, as the hereditary organization seemed to exude the inherent threat of aristocracy, a system the country had just fought a war to be rid of.[26] From the outset, it drew the ire of those who feared a revival of tyranny against America. South Carolina chief justice Aedanus Burke, who had previously served in both the state militia and the Continental army, took issue with the Cincinnati and saw it as an attempt to subvert republicanism through aristocracy. He attempted to publish his ideas anonymously, under the name Cassius, in *Considerations on the Society or Order of Cincinnati*, but the pamphlet spread quickly throughout the states in popularity and impact and his true identity was revealed. Being of Irish birth and having just defended America against Britain, Burke's reaction seems perfectly logical and consistent with the sentiments of a fair amount of the population.

Considerations' antirepublican accusations were multifaceted. Obviously the most glaring concern centered on the society's potential for aristocracy. But Burke contended that the Cincinnati was even more opposed to the American government, as it "usurp[ed] a nobility without gift or grant, in defiance of Congress and the States." The society was formed independently from the government and the people. Since the group was self-created, Burke feared that it would be beholden to no one: "This is the natural result of an establishment, whose departure is so sudden from our open professions of republicanism." But more was at stake than just the fall of republicanism: "The Order is planted in a fiery, hot ambition, and thirst for power; and its branches will end in tyranny."[27] Harking back even further than the ever-present Cromwellian fears, Burke alluded to Caesar; for him it was a foregone conclusion that the Cincinnati would eventually seek to assert control over the nation through military means. The group had more in common with the Roman dictator than with Cincinnatus, the republican hero. After all, did Cincinnatus, "that virtuous Roman, having subdued the enemies of his country and returned home to tend his vineyard and plant cabbages; did he confer an hereditary order of peerage on himself and his fellow soldiers?"[28]

Burke boasted that America was home to "scarcely a distinction among us" and a democratization of "military virtue" and a "sense of dignity." All citizens were capable of safeguarding the ideals of the Revolution; there was no need of "the incessant watching of a dignified Order of Patricians."[29] Coinciding with these professed egalitarian principles was a general sense of an equally democratized notion of honor. Burke argued that the presence of the Cincinnati undermined this transformation of American honor. He warned that, according to the society, "the people of America . . . are not fit to be trusted with their own national honor."[30] Thus, the sense of equality formed before the Revolution and preserved through war was under attack. Contrary to the Cincinnati's espoused goals, Burke claimed that it was "not the way to promote and cherish Union and National Honor. Out of it will arise discord and not union." His pamphlet also held the American people accountable: "That they should commit such a vile abuse of their liberty as to allow it, is a reproach upon human nature; and would in the eyes of posterity, be a national dishonor to us."[31] As they had proved in the Revolution, the people had a duty to maintain national honor above all else.

Although Burke did attribute a malevolent intention to the Cincinnati, he did not believe that all of its members were aware of its sinister plan. In an accusation very similar to those leveled against Freemasonry to the present day, Burke claimed that the society "seems to be the offspring of patriotism, friendship, and humanity. And that many of the officers who have not closely viewed the subject, favour it from those principles, I have no doubt. . . . It is in reality, and will turn out to be, an hereditary peerage, a nobility." Burke was convinced that "the Cincinnati will soon be corrupted . . . for in less than a century it will occasion such an inequality in the condition of our inhabitants, that the country will be composed only of two ranks of men; the patricians or nobles, and the rabble."[32] It was not a question of if, but only of when.

The Society of the Cincinnati wasted little time in attempting to defend its organization and its founding principles. Another anonymous author, likely Pennsylvania society member Colonel Stephen Moylan, refuted the charges in his own equally unoriginally titled pamphlet, *Observations on a Late Pamphlet, Entitled "Considerations upon the Society or Order of the Cincinnati."* The author labeled Burke's pamphlet as being "impregnated with venom" and entirely untrue in its conclusions.[33] The new pamphlet asserted that the ideals of the Cincinnati were exactly as they were stated: "to promote and cherish between the respective states, that Union and national honor." Its motives were transparent and free from the "caballing" that Burke alleged.[34] The author seems honestly perplexed by the vigorous denunciation of the society. How could they give birth to a Caesar, he asked, when "Caesar disbanded no army . . . till he had accomplished the mischief he meditated"? Who among them could even become a Caesar? Only Washington possessed the ability, but then he was "our *greater Caesar!*" What evil could they charge the former commander in chief with? "Having restored the Goddess Liberty to her country and built her a permanent habitation there," or perhaps the fact that "he quietly retires to the rural shade, the glory and wonder of the age"?[35]

The officers had embraced civilian supremacy and not professed any contradictory position. The author offered that the Cincinnati had no authority, as "POWER *is conferr'd by Congress and the representatives of the people.*" How could they bring about tyranny when they submitted themselves to the will of Congress and the people? The members even supported the same democratization of honor that Burke professed as a core republican ideal. The pamphlet states, "Honours indeed, like impressions upon coin, may give an ideal value to base metal, but it is gold and silver alone that will pass without any recommendation but from its weights."[36] An individual could be given title, rank, and prestige, but that did not grant him honor. Only his true character could influence his reputation. Thus, false honor was worthless, and true honor was of inherent value and was acquirable by all. The Cincinnati's honor was derived from the character and actions of his members, just as was true of the nation as a whole. Thus, the society was "a distinction *without power,* and without any other luster than what it borrows from virtue."[37]

Despite this defense and the organization's support of democratized honor, the Cincinnati did not dispute that hierarchy remained, and it refused to apologize for what was regarded as a basic fact of eighteenth-century existence. The author of *Observations* unremorsefully remarked, "I dare say that even Cassius will not contend that, absolute, perfect, equality is possible to the government of any state."[38] Washington certainly was not opposed to the society's elitist nature.[39] He was a Freemason and also had been a member of a gentlemen's club in Williamsburg and was thus familiar with the dualist notion that afforded equal inclusiveness to members and excluded the uninitiated.[40] This was the world that Washington had grown up in, and he saw no inherent connection between hereditary aristocracy and hierarchical society or any contradiction between the membership in the society and his personal or national honor. He was puzzled how the society could "have any tendency unfriendly to the purest spirit of republicanism."[41]

The author of *Observations* asserted that the "*silence*" of Congress and the people in regard to the Cincinnati was "the strongest argument of the *innocence of the institution*."[42] However, this was far from the truth; although Burke may have been the Cincinnati's most vocal antagonist, he was far from a lone voice crying out in the wilderness. Criticism emanated from politicians, soldiers, and citizens alike.[43] The society's most prominent detractors included Samuel and John Adams, Franklin, and Thomas Jefferson. Franklin described the society as "an Order of hereditary Knights, in direct Opposition to the solemnly declared Sense of their Country."[44] Jefferson shared a similar sentiment and made an appeal to Washington that he remove himself from the "disapprobation" directed at the society. In a heartfelt plea, Jefferson intimated that it was only Washington's "moderation & virtue" that "prevented this revolution from being closed as most others have been, by a subversion of that liberty it was intended to establish." Jefferson reminded Washington that, though he was unarguably honorable and virtuous, he was "not immortal, & his successor, or some of his successors, may be led by false calculation into a less certain road to glory." Regardless of the society's intentions, Jefferson advised that it needed to seem more benign and be "modif[ied]" "so as to render it unobjectionable"—in other words, it must give up any concept of hereditary membership.[45]

Although Washington felt no personal guilt over his membership in the Society of Cincinnati, he was still conscious of his reputation as a national symbol.[46] Washington understood that any hint of a departure from republicanism on his part could threaten the country. The public outcry against the "aristocratic" society forced the self-proclaimed "republican General" to become defensive of his personal honor and conscious of national honor.[47] As president of the society, he took up Jefferson's suggestions and urged its members to restructure its constitution in order to "discontinue the hereditary part in all its connexions."[48] Washington warned that if such a measure was not enacted, it would severely damage the honor of the organization to a point that "we might I presume as well discontinue the order."[49] Based on Washington's personal intervention, the reforms passed in the general assembly were publicized and drew approval from the American people.[50]

However, much like the Articles of Confederation, these changes could not go into effect without unanimous approval on the state level. What many citizens failed to notice, largely due to a lack of press coverage, was that many of the state societies refused to implement these amendments, effectively killing the reforms adopted in the national meeting. The state societies claimed that they understood the reasons behind the proposed changes, but they could not support them as a matter of honor.[51] Hamilton "approved the motives" but could not concede on principle.[52] The New Hampshire society defended its actions: "To yield to Arguments that have no force, to acknowledge dangers that cannot exist, to recede from a Plan founded on the most laudable principles ... [would be] the mark of suspicion on the most virtuous actions." Its members supported one of Washington's original alternatives: it would be "more honourably done by laying the ax to the roots of the tree and abolishing the society at once" than to alter it based on misconceived prejudices.[53]

Washington lamented the perception that "the honour of American officers stands committed, and in danger of being [mutilated] publicly."[54] He therefore withdrew his presence, remaining the society's president largely as a figurehead. He no longer attended meetings, and he discussed his desire to avoid reelection, a wish that was not granted despite his protests.[55] This was a sacrifice, but one he made for the sake of national honor.

The state societies' failure to ratify the proposed amendments and Washington's distancing himself from the public face of the Cincinnati did not mean that the organization's detractors were justified. In fact, the Cincinnati showed every indication of being fully supportive of principles of national honor. Hamilton wrote to each of the thirteen groups, "The members of the Cincinnati, always actuated by the same virtuous and generous motives, which have hitherto directed their conduct, will pride themselves in being ... the steady and faithful supporters of her Liberty, her Laws and her Government."[56] The New Jersey society likewise maintained notions of civilian supremacy and "express[ed]" to John Adams "our entire satisfaction with ... the government ... [and] obedience to any call of our country, in vindication of its national honor."[57]

From the start, the members of the Cincinnati did not view their conception of honor as any different from that of the rest of society. Rhode Island society president Nathanael Greene even drank a toast to "honor" that was equally "sacred to both citizens and soldiers."[58] They did not view membership as a title but rather as a distinction earned by merit, for true honor could only originate from merit and was open to anyone of quality, a fact that even the society's French members had come to understand.[59] Hamilton would go on to argue that honor was available to all citizens, for "the character of Patriot ought to be an equal title to all its members."[60] Honor could translate from military to civilian life and vice versa; there was no difference in the minds of the Cincinnati. At the society's 1786 induction ceremony, Colonel Benjamin Walker highlighted this point: "The tenor of our past lives will be a pledge for our future conduct; for men who have done and suffered so much in such a cause, can never, (however their services may be requited) deviate from the paths of honor and public rectitude."[61]

Aside from the attention given to hereditary membership, the Society of the Cincinnati's understanding of honor was very much the natural evolution of its original European form. Honor had always carried with it an inherent notion of rank and distinction, which the Cincinnati and even Washington fully embraced. Their understanding of honor was formed through a combination of personal slights, merit through service, and exaltation of the national cause. Hierarchy remained, but the ability to acquire honor was fundamentally expanded. Although the Cincinnati viewed this model as applicable to all of society, others had come to form different interpretations of honor in post-Revolutionary America. The crisis surrounding the hereditary dynamic of the Cincinnati directly led two of its detractors, Franklin and Jefferson, to formalize their own thoughts as to the true definition and manifestation of honor.

Still in France, Franklin learned about the Cincinnati from his daughter Sarah Bache. He was not discouraged by the wish for distinction by the former officers. Since the dawn of the Revolution, many had fought vigorously and thrown out accusations against others of prizing personal honor rather than collective honor. Franklin viewed the argument as simply semantics. He wrote that honor "is in its Nature a personal Thing." For Franklin, honor always had a personal component, but it could be placed within a larger framework to support the national good. This was nothing shocking; it was a principal component of honor culture and nothing to be feared. The matter at issue was the Cincinnati members' belief that they could bestow "Honour on their Posterity."[62]

Franklin, who had made so much of himself despite being of humble origins, always showed an inherent hostility toward the rewards of lineage. He wrote, "For Honour worthily . . . is in its Nature a personal Thing, and incommunicable to any but those who had some Share in obtaining it." You could only earn honor through your own action or merit; thus, it was impossible for descendants to have any claim to the honor of ancestors, since they contributed nothing toward its acquisition. As Franklin explained, "Honour does not *descend* but *ascends*"; thus, only the individual and those (such as the individual's parents) whose "Education, Instruction, and good Example" made that person "capable of Serving the Publick" had any claim to it.[63] By this definition, honor became incompatible with heredity and birth status. In addition, it made honor directly dependent on a person's duty to the community.

While Franklin had stated that all honor was personal, he also asserted that all honor was also collective. Thus, for people to have true honor, they not only had to display their own proper conduct but had to do so for the greater good. Franklin's concept of ascending honor was a drastic reinterpretation of the traditional European connotations of heredity. Though Franklin was in Europe, his departure from European thought marked a prominent moment of change for American honor.

He had flirted with this idea of ascending honor since his youth in Boston. By 1723, he had publicly formulated this ideological framework, but for whatever reason he did not voice his musings again until spurred by news of the Society of the Cincinnati over sixty years later in 1784. But, as was quite common with Franklin, his ideas were multifaceted. "Ascending" continued to have a double meaning. As mentioned in chapter 1, "ascending" also referred to the type of honor—meaning it was ennobling and virtuous. Descending honor in turn was nothing but selfishness that failed to aid the nation in any practical way.[64] In fact, Franklin warned that "*descending Honour* . . . is not only groundless and absurd, but often hurtful to that Posterity, since it is apt to make them proud, disdaining to be employed in useful Arts, and thence falling into Poverty and all the Meannesses, Servility and Wretchedness attending it."[65]

Franklin also viewed ascending honor as having practical applications for a republic. He explained, "This *ascending Honour* is therefore useful to the State as it encourages Parents to give their Children a good and virtuous Education."[66] Since childhood, Franklin had always viewed virtue as the more eminent of the two ideas, but virtue was essential in the acquisition of honor. For a republic to survive, it needed to be composed of citizens who possessed both virtue and honor. By removing any remnants of descending honor, ascending honor inspired merit not only for individuals but also for their parents to promote honorable actions. In this respect, as he had done throughout his life, Franklin continued to promote education (of various sorts) as the root of all honor. In this way, he believed that America would prosper and honor would be its foundation.

The following year, Jefferson made a dramatic leap in his own thinking that had noteworthy repercussions on honor as well. As a Virginian, he had grown up surrounded by the most traditional form of honor. In his social relationships and at school, hierarchy, reputation, and public perception were understood as inherently linked to honor. So ingrained were these concepts that, to a degree, Jefferson always retained an element of this notion that honor was equivalent to reputation. However, he also came to develop a surprisingly modern view that is fairly consistent with our present-day conception of honor.

Jefferson's new idea of honor is very similar to our modern understanding of conscience. While he had grown up with the public face of honor, he came to reject it. Honor for him was entirely internal and dependent only on one's personal sense of morality. He viewed this idea of honor as a necessity and the core element of self-education. He wrote, "Never suppose that in any possible situation or under any circumstances that it is best for you to do a dishonourable thing however slightly so it may appear to you. Whenever you are to do a thing tho' it can never be known but to yourself, ask yourself how you would act were all the world looking at you, and act accordingly." Although Jefferson was dismissive of his internal honor's public component, he recognized that the communal perception of the individual was still the norm. Thus, he made his appeal in the language of public honor; one must act as if "all the world" were looking. Despite his wording, Jefferson's honor was fundamentally internal.[67]

Although Jefferson's emphasis on the self is striking, he did not intend for this internalized ethic to simply be a revision of personal honor. To be truly honorable, "give up money, give up fame, give up science, give up the earth itself and all it contains rather than do an immoral act." Jefferson's honor was clearly indistinguishable from ethics, morality, and conscience. But also, like Franklin, Jefferson was insistent that one must "pursue the interests of your country, the interests of your friends, and your own interests also with the purest integrity, the most chaste honour."[68] Thus, one must behave honorably, but in the confines of benefiting the nation. National honor was of central importance, but it could only be achieved by the collective honor of individuals.

The common theme between these different variants of honor was that national honor should take precedence. However, the issue of exactly what national honor was remained in question, due to a variety of individual and collective thoughts. The good of the nation and national honor were central. But what was national honor? This struggle became reflected politically in the turmoil surrounding the Articles of Confederation. The issue would be brought to a head by a matter of honor that had both personal and national implications.

In the fall of 1786, cash-strapped and debt-ridden farmers in rural western Massachusetts took up arms against the government.[69] These farmers had lost their lands due to foreclosures initiated by Massachusetts's attempts to pay off its own considerable debt by raising taxes. They began by attacking and seizing courthouses, thereby stopping legal proceedings since the judiciary was responsible for their land foreclosures. Led in part by former Continental army veteran Captain Daniel Shays, these outraged citizens viewed themselves as reviving the ideals of the Revolution and serving as champions of the spirit of 1775 and 1776. They publicly announced, "The end of Government is the good of the people."[70] The emphasis on the greater good was a clear acceptance of the Revolutionary conception of collective honor.

Before the hostilities, they had petitioned the Massachusetts state government with a list of grievances, just as the Americans had done to Parliament.[71] In what became known as Shays's Rebellion, over a thousand farmers who believed that their own government had ignored their grievances, as the British Parliament had done, perceived the insult as a matter of honor and attempted to rectify it.

Shays's Rebellion was not a flash in the pan or even an isolated incident but rather represented mounting tensions between the citizens, state government, and the national Articles of Confederation.[72] This western Massachusetts segment was part of a wider and regionally diverse expression of resentment that manifested itself in violence throughout nearly half of the Northern and Southern states.[73] In addition, along with the later Whiskey Rebellion, it was part of a joint attempt to regulate the new government while ensuring justice and fairness against the backdrop of the ideals of the Revolution.[74] The Shaysites, as they came to be called, viewed themselves as behaving honorably and continuing the patriot tradition. Shays explained that although he and his fellow rebels may technically be breaking that law, they were displaying "Virtue which truly Charaterises [sic] the Citizens of a Republican Government" and therefore "hath hitherto marked our paths with a Degree of Innocence."[75]

While the Shaysites believed they were championing the cause of honor, resistance to their actions was also based on interpretations of honor, though conflicting ones. The violence inflicted by the rebels was considered nothing less than a conscious "insulting" of the government, its officials, and justice. Even more offensive to national honor was the effect the rebellion had on America's reputation abroad, as it suggested a failure of republican government and the Revolution. Washington recognized that the resistance to the government and the government's inability to stifle the rebels was a slight to national honor. He lamented, "To be more exposed in the eyes of the world & more contemptible than we already are, is hardly possible."[76]

The Shaysites were accused of using the language of national honor for their own purposes, not out of a real sense of conviction.[77] Instead, they were blamed with having purely selfish motivations. The rebellion was viewed by its dissenters as a collection of disgruntled debtors and would-be tyrants seeking to avoid their obligations as citizens. The Shaysites' goals were described as an attempt to "*insert themselves* in posts of honor and profit, through the medium of war, confusion and anarchy."[78] Opponents made it clear that Shays's view of national honor was nothing more than a disguise for personal advancement and honor.

Not only that, but the group's personal and collective character and motivation were called into question. In a newspaper article in the *Independent Chronicle and the Universal Advertiser*, an anonymous detractor unhesitatingly stated, "These men are weak as well as wicked. Their attempts, to place themselves in the same situation with the people of America when they commenced the late revolution, must prove them to be destitute even of common reflection." In fact, they were "acting the part which Great Britain acted," since they were trying to "overthrow" an agreement between the people and the government.[79] Thus, those in opposition to the rebels were the ones really advancing the maintenance of Revolutionary ideals and national honor.

The Society of the Cincinnati was particularly active in condemning Shays's Rebellion. Although Shays and some of his supporters actually met the society's membership requirements, prominent members of the Cincinnati were responsible for raising and leading troops against the Shaysites.[80] Before long, all remnants of the Shaysites were crushed, due in large part to the Cincinnati, under an army commanded by Revolutionary War veteran and president of the Massachusetts society General Benjamin Lincoln, which "gain[ed] him fresh honour."[81] No sympathy was shown to the former Continental soldiers among Shays's band; the Cincinnati made it clear that it was devoted to America, not to its dishonorable brother officers. In fact, two of the rebels (brothers Luke and Elijah Day) had applied to the Cincinnati (or possibly were even members), but the society labeled them as "odious and obnoxious," publicly declared they were "never" members, and banned them for conduct unbecoming of "a Gentleman and a Man of Honour."[82] Shays's Rebellion had a positive influence on the Cincinnati, as the society's role in stopping the rebels proved it loyal to true principles of national honor. Knox shared this new public perception with Washington: "The clamor and prejudice which existed against it, are no more." Instead, the Cincinnati assumed a new mantle as champion of national honor: "The men who have been most against it say, that the society is the only bar to lawless ambition and dreadful anarchy."[83]

In 1787, a risky but necessary attempt on the federal armory in Springfield ended in a Shaysites defeat and marked the beginning of the end of the movement. The quashing of the rebellion was credited to both the military and civilians; it was said that "the zeal manifested" by the citizens "for the support of constitutional government, and the alacrity shewn by them when called upon to defend it, will reflect on them the highest honour."[84] Although Shays's Rebellion technically lasted only a year, its influence on the American people's perception of national government and honor had long-lasting implications.

Almost simultaneously with the outbreak of Shays's Rebellion, a small group of delegates (including Hamilton, James Madison, and John Dickinson) met in Annapolis, Maryland, to discuss revising the Articles of Confederation. By February 1787, roughly five months later, they had decided that a constitutional convention needed to be called to change the current government. While Shays's Rebellion was not the sole cause of the Constitutional Convention of 1787, its outbreak and the difficulty of its suppression publicly highlighted numerous failures and flaws in the Articles of Confederation, especially on economic matters and state and national cooperation. There were many different factors at play during the coming constitutional debates, but honor and virtue were chief among them.

Over a decade after the Declaration of Independence was signed, state delegates—some old and some new—returned to Philadelphia in May 1787 with another mission that was no less important in establishing the foundation of the United States. Eleven years earlier, they had raced to that city for a matter of honor, and now they were repeating the process. As early as 1785, Virginian James Madison, a former member of the Continental Congress and delegate at the Annapolis Convention, had singled the "Confederacy" out as the source of "confusion which has so long mortified the friends to our national honor and prosperity."[85] In 1786, Washington blamed the country's "departure" away from "virtue" on the articles, and further labeled them as the cause of "the want of disposition to do justice" that was now "the source of the national embarrassments."[86] Tension and frustration continued to grow, and the violence of Shays's Rebellion had convinced many of the necessity of change. By 1787, Madison believed that the Constitutional Convention was necessary to "perpetuate the Union, and redeem the honor of the Republican name."[87]

By September 1787, through debate, compromise, and negotiations, the delegates created the document that would become the U.S. Constitution. What began as an attempt to revise the Articles of Confederation ended with the creation of a fundamentally new system. All that remained was for this new government to be ratified by nine of the thirteen states. The Constitution contains no reference to virtue and only a single, insignificant mention of honor, but both the document and the government it represented were understood and presented to the people as a matter of national honor. As ratification loomed, proponents and opponents of the Constitution used the language of honor to justify or vilify it across the nation.

The resulting battle of public opinion waged by the Federalists (supporters of the Constitution) and Anti-Federalists (those opposed to it) was a contest over the meaning and nature of national honor. Madison, Hamilton, and Jay composed the Federalist vanguard. As the coauthors of numerous essays on the Constitution that came to be known collectively as *The Federalist Papers*, they were the ideological leaders of the constitutional cause. The Anti-Federalists fought back in their own publications, but they lacked the centralized vision and unity of their opponents. Still, the Anti-Federalists wasted little time in labeling the Constitution as aristocratic and subversive of republican and democratic tendencies.

Both sides made it known that honor was at stake. An Anti-Federalist, possibly Benjamin Workman, under the pseudonym Philadelphiensis, accused the constitutional framers of sacrificing their honor. They were portrayed as abandoning national interests for their own benefit. The author wrote, "I assert roundly, that another assembly of men never met in this, or any other country, possessing so fully the confidence of so many freemen: and to their shame be it said, they abused this confidence; their own private interest, private emolument, and hopes of dominion, overcame every consideration of duty, honor, and gratitude."[88] The tone and the repeated use of the word "private" in essence show that the author was claiming that the framers and their Federalist supporters were concerned only with their personal honor.

In turn, Hamilton, Jay, and Madison wrote *The Federalist Papers* under the alias of Publius, and they first appeared in the form of newspaper articles. Jay countered the accusations of holding only principles of personal honor. He did not deny that the framers each held a personal sense of honor—in fact, he praised it. He lauded the framers as "distinguished by their patriotism, virtue, and wisdom" and proven by their service to the nation during the Revolution. However, he asserted that national honor was always at the forefront of their minds. They were not the victims of "passions" or "awed" by "the prospect of obtaining" power. The framers' (and likewise the Federalists') sole motivation was "love for their Country."[89] As we have seen, the concept of the love of one's country is intimately, almost indistinguishably, tied to national honor.

Anti-Federalists continued to target their opponents by questioning their devotion not only to national honor but to personal honor as well. Those who denounced Philadelphiensis's accusations were singled out for being nothing more than a "base parasite and tool of the wealthy and great, at the expense of truth, honor, friendship."[90] Others claimed that the Federalist adoption of the phrase "national honor" was severely mistaken: "In public disquisitions, especially political controversies, one of the parties generally adopt some *cant word or phrase*, whereby they may be distinguished from their opponents . . . the *word or phrase* is nineteen times out of twenty wrong applied." Constitutional supporters were compared to nothing less than the previous decade's greatest villain: British Parliament. Anti-Federalists pointed out that under the vilified British prime minister Lord North's administration, "*national honor,* was bazed about, when not a fragment of *honor, principle,* or even *national courage* could be traced at court."[91] This was a clear indictment of their opponents, but they went a step further and directly linked false notions of national honor with federalism. Federalist support was reduced only to personal interest because they were choosing to support an idea that they developed; their beliefs were nothing more than "vanity" and were inconsistent with "honor and conscience."[92]

Federalists insisted that the Constitution and their support of it were based only on the goal of preserving national honor. As Hamilton retorted, "Men often oppose a thing merely because they had no agency in planning it, or because it may have been planned by those whom they dislike. But if they have been consulted and have happened to disapprove, opposition then becomes in their estimation an indispensable duty of self-love. They seem to think themselves bound in honor, and by all the motive of personal infallibility to defeat the success of what has been resolved upon, contrary to their sentiments."[93] Thus, in their argument, the Federalists, exactly like their counterparts, made sure to accuse their rivals of only having the interest of personal honor at heart. Using an identical technique to that used by the Anti-Federalists, Hamilton claimed that their fervent opposition was based only on the fact that their ideas were not met with favor, and they were defending them as if they were "bound in honor."

Despite the bickering back and forth, the Constitution itself and its potential power caused the most profound debate surrounding the preservation of national honor. Anti-Federalists contended that the Constitution was too strong and threatened to trample the rights of the people. Philadelphiensis contended, "If America is to become a respectable nation, the people must retain their freedom in the fullest extent possible; this is the *sine qua non* of our respectability; on this alone must the strength, honor, and national character of this country depend."[94] For Anti-Federalists, national honor was dependent solely on the behavior and actions of the citizenry. Richard Henry Lee, calling himself the Federal Farmer, supported a democratized version of honor and virtue that superseded class and birth.[95] The fear was that a strong central government, composed of the elite, could impose its will on the country, thereby removing the influence of the rest of the people. Chief among their concerns was that the office of the president seemed an opportunity for a Caesar-in-waiting.[96]

The Federalists responded by painting a portrait of lawlessness and stifled potential under the Articles of Confederation. Under the articles, the state legislatures and their representatives held too much power. Hamilton complained, "The faith, the reputation, the peace of the whole union, are thus continually at the mercy of the prejudices, the passions, and the interests of every member of which it is composed." For him, such a situation put the nation's honor in question: "Is it possible that the people of America will longer consent to trust their honor, their happiness, their safety, on so precarious a foundation?"[97] The people were in danger of losing their own honor because of the collective link between the government and the citizenry.

Hamilton, Madison, and Jay justified the Constitution by pointing to the personal and collective honor and virtue of those men chosen to represent the people. Jay tried to soothe the citizenry, saying that "every consideration that can influence the human mind, such as honor, oaths, reputation, conscience, the love of country, and family affections and attachments, afford security for their fidelity."[98] Likewise, Hamilton professed that all government positions would only be filled by men of virtue.[99] Furthermore, he asserted that the preamble of the Constitution itself was an ethical pledge between the people, "who surrender nothing . . . and . . . retain every thing," and the United States out of a "regard to the public good," writing that the document's opening words "would sound much better in a treatise of ethics than in a constitution of government."[100] Madison echoed these words: "The aim of every political constitution is or ought to be first to obtain for rulers, men who possess most wisdom to discern, and most virtue to pursue the common good of the society."[101] What would keep the government in line? Jay contended that "the constitution has taken the utmost care that they shall be men of talents and integrity . . . and so far as the fear of punishment and disgrace can operate, that motive to good behaviour is amply afforded by the article on the subject of impeachment."[102] In allowing for the process of impeachment, or removal from office, the Constitution institutionalized shame and disgrace with a more tangible punishment.

Hamilton viewed this as a moment of great opportunity, rather than the precipice of tyranny: "Happy will it be for ourselves, and most honorable for human nature, if we have wisdom and virtue enough, to set so glorious an example to mankind!"[103] The framework of the Constitution boasted a continuous bond between the people and the government. Honor and virtue were at its heart. The division of powers, and even the fact that the Constitution could only be adopted with the ratification of nine states, continued to illustrate the importance of the greater good. According to Madison, it was done to prevent the few from influencing the many and avoid the "indignation of every citizen who has felt for the wounded honor and prosperity of his country."[104] Remembering his Montesquieu, Hamilton claimed that the Constitution had further democratized honor. Since the president was not "the fountain of honor," like a king, but only part of a wider government, the checks and balances kept the national goal as central.[105] It was a recognition that honor was accessible in America. He concluded, "The institution of delegated power implies that there is a portion of virtue and honor among mankind which may be a reasonable foundation of confidence."[106]

Hamilton was also concerned with perception, especially of America's reputation abroad; if America stayed under the articles, "is it possible that foreign nations can either respect or confide in such a government?"[107] The Constitution was a necessity to defend America's national honor to other countries. Former Continental army officer Colonel David Humphreys would later recall that the rule of the articles was America's "hour of humiliation. The confederacy was found to be a government in name, rather than in reality."[108] Another former soldier, William Hull, concurred that policy under the articles was "derogatory to our honour and interest."[109] Hamilton believed all of Europe was mocking the nation: "Men admired as profound philosophers have, in direct terms, attributed to her inhabitants a physical superiority; and have gravely asserted that all animals, and with them the human species, degenerate in America—that even dogs cease to bark after having breathed a while in our atmosphere." To refuse to support the Constitution was to allow America and its citizens to be insulted. He tried to galvanize the people, arguing, "It belongs to us to vindicate the honor of the human race, and to teach that assuming brother moderation. Union will enable us to do it. Disunion will add another victim to his triumphs."[110] His words were a clear attempt to collectivize personal honor and make it subservient to the good of the nation.

By late 1787, the Constitution had gone before the states for ratification. The process proceeded relatively smoothly, with the exception of Rhode Island, which refused to even call a ratification convention. This reluctance led to charges against the state, which was accused of being dishonorable and blind to the true interests of the nation. Francis Hopkinson complained to Jefferson, "Rhode Island is at present govern'd by Miscreants void of even the external appearances of Honour or Justice."[111] Ultimately, all thirteen states would ratify the Constitution, in large part due to the influence of Cincinnati members serving as delegates.[112] The Society of the Cincinnati and its members had long supported the concept of national honor that the Constitution promised, and they rallied to influence its acceptance on the state level. Most importantly, the ratification of the Constitution illustrated the widespread acceptance of the ideals of national honor that had been building since the resistance to the Stamp Act. National honor, as duty to the country over personal interests, was validated on the national, state, local, and individual levels.

With national honor accepted as governmental policy, the next step was implementing it within the population. The most effective methods were already tried and true by the early republican era; schools and literature, the principal points of introduction to European honor, again became the most common means of educating the citizens on Americanized national honor. In stark contrast to Washington's and Franklin's views during the colonial era, Jefferson saw the United States as now the preferred site for citizens' education, for "an American coming to Europe loses in his knowledge, in his morals, in his health, in his habits, and in his happiness."[113] As previously discussed throughout this inquiry, especially in chapter 2, colleges had been advancing a notion of collective honor centered on the academic institution since the mid-eighteenth century, but now they were also advancing ideas that had become altered by the Revolution.

The transition from collective college honor to national honor was by no means a drastic leap. In fact, as we have seen, it was this collectivized conception of honor first learned in schools that helped many of the founders transition their own thinking toward national honor. Colleges had continued the practice of stressing collective honor, and discipline was severe for those whose misdeeds "reflected unspeakable dishonor on the religious and moral character of this University in the public mind."[114] Instructing future generations to venerate national honor became one of the chief aims of American schools, as dictated by internal and external sentiment. Speaking on schools in Pennsylvania, Dr. Benjamin Rush wrote, "Next to a duty which young men owe to their Creator, I wish to see a regard to their country, inculcated upon them."[115]

Honor and virtue had been prominent in the curriculum and rules of American colleges for over a century, and again these two concepts were inherently linked. But by this period even Northern students readily accepted that "by following the paths of virtue, we also may attain true honor."[116] Despite scholarly differences between these ideologies, the Northern and Southern understandings were fairly similar, if not simply a matter of semantics.[117] Again these ideas were considered ethical. They were specifically taught in classes on ethics and moral philosophy, and at Columbia these subjects became so popular that private lectures were called for outside the school by "a considerable number of gentlemen" in New York.[118] But the United States' nascent independence now precipitated greater emphasis on this notion of duty to the nation. Education itself was even viewed as a matter of national honor. In 1785, the newly founded University of Georgia's charter declared that educating the youth in "the love of Virtue and good Order" created "national prosperity." Unlike during the colonial era, the Georgians intimated that American colleges alone must be responsible for this charge; sending students abroad for a foreign education cast dishonor on the nation. It would be the American schools that would "form the youth, the rising hope of our Land to render the like glorious & essential Services to our country."[119] Likewise, Dr. James Madison, president of the College of William and Mary, proudly wrote to former student Jefferson, "I believe you will rejoice to hear it, that ye Spirit of Republicanism is infinitely more pure as well as more ardent in the rising Generation than among any other Class of Citizens."[120]

Elsewhere, national honor was no less visible. At Queen's College in New Jersey, orator William Linn, a former Continental army chaplain and current president of the school, stressed the unpartisan nature and disinterestedness of promoting "the honor and happiness of the American nation."[121] Harvard used its commencement ceremonies as public displays of the ideals fostered within its halls. Speaking to their peers, faculty, family, and distinguished guests, students John Harris and William Hyslop Sumner (and later George Sullivan and Nathanael Williams) led a discussion entitled "The Importance of a National Character to the United States," and at the following year's commencements, James Richardson delivered an oration called "National Honor."[122] Throughout the country, national honor was conspicuously on display, showing its prominence within academic culture.

A greater focus on national honor was not the only evolution within colleges. During and after the war, American colleges began to embrace a more open, egalitarian perception of honor. Honor and virtue were now democratized. On July 4, 1791, Linn, again at Queen's College, proclaimed that regardless of one's *"goodly heritage,"* "every one stands upon equal footing, and can prove successful, only by the piety, virtue, learning, and liberalism."[123]

The U.S. Military Academy at West Point, founded in 1802, evaluated its cadets based on merit, and conduct was considered the most important determinant.[124] Harvard, which previously ranked its students based on social status, now claimed, "To reward virtue & applaud merit is ever the delight of a generous mind."[125] There was a sense that honor, virtue, ethics, and morality were consistent for all, regardless of status, region, or religious affiliation.

Jefferson would come to have the greatest impact on perceptions of honor in the early republic with his advancement of an internal ethic. By 1779, the College of William and Mary had formalized an honor code, credited with being the first in America and attributed to Jefferson, that saw each student answering to his own sense of internal honor. In the early nineteenth century, this code still centered on a student declaring "his guilt or innocence" by "giv[ing] evidence on his *honour*" so "that the College may not be polluted by the presence of those who have shewn themselves equally regardless of the laws of honour, the principles of morality, and the precepts of religion."[126] Beginning in 1802, the College of New Jersey, already home to an honor- and shame-based punishment system, adopted a similar code, which required all to "solemnly pledge your truth and honour."[127]

By 1783, Rhode Island College had a system that saw students policing other students on honor infractions.[128] Other colleges soon followed this model, which became a fairly consistent example throughout the country.[129] In 1803, Yale's seniors even authored their own constitution, whereby they would "give information concerning each other"; it stated, "Should we hear an evil report of anyone of our number we will inform him . . . and reprove him."[130] Students were expected to inform on each other's wrongdoing as a means to preserve their own and the school's honor. In institutions where these codes were not formally enacted, it was not for a lack of trying. Harvard's government also appealed to its students "to reflect on the natural tendency of certain principles, too prevalent in the Society, particularly . . . 'that it is dishonourable to give evidence, when called upon by a lawful Authority.'" It declared that such a view was false, "that such a principle . . . must be highly injurious to the best interests of any Society, civil or literary, and that, so far from being allied to any sentiment of true honor or friendship, it in reality bespeaks a combination against the common good."[131] Thus, the pupils in a variety of institutions were taught that this self-imposed honor code should be carried over into daily life, as it was the duty of every citizen to protect national honor.[132]

Even when students were not directly enforcing their own honor system, disciplinary practices also evolved in relation to the greater dependence on an internal ethic. At Yale, a larger focus was placed on the self-preservation of reputation than on public shaming or monetary fines, illustrating a more inclusive conception of honor.[133] Harvard also appealed to its students' "own honor" rather than resorting to punishment.[134] By holding up these ethical principles and those who followed them, schools forged a culture of emulation that also created the possibility for advancement in school and society.[135]

Although traditional punishments still remained, in general, a student's word of honor was more accepted after the Revolution. Oaths of honor became standard and were the principal means of college governance. The U.S. Military Academy, founded with the help of Jefferson, combined the civilian and martial tenets of honor through both its curriculum and its honor code. The "Gentlemen Cadets" were educated in ethics, and they were also expected, as superintendent and alumnus Alden Partridge instructed them in 1816, to "pursue with undeviating course the paths of virtue and true honor; and rest assured that although the vicious and the vain may affect to ridicule and despise you they will inwardly respect you, and that you will thereby ensure the applause of the good and the great." And, in a very Jeffersonian sentiment, Partridge reminded the future officers, "What is of more importance [is] the approbation of your own consciences."[136] At the Jefferson-founded University of Virginia, an honor code was implemented, also in line with Jefferson's personal thinking: "When testimony is required from a Student, it shall be voluntary, and not on oath, and the obligation to give it shall be left to his own sense of right."[137] Honor was regarded throughout the nation as virtuous action and an internal ethic by which all were governed.

The formalization of honor, virtue, and ethics could also be found outside the classroom. Honor as an ethical concept pervaded the early republican professional world, with a focus on moral character and merit overtaking the older models of patronage and hierarchical status. This was consistent with John Adams's 1787 assertion in *A Defence of the Constitutions of Government of the United States of America* of the existence of a "natural aristocracy" of individuals grounded in "virtues and abilities," not by "attachments to noble families, hereditary lines and succession."[138] John Lowell, a Federalist lawyer, agreed and unsurprisingly credited it to "our federal constitution," which was "formed agreeably to the principles of moral justice." Now, advancement was based on merit, ensuring that "offices of distinction are open to every citizen." For Lowell, positions were not "used as the props of decaying dignity," as in the older system of patronage, but were "conferred as the reward of virtue."[139] More opportunities for society as a whole also allowed for expanding ethical interpretations. Belonging to the same occupation specifically opened individuals to another sense of collective honor. As discussed in chapter 2, before rising to the bar, Adams was taught, "a Lawyer ... ought to have some Book on Ethicks ... always on his Table."[140] He would indeed pass these ideals along to his own children, Charles and John Quincy Adams, reminding the latter, a future attorney and politician, in almost the exact same words, "you should have some Volume of Ethicks constantly on your Table."[141] Ethics was viewed as a necessity for many professions, that of lawyers chief among them; as John Quincy Adams would record in his diary, "it was necessary for a person going into the profession of law, to have principles strongly established," or else they may be corrupted by "the good and the bad, the right, and the wrong" of their occupation.[142]

While the connection between law and conduct is readily evident, ethical conceptions went beyond the courtroom. In business and politics, the payment of debt was cast as a matter of "morality" that was beholden to a "system of Ethics."[143] Relationships and businesses were made and unmade based on such interpretations. Journalist Samuel Morse dissolved his association with the *Farmers Journal* because he was "dissatisfied with his partner's [Stiles Nichols's] business ethics."[144] Government officials were expected to possess "political ethics," regardless of whether they were stationed domestically or abroad.[145] In 1783 John Adams assembled a list of qualities desirable in an American ambassador, including being "well versed in the Principles of Ethicks." All the trappings of "genteel address," manners, language fluency, "private Ambition," civility, and so on were purely inconsequential. Madison responded that this list "ridiculously" portrayed "his [Adams's] own likeness." Adams argued to Elias Boudinot, president of the Congress, "If Knowledge is in the Head, and Virtues are in his Heart, he will never fail to find a way of communicating his Sentiments to good Purpose."[146] Regardless of Adams's own self-aggrandizement, the assertion of these ideals illustrates their widespread acceptance. Similarly, officers and soldiers were instructed in military ethics that could be branch specific, such as "Naval Ethics."[147] Even preachers were encouraged to be equally versed in secular, "philosophical Ethics" and religious, "Christian Ethics."[148] Such codes of conduct could be found extensively in America, and some, such as medical ethics, became even more formalized in the nineteenth century and beyond.[149] Doctors, for instance, were expected to maintain "a good moral character" and avoid "immoral or ungentlemanlike conduct."[150] It was evidently also known that prospective employees had to follow these guidelines, as even job seeker Richard Dinmore, an English native, stressed in his application letter that he was "strongly disposed towards a doctrine of Ethics."[151]

Honor went beyond the realm of wealthy gentlemen. As it was democratized in the war's aftermath, tradesmen of all kinds began to view their work as inherently linked with honor. Or, as John Quincy Adams stated, "every profession has some such false [in his opinion] point of honour."[152] "Mercantile men" would only ship their cargo with men they owed money to, as "a point of Honor."[153] Sailors, again as a "point of honor," only trusted other sailors, and "a Captain thinks it almost dishonourable to be obliged to ask the opinion of another."[154] Virginian plantation overseer Thomas Mitchell worried that a failed crop of tobacco and corn would cause him to "loose [*sic*] [his] Character."[155] Repairmen were also held to such a standard; a Mr. Latrobe was instructed to fix Princeton's roof because "he is bound in honor, to do something decisive, if it be possible & to do it immediately."[156]

Just as in schools and professions, literature was used as a wide-ranging means to educate the population on honor and virtue. Illustrating the connection between literature and professional codes, printers came to regard their occupation as being responsible for the "rapid distribution of intrinsic virtue" and for providing "ethics to the universe."[157] Even Jefferson, a prominent supporter of formalized education, believed that ethics was one of the subjects "which may be acquired by reading alone" because "its dictates are written in the heart of every good man, & the head of every wise one." Reading improved and "strengthen[ed] his moral sense by exercise."[158] These ideals were available to all. It would be through such literature that Franklin's ideas were circulated among the population as a whole. Over the course of his life, Franklin had a knack for disseminating his thoughts to the public. Whether as Silence Dogood or through the *Pennsylvania Gazette* or *Poor Richard's Almanac*, Franklin always possessed an unrivaled skill in using the printed word to comment on and effect change in society.

In 1784, Franklin restarted his *Autobiography*, a dormant project begun in 1771, after being persuaded by friends that it would be "useful and entertaining not only to a few, but to millions."[159] Published in 1791, it tackled questions of virtue and the means for perfecting them in the self and society (examined in greater detail in chapter 1 of this book). The *Autobiography* became a vehicle for educating the American people, especially the youth; it would "not merely teach self-education, but the education of a wise man." Thus, Franklin's writings established "a noble rule and example of *self-education*" that would help foster the virtuous and honorable individuals that the new republic needed to maintain its lofty ideals.[160] Only three years after its publication, the New York–based *American Minerva* newspaper proclaimed, "The proverbs of Solomon [are] a good table of ethics, tho inferior to . . . the maxims of Doctor Franklin."[161] His writings were viewed as a guide to creating not only educated men but also great men.

The *Autobiography* also continued to advance the principles of democratized honor and virtue. By analyzing his own personal advancement from his meager origins, Franklin was arguing against ancestral hierarchy. His work and life inspired others to be "ashamed of no origin." Franklin's life and its immortalization in print "prove[d] how little necessary all origin is to happiness, virtue, or greatness."[162]

Despite Franklin's death the year before its publication, his *Autobiography* retained his message for posterity, and in many ways it made him even more influential. It also resonated outside America. Before Franklin's death, Benjamin Vaughn, a personal friend in Britain, said of the unpublished version, "It will moreover present a table of the internal circumstances of your country, which will very much tend to invite to it settlers of virtuous and manly minds." Franklin's work was viewed as being a how-to guide for the acquisition of virtue and even a replacement for classical literature.[163]

Franklin's resumption of work on his *Autobiography* in 1784 occurred the same year as his formalized expression of ascending honor. This intersection was far from coincidental, and it again shows the connections between honor and virtue. The *Autobiography* had caused Franklin to reevaluate his own life, as well as consider the message he would leave for posterity. Friends had convinced him the previous year that his uncompleted draft held the potential to serve as an example of self-education that could be followed. Likewise, Franklin's definition of ascending honor was also inherently a teaching model. As a father giving sage advice to his daughter, Franklin argued that ascending honor was "useful to the State as it encourages Parents to give their Children a good and virtuous Education."[164] Franklin's assertion was important on several levels. It reaffirmed honor as open to all based on merit, linked honor to the good of the nation, and claimed that educating the coming generation was an honorable act.

Throughout the letter, it is important to note, Franklin makes no differentiation between the roles of each person's parents. Mother and father are viewed as equals in the education of their children and, as such, equals in honor, according to his principles of ascending honor. Just as tellingly, Franklin revealed his new conception of honor specifically to his daughter, Sarah Bache, an active female organizer and supporter of the Continental army during the war. The coming of the American Revolution had allowed women to enter into honor culture through service to the cause. Whether through boycotts, tending to the wounded, or (in rare cases) fighting, women became accepted as honorable. They had proved to themselves and others that they were an asset to the greater good.[165] The new republic again offered this same opportunity through continued service to the nation.

Abigail Adams wrote, "Let every one consider it as a duty which they owe to themselves to their Country and to posterity to practise virtue, to cultivate knowledge ... by which not only individuals, but a people or a Nation can be prosperous and happy."[166] Women, as daughters, wives, and mothers, could continue to gain honor through duty to the nation. Adams, Warren, and other women now concluded that "personal Merit and virtue create[d] the only distinctions."[167] However, due to the continued inequality of the sexes, women's avenues for advancement were limited. Still, the cultivation of the next and current generation was viewed as a matter of honor in which women could readily engage. This phenomenon, originally termed "republican mother-hood" by historian Linda Kerber, has been shown by subsequent historians to be more consistent with a notion of republican womanhood.[168] In this respect, women became political actors and gained honor by engaging in their traditional gendered roles.

While the exact origins of republican womanhood are debated, historian Rosemarie Zagarri has persuasively argued that its roots lie within the Enlightenment tradition, especially from Montesquieu and moralists such as Adam Smith and William Robertson (both Franklin acquaintances from his time in London).[169] Thus, it is unsurprising that this thinking was readily known and embraced by the Revolutionary generation. Franklin's concept of ascending honor, in its nature and tone, is certainly receptive to this conception of republican womanhood. While it is impossible to say whether Franklin's ideas were a direct catalyst for this movement, it would be disingenuous to discount them—especially as they have been overlooked.

Regardless of any historiographical debate, republican womanhood was inherently linked to honor and virtue. Feminine honor was not simply the traditional view of preserving chastity and faithfulness; the nature of republican womanhood implied a public and personal dynamic.[170] Through service during the war, women had shown that they possessed virtue and honor equal to that of men. The sexes may not have contributed in the same ways, but the commitment of each was viewed as honorable.

Women recognized that although they may not be the political equals of men, they held the same status in terms of patriotism, honor, and virtue. Judith Sergeant Murray argued that women had "a nice sense of honor," which displayed "its innate, its native grandeur."[171] At the foundational level, said Murray, women and men were the same and had equal capacities to obtain honor and virtue.[172] By the early nineteenth century, novelist turned educator Susanna Rowson similarly instructed her female students in Massachusetts that "virtue gives dignity to every talent" regardless of status or gender.[173] Honor and virtue were considered accessible to all; thus, the early republican advancement of national honor was just as readily open to women as men. But Murray and others recognized that gender equality did not exist; as in the Revolution, a woman's path to honor would be decidedly different from a man's. Women could support national honor by educating others to hold noble aspirations and serve the nation, raising their children to be patriots, inspiring their husbands to virtue, and sending their loved ones off to war. These practices may have been viewed as feminine, but this did not make them any less important.

Women may not have actively fought for America, but Hannah Adams stated they were soldiers in "spiritual warfare" that saw them "zealously engaged in this good cause."[174] According to Murray, "When they part with him in whom is centered their dearest hopes, who blends the characters lover, friend, husband, and protector—when they resign to the hostile career the blooming youth whom from infancy they have watched with all a mother's tenderness . . . in those moments of anguish, their heroism and their fortitude are indisputably evinced."[175] While there was a gendered dynamic to republican womanhood, it was not a feminization of honor and virtue but rather an inclusion of women in a previously masculine domain.[176] Ann Negus, an example of a republican woman, stated, "We [are] not seeking the praise of men, but by your noble and disinterested example, have acquired the laurels of honor."[177] Women made sacrifices for their country no less valuable than any man's; they possessed the "equal share that every citizen has in the liberty . . . of our country" and thus were entitled to equal shares of honor.[178]

Marriage and motherhood proved the most acceptable means for women to gain honor. Abigail Adams stated, "Marriage was a Natural state, an honorable State," and from this place of traditional honor a woman could enact service to the nation.[179] Her daughter, Abigail Adams Smith, obviously took this message to heart, as she concluded that a husband and wife were "connected by ties of Honour."[180] Women were expected to seek out "virtuous conduct" and a "man of honour . . . strickt honour," most of all in their partners, thereby ensuring that men would aspire to these ideals to gain and retain a lady's affection.[181] Washington's granddaughter Nelly Custis, who certainly was familiar with ethical concepts and concerned about male character, concluded that her future husband was "in every respect calculated to ensure" her "happiness," because "he is universally esteemed for those virtues which do honour to the Head and Heart."[182] The desired concepts of honor and virtue were the internal ethics heroicized by the Revolution, not the physical trappings of gentility, as women warned each other of the dangers of appearance and false honor.[183]

Through their own behavior, women were in essence regulating the deeds of others, maintaining America's virtue, and thus advancing national honor. Dr. Rush, a proponent of feminine honor and virtue since the war, was one of the first to campaign for the vast potential that women held. Rush was aware that "the opinions and conduct of men are often regulated by the women in the most arduous enterprises of life; and their approbation is frequently the principal reward of the hero's dangers, and the patriot's toils."[184] During courting and marriage, a woman's insistence on a man of honor and virtue could virtually ensure its continued importance. This was not an entirely male construction simply imposed on women. During her time in Europe after the war, Abigail Adams had personally experienced what she regarded as a waning of virtue. She concluded that this lack of virtue in men was a symptom of the failing of virtue in women. Women could hold themselves to high principles and inspire others to follow in their wake, and America must do this to avoid the "licentiousness" of Europe.[185] The "ladies of honour, worthy women, and honourable daughters of America" were invited to preserve national virtue for "the defence of life and liberty."[186]

While supporting the nation, this aspect of republican womanhood was also reinforcing conventional shaming practices that ran concurrently with honor culture. For only through honorable and virtuous action could a man gain the hand of a republican woman. As Rush mused, "Our young men would then be restrained from vice by the terror of being banished from their company."[187]

The female influence of mothers was just as powerful, if not more so.[188] Rush also concluded that "the first impressions upon the minds of children are generally derived from the women. Of how much consequence, therefore, is it in a republic, that they should think justly upon the great subjects of liberty and government!"[189] From their mothers, children could learn the importance of duty to the nation, honor, and virtue. Boys could grow up to be great statesmen and girls could perform the same national service as their mothers. Florence Cooke of Charleston, South Carolina, remarked that she would be "happily engaged in employing all the influence & Care of a Mother, to render them fit for the defence and Support of their Country."[190] Abigail Adams lectured her son John Quincy that "your honour your integrity and virtue" can "always prove your safe guard," and that virtue could make one

"Great."[191] Likewise, Virginian matriarch Betsy Watts reminded her daughter, Sarah, to maintain virtue and avoid the failings of youth.[192]

Women's influence could even be felt in areas of society with which they seemingly had no discernable relationship—extending even into the military. Abigail Adams maintained the Revolutionary ethos of a moral war in which "true Courage is always humane."[193] Elizabeth Trist wrote to her West Point–educated grandson, Nicholas P. Trist, also Jefferson's grandson-in-law, instructing him on her proper principles of warfare. Again advancing national honor, as well as the Revolution's emphasis on defensive war, she asserted, "I hope you will never take up arms but in defence of your Country." It was "dishonor" to go to war "to agrandise your fame," as fighting should only be undertaken for a noble cause. And if the nation required protection, she instructed (echoing honor-shame culture), "do your utmost in its defence I shou'd be asham'd of you, if you did not."[194]

While there were misogynistic undertones to these principles, which placed a greater emphasis on the cultivation of boys and men, they still granted new opportunities for female education.[195] Samuel Magnaw, the vice-provost of the University of Pennsylvania, suggested that the education of young women should be supported by "all who wish well to the prosperity of their Country."[196] Future mothers and wives had to be educated in order to instruct their children.[197] An ad in the *Connecticut Gazette* for the Academy of Plainfield, which offered ethics classes to young ladies, echoed this point, reminding its readers that women forged "the character and manners of the other sex."[198] Just as for boys, schools and literature became the tools for instilling these notions in the minds of the female population.[199] During this period, there was virtually no difference between men's and women's literature; both sexes read the same books, providing a consistency in thought. Female schools, such as the Young Ladies' Academy and the Ainwell School, both in Philadelphia, and the Schenectady Female Academy in New York, built a curriculum, virtually identical to that taught to male students, that stressed morality and virtue as overriding themes through subjects ranging from history to rhetoric.[200] Texts used in schools, including the *Young Gentlemen and Ladies Instructor*, even contained lessons on the value of the teachings of a mother.[201] John Poor, the principal of the Young Ladies' Academy, delighted that his students, as a result of their "virtuous exertions, excite the rising fair to emulate (with equal excellence) your very noble examples."[202] As a woman named Louisa Hartley proudly boasted, "Age and education had so far matured my understanding, as to make me prefer the virtuous mind, even though his fortune were contracted, to the man who had habituated himself to vice."[203]

Women, as teachers and role models, could impart to the future generations the importance of ideological ideals. Merit was equated directly with honor, and, even more radically, Priscilla Mason, a Philadelphia Academy salutatorian, called for women's "equal participation in honor."[204] In school, women learned, as Ann Harker (another Young Ladies' Academy student) remarked, to "defend our honor with amazonian courage."[205]

The prevailing perception became that republican women, in cultivating honor and virtue in their children and spouses, were aiding the collective good of the nation. Women were therefore viewed as honorable not only due to their merit but also based on Franklin's conception of ascending honor, which lauded the educators of youth. Republican motherhood and Franklin's ascending honor would both retain traction throughout the early republic, illustrating a greater sense of openness in honor culture.[206]

Despite the continued democratization of American society, there was still a clear hierarchy.[207] For example, what role did slaves and free African Americans play in this new discourse?

Much as for women, the path to inclusion for free African Americans was dependent on ethics. Free African Americans believed that their place in society would be built on the morality of their actions. In Boston, the importance of ethical behavior became the focal point of the first chartered meeting of the African Lodge of the Honorable Society of Free and Accepted Masons on June 24, 1789. Led by Grand Master Prince Hall, a former slave and Revolutionary soldier, the first all-black Freemasonry lodge was originally founded in 1775, but it had to wait until well after the war for formal recognition. In many ways, the African Lodge existed as a dual symbol of inclusion and exclusion. The ideas espoused by Freemasonry (and its many members, ranging from Franklin to Washington) promoted brotherhood, but the exclusion of African Americans from other lodges further illustrated ideological hypocrisy.[208] Despite this fact, the African Lodge and its members represented a continuity of similar ideals within the white and black communities.

As the valiant conduct of black soldiers, like Hall, had helped to sway the opinions of many white founders during the Revolution, it is not surprising that a similar tactic was employed again. Hall would naturally use his service and that of all African Americans in the Revolution to stress their equality in honor and society, reminding others of their "conduct in the late war; for then they marched shoulder to shoulder, brother soldier and brother soldier, to the field of battle."[209] However, the African Lodge's opening sermon, delivered by fellow Mason Rev. John Marrant (although Hall would take credit for writing nearly the entire oration), established ethics, not martial valor, as the group's guiding principle.[210] Marrant warned the Masons to not be "careless of their own reputation," for those who give in to "vice" forsake themselves and Freemasonry. Those who so "disgrace[d] themselves" thereby "reflect[ed] dishonour on Masonry in general." He concluded that those who were lost to morality were also lost to honor and were therefore "in reality no Masons." All Masons needed to be "persons of a virtuous character," for "religion and virtue" existed as "the force of [their society's] principles and conduct."[211] This oration was later published as a source of education for other black Masons as far away as Philadelphia and Providence.[212]

Hall would continue to build on these ethical themes, and he reminded the African Lodge that the path to inclusion was to "be good subjects to the laws of the land in which we dwell." Black Masons needed to "giv[e] honour to whom honour is due," and they must prove themselves to be noble in order to receive similar treatment.[213] Marrant had previously offered examples to aspire to, such as Tertullian, Cyprian, and Origen, African historical figures meant to complement the founders' focus on classical heroes.[214] According to Hall, African Americans had to behave ethically even in the face of adversity for the benefit of the greater good of society. Mob violence leveled against blacks should not be returned in kind. Hall reminded his brethren that they "had rather suffer wrong than to do wrong," for to do otherwise would be for "the disgrace of our reputation." Black Masons, and African Americans generally, needed to prove themselves "good citizen[s]" by doing "honor to the laws of the State" where they reside.[215]

Proponents of African American education viewed schooling as the path to inclusion in society. White educators often described blacks as possessing "good character" or "moral conduct," and the creation of schools for the purpose of "instruction on moral and religious subjects" was viewed as essential for the acquisition of their "freedom and rank in Society."[216] While Hall certainly agreed with the need for morality, he went a step further and refused to allow the excuse of a lack of education to permit one to act unethically. Speaking to the African Lodge, but perhaps referring to African Americans more generally, he declared, "Although you are deprived of the means of education; yet you are not deprived of the means of meditation; by which I mean thinking, hearing and weighing matters, men and things in your own mind."[217] Each person, regardless of background, was accountable for judging the rightness of his or her actions.

These ideals were not exclusive to black Masons but also existed within the free African American community at large. Like Hall, Rev. Lemuel Haynes, another former Revolutionary soldier, then a church pastor in Vermont, also stressed ethical conduct. His own view of virtue was "nearly" identical to Jonathan Edwards's, meaning that he would have believed that "virtue" is "of a moral nature."[218] On the twenty-fifth anniversary of independence, Haynes reasserted Edwards's conceptions, stating, "When a man distinguished himself by a proper regard for the general good, he is then worthy the name ["greatness"]." Haynes advanced the new, democratized version of honor, in which "virtue and philanthropy" alone were "considered the true criterions of distinction," for a man "will be esteemed great who is servant of all, who is willing to devote his talents to the public good." Haynes understood the path to greatness as an inherent connection between honor, ethical conduct, and a devotion to the greater good. The Vermont pastor believed that "the true *nature* of republicanism and independence" needed to "import something noble and excellent," meaning only what was "promotive of order, virtue, and morality."[219] Over a decade later, James Forten, a born freeman from Philadelphia, continued the call for honor and advancement based solely on merit and the greater good. He pointed out, "There are also men of merit among the African race, who are useful members of Society." African Americans could equally be men of "reputation," as they were "as good citizens as any man can be."[220] After the Revolution, ethics, honor, and virtue were viewed as the great social equalizer. Thus, the African American understanding of the linkage between honor, virtue, and ethics was in many ways consistent with the white population's.

While free African Americans used ethics to navigate their way in a white-dominated society, the countless enslaved faced an uncertain future that inherently contradicted the professed ideals of the American Revolution. The founders had framed the Revolution as a matter of honor against a British imposition of slavery. The rhetoric against slavery, the absolute opposite of honor, had been used to galvanize the people to action. But actual slavery still remained in America—a point of hypocrisy that posed a challenge to the nation's supposedly ethical ideals. It also raised a point of contention regarding what the definition of true honor actually was. Slavery represented one of the greatest challenges to the United States' national honor. It was a divisive element in society, and one that compromised America's moral high ground.[221]

The connection between slavery and liberty during the Revolutionary era was not lost on many Americans—even if they chose not to acknowledge it. In 1772, David Cooper, a Quaker from New Jersey, cast slavery as the robbery of freedom.[222] A year later, an anonymous self-named "lover of constitutional liberty" in Boston called slavery "so base and scandalous a Trade, which reflects the highest Disgrace on any People."[223] Franklin, who would go on to lead the Pennsylvania Abolition Society, held virtually identical sentiments, and he "hope[d] in time that the Friends to Liberty and Humanity will get the better of a Practice that so long disgrac'd our Nation and Religion."[224] As patriots used the rhetoric against slavery to advance their opposition to British law, the relationship between bondage and dishonor was repeatedly and consciously brought to the forefront. Slavery was not simply a personal matter but also a national one, with the potential to disgrace those who submitted to it and bring honor to those who opposed it.

During and after the Revolution, the inherent contradiction between American liberty and the continuation of slavery was a festering wound. Antislavery supporters believed that America must rid itself of slavery to truly be a symbol of freedom. In his collection of antislavery literature, William Law quoted the common motif, "If Slavery admits of a moral or a rational Justification, every Crime, even the most atrocious, may be justified."[225] Early abolitionists cast slavery as a "national evil" and a blight on national honor. Quoting from the book of Proverbs, Alexander McLeod, the pastor of the Reformed Presbyterian Congregation in New York City, intimated *"that righteousness exalteth a nation, and that sin is a reproach to any people."*[226] In *A Serious Address to the Rulers of America*, Cooper again cautioned Americans to "beware: Let it appear to future ages ... that you not only professed to be advocates of freedom, but really were inspired by the love of mankind, and ... as you disdained to submit to unlimited control of others, you equally abhorred the crying crime of holding your fellow men, as much entitled to freedom as yourselves." For Cooper and other like-minded individuals, the continuation of slavery threatened the Revolution.[227] Slavery was cast as a sin, not just against God but also against the United States, its ideals, and its reputation.

While domestic opposition would lead to disunion decades later, the emerging nation viewed the opinions of the world as just as vital as those of the country's citizens. Conscious of America's nascent international standing, Cooper warned that "the eyes of the world are singularly attentive to his [America's] conduct" and the "honor of America" was at stake. The Revolution had placed the United States in the spotlight, and it was a national obligation to behave properly and "demonstrate to Europe, to the whole world, that America was in earnest ... when ... she plead the cause of human nature, and ... insisted, that *all mankind* came from the hand of their Creator *equally free.*" Thought and action must be consistent; America must have "a sound mind in a sound body."[228] This same idea had been the guideline for policy in war and peace—and it could not waver. Law feared America's position as a continuing ideological symbol was jeopardized, for with slavery "we teach

other Nations to despise, and trample under Foot, all the Obligations of social Virtue."[229]

The British, still reeling from a defeat that seemed to prove America's accusation of an ethical fall correct, were anxious to reclaim their lost honor.
The continuation of slavery in America became one of the primary means for
Britain to reassert its supremacy in honor and virtue over its former colonies.
Thus, abolitionism took on a dual political and moral significance.[230] Even
during the war, Americans were aware of the criticism slavery brought from
abroad. In 1777, an anonymous author compelled his countrymen to address
the issue and prove themselves "worthy of their independence, and convince
Britain, that we really are that 'VIRTUOUS PEOPLE,' we have declared ourselves
to be."[231] In *Short Observations on Slavery*, Anthony Benezet, a French-born
American abolitionist and Franklin's friend, offered a clear-cut synopsis of
the conflict between American thought and action. Citing the Declaration
of Independence's famous clause "that all men are created equal," Benezet
concluded that this idea must be "diversified by colour and other distinctions." How else could America justify slavery? America had to answer for "a
conduct abhorrent from these sacred truths" of the declaration and the Revolution. By casting slavery as "inconsistent . . . with every idea of Liberty,
every principle of humanity," he questioned the American Revolution's ideals
and attacked the righteousness of its cause. The Americans had gone to war
with Britain over legislation framed in the rhetoric of slavery, but the United
States was behaving worse, "dragging these oppressed Strangers from their
native lands . . . under the sanction of unjust laws." The accusation had an
obvious subtext: How could America justify the revolution while slavery
remained? For Benezet, the abolition of slavery was "a step which every principle of honour, reason, and humanity call for."[232]

Benezet was not alone in his perceptions. Ottobah Cugoano, a former slave
turned British abolitionist, concurred and presented the abolition of slavery
as not only a matter of honor but also an opportunity for Britain to prove itself better than America. He billed abolition "as an act to bring great honour
and blessings to that nation, and to all men whosoever would endeavor to promote so great good to mankind; and it might render more conspicuous advantages to the noble Britons, as the first doers of it."[233] Ending slavery would
bring Britain honor and redemption after the Revolution.

Recriminations did not only come from enemies; the French also weighed
in on the slavery issue, placing a greater burden on America's reputation. The
Marquis de Lafayette was openly critical of slavery and wished for the

slaves' manumission.[234] The Marquis de Condorcet, a French philosopher, authored a text condemning slavery, which Jefferson personally translated. Symbolically addressing the slaves of America, Condorcet wrote, "Nature has endowed you with the same genius, the same judgment, the same virtues as the Whites." In addition to casting African Americans as equals in virtue, he also contended that proslavery supporters "disgrace themselves" and lack "honor by [not] defending you."[235]

Casting slavery and abolitionism as a matter of honor was a common practice of slavery's supporters and detractors on both sides of the Atlantic. Still, many slaveholders, firmly entrenched primarily in the South, were reluctant to give up their wealth and power, and they instead argued that the institution advanced the nation's prestige.

Assuming a language of patriotism and collective honor, slavery supporters cited the practice's vast economic benefits as a source of the "Glory of our Nation." Cugoano similarly lamented that slavery "manifest[ed]" the appearance of false honor, which he termed "infamous dignity," through slaveholders' economic advancement.[236] British abolitionist Thomas Clarkson labeled America as "dishonoured with this stain of inhumanity" and also noted that slavery, "though dressed in the outward habiliments of *honour*, will still be *intrinsically base*."[237] But wealth was never recognized as a determinant of honor, and this point held true on the national level. In line with this thinking, John Wesley argued, "Wealth is not necessary to the Glory of any Nation; but Wisdom, Virtue, Justice, Mercy, Generosity, Public Spirit, Love of our Country. These are necessary to the real Glory of a Nation; but the abundance of Wealth is not."[238] Greatness could only come from true honor and virtue, and slavery would mar the ideals of the nation.

Other proslavery individuals criticized the innate capacity of African Americans for ethical behavior, and they used this as a justification for their bondage. Abolitionists, in turn, used this stance as further evidence against slavery. McLeod did not deny that some African Americans were lacking in moral principles, but he said that it was not due to any fault of their own or any natural predisposition. He and others contended that it was slavery that prevented the African Americans from gaining virtue and morality, due to the interference of their owners. McLeod wrote, "Their moral principles also suffer. They are never cultivated. They are early suppressed. . . . We have no right to expect morality or virtue from such an education and such examples."[239] In addition to preventing the acquisition of these ideals, slavery also had the ability to warp African Americans' perspectives. Remembering her time as a slave in the early nineteenth century, Sojourner Truth "firmly believed that slavery was right and honorable. Yet she *now* sees very clearly the false position they were all in."[240] Without slavery, it was argued, African Americans would be free to cultivate themselves into virtuous citizens who would benefit the nation in practical and ideological means. In *An Essay on the Slavery and Commerce of the Human Species*, a book that was widely read throughout the Anglo-American world, Clarkson counterargued that Africans possessed such a notion of "honour" that "thousands of the enlightened Europeans would have occasion to blush."[241] Slavery robbed a person of honor.

For many of the founders, slavery was an issue that was indicative of the struggle between personal and national honor. At the heart of the conflict were Southern slaveholders, who personally (often privately) claimed to abhor slavery. Critics singled out this group for particular censure, chiding them that antislavery ideals and slave owning were incompatible.[242] Discussing slavery before the war, in a moment of crystallized evaluation and prophetic foreshadowing, the unnamed Bostonian Lover of Constitutional Liberty expressed anguish over that institution's continuation: "I would hope better Things of those worthy *Gentlemen*, many of whom in Times past, to their immortal Honor be it spoken, have distinguished themselves for their steady and disinterested Conduct . . . whose noble and patriotic Resolves will hand their Names down to Generations yet unborn."[243] Yet these men, who were honorable in all other stations of life, failed to eradicate a bitter bondage that threatened their personal and national character.

Slave-owning patriots, such as Washington, Madison, and Jefferson, could not escape the personal hypocrisy. For men who had placed such emphasis on transforming thoughts into actions, the lack of any tangible efforts to end slavery is puzzling in light of their devotion to honor. But it is honor again that provides the answer. Each man's path toward antislavery was individualized, but the inaction was jointly cast as a matter of national honor.

Washington was a firm believer in social hierarchy, and he had grown up in a world that embraced slavery as an essential fact of life.[244] At the start of the American Revolution, he showed no signs of wavering. But as the war progressed, his perception of African Americans began to change and he was forced to accord them a degree of honor—thereby complicating his thinking. Slavery and honor were incompatible. Likely spurred by the honorable service of African American soldiers, Washington privately expressed a desire for abolition in 1778, as he wrote to a family member, "I wish to get quit of Negroes."[245]

While privately discussing Lafayette's opposition to slavery with Jefferson, Madison stated that the Frenchman's abolitionist ideas did "*him real honor*, as it is a *proof of his humanity*."[246] At the Constitutional Convention in 1787, Madison was even less subtle in his opinions. As the attendees of the convention debated an ultimately successful motion to move the limiting of the importation of slaves back eight years to 1808, he was already thinking of the elimination of slavery and of America's honor. Madison pleaded with his fellow delegates, "Twenty years will produce all the mischief that can be apprehended from the liberty to import slaves. So long a term will be more dishonorable to the National character than to say nothing about it in the Constitution."[247]

Jefferson was by far the most outspoken of the group. His opposition to slavery was well known as early as 1776. His original draft of the Declaration of Independence had even contained a passage denigrating slavery, although he blamed the practice on George III.[248] In *Notes on the State of Virginia*, the only book he ever published, Jefferson declared slavery to be a "great political and moral evil." He further contended that slavery "destroys the morals" of all who are touched by the institution (essentially everyone in Southern society). Finally, he prophesied a new revolution in America, one equally founded on liberty, in which the slaves would rise up and take their freedom. Jefferson was so assured of the base nature of slavery that he considered such a fate as God's "justice."[249] After reading it, John Adams enthusiastically wrote to Jefferson, commending him for his thoughts on slavery, which Adams believed "will do its Author and his Country great Honour." Adams continued, "The Passages upon Slavery, are worth Diamonds. They will have more effect than Volumes written by mere Philosophers."[250] Jefferson's views seemed poised to bring about a great change in America.

While Franklin contributed the last years of his life to fighting against slavery as president of the Pennsylvania Abolition Society, why did these other prominent founders not act? Perhaps it was a protection of the independence slavery afforded them, which was crucial to their personal honor and reputation? McLeod would certainly have thought so when he labeled dissenting slaveholders as being "strongly influenced by personal motives" (another way of saying personal honor).[251] Or maybe, like Patrick Henry, they opposed slavery but refused to live without slave labor? Historian Francois Furstenberg has also compellingly asserted that post-Revolutionary Americans "defined virtue as a willingness to resist tyranny"; thus, "people gained either freedom or slavery through individual action." As a result, "white Americans need not see any contradiction between revolutionary ideology and the persistence of slavery." Furstenberg contends that as Americans had fought for their independence from Britain, slaves "by choosing to submit . . . deserved slavery."[252] This interpretation seems very consistent with the expansion of honor to African American soldiers. For, as noted in chapter 4, Madison believed that after fighting for his independence, "a freedman immediately loses all attachment & sympathy with his fellow former slaves."[253] Whatever their reasons, the founders' responses seem consistent with their thinking on and overwhelming concern for national honor.

Though Washington personally acknowledged African American humanity and wished to abolish slavery, he was pragmatic about the damage such a step could levy against his reputation and the fate of the new republic.[254] Similarly to his handling of the Society of the Cincinnati, Washington tried to distance himself from the matter due to his national status and influence. He was aware of the fear his Southern brethren felt over the possibility of an insurrection or liberation of the slaves, as well as of its ability to disrupt the social hierarchy.[255] As he did not wish to unsettle a still-infant nation, Washington never used his power as president to attempt antislavery legislation and never spoke against slavery publicly; once again, he chose national honor over personal honor.[256]

Although Madison personally regarded the governmental failure to combat slavery as a national dishonor, he still chose to publicly support constitutional authority. In *The Federalist Papers*, Madison, conscious of the need to stabilize the nation, called the 1808 clause "a great point in favor of humanity." Furthermore, obviously aware of British criticisms of American slavery, Madison cast America as a moral champion in an effort to improve its international reputation. He half-heartedly extolled it, stating, "Happy would it be for the unfortunate Africans if an equal prospect lay before them of being redeemed from the oppressions of their European brethren!"[257]

Despite Adams's boisterous praise, shortly after the publication of *Notes on the State of Virginia*, Jefferson nervously wrote to Madison, regarding the passages on slavery, "But there are sentiments on some subjects which I apprehend might be displeasing to the country." Thus, one may attribute Jefferson's inaction to a desire for national honor. Reputation is certainly at the forefront, and Jefferson likely would have contended that backing away from his personal views was for the greater good. But in the same letter, he still voices a fear, perhaps the real one: "I do not wish to be exposed to their [my countrymen's] censure."[258] Jefferson remained publicly silent on slavery, though he privately professed to "encounter every sacrifice" to bring about abolitionism. But Jefferson, as a public official, continued to state the national cause as his reason for inaction.[259] He wrote, "I serve having not yet been able to give their [the American people's] voice against the practice, it is descent for me to avoid too public a demonstration of my wishes to see it abolished."[260]

Despite Jefferson's reasoning, his response seems the most untenable. Neither side of the slavery debate accepted Jefferson's views. Proslavery supporters looked at him as an abolitionist, while those opposed to slavery saw him as a proponent.[261] In addition, Jefferson's ideals were different from those of the others who held to a democratized but still eighteenth-century conception of honor. His definition of honor stressed an internal ethic that required individuals to adhere to their own values. Thus, according to Jefferson's own standards, he was in essence behaving dishonorably by ignoring his conscience.

Slavery remained a contentious political issue for the next half century. Honor, in some fashion, was always at its center. In the early nineteenth century, abolitionists, such as Edward Darlington, continued to cry out that national honor was in jeopardy due to those who, "despite of laws divine and human, continue to prostrate national character, by a trade so baneful in its tendencies, and murderous in its effects." Darlington and others like him continued to remind Americans that support for abolitionism was "the duty of every citizen averse to such nefarious practices, attached to the honour of his country, and anxious to promote its prosperity."[262]

As the battle over slavery continued throughout the early republican era, Federalists and Republicans would also battle over contested views of national honor. This debate would be highly contentious. Politics in general began to take on a duality that saw political opponents label each other as being guided by personal motives rather than the greater good. While national honor was interwoven throughout numerous political debates, the concept always took on a special meaning when faced with international scrutiny.

By the summer of 1789, Washington was only months into his first term as U.S. president and France was in the grip of revolution; both events would have a tremendous impact on the interpretation of American national honor. The inherent diplomatic and honor-based conundrum centered on whether the United States had an obligation to aid the French people, as they had supported America during the American Revolution. The issue became even more complicated as the monarchy was abolished and the French Revolution became more radicalized. The event became politicized domestically, as Republicans favored the revolution and Federalists opposed it. The United States had a decision to make that placed national preservation and ideological obligation in conflict. As illustrated in the debate over slavery, America's international reputation was a major catalyst in the debate over national honor. Furthermore, the issues with France show an early moment of the continuity between honor and ethics, as national honor segued into a debate over, as Jefferson termed it, "national and private ethics."[263] Combined with the constitutional crisis, the polarization caused by the French Revolution would essentially create American partisan politics.

The French declaration of war against Britain and the execution of King Louis XVI in 1793 exacerbated matters, as the recently reelected president Washington, conscious of the precarious position of the new nation, sought "to maintain a strict neutrality."[264] National honor was called into question due to the French intervention during the American Revolution. Did the United States owe a debt of honor to France? Was the alliance of 1778 still applicable?

Republican secretary of state Jefferson, only four years removed from his diplomatic mission to France, supported the French Revolution. Having witnessed the early rumblings of the movement, Jefferson was taken by the ideological parallels between France and his own country. He saw the French Revolution as a continuation of the American, and he believed that its failure could hinder democracy in the United States. Jefferson was convinced that the United States had a debt of honor to France that had to be paid by maintaining the alliance of 1778, for "to be grateful, to be faithful" was the foundation of the only "system of ethics for men and nations."[265] In fact, he claimed to the Marquis de Lafayette that he only accepted his new position because of his belief that Washington's "national and private ethics were the same."[266]

From his residence in Paris, Gouverneur Morris, the ambassador to France, was on the frontlines of the radical, unfolding drama, and he understood that America's honor was at stake. As various European delegates fled France, Morris, although eminently friendly with the king and many aristocrats, stayed resolute in his appointment. Even as others, likely foreign diplomats, admonished him "that the Honor of my Country and my own require that I should go away," he remained because he was "unauthoriz'd in this Respect" and had a duty to maintain. Morris dismissed the chidings as "influenced by Fear"; his understanding of national honor was solely based on "the Interests of my Country" not "my personal Pleasure or Safety."[267] The issue became much more than ideological when considered in relation to the matter of America's financial debt to France. Much like the debt of honor, did this financial debt contracted under the king still need to be paid to the Republic of France? William Short, ambassador to Holland, contended that paying the French Republic was akin to giving money to a thief, but Morris persisted in reimbursing the current government in order to fulfill America's obligations and maintain its national honor.[268]

As tensions heightened, Washington turned to his cabinet. Indicative of national sentiment, the cabinet secretaries were also split in their opinions. Did the king's execution change American and French relations? Secretary of the Treasury Hamilton and Secretary of War Knox concurred that because of the death of Louis XVI, "our treaty with France is void"; Jefferson and Attorney General Edmund Randolph, on the other hand, both dissented, in favor of the treaty being made with the nation, not a king. Washington nominally sided with Randolph and Jefferson, but he still took a stance of neutrality on the grounds that the 1778 treaty with France was a defensive alliance only.[269] By declaring war, France had in effect removed any U.S. obligation. Jefferson tried to delay any formal announcement, as he desired to extract more favorable terms from France or Britain in exchange for a more partial national policy. As biographer Ron Chernow remarks, "Thunderstruck at the notion of auctioning American honor, Hamilton favored an immediate decision."[270]

The cabinet unanimously agreed on American neutrality, but the means of executing it caused dissension. On April 22, 1793, just a few days after the cabinet meeting, Washington signed a neutrality proclamation, which stated, "The duty and interest of the United States require, that they should with sincerity and good faith adopt and pursue a conduct friendly and impartial toward the belligerent powers."[271] Although America received a diplomat, Citizen Edmond-Charles Genet, from the French Republic (basically offering them formal recognition), the United States pledged to treat France no differently from its recent enemy, Britain.

After news of the proclamation was publicized, vast sections of the people mourned for what they believed was their lost national honor. "Ungrateful Americans!" charged "A Citizen" in the press.[272] Ingratitude was often regarded as the most detestable sin that could be committed by a gentleman; it was inherently linked to concepts of dishonor, and its meaning and implications were commonly understood. The Philadelphia-based newspaper the *National Gazette*, in particular, became a platform for the outrage directed against Washington's perception of national honor. "An American" suggested that the newspaper reprint the U.S. treaties with France, because he incredulously worried that "many persons, from distance of time," must have forgotten them. It may be in the "interest and duty" of the United States to stay neutral, but "this neutrality can only [be] observed by our conforming to the treaties we have made."[273] If the United States did not maintain its obligations, then it was without honor.

The aspersions cast on American honor were not just domestic. Upon his arrival in Philadelphia, Genet was greeted by adoring and cheering crowds (and cold civility from Washington). With carefully chosen words, the diplomat tried to capitalize on the favorable crowd: "If gratitude be not acknowledged a virtue among despots, it is evidently such among freemen." In other words, the people wished to pay their debt of honor, but the government clearly was willing to sacrifice the nation's honor and was held in the same regard as "despots."[274]

Staunch Federalist Hamilton came to Washington's defense. He correctly recognized that the most important issue at hand was that the people were anxious to know if "the policy of the government is not inconsistent with its obligations or its honour." Hamilton argued that the United States was behaving honorably by staying out of the conflict; he went even further by suggesting that aiding France in any way would bring about national dishonor. For Hamilton, the French had declared an offensive war, negating their defensive alliance; in addition, the treaty ceased to exist with the king's death. There was no ingratitude; Louis alone authorized aid to the American Revolution (Hamilton didn't fail to mention that it was out of a sense of self-interest, that is, anti-British sentiments, not similar ideals), and any agreements were not transferable to his deposers. Hamilton also fired back at Genet: "The preachers of gratitude are not ashamed to brand Louis the XVI as a tyrant, and La Fayette as a traitor."[275]

In response, Madison, whose thinking was very similar to Jefferson's, retorted with (surprisingly modern) charges that such views were un-American. They were held only by "denigrated citizens," naturally without honor, "who hate our republican government, and the French revolution." The treaties with the French were still valid because "a nation, by exercising the right of changing the organ of its will, can neither disengage itself from the obligations, nor forfeit the benefits of treaties." Regardless of who sat at its head, America had an obligation to France—one that honor required to be fulfilled. Hamilton's principles were vilified as "strik[ing] at the vitals of its constitution, as well as its honor and true interest." Madison equally bandied about themes of national honor, seeking to remind the people that "governments are established for the national good and are organs of the national will." Since the nation favored the French Revolution's notions of liberty, the government was denigrating the people's and the nation's honor.[276]

The acrimony leveled against the neutrality proclamation is interesting when compared with the spirit of isolationism that followed the Treaty of Paris.

Franklin had been accosted for being too close to the French during the Revolution and peace negotiations, which he called "little Short of Treason to my Country," forcing the elder statesman to appeal to his fellow delegates to certify his honorable conduct.[277] Fortunately, Franklin's death in 1790 spared him any such indignation over the French Revolution. Even Madison put forth a resolution for "the true interest of these states," which intended them to "be as little as possible entangled in the politics and controversies of European nations."[278] But France under Louis XVI was viewed as something very different from the French Republic. As one critic wrote to Washington, "The spirit of 1776 is again roused," and with it isolationism was cast aside for a union of liberty in which the "American whigs of 1776, will not suffer French patriots of 1792, to be vilified with impunity, by the common enemies of both."[279]

Despite the public animosity directed at the proclamation of neutrality, and the more vocal opinion that America owed a debt of honor to France, Washington remained steadfast. The president likely took added resolve as he paged through his copy of Thomas Nettleton's *Treatise on Virtue and Happiness*, which reminded him, "The *ties of gratitude*, how binding soever they may be, should never lead us to do anything contrary to the *rules of justice*, and honour; for whenever that happens, we shall not fail to blame, and reproach ourselves afterwards."[280] These words were enacted in Washington's policy, as he believed that national honor required doing what was best for the nation rather than what was popular. As president of the United States, he was conscious of the need to preserve "national rights and honor."[281]

Throughout the next two decades, the specter of foreign entanglement, largely with Britain or France, loomed over the American political scene. Washington's farewell address called for a preservation of neutrality for the sake of national honor.[282] His 1799 death and apotheosis left a symbol of dedication to national honor and "public Virtue," so much so that even a lock of his hair could be considered a "sacred talisman of virtue."[283] But almost immediately after Washington's death, New Hampshire–born preacher Joseph Buckminster warned that "an unpleasant diversity of sentiment and difference of opinion have arisen in this country respecting the line of political conduct, most directly tending to secure our national honor, prosperity, and peace."[284] The matter of defining national honor remained.

The conflicting visions of national honor and partisan accusations of dishonor exacerbated by the French Revolution would carry over into all areas of American politics during the early republic. Diverse thinking on France increased and defined the gap between Federalists and Republicans, and even more specifically between their figureheads, Jefferson and Hamilton. The affair had convinced Jefferson that Hamilton had leveled "a fatal stroke at the cause of liberty." He was no friend of republicanism; he would kill it. Jefferson was left muttering, *"Et tu Brute."*[285] Hamilton in turn viewed Jefferson as politically prostituting America's national honor. Jefferson and the Republicans would cast Federalists, such as Hamilton and John Adams, as overtaken by British corruption and a secret desire for monarchy. Federalists, meanwhile, used the radicalism of the Republican French support to instill fear in the people of possible horrors to come. The *North-Carolina Journal* credited Jefferson with personally getting Americans to support the French Revolution, but it warned that although it was initially "taken for granted that their cause was just the same as our own," the people "learnt, from this new republican school of French ethics, to transfer our gratitude from our real benefactor to their murderers."[286] The New Hampshire–based newspaper the *Oracle of the Day* even ran hundreds of columns entitled "The Moralist . . . National Ethics," which regularly bashed the French Revolution and sought to educate "your sons and daughters" on national ethics, urging, "Let the pure principles, the virtuous manner . . . be retained and perfected. Be not carried about by every wind of [Francophile] political doctrine."[287] The dramatic and hyperbolic Adams even claimed that the American Revolution did not share "a single principle" with the French Revolution.[288] While definitions of national honor and ethics widened partisanship, mounting political squabbles infringed on America's national honor.

Although the debate over national honor began as primarily professionally and politically focused, with even Jefferson admitting that Hamilton was "disinterested, honest, and honorable in all private transactions," it soon began to transform into a more personal matter of honor.[289] As the nineteenth century dawned, a heightened sense of self was evident in American politics; the rhetoric of national honor certainly remained, but in many places it became secondary to maintaining one's own status and office. Thus, it would become possible for a politician like Aaron Burr to be regarded as "politically honest" by one party, despite having "inordinate personal ambition," while another cast him as lost to "political ethics" based on his "unbound ambition."[290] Reputations were slandered, mocked, and attacked in order to gain political currency, as politics would slowly begin to devolve from an arena focused on national honor into an affair of personal honor.[291]

With peace came questions about how the United States of America was to be governed and what ideals should represent its foundation. While most citizens agreed that honor and virtue were defining elements, they differed greatly on how these concepts related to governance, policy, and society. Contestations over the interpretation of national and personal honor would in turn spark infighting, dissension, and rival belief systems highlighted by the development of political parties. For, as Jefferson would write to his old friend John Adams after years of separation due to a political feud, "one of the questions on which our parties took different sides, was on . . . ethics."[292]

CHAPTER SEVEN

The Counterrevolution in American Ethics
Reinterpretations of the Next Generations

Following the turmoil of the Constitutional Convention and the French Revolution, American partisanship was firmly divided between Federalists and Republicans. From political jostling came two conflicting visions of national honor; soon debate and recriminations surrounding national honor digressed into personal matters of honor. At a time when Mercy Otis Warren declared that "every free mind should be tenacious of supporting the honor of a national character," she feared that "party feuds have thus divided a nation, urbanity, and benevolence are laid aside; and, influenced by the most malignant and corrupt passions, they lose sight of the sacred obligations of virtue."[1] Politicians on both sides were eager to achieve political gain by advancing their own reputations, often at the expense of their opponents. Dueling became the most visible symbol of this shift toward personal honor. From fights on the floor of the House of Representatives to private affairs between gentleman politicians, as noted by historian Joanne Freeman, dueling became a political tool.[2] This heightened sense of personal honor also had a direct influence on the interpretation of the meaning of national honor, which would in turn have profound effects on the United States' reputation and status internationally.

Despite its visibility and inherent drama, dueling was never common in America, and justifications of it often made substantial departures from the codes of honor championed by the American Revolution. Dueling did not define honor culture. A great portion of the Revolutionary generation would come to view dueling as thoroughly dishonorable. But, like America's return to virtue after Benedict Arnold's treason, the nation and its citizens would require a jolt to personify and exemplify the dangers of allowing personal honor to come before the country's.

On July 11, 1804, two Revolutionary War veterans kept an early-morning appointment on the banks of the Hudson River in Weehawken, New Jersey. On a discreet, tree-enclosed beach, accessible only at low tide, Federalist general Alexander Hamilton, former secretary of the treasury, and Republican colonel Aaron Burr, the current vice president of the United States, renewed a decades-old acquaintance. Drawn together that morning by a combination of political and personal motivations, each man gripped a flintlock pistol with the hopes of solving a matter of honor.

An off-color dinner party remark by Hamilton that labeled Burr "a dangerous man and one who ought not to be trusted" had reignited a hostility that had previously simmered below the surface. Burr believed his honor had been impugned, and he wanted satisfaction through a duel. After a several-weeks-long negotiation, the two men took aim. Hamilton followed through with a plan he had developed the previous night. Whether from grief over the recent death of his son in a duel, a fear of shame, or his own morality, Hamilton wasted his shot and purposely fired wide. Reconciliation was now firmly in the hands of Burr, who took aim, shot, and fatally wounded Hamilton.[3]

In that moment, marked simultaneously by death and dishonor, the face of American dueling and politics changed forever. As one critic reminded Burr, "In that . . . fatal moment, in which Hamilton fell, your character, began to bleed. The wound it received, is mortal; not time, no means can heal it."[4] On July 11, 1804, one bullet had taken two lives.

The prevailing image of honor culture within modern society is that of the duel: two men facing one another with drawn pistols, ready to kill or be killed over a personal affront. This singular portrayal has done much to discredit the validity of honor as a form of ethics within a large section of the general public and academia. Honor has become inherently linked to the duel, and if dueling is nothing more than fashionable murder, how can honor be considered ethical?

Contrary to the personal beliefs of professed early modern duelists and their modern detractors, this form of single combat was historically and consistently denounced by American (and European) society as dishonorable from the seventh through the early nineteenth century.[5] Prominent individuals such as George Washington, Benjamin Franklin, John Adams, Thomas Jefferson, and even Hamilton decried dueling as nothing more than false honor and an infringement on both Christianity and American law.[6] In 1797, the editor of the Franklin-founded *Pennsylvania Gazette* even banned all articles mentioning dueling "in order to shield himself from the censure of having voluntarily aided in the extension of this abominable custom."[7]

Especially in the wake of the Hamilton-Burr affair, dueling was cast as dishonorable not only to the individuals involved but also to the nation as a whole. The death of Hamilton, a prominent founder, gave a public face to the private menace of dueling and started the cry for the end of the practice though the language of national honor, virtue, ethics, and morality.[8]

Hamilton's fall shocked the nation. He was a man of unquestioned fame and was still in the prime of his life; he was viewed as having much left to contribute to the country.[9] The public and press compared the "unfeigned sorrow" for his death and the corresponding elaborate state funeral with that of Washington's demise in 1799.[10] Even more pointedly, Gouverneur Morris, who had previously performed the same service for Washington, was selected to deliver the eulogy for his friend Hamilton. Morris called Hamilton the "brightest ornament" and espoused his dedication to America.[11] Speaking before the Society of the Cincinnati, Dr. John M. Mason, pastor of the New York Scotch Presbyterian Church, also compared the two men, stating that America was a land where "Washington presided, and your Hamilton shone." He continued, echoing a joint sensation of loss, "When Washington was taken, Hamilton was left—but Hamilton is taken, and we have no Washington. We have not such another man to die!"[12]

While individuals ranging from kings to statesmen to clergy had condemned dueling for centuries, it took the death of Hamilton to galvanize the American people against the antiquated practice. Immediately after news of the duel and Hamilton's subsequent demise, the American people, from the press to the pulpit, labeled the affair as inconsistent with ideas of honor, religion, and law. It caused naval officer Thomas Truxton to remark on the reaction: "I never knew a business of this kind so treated in any part of the world."[13] Only hours after Hamilton died, Benjamin Moore, New York's Episcopal bishop and the president of Columbia College, proclaimed, "Let those who are disposed to justify the practice of dueling, be induced, by this simple narrative, to view with abhorrence that custom."[14]

But America and Europe had a long history of championing, or at least tolerating, the duel. What made the Hamilton-Burr duel so different? As most prominently chronicled by Freeman, dueling during the early republic was not an inevitable death sentence—in fact, the whole incident could be, and often was, resolved without a shot being fired. The mere threat and subsequent negotiation of a duel had become a political and social tool that often proved just as effective without violence.[15] The public even mocked the notion that harm would result from a duel; the Federalist newspaper the *New York Commercial Advertiser* chided, "Besides, of fifty duels, not five prove mortal, owning to pusillanimity of the parties, who tremble into each others arms on the slightest interposition of seconds."[16] On July 12, 1804, a day after the duel, but before news had reached Massachusetts, the Newburyport newspaper the *Political Calendar*, in a display of unwitting dark humor, lampooned another duel with a similar ending: "One second proposed their shaking hands, on which the other observed 'there is no occasion; their hands have been shaking all the time.' "[17]

There was a very real perception that death, injury, or even violence of any kind was an unlikely result of a duel. Illustrating this point, Hamilton had been involved in nine prior duels (six as a principal and three in a secondary capacity), none of which escalated to the drawing of pistols.[18] But in his final duel, Hamilton was killed—a rarity that escalated the importance of the event in the public's perception. Still, the public did not react as it usually did to any death by dueling. The exchange between Hamilton and Burr was actually only one of the fatal duels to have taken place in America that same year. The public response to the shedding of blood in such a way was usually repulsion and derision. However, no other duel in American history caused such a surge in antidueling sentiment. The negative message had always existed, but it lacked the immediately recognizable symbol of a life wastefully squandered. The personages of Hamilton and Burr, and the former's death, loomed so large that opposition to dueling was propelled into a place of prominence.[19]

Despite the seeming pervasiveness of dueling in American society and culture, it was never more than a tool of a rather vocal minority. After the Hamilton-Burr duel, the political-centric Virginian newspaper the *Alexandria Advertiser* estimated the number of dueling proponents, albeit likely hyperbolically and less than scientifically, at fewer than one hundred individuals in total. In any event, there was a very real belief that the reach of the *code duello*, or the rules of dueling, in America was due to the fact that the majority (antiduelists and apathetic onlookers) had failed to take action.[20] The *United States' Gazette* seconded this point: "The much greater part of mankind seldom think or reason with ardency, on points in which they are not immediately interested. . . . The false notions of one man or set of men, do not mend the errors of others." Hamilton's death woke the American people—just like other shocking moments, such as Arnold's treason, had done in the past— and "cause[d] many persons to think on the subject more closely."[21] In his sermon *The Danger of Ambition Considered*, Hezekiah North Woodruff, a pastor from Scipio, New York, championed the turning-point potential this moment possessed: "O that his example might wake the feelings, and rouse the attention of every immoral and unbelieving heart!"[22]

The public was certainly roused, as dueling came to the forefront of national news and discussion. But at the outset, the reaction, like the cause of the affair itself, was divided along political lines. The general public, spurred by Hamilton's supporters, vilified Burr, causing him to be "found *guilty of the murder of general Alexander Hamilton*" by the deliberations of "a very respectable jury," his "fellow citizens."[23] Despite Republican attempts to defend Burr, Federalists successfully saddled him with a faulty sense of national honor.[24] As the *Trenton Federalist* wrote, Burr was "a man of no fixed principle—no consistency of character—of contracted views as a politician—of boundless vanity, and listless of the public good; one, who is pursuing . . . projects disreputable to himself and injurious to the country." The paper went even further, dredging up the old Republican-French connection, as Burr was accused of "intriguing—thirsting for military glory, and Bonapartian fame!"[25]

Conversely, Hamilton was cast as the reluctant duelist who wasted his shot to preserve Burr's life and his own morality. In both eulogies and newspaper commemorations, much was made of Hamilton's avowal that he was "strongly opposed to the practice of duelling," and it became an early rallying point to exonerate his behavior and cast him as a martyr.[26] Despite these attempts to absolve Hamilton, he too was scrutinized under the lens of honor and morality, in what represented an opportunity for political unity.[27]

A pamphlet appropriately and tellingly titled *The Sixth Commandment Friendly to Virtue, Honor, and Politeness* took aim and lambasted as dishonorable not only dueling but also all duelists—including Hamilton. The author, Rev. Samuel Spring, a Revolutionary War veteran and Burr's former college classmate, hoped "to prevent or at least check the growing danger of misquoting Hamilton. For the Duellist and the Christian are different characters, and must not by any means be blended and confounded."[28] Contrary to any passionate pleas or deathbed confessions, the pamphlet contended that Hamilton had behaved in a dishonorable and un-Christian manner by participating. Philadelphian gentleman Joseph Hopkins, in the preface to his poem the *Hamiltoniad*, also lashed out at Hamilton. He wrote with a genuine credulousness, "I cannot withhold surprise, that a character such as was General Hamilton's . . . could commit such a fault . . . an error, which the cloak of spirit, is cowardly—and under the appearance of honor, disgraceful—which is despised by every virtuous man."[29] While he recognized the past honorable and virtuous behavior that Hamilton had exhibited in service to his country, he refused to exonerate him. Hopkins contended that dueling was false honor and an act of cowardice.

As the reaction to the Hamilton-Burr duel spread, so did the perception that such a practice was dishonorable and cowardly; a growing opposition to affairs of honor resulted. Dueling, which for so long had been viewed by some as a way to prove courage and gain honor, now became an obstacle to advancement. Participating in a duel was no longer regarded as a path to honor but was instead recognized as undoing the righteousness of a lifetime. Hopkins's poetry gave emotion to this sentiment:

> How hast thou sullied that fair Wreath of Fame,
> Which seem'd to shroud thy ever deathless name!
> How hast thou lessened, by a mournful deed,
> That glory which thy actions did succeed!
> Alas! Alas! I mourn thee thus, thus gone!
> Thy Worth, thy Virtue, and my loss I mourn.[30]

Burr and Hamilton became tangible symbols for the evils of dueling and the potential for the loss of reputation.

Attacking dueling based on religion was a popular tactic; sermons throughout the nation used the Hamilton-Burr duel as a modern-day parable. Dueling was inherently anti-Christian; regardless of the nature of one's participation or intent, duels were responsible for either a murder or a suicide.[31] Similar appeals had been commonplace since America's first fatal duel, in 1728.[32] The connection between antidueling and religion was so well known that Hamilton and others professed to oppose the practice based on Christian ideals— while still participating in it. Thus, it could be concluded that the spiritual argument, although readily understood by the public, was less than persuasive. Duelists consistently felt themselves bound by the rules of honor, which they believed overruled their religious scruples. Other methods of deterrence proved necessary.

Dueling and honor had always been intimately connected. Since dueling's origins, honor had been professed as its cause, motivation, and justification. But the various definitions and interpretations of honor often clouded the true nature of the ethic. As the Hamilton-Burr duel was both literally and figuratively an affair of honor, labeling the practice as dishonorable became the most prominent and persuasive rebuttal. The approach of the *Enquirer* of Virginia was logical and straightforward, beginning with the question, "What is honour?" Honor was defined by that newspaper as "the noble mind's distinguished perfection," but also included "the faculty of discerning every combination of circumstances, however complex or unexpected, with intuitive quickness, and pursuing with heroic energy, the path of propriety and justice." This understanding of honor, which combined ethical interpretations and illustrated the concept in terms of morality and justice, was incompatible with the duelists' understanding. The newspaper asked, "Now, will it be contended that the practice of dueling, the perpetration of deliberate suicide and murder, can be, in any possible combination of circumstances the duty of an enlightened man, the line of conduct which justice and reason prescribe?"[33]

Most of the general public rallied around the idea that dueling was inconsistent with honor. In addition to his religious sentiments, Woodruff argued, like Hopkins, "How false—how criminally false, are those growing sentiments which make honor an equivalent for life!"[34] Dueling was false honor. Philadelphia minister James Abercrombie quoted a contemporary jurist, stating, "By this infamous vice of dueling . . . how is the name of Honour prostituted! Can honour be the savage resolution, the brutal fierceness of a revengeful spirit? True honour is manifested in a steady, uniform train of actions, attended by justice, and directed by prudence."[35]

Reluctant duelists often cited their fear of being branded craven for refusing to fight; they acted not out of any personal malice but as a form of self-preservation. Duelists often resorted to the use of historical precedent to justify single combat, countered the author who went by the pseudonym Philanthropos (likely peace activist William Ladd), providing his own view of antiquity.[36] He remarked how Caesar Augustus refused Mark Anthony's challenge with the retort "*that, if he was weary of life, there were other ways to death, besides the point of his sword.*" Philanthropos asked, "Was Caesar a coward? Has his refusal to fight Anthony, ever been, in any age, or in any country, accounted an instance of cowardice?" The answer was clear-cut: "No. All ages have admired it as an act of a discreet and gallant man, who was conscious of the importance of his life; and who knew how to treat, with deserved contempt, the humour of a petulant and revengeful antagonist."[37] Making his argument more current, the author posited the true fate of refusing a duel. He wrote, "His honour is sullied, his reputation tarnished, because he refuses to kill, or to be killed! Among whom is his character injured?" It was concluded that no honor would be lost with the "judicious and worthy of mankind," but only "among a few rash and precipitate creatures; the pupils of La Mancha's knight; the sons of chimera and cruelty; whose applause is infamy and their detraction the highest praise they can bestow."[38]

Dueling was a remnant of Gothic barbarism, not compatible with the American concepts of republicanism, honor, and justice. For a society that often looked to the classical age for its sage advice, Abercrombie offered, "The polite nations of Greece and Rome knew nothing of it: they reserved their bravery for the enemies of their country and then were prodigal of their blood. These brave people set Honour up as the guardian genius of the public, to humanize their passions, to preserve their truth unblemished, and to teach them to value life only as useful to their country."[39] Since the run-up to the Revolution, Americans had embraced a concept of honor and virtue that was inherently linked to serving the greater good of the nation. National honor and selfless virtue were considered the ideological pinnacle of the United States.

On the other side of the coin, dueling was considered a matter of personal honor, which in turn drew accusations that it was simply a case of "ambition" and "self-aggrandizement," as you should only sacrifice your life for the nation and God.[40] Antiduelists contended that affairs of honor were merely an attempt to improve an individual's reputation; since fatal duels deprived the nation of valuable citizens, they were therefore a social blight.[41] Never before had a duel taken a person deemed as important and influential to the country as Hamilton. In addition, as both Burr and Hamilton were politicians and notable public figures, it triggered an increase in arguments regarding the selfish nature of the duel. Abercrombie pleaded, "And, if neither the dictates of Reason, the persuasions of Religion, nor the absurdity of those impious principles of False Honour . . . let him listen to the voice of Humanity—let him consider the duty which he owes to society."[42]

More pointedly, antiduelists, who argued that individual reputations were lost rather than gained by fighting, contended that the persistence of the practice infringed on the honor and reputation of America. In their official capacity, Burr and Hamilton represented the United States, and so their conduct reflected on the nation as a whole. Philanthropos asked, "Has your conduct been ornamental to your high office; or has it been disgraceful? Have you not disgraced yourself; have you not disgraced your high office; have you not disgraced your country?" Dueling placed national honor in jeopardy; it darkened the country's reputation among "the friends of America in Europe, and in every other quarter of the world." The duelists, "however regardless of . . . personal honour . . . ought to have paid more respect to [their] official character."[43]

The antidueling sentiment was more than simply theoretical, as it had tangible results within American society. The Society of the Cincinnati, of which both Burr and Hamilton were members, was the first to take action. Having lost perhaps their most illustrious member, the society's vice president, Charles C. Pinckney, issued a formal statement opposing dueling. The society virtually banned dueling within its ranks by making its members take an oath to neither issue nor accept a challenge—in essence using honor to combat false honor. Such a stance from a collection of former military officers, a group much maligned for its supposed pro-dueling views, did a great deal to raise awareness and gain public support.[44] The press urged others to follow the Cincinnati's example, and soon members of additional groups, such as the American Revolution Society and the Presbyterian Church in the United States, affirmed their commitment to the elimination of dueling.[45]

Pinckney was also active in his home state of South Carolina, where he used his influence to spread the antidueling message. Contrary to the popular opinion that dueling was a Southern phenomenon, the specter of the Hamilton-Burr duel even loomed so large that some pro-dueling Southerners were turned against the practice as a matter of honor.[46] South Carolinian David Ramsay led the distribution of a memorial and pledge "to abolish the abominable nature of single combat." He boastfully wrote to Philadelphian Benjamin Rush, explaining that he was "agreeably disappointed" that his initial "fear" of publicly supporting such measures was unfounded due to the lack of "opposition" he encountered. Of the eight men who drafted the pledge, three were former duelists, "one had killed his man & two others had frequent duels which though not fatal were not bloodless," illustrating the dramatic reversal that this singular event had on Southern honor culture. Furthermore, it was broadly embraced by the population: "Some have signed the memorial who had declared that they would fight any gentleman who challenged them & that they would challenge any Gentleman who insulted them." Ramsay gleefully reported that this served "as a proof that our people are changing their sentiments on the subject of Duelling."[47]

The Hamilton-Burr duel opened up an active and diverse debate about how to prevent duels on a wide scale. Clergymen and religious laymen had been attempting to leverage the sixth commandment, "Thou shalt not kill," for years.[48] Antidueling laws had also been on the books before 1804, but this event spurred new legislation in Massachusetts, Rhode Island, and Pennsylvania. But, as conclusively illustrated by historian Matthew Byron, such laws were largely ineffective in the early republic due to a lack of enforcement.[49] Dueling supporters and apathetic onlookers in government and law enforcement proved the largest obstacle. Even before Hamilton's death, the Massachusetts newspaper the *Republican Spy* was disgusted that "this wicked, and weak as wicked, practice is sanctioned by those whose special duty it is to suppress it."[50]

Regardless, duelists had shown little regard for existing legislation, earning the moniker of the "contemnor[s] of thy country's laws."[51] Philanthropos added to this perception, stating, " 'The life' . . . of an American 'gentleman, is the only thing in which he seems to have the least property. Make an attempt on his estate, and he seeks a judicial remedy; set fire to his house, and he seeks a judicial remedy also; but if you doubt his veracity, no law can give him redress.' "[52]

While some still hoped that the stiffer legal punishments would curtail the problem, others were convinced that change could only come from within society—not by having it imposed. There was recognition that duelists already ignored statutes; in Virginia the questioning was quite active: "But why, in the name of conscience, do we talk of special laws for the prevention of dueling?—Merciful Heaven!—Are there not everywhere standing laws against murder?"[53] It was concluded that an end to dueling "can be effected only, by means of reasoning, expostulation and example. The eradication of inveterate errors, the correction of prevailing immoralities . . . that lye beyond the sphere of government, legislation, and police."[54] Antidueling had to come not as a mandate of the government but as an ideological shift within individuals.

The goal was to win hearts and minds, as "to attempt by authoritative prohibitions and penal regulations to extirpate immoralities that have their root in general prejudice, is of all projects the most preposterous."[55] Since honor was the reason cited for duels, honor was used as the reason to avoid them. Hopkins suggested that the people had "to stamp each duelist with some dread disgrace. Then shall your country overcome this ill."[56] Again he was speaking of public shaming, a crucial component of the eighteenth- and nineteenth-century language of honor—reputation could enact changes that laws would be powerless to impose.

"But how, we are asked, can dueling be abolished?" The most original method was to interchange the duel's focus on false honor with the understanding of true honor. Forgoing a duel would not be considered a cravenly act, but one that showed an inner strength of character and respect for the nation and God. Virginia's *Examiner* asserted, "Courage consists in being able to encounter with readiness & energy, and endure with unshaken firmness, the difficulties, dangers, disappointments and distresses incident to the performance of our personal and social duties." By refusing to duel, you maintained your honor and morality, which in the popular understanding was akin to virtue. True courage and honor were demonstrated in remaining steadfast to an ideal ethic, while "cowardice may be defined the evasion, violation or desertion of a personal or social duty." This interpretation also accounted for the reluctant duelist, like Hamilton, as those who participated "not from a clear conviction of the propriety of dueling, but from a servile dread of contempt which the refusal to fight may excite in the minds of prejudiced persons, is in the most odious and emphatic sense of the term he most, detests and despises, a Coward."[57] Thus, the language of honor employed by duelists was turned against them.

As has been evident throughout this discussion, the press and publications were considered an effective way to spread the antidueling message extensively within a highly literate America. But from the start, the movement rested on the personages of America's great men. The ignominy heaped on Burr and both the lamentation and criticism of Hamilton fit this role perfectly. They were esteemed men of the nation who had both fallen (one physically, one symbolically) as a result of dueling. Their example spurred others within the Revolutionary generation, such as Pinckney, to publicly oppose the practice. "Let it be recollected, that as this memorable and modern custom, was originally established by the example of influential individuals, its abolition can be effected only by the heroic efforts of enlightened and accomplished men."[58]

On the whole, the antiduelists' ideological inundation worked on the members of the Revolutionary generation who viewed dueling as inconsistent with national honor. There was an active antidueling message communicated through the press, publications, sermons, orations, organizations, and individual correspondence to illustrate the American disapproval of dueling.

Looking at the number of actual duels at the time could be deceiving. There was no great change in the amount from 1804 to 1805. From 1800 to 1809, the number of duels per year never dropped below three and never exceeded sixteen.[59] While there were sporadically large increases in the percentage of affairs of honor over these years, dueling was actually a minor occurrence with relatively stable rates. But rather than focusing on numbers, it is more important to examine the dissemination of antidueling sentiment within the nation.

Naturally, dueling did still occur, but the Hamilton-Burr duel was the impetus behind the antidueling crusade. To prevent the influence of duelists in positions of power, an antidueling association was formed in New York for the sole purpose of encouraging members to withhold their votes from such individuals. It was concluded that the "class of avowed duellists is too small to impoverish the councils or offices of the state by their absence. Nothing will be lost by leaving them out." The association's members also took an active stance in fighting against any pro-dueling sentiment, stating, "We cannot submit to such a libel upon the understanding and the morals of this nation." The image of the politician duelist in the style of Burr and Hamilton was cast as "infamous," as the critics' method was to appeal "to the very principle on which they profess to build their practice, a sense of honor."[60]

Throughout the years, antiduelists continued to dispute the duelists' definition of honor as "not religion," "not virtue," "not courage," and "not humanity." The *New York Commercial Advertiser* called the duelists' understanding of honor "a mixture of pride, profligacy, and malignity." The antiduelists' definition of honor was the same version espoused by the American Revolution, a form of honor that was consistent with virtue and humanity. The public was reminded, "Honor, in the true sense of the word, means character—and this being the definition of philosophers, and men of understanding, I prefer it to the specious, though fashionable explanations of every profligate in the world, whether he wield a sword or a quill. If honor be character, who is it that can hurt that?"[61]

The biggest impact the Hamilton-Burr engagement had on dueling culture in America was more philosophical than practical. Most of society was in clear and vocal opposition to the practice. But despite all of this negative attention, dueling remained. Before 1800, there were only seventy-five duels in American history; through the nineteenth century, the number surged to over seven hundred.[62] As the next generation came of age, it began to embrace the romanticism of the duel. Young people turned a deaf ear to society's cries against it, in favor of using dueling for their own advancement personally and politically.[63] Around 1800, some pro-duelists even claimed the practice was consistent with "modern ethics."[64] The honor of the American Revolution and its generation was an idealized internal ethic that supported the collective good. Dueling was taken up, with rare exception, by the sons of the Revolutionary generation, who had matured amid strife between political parties and came to exalt external displays of honor. Connecticut Presbyterian minister Lyman Beecher noted that young men's notion of honor was most "especially" and "dreadful[ly]" "perverted," leading to challenges between "those whom our grandfathers would have called boys." The duel became the method for young men to advance themselves in an honor-based world. Beecher anguished, "Expertness in firing the pistol is a qualification of indispensable attainment."[65]

But what accounted for the popularity of dueling among the youth of America? For starters, they lacked the glorious cause of the American Revolution as a vehicle to prove their valor and gain honor, so they sought to display their bravery in ways that were more readily available.[66] Historian of the concept of merit Joseph Kett asserts, "Ambitious members born around the time of [or after] the Revolution were no less eager for fame," and this was also part of an expansion in "disruptive individualism."[67] There seems to have been a conscious effort to live up to the Revolutionary generations. In 1788, despite the new preference afforded to merit over birth, William Barton, a Pennsylvania lawyer and member of Philadelphia's American Philosophical Society, still predicted that "*reputation* obtained by a man, for his public Services, will operate on his descendants." As these children came of age, he correctly foresaw that the status of their fathers would "promote in them a commendable ambition, to *increase* the honor of their Name and Kindred."[68] The youth of America needed to not only match but potentially exceed their predecessors. Given the impact of the Revolution, it was a tough act to follow. Future senator Daniel Webster, born just three months before the Battle of Yorktown, not only looked up to men like Washington but also enviously recalled the exploits of his "striking" officer father, who led New Hampshire militiamen in "almost every campaign" of the war from Bennington to White Plains to West Point. Years later, Webster still expressed disproportionate pride over simply being compared to his father in "complexion." Although Webster was only on the receiving end of two challenges, other young men certainly looked to their elders in similar ways, but they didn't heed the cautionary tales of dueling; they saw the names of the illustrious men who had fought in the past and wanted to emulate them.[69] Because of this "infatuation," Beecher concluded, "dueling is steadily progressing; the example of great men and rulers is sweeping all before it, and is bending its destroying courses to the vale of common life." Unlike in Europe, honor had become democratized in America, though hierarchy still existed and honor was far from equal; it was accessible.[70]

During the Revolution, service to the nation granted the path to honor, but, in the mind-set of the youth, the duel could show a person's quality before society through the display of personal honor. Despite the advancement of the cause of national honor in learning and literature, there seemed to be a disconnect between the generations in their understanding of honor. Although the teachings on honor, especially in schools, largely stressed it as a secular ethic or morality, young men forged their own interpretations. The members of this new generation, as historian Jason Opal has illustrated, were eager to "transcend their surnames in post-Revolution America," while casting aside "honest work" as dishonorable in favor of "fame, glory, [and] distinction." Such ambition "enticed" one toward personal honor and away from "public duty."[71] Noting "the appearance of change in public opinion" and unofficially identifying 1805 as a dramatic turning point, Mercy Otis Warren complained, likely picking up on the shift in the rising generation, "They have too far lost that general sense of moral obligation, formerly felt by all classes in America."[72] The maintenance of honor shifted from being a duty for proper conduct to being a matter of the preservation of reputation, even if it meant breaking the law. Faced with this lack of discipline, Mr. Hillbanks, a teacher at the University of Pennsylvania's grammar school, complained that there "was a false sense of honour, generally prevailing in Schools" among the students. His colleague Joseph P. Engels concurred and admonished the students "that it was the same sense of honour that prevailed among bands of thieves." As if to prove his point, this comment incited a vicious attack on him by two students wielding unlikely weapons: umbrellas. The two students, brothers Hammond and Charles Shoemaker, considered the assault a matter of honor since they felt insulted by Engels's accusation.[73] Dueling in schools, especially at the college level, was formally outlawed through statutes and not universally accepted, but it (or at least public displays of honor-centered violence) was not a rarity in the early republic.[74]

The year 1808 saw the highest number of duels for the century's first three decades, and it was likely not a coincidence that it followed another national event that held clear implications for personal honor.[75] The *Chesapeake-Leopard* Affair of 1807, when a U.S. Navy frigate was attacked by a British vessel, became not only a rallying point for personal honor but also one of the sparks of the War of 1812.

On Monday, June 22, 1807, the USS *Chesapeake* (of the U.S. Navy), only a day after leaving port, cut through the Atlantic waters off the Virginia coast, powered by light breezes from the southwest. At the helm was veteran naval officer Commodore James Barron, who outranked the vessel's commander (Captain Charles Gordon, who was still on board) and was thus in control of the Europe-bound ship. In the early afternoon, a lone ship on the horizon could be spied from the top deck. Despite the freedom granted by the favorable winds, this unknown ship appeared sedentary in the ocean, as if it were waiting for something. As audible winds began to whip from the northeast, the *Chesapeake* drew nearer. After three o'clock in the afternoon, some nine miles northwest of Cape Henry on the eastern tip of Virginia, the *Chesapeake* met the HMS *Leopard* of the British Royal Navy. As the ships came alongside and hailed each other, there was nothing in the *Leopard*'s appearance that seemed untoward. The commodore simply assumed the British vessel had some message or correspondence to deliver—nothing unusual. There was peace between the United States and Britain; an uneasy peace that had lasted since the conclusion of the American Revolution over two decades ago; a peace that was about to become much more tenuous.

Before long a message was delivered from British captain Salusbury Pryce Humphreys to the American ship that removed any doubt of the *Leopard*'s intentions. They were looking for British deserters, several of whom were aboard the *Chesapeake*—and their request was tinged with inherent threat. Barron promptly refused to recognize any British authority and anticipated only a volley of words. What followed next was a tragic comedy of errors, of orders given and misunderstood, bravery by some, negligence by many, and surprise by all. The *Leopard* unleashed a warning shot, followed by three full broadsides from half of its fifty-two guns. The timing between the first and second shot was under dispute, but there was no mistake that a British vessel had attacked an unsuspecting American ship during peacetime. There in the Atlantic, the *Chesapeake* and the *Leopard* were at war.

As the British barrage assaulted the *Chesapeake*, confusion reigned above and below decks, as the officers and crew struggled to ready their ship for battle. As broadside after broadside crippled the *Chesapeake*, Barron stood proudly facing the enemy fire, desperately shouting and flailing about in an attempt to entice the British to halt their fire. He took wounds in his right thigh and leg, but still he stood in harm's way, pleading for a British respite or an American counterattack. Neither would come. The *Chesapeake*'s guns weren't prepped, the men weren't at their positions, and the deck was crowded with baggage and cargo. Without the threat of retaliation from its forty silent cannons, the ill-prepared ship could not offer a resistance. Barron was left with no alternative; he shouted to another officer, "Go down to the gun deck, and ask them for God's sake to fire one gun for the honour of the flag, I mean to strike." As the American flag descended from atop the ship's mast in disgrace, a single shot filled the void left by the *Chesapeake*'s inaction. The last attempt at seizing some valor had been lost, as well as control of the ship, the sailors it had tried to conceal, and, most important of all, the nation's honor.[76]

Even before the smoke from the cannons cleared, all Americans immediately and unquestionably understood this naval battle as a matter of honor. It directly challenged the reputation of the United States. The *Norfolk Gazette and Public Ledger* informed readers, "The honour of our nation [was] insulted beyond the possibility of further forbearance."[77] This outbreak of Anglo-American hostility, which became known as the *Chesapeake-Leopard* Affair of 1807, represented a crucial moment in American international policy. It also served as a blatant example of the "*monstrous* doctrine" of naval impressment that challenged "any [nation's] regard to her own honor" and as an initial spark for the outbreak of the War of 1812.[78] Although the political and diplomatic fallout from the event was eventually settled peacefully, the outrage and feelings of American dishonor did not vanish. The American people continued to view this attack as a clear degradation of their sovereignty, their flag, and their national honor. The indignation of the loss of the USS *Chesapeake* represented a conscious debt that "will *never* subside until ample satisfaction has been made" and helped pave the way for the coming of war.[79] While the *Chesapeake-Leopard* Affair stirred American war hawks and eventually let slip the dogs of war, it also provides remarkable insight into American perceptions of and connections between national and personal honor in the early republic.

The contested notion of national honor revived the supremacy of personal honor, and the *Chesapeake-Leopard* Affair represented a moment when this reversal was displayed on a public stage. The *Chesapeake-Leopard* Affair fueled the ongoing battle over definitions of national honor that began with the Constitutional Convention and the French Revolution. From the start, the cries for the reclamation of honor through war could be heard up and down the Eastern Seaboard.[80] In Norfolk, Virginia, close to the *Leopard*'s postincursion docking at Lynnhaven Bay, martial fervor was high and a war was assumed to be imminent. Captain Robert Taylor, of the N.V. Troop of Cavalry, "invite[d] all those who feel for the insulted honour of their country, and who have formed the manly and proud resolve to sustain it, to appear on the field and enroll themselves among its defenders."[81] Major General Henry Lee, of the Virginia militia, likewise declared, "We shall present to our unjust for a front of bayonets in the hands of freemen, estimating peace with honour, as the highest national good, and estimating peace with dishonour, as the deepest national curse."[82] "Peace with honor" was viewed by this contingent as the greatest good, and thus the pinnacle of national honor. But they would not accept a peace dependent on accepting national disgrace. To allow the British to violate "our sovereignty and our honour" without retaliating was unthinkable, even if peace could be restored.

From the start, the incident created two camps: one that favored war and another that hoped to maintain peace. The cry for satisfaction was the loudest, and those who hoped for peace were branded as Tories and traitors.[83] Still, both sides claimed to be advancing the cause of national honor. A gentleman from New York wrote in a letter, which was eventually published as a pamphlet called *The Voice of Truth*, that honor was indeed "the true interest of the country," but that by enlisting former British sailors, America may have given the *Leopard* cause under a similar language of honor.[84] America had offended British sovereignty, and Britain had offended American sovereignty—the ledger was even.

John Lowell, in his aptly titled *Peace without Dishonour—War without Hope*, also asserted that "our national good faith" (or national honor) was his "only aim" in writing the 1807 publication. He was among the minority that believed that some diplomatic policy should be worked out with Great Britain. Lowell concluded that British officers should have to offer proof in order to reclaim their deserters, and if an American captain would find such evidence conclusive, he should indeed turn over the men. He stated, "There is nothing in this procedure derogatory to our national honour."[85] Despite the more moderate nature of these appeals for peace, they only questioned what was in the country's best interests. They did not suggest that the *Chesapeake-Leopard* Affair was anything other than a national dishonor.

While honor was of critical importance to all Americans, the principals involved with the *Chesapeake* were military men, typically more sensitive to slights to their reputation and honor because of the inherent rank-based structure of the military. Commodore Barron, the highest-ranking American officer aboard the Chesapeake, would face a wrath that exceeded, or at least rivaled, that reserved for Great Britain and the *Leopard*. Throughout his naval career, Barron had shown a careful attention to his reputation to ensure that "his Conduct has ever been that of a Gentleman."[86] The Virginia-born Barron came from a naval family and had served with distinction since the American Revolution, when he enlisted as a midshipman at only twelve years of age. As both a military and merchant seaman and officer, he was regarded for his ingenuity and bravery.[87] Barron was promoted to the rank of captain in 1799, and by 1807 he had been in command of warships in the still-infant U.S. Navy for over eight years.

In 1807, Barron was by no means a novice, and his actions (or inactions) and conduct on June 22 made him a target for criticism, hostility, and official discipline. Barron's most fervent detractors originated from among the *Chesapeake's* junior officers. The day after the affair, a collection of five wary, self-preserving, and enraged officers (Lieutenants Benjamin Smith, William Crane, William H. Allen, James Creighton, and Sidney Smith), along with Sailing Master Samuel Brooke, penned a letter to Robert Smith, secretary of the navy, formally declaring the defeat of the *Chesapeake* and the loss of national honor as Barron's fault. These men were "compelled by imperious duty, the honour of their Flag, the honour of their countrymen, & all that is dear to themselves to request that an order may be issued for the arrest of Commodore James Barron."[88] Someone had to atone for the loss of national honor, and these officers made it clear that it would not be them.

The officers claimed they came forward with their complaint because they felt "deeply sensible of the disgrace, which must be attached to the late (in their opinion) premature surrender of the US Ship Chesapeake." They recognized the dishonor of the event but were not willing to assume any of the blame personally. According to them, dishonor came from the premature surrender and the commodore's neglect of duty in readying the ship for battle and returning fire. They instead declared that they were "desirous of proving to their country and the world . . . [that they were] worthy of the Flag under which they had the honor to serve."[89] Others outside this immediate circle echoed the charge. Lowell, although predisposed to peace with Britain, leveled similar accusations against Barron, who, "after having resolved to defend his ship, ought to have nailed his flag to the mast, and to have sunk his adversary, or to have gone down himself with his flag undishonoured. It is the disgrace which this conduct seems to fix upon us, which makes us feel so pungently."[90]

The officers' accusation against Barron on the basis of honor was indicative of several themes of the post-Revolutionary era. The simple fact that numerous subordinate officers felt secure enough to bring charges of dishonor against a superior officer shows a drastic democratization of honor in comparison to the pre-Revolutionary European hierarchy. The conspicuous use by the officers of the rhetoric of devotion to principles of national honor shows the continued importance placed on sentiments of the greater good within society as a whole. There was certainly a belief in these principles, but the use of such language was also essential to illustrate that their accusations were for the good of the country—and to shield themselves from charges of self-preservation. But beneath the officers' attempt to demonstrate a selfless devotion to national honor, their charge illuminates a resurgence in the importance placed on personal honor.

The *Chesapeake* officers' understanding of personal honor allowed them to separate themselves from the greater disgrace of the defeat of their ship. The striking of the *Chesapeake*'s flag was a national dishonor, but these officers believed that they could remove any tarnish from their names by proving that they personally acted honorably. Their protests directly contributed to Barron's facing military discipline over the incident.

The belief that honor could be saved through proper behavior had actually been quite common since the early days of the War of Independence. As illustrated in chapter 4, the result of a string of defeats during the Revolution in which the army still performed admirably led many Americans to realize that honor could be gained through battle, even a loss, provided that the combatants behaved well. As Humphrey Bland's *Treatise of Military Discipline* states, "When an Officer has had the Misfortune of being Beat, his Honour won't suffer by it, provided he has done his Duty, and acted like a Soldier." Officers were disgraced only by "neglecting the common Methods used to prevent" defeat.[91] Likewise, following orders could also protect one's reputation from disgrace in a battle's loss. Bland comments, "We shall gain Honour and Reputation enough, if we adhere strictly to our Orders; but Disgrace may attend the exceeding of them, as well as the falling short."[92] From the Revolution's war of posts, American civilian society and government had also come to accept these ideas. However, in accordance with this thought process, it was also believed that the dishonor of one could infect the whole—thus, the misconduct of a single man could bring dishonor on the entire ship.

Contrary to this conception that exalted collective honor over an individual's, the officers of the *Chesapeake* sought to escape with their reputation intact while also indicting Barron for his alleged misdeeds. The junior officers' accusation made it clear that they intended to win back their honor by proving not that the ship behaved well but rather that their commander had failed, thereby absolving themselves from blame. This treatment of collective honor is starkly different from the definition understood by the Continental army and navy during the Revolution. Such thought and action was indicative of a rise in the importance placed on personal honor.[93]

These junior officers came of age after the Revolution, and thus they did not have this sense of collective honor engrained in their consciousness. In this instance and in other examples from the era, the younger generation was particularly sensitive about their honor, as they sought to prove themselves in relation to the Revolutionary generation. On the reverse, Commodore Barron had served in the American Revolution as a very young man. The mentality that national honor, the greater good, and collective conduct and reputation were all linked would have been instilled in him by his officer father and his comrades.[94] Thus, initially he did not attack the conduct of his officers, possibly because "he assumed they would close ranks with him to protect their own reputations" under the philosophy he had grown up with, in which the dishonor of one could bring dishonor to all.[95] But as the rancor against him escalated, Barron reacted to their attacks in kind and attempted to maintain and defend his own honor. He agreed that the *Chesapeake* had been dishonored, but he was convinced it was not due to his behavior or orders.[96] The injured Barron lashed out: "I write in Pain not being able to Sit up but have to Lay on my Side, my worst wound is what you call Shaking but to me that have so many darts in the heart and them shot by my Country men without knowing the Merits of my Case." He was injured more by the treatment he received from his officers and the nation: "The Conduct of the British was cruel and in the extreme it is certainly infamous in every Point of View, but the Manner in

Which the Government has acted and is about to act towards me does not fall far Short of it."[97]

The resulting court of inquiry and court-martial became an opportunity for the junior officers and Barron to attempt to publicly defend their honor.[98] Further illustrating the democratization of honor that had taken place since the Revolution was the fact that of the eleven-man military tribunal sitting in judgment, only one outranked Barron. Inferiors held control over the fate of their superior. The junior officers' position had been clear from the start: they and the crew had behaved honorably; it was the negligence, indecisiveness, and cowardice of Barron that had cost the *Chesapeake* the engagement. Barron's defense began with a declaration that he welcomed the inquest in order to clear his reputation. He offered the court, "For six months the silent victim of misrepresentation and misconception; I shall have this day an opportunity of vindicating my honour. . . . Conscious of my own innocence . . . I enter on my defence with . . . confident anticipation of rescuing my reputation from unmerited reproach."[99] Barron even used the court-martial to link his personal honor with national honor, remarking that his defense was "due to truth, to my own honour, and to the American nation."[100]

Throughout the trial, two distinct portrayals of the *Chesapeake-Leopard* Affair emerged. One was supported by the junior officers, who described the event as the result of Barron's failings. The other unfolded as Barron accused the officers and crew of incompetence and of failing to follow orders. But although he voiced protests, he never directly attacked his accusers' honor, instead insinuating that they were overcome by self-preservation, "pride and egotism." He stated, "If I did not acknowledge my respect in their honour, and truth, I should conceal the opinion which I really entertain of them." But it was this very collection of men he now regarded as honorable who had publicly dishonored Barron in a signed letter—a physical bond of the officers' honor and Barron's dishonor. Barron, conscious of this perception, continued, "But though I believe them honourable and just, I know them to be mean; they are not exempt from the infirmities of our nature; it is not in human virtue to be indifferent to the result of a prosecution, for the maintenance of which, we are pledged to the world."[101]

Captain Gordon, although not one of Barron's pledged accusers, was lumped into this same group. Barron recognized that "the web of his destiny is interwoven with mine. My condemnation is the pledge of his acquittal."[102] Thus, Barron concluded that his detractors all had a vested interest in his conviction, as it would exonerate their conduct and personal honor.

For a United States that was led by President Jefferson and not yet ready to risk a war with Great Britain, the court-martial and diplomacy with Britain remained the only available avenues to attempt to reclaim lost honor.[103] Thus, it is not surprising that a public explanation was needed, or, more pointedly, that a victim needed to be sacrificed to this cause.[104] The court, hedging its bets, concluded that although the commodore displayed personal courage, the defeat was a result of Barron's "great inattention to duty." Any deficiencies on the part of the officers and the crew were virtually disregarded, and their conduct was declared "proper, commendable and honourable."[105] Thus, the national and collective sense of honor that had so dominated the Revolutionary era and the earliest years of the republic was allowed to wane in favor of this revived personal honor that allowed an individual to be held accountable for the *Chesapeake's* failure. Almost in recognition of the necessity of his conviction, Barron was not sentenced to death or dismissal but was publicly shamed and suspended without pay for five years. In many ways, this return to a conception of personal honor seems to have been a conscious choice within the country in order to vindicate a national disgrace. If war was not an option, honor had to be restored in some other way—the court was the most readily available method.[106]

Although the verdict had officially placed most of the blame and dishonor on Barron personally, it did not fully heal America's injured reputation. Nor did the 1811 receipt of reparations from the British and the return of two of the four *Chesapeake* sailors taken prisoner (Daniel Martin and John Strachan) alleviate any of the shame. (Jenkin Ratford, the only British subject in the group, was hanged; William Ware died in 1809.)[107] The memory of the *Chesapeake* remained a festering wound. U.S. Navy captains constantly sought vengeance for the affair. In 1810, Captain John Rodgers (the president of Barron's court-martial) was labeled "the man who avenged the Chesapeake" for his taking of a Royal Navy sloop called the *Little Belt*, which reportedly fired on the USS *President*.[108] In the American mind-set, it seemed that only violence could bring about absolution. Thus, though clouded in the language of national honor, the matter remained quite personal. Only a direct confrontation with Britain, a duel between nations, could bring about a sense of redemption.

The War of 1812 has been generally understood as a matter of honor in the historiography, but it has not been recognized that the war was more than just a single matter of honor.[109] It was a conflict not only between nations but also between Americans and their conceptions of individual and collective responsibility.[110] The *Chesapeake-Leopard* Affair and the coming of the War of 1812 had in essence revived the cult of personal honor that had been extensively denigrated after the death of Hamilton. The *Chesapeake-Leopard* Affair and the War of 1812 represented a revival of personal honor, but cast in the Revolutionary rhetoric of national honor. The Committee on Foreign Relations in the House of Representatives reported that the United States was "engaged in the war for the sole purpose of vindicating their rights and honor" because, it asserted, "it becomes a free and virtuous people to give an useful example to the world."[111] The indelible image of the British burning Washington, D.C.—as clear a challenge to honor as any single event in any war—became the most striking example of the dangers of individuated personal honor gaining precedence. If America's capital could be burned, what did it say about national honor? Secretary of War John Armstrong attributed the disgrace to the prioritization of self-interest over national honor: "Without all doubt the deterring cause of these is to be found in that love of life which, in many of the corps, predominated over a love of country and of honor."[112]

The rise of the sons and daughters of the Revolutionary generation and their quest for prominence and personal honor were on display throughout the conflict.[113] Like the unsteady officers of the Revolution, young men threw away their commissions over trivial matters out of "a Sacred Regard to [their] own Honor." Captain Abraham Hull, just twenty-eight years of age, died "trying to retrieve his family's honor," which was lost by his general father's surrender of Detroit to the British. As previously mentioned, the rise in dueling at the time was also a clear indication of the reemergence of personal honor. Historian Alan Taylor regarded such practices as "putting honor ahead of nation."[114] It is interesting to note that military honor was hardly spoken of during the American Revolution, but its rise coincided with that of personal honor in the early national period with the War of 1812, peaking in the Civil War (with noticeable spikes during wartime into the twentieth century).[115] Illustrating their inclusion in honor culture, women joined in promoting the value of personal honor. The song "The Love of Country," despite its patriotic name, was a careful recrimination of personal honor and the inherent threat of shame. It reminded men and women,

A soldier is a gentleman,
His honor is his life,
And he that won't stand to his post,
Will ne'er stand by his wife.[116]

In this clear personalization of national honor, women became the judges of masculinity: a bad soldier was a bad husband.

There continued to be differences between the Revolutionary generations and their more youthful counterparts; constitutional architect President James Madison "exhort[ed] all the good people of the United States, as they love their country, as they value the precious heritage derived from the virtue and valor of their fathers . . . that they exert themselves."[117] Madison was exalting a past Revolutionary ideal, his use of the word "good" speaking to a sense of morality and his use of "virtue" representative of an ethical principle. Just as during the Revolution, America needed to defend itself in the proper way. Also illustrating the expanding nature of honor, African American Revolutionary War veteran turned reverend Lemuel Haynes criticized the younger generations when he said, "The words love to our country . . . go cheap at the present day." As historian Nicole Eustace claims, Haynes believed the war and the country were "tainted by private passions"—self-interest over the greater good.[118] But General Andrew Jackson and the victory during the Battle of New Orleans overshadowed these criticisms. For afterward even an American prisoner of war in Britain remarked, "Nothing now is thought of or talked of, but *New Orleans* and *Jackson*, and *Jackson* and *New Orleans*. We already perceived that we are treated with more respect, and our country spoken of in honorable terms."[119] The conception of honor was reverting back to a notion of defense of reputation, and this revival of personal honor did not end with the conclusion of the war.

Nor did the War of 1812 conclude the battle over the *Chesapeake's* honor. It would take a duel between two of the principals to finally settle the affair. Several years after peace had been reestablished, Captain Stephen Decatur (a member of the court-martial tribunal) attributed Barron's absence during the war to cowardice. (Barron wanted to return to service, but he was trapped in Europe by the war and later by poverty induced by his suspension.[120]) The affront escalated into a duel, a practice that both men claimed to find "barbarous." Yet neither backed away from what seemed inevitable. On the morning of March 22, 1820, the two men met on the field of honor in Bladensburg, Maryland (just outside Washington, D.C.). Both expressed remorse for the chain of events that had led them there. Ordinarily such an admission could have brought about reconciliation (Barron had shown a predilection for such settlements in an 1806 duel), but no peace was brokered—there could be no peace without honor. After the smoke of fired pistols cleared, Barron stumbled back (wounded in the thigh yet again) and Decatur lay on the ground clutching his abdomen, a fatal bullet lodged in his groin. Decatur would not last the day, but Barron would survive, regain his honor (in some circles), and return to the navy—before resigning over a personal slight of rank.[121]

The upsurge in the perceived importance of personal honor directly translated to an increase in dueling, which prompted further attempts to stop its influence. But as more duels took place featuring prominent men, more models were created for the youth. Military officers and politicians, perhaps not of the Revolutionary generation but still esteemed, continued to create an appealing image and example for others to follow. Still, antiduelists attempted to brace the nation through legal means as states, organizations, and schools created new or stronger penalties—with questionable results.[122] But, as we have seen, the most effective method of hindering dueling was appealing to honor. And as the definition of honor shifted away from the Revolutionary ideal, the matter became more complex. By 1829, even the president of the United States, Andrew Jackson, had taken a life in a duel. Thus, dueling remained "the great national sin" that led to "the whole land [being] defiled with blood."[123] And the true nature of honor, both national and personal, remained a point of contestation. However, as the societal divide between the Revolutionary generation and their children increased, the nation was left with a collection of young people who sought to assert themselves in the world through a more archaic notion of honor.

While the rising generations sought to return to this antiquated concept of honor, the old guard of the Revolution still clung to ethical foundations—but often in ways that, at least on the surface, seemed to challenge notions of equality. In 1813, former president Jefferson, who had previously avoided war in the wake of the *Chesapeake-Leopard* Affair, wrote to former president John Adams lamenting the role of physical combat as the determining factor of honor. Jefferson complained that "bodily powers" and "bodily strength" had gone out of fashion "since the invention of gunpowder has armed the weak as well as the strong with missile death."[124] As guns made all men equal on the field of battle, Jefferson found it difficult to believe that the mere pull of a trigger should grant any preferment or reputation. Just over two weeks earlier, in another letter to Adams, he described editing the New Testament down to simply Jesus's own words, without a trace of divinity. In what would become *The Life and Morals of Jesus of Nazareth*, Jefferson claimed to have untangled "the most sublime and benevolent code of morals which has ever been offered to man," and this martial form of honor ran in opposition to it.[125] Nearly thirty years before this, Jefferson had equated honor with conscience, a matter of ethics and a term he would also apply to his "Philosophy of Jesus."[126] Adams held a similar devotion to morality, albeit with a religious difference. They agreed that it was those who held to these principles who should advance in society.

Both men looked to a "natural aristocracy" founded exclusively on "virtue & talents."[127] Natural aristocracy was far different from the "artificial aristocracy" of monarchical Europe, which was "founded on wealth and birth, without either virtue or talents."[128] Adams asserted that America's "leaders, or more properly followers, were men of too much honour to attempt it [artificial aristocracy]."[129] They both also denounced hereditary titles; the natural aristocracy reflected the democratization and collectivization of American ethics, and this was an aristocracy that anyone could enter.[130] Jefferson had first expressed this concept in 1779, but the term hadn't been formalized until 1787 in Adams's *Defence of the Constitutions of Government of the United States of America*.[131] Just after the outbreak of the War of 1812, Jefferson hoped that the national government would be led by these natural aristocrats, who were "the most precious gift of nature."[132] Like Franklin's concept of ascending honor, the natural aristocrats were afforded preference by the ethics of their deeds, not their birth status. Adams, in a Lockean sense, asserted that people are "all born alike morally innocent, but do not all remain so. They soon become as different and Unlike and unequal in Morals as Virtue and Vice, Merit and Guilt. . . . These Inequalities are the Sources of the Natural Aristocracy."[133]

Still, despite a great deal of commonality, the debate over natural aristocracy echoed arguments between Federalists and Republicans. What role would such a collection play in government and society? Jefferson, who had been critical of the Cincinnati, acknowledged the potential for an artificial aristocracy to form and become a "mischievous ingredient in government." In order to prevent this, he believed, "the best remedy is exactly that provided by all our constitutions, to leave to the citizens the free election and separation of the aristoi from the pseudo-aristoi. . . . In general they will elect the real good and wise."[134]

Although Adams also felt that "mischief" could arise in government, he believed that the formation of a true artificial aristocracy was a "remote" possibility "many hundred years" away. It could only result from the "corruption" of the natural aristocracy, with "Wealth and Power [being] made hereditary municipal Laws and political institutions." He worried instead about the tyranny of the people.[135] Adams pointed to the lack of "pure" elections in the United States; playing on Jefferson's emotions personally, he asked, "Do you recollect in history, a more Corrupt Election than that of Aaron Burr to be President[?]"[136] For over a decade, Burr's understanding of honor and personal interests had been attacked. It was not difficult to label Hamilton's killer, who had previously attempted to steal the presidency from Jefferson in

1800 and had been unsuccessfully prosecuted for treason in 1807, as aspiring to an artificial aristocracy. Jefferson, who had shown great personal animosity toward Burr, certainly wouldn't have disagreed about his former vice president.[137] But, for Adams, the problem also ran much deeper. He feared that "Aaron Burr had 100,000 Votes from the Single Circumstance of his descent from President Burr [of Princeton] and President Edwards [of Yale]." The issue was that such a man could still garner votes based on familial lineage. Adams saw "a fewdal Aristocracy," or at least aspirations toward one, in New York and similar situations in Virginia, New England, and Pennsylvania. Adams warned that there were still those among the citizenry who would "Sacrifice of every national Interest and honour, to private and party Objects."[138] The natural aristocracy was a reflection of the Revolutionary changes in American honor. It stressed national over personal honor and exalted ethical conduct.

Anyone could become a natural aristocrat, but obviously not everyone was a member due exclusively to personal ethical choices. Adams acknowledged this democratic foundation, as men and women could equally aspire to inclusion, although there was certainly a gendered prejudice. But using the example of his alma mater Harvard, he concluded that the easiest path was through education. As illustrated in chapters 2 and 6, schools formed the foundation of the new ethical concept of honor, thus it is not surprising that he considered them the breeding ground of the natural aristocracy. But just how many were part of this select group? Adams asserted that "there never can be ... more than one fifth; no nor one Tenth of the Men regularly educated to Science and Letters," and it was these individuals who had the virtue and "Abilities" to gain "Distinction" and "Privilege." To find them, one only had to look in "Schools, Academies, Colleges and Universities" and "in the shape of Ministers Lawyers and Physicians."[139] Adams's description of education as the foundation of ethical identity remained consistent with ideas held in America since the colonial era. Still, it also linked his understanding of a natural aristocracy with the codes of honor and ethical rules of occupational professionalization. Adams's mention of physicians was particularly noteworthy, as within the medical community his vision of a natural aristocracy based on ethics, virtue, and talent was actually attempted. And both he and Jefferson would carry on a correspondence with many of the figures responsible for their institutionalization.[140]

Even today, the medical practice has a strong connection with codes of ethics. The first U.S. version appeared in Boston in 1808 as the "Code of Medical Police," but it was the 1819 creation of the Kappa Lambda Society of Hippocrates that formalized ethics in a collective sense of professional honor throughout the country.[141] Founded in Lexington, Kentucky, by Dr. Samuel Brown, professor of medicine at Transylvania University, the group was "a revival of, & an improvement upon the one formed by Hippocrates."[142] While, as its name would suggest, the Kappa Lambda Society did adopt some of the ideas of the classical Greek physician, such as to "abstain from every voluntary act of mischief and corruption," it was very much invested in the honor culture of early America.[143] Based on its constitution, their motives were "laudable and honourable to humanity," as all its members were to "embrace honour, science, friendship and virtue." By holding to these ideals, the physician-members hoped to promote the greater good of society.[144]

Brown, who was partly educated at the University of Edinburgh, borrowed heavily from British doctor Thomas Percival's 1803 publication *Medical Ethics, or, A Code of Institutes and Precepts*, credited as the first medical code of ethics (it had also been adopted in the "Code of Medical Police"), and he even helped publish the first U.S. version of Percival's rules in 1821. In the text, honor was treated the same as morality, the "*moral rules of conduct*" were to be "fully adopted in private or general practice," and maintaining them "should be deemed a point of honour." The path to obtaining the foundation of this moral conduct was through "a regular *academical education*," which gave "professional ability" and a "just claim to pre-eminence among physicians."[145] While similar groups existed in England and many ideas came from a British physician, the American version does not seem to be exactly their offspring. The British versions focused on "inherited talent" and "moral character," whereas the American society stressed each physician's personal behavior and moral conduct.

Although certainly indebted to the British model, Brown was very much a product of the American ethical tradition as well. He had attended Dickinson College in Pennsylvania and even studied medicine under Rush, and thus would have been familiar with the version of honor taught in American schools, as is evident by his focus on moral conduct rather than "inherited talent." Brown, a correspondent of Jefferson, seemed to conform very much to the model of natural aristocracy that was advanced through education. Adams was also aware of their ideals, as he received a letter from New York's Dr. Samuel L. Mitchell, a former Columbia professor, who detailed their formation of a "National Convention" to create a "Code of Medical Ethics."[146]

Like the natural aristocracy, the Kappa Lambda Society was theoretically open to all, but all could not be members. It existed, like the Society of the Cincinnati, as an organization just for a specific group, with membership "confined to medical men," but it lacked the element of blood descent.[147] And, like the Freemasons, it functioned as a secret society. Members had to take an oath that they would "endeavour to exalt the character of the Medical profession by a life of virtue and honour."[148] Their notion of honor and virtue was consistent with ethics and morality, with none of the trappings of birth or heredity.

As its founder and a professor, Brown exercised a great deal of influence on its members and his students, which greatly expanded the group's reach. For example, one such individual, Dr. Samuel Jackson, professor of medicine at the University of Pennsylvania, created the Philadelphia branch of the society as a result. Soon other branches could be found in cities such as New York and Washington, D.C. By 1823, Dr. G. F. H. Crockett boasted to Jefferson, the Kappa Lambda Society had taken "root in most of the medical schools in the Union."[149]

Again, like the Cincinnati, Freemasons, and the idea of the natural aristocracy, the Kappa Lambda Society came under scrutiny for its understanding of honor. Although technically open, it was also exclusionary to nonmembers. Internal debate within the various societies over the use of a secretive oath or a public code spoke to individualized concepts within the group as a whole. An oath suggested that each member needed a personal sense of honor to become a member, whereas a code allowed anyone to follow the tenets and act honorably. The issue came to a head in 1830, when an article entitled "Secret Medical Society" claimed that the Kappa Lambda Society, speaking specifically about employment at New York Hospital and the Lying Hospital, exercised an "unjust monopoly of the emoluments and honours of the profession." In so doing, the society was trying to "put a patina of honor on the shameless pursuit of personal advantage."[150] The opposition in the Medical Society of New York claimed Kappa Lambda removed the *"rewards of merit."*[151] It was further argued that it acted counter to the Medical Ethics of New York, which asserted, "Honor and justice particularly forbid one medical practitioner's infringing upon the rights and privileges of another who is legally accredited, and whose character is not impeached."[152] The inherent nature of exclusivity was viewed as preventing those of true character from advancing. The challenge was one that had taken place numerous times since the Revolutionary era: a debate over the nature of honor. While the society did cast honor as an ethical ideal, the issue of favorable employment echoed older questions regarding patronage and the prioritization of personal advancement over the greater good. If advancement was purely based on an ethical notion of honor arising from each person's behavior, should not all people have equal claim? Although the society did persevere into the mid-nineteenth century, its opposition denounced what they felt was a false notion of democratized honor and concluded, "The grand principle of Kappa Lambda ethics . . . is . . . that 'Success is the criterion of merit.'"[153]

The Kappa Lambda Society illustrated two concurrent yet conflicting views in nineteenth-century American society. The group existed between the ethics of the natural aristocracy and the revival of personal honor characteristic of the post-Revolutionary generations. While it showed that honor culture was adapted into professional codes, it also showed the return of older ideas of personal honor. Like the debate over dueling, national honor, and personal ethics, the society showed that while education could instill ideas, individual interpretation was responsible for an ongoing change in definitions and ultimately understanding.

In the last year of his life, the elderly Jefferson presided over a board meeting for the University of Virginia that dealt with a sense of false honor and ethics that had developed among the youth. The school's Visitors (trustees) acknowledged that "a prejudice prevails too extensively among the young, that it is dishonorable to bear witness, one against another, while this prevails, and under the form of a matter of conscience, they have been unwilling to authorise constraint . . . however unfounded in reason or morality." The Visitors believed that the students' concept of honor had wandered from one consistent with ethics and morality. They concluded that "this loose principle, in the Ethics of schoolboy combinations," was a danger to the "good & safety of society."[154] As one of the last of the founders looked on, he saw that his students were no longer thinking of honor in that same way. This change manifested itself broadly in society and, as the youth came into adulthood, this new thinking came with them. Andrew Burstein seconds this point, concluding, "The second generation of national leaders, whose political upbringing took place not during the unifying 1770s but during the divisive 1790s, was unable to resist the sectional pull that in due time would result in civil war."[155] The turmoil between political parties had solidified competing definitions of honor and virtue that in many ways harkened back to the pre-Revolutionary era. In explanation, Harvard professor Dr. Benjamin Waterhouse complained to former president Madison that Americans now received their poor ethical education from newspapers run by "a set of rascally editors."[156] Honor was changing once again.

March 16, 1824

Only months before his first attempt at the presidency, the "Hero of New Orleans," the most celebrated figure of the War of 1812, had traveled to Washington, D.C.—the nation's capital and concurrently the site of America's most embarrassing defeat. Within the President's House, a structure no longer marred by the charring or shame of British torches, former major general Andrew Jackson stood before James Monroe, the last of the "founders" to occupy the executive office, for a ceremony that was carefully orchestrated and full of "pomp and perade." Jackson had only the night before celebrated his birthday, and now, at eleven o'clock the following morning, he was fittingly about to receive a long overdue gift. Numerous attendees, ranging from First Lady Elizabeth Monroe to Secretary of State John Quincy Adams, looked on as the president presided over the presentation of the Congressional Gold Medal (a precursor to the Medal of Honor) to Jackson for his "distinguished gallantry, skill, and good conduct" at the Battle of New Orleans. Congress had initially awarded the medal to Jackson in February 1815, but now, nearly a decade later, the general could gently run his finger over the golden relief of his younger self etched in full military dress. The medal represented not just the thanks and praise of a grateful country but also the new spirit of the nation—whereby a man could rise far above his birth.

Jackson steadied himself, attempting to both conceal and overcome "a tremor" that "allways seise[d]" him when forced to speak publicly. The general spoke of his "peculiar pleasure" at receiving the award but claimed it "in the name of those patriotic officers & soldiers" who fought beside him in Louisiana at "one of the proudest moments of [his] life." In the same room was his biographer, John H. Eaton, author of 1817's *Life of Andrew Jackson,* a former soldier under the general, and a Tennessee senator. Here was a man who had done as much as any to immortalize Jackson's fame—a friend (and future secretary of war) who had proclaimed to the world that the general's "moral character is without reproach" and "unstained by dishonor." Eaton certainly watched the presentation with admiration, though after the ceremony Jackson claimed to despise such "shows." But while the general attempted to sound humble as he recounted his victory over "the ruthless savage" and the "British foe," he undoubtedly smiled to himself, enjoying the praise heaped on him. For Jackson had ascended to the upper echelons of American society not through birth or ethics but through combat. He stood receiving one of the nation's highest honors despite his checkered past. For Jackson had killed before, and not just for the nation—for himself. His actions were often questionable and challenged the long-held ethical beliefs of the Revolution. Even Eaton reluctantly admitted that within Jackson "vice and virtue" were "found in the same bosom."[1]

Although he had briefly served as a teenager in the partisan fighting on the Carolina frontier during the American Revolution, Jackson's youth, his capture, and the relatively minor impact of his service kept him firmly outside the traditional prestige of the Revolutionary generation. This in turn made him even more defensive of his status and pushed him to live up to an exalted memory to which he had gotten painfully close. But robbed of his chance by being born too late, Jackson was left to seek out his own honor and fame through other means. He had witnessed the Revolution with his own eyes, but Jackson was more representative of the new men of America who came of age after the war. In some ways Jackson was between two generations, old and new, and he held the characteristics of both. He was able to advance based on service in both the Revolution and the War of 1812, but he didn't hold himself to the same ethical basis of honor that defined the Revolutionary generation. He fit the mold of Bertram Wyatt-Brown's concept of primal honor: highly personalized, sensitive, and often violent. In the words of that same historian, "No one in American history and certainly no other president can be more closely identified than Andrew Jackson with the dictates of [primal] honor." From his martial prowess to his affinity for dueling, Jackson was a personification of the principle "that honor adhered to a warrior on the battlefield."[2] His striving, his ambition, and his use of violence were symbolic of the spirit of the new American man—one who desired honor and sought out available opportunities to earn it.

Born in the South Carolina backcountry to a recent Scots-Irish immigrant family that considered themselves among the Old World gentry, Jackson's thirst for honor and acclaim had driven him. While he considered himself a gentleman, his social status in America was murky, forcing him to become even more defensive over his reputation.[3] He was taught by his mother, "If ever you have to vindicate your feelings or your honor, do it calmly . . . but sustain your manhood always."[4] Sitting around the fire on many a cold "winter's night," Jackson embraced an older, European model of honor instilled in him by his mother, transported via Scots-Irish migration and folkways.[5]

These lessons were not forgotten. Many years later, Jackson was regarded by Josiah Quincy Jr. (two generations removed from the patriot of the same name) as "a knightly personage" who was "prejudiced, narrow, mistaken on many points," while still possessing a "high sense of honor."[6] These were not the ethical ideals of the Revolution; they represented a devotion to personal honor acquired at the end of a gun barrel. Dueling was a tool for both glory and social mobility.[7]

As a young lawyer in Tennessee, Jackson was never afraid to offer a challenge or face a bullet, sword, or fist (possibly even a rock) in the field or street.[8] Echoing the maternal guidance imparted during his youth, Jackson proclaimed, "I feel the Sweetness and necessity of protecting my feelings and Reputation whenever they are maliciously injured."[9] In an 1806 duel, this time with pistols, he again followed his mother's advice. He was "calm" as he held his shot (taking a bullet to the chest for his trouble) before taking aim, firing, and killing his opponent, Charles H. Dickinson. Jackson was criticized for his "unethical" behavior during the affair: he had worn an oversize coat that disguised his silhouette (making him a more difficult target) and demanded a refire after his pistol went off half-cocked.[10] Jackson dismissed the charges: "I should have hit him, if he has shot me through the brain."[11] For a nation only two years removed from the Hamilton-Burr duel, this was too much. Nineteenth-century biographer James Parton recalled, "It is certain that at no time between the years 1806 and 1812, could General Jackson have been elected to any office in Tennessee that required a majority of the voters of the whole state."[12] But that was before war was declared.

The War of 1812 provided Jackson, like many others of the rising generation, with the path to advancement. His view of honor as a defense of reputation and his sense of the duty of avenging a wrong meshed with the wider, prevailing rebirth of personal honor. In her work *Manifest Manhood and the Antebellum American Empire*, author Amy Greenberg notes similar changes throughout society: "In the early years of the republic, men grounded their own sense of manliness in virtue, honor, and public service. By the nineteenth century, these ethical ideas came into conflict with a limited and gender-specific notion of 'primitive masculinity.'"[13] Jackson perfectly embodied this nineteenth-century man.

During the war, Jackson's campaign against the Creeks after their attack on Fort Mims in 1813 was one that he viewed as equal parts justice and vengeance.[14] Jackson had grown up in the shadow of Griffith Rutherford's 1776 raids on the Cherokee, and he was, at least partially, aware of his actions in the Carolinas.[15] But Jackson did not heed General Nathanael Greene's admonishments of Rutherford at the time that there needed to be "moderation" and "humanity" in combat.[16] Recuperating from wounds suffered in personal combat, Jackson's message to his soldiers was very different: "We are about to furnish these savages a lesson of admonition," for Americans "have borne with their insults, and submitted to their outrages." It was now time for "our vengeance," for it is "worthy the character of American soldiers, who take up arms to redress the wrongs of an injured country." This was the language of the duel enacted on a wider scale.[17] Although he warned, "we must not permit disorderly passions to tarnish [our] reputation," it was not from a perspective of maintaining the rules of war. Jackson expected discipline, yes, but not restraint against his enemies: "We must and will be victorious."[18]

All the while, Jackson, like many of the new generation, still invoked and measured himself against the founders: "How glorious will it be to remove the blots, which have tarnished the fair character bequeathed us by the fathers of our revolution!"[19] He saw himself as preserving America's reputation and his own honor. During the Revolution, officers recalled Emer de Vattel's warnings of "savage and monstrous excess," and Greene's arguments that "cruelty was dishonourable."[20] But for Jackson, his enemies were "inhuman," and he ordered, "If the enemy flee before us, we will overtake, and chastise him."[21] In other words, there would be no quarter; retreating warriors should expect no mercy—honor came through revenge and victory. Famed frontiersman Davy Crockett, then a soldier in the expedition, recalled that they "shot them like dogs."[22] In their wake, Jackson and his men left trails of dead Creek men, women, and children. The American reprisal was great; even Lieutenant Richard Call, an officer under Jackson, remembered being "heart-sick" as he saw that "cabins had taken fire, and half consumed human bodies were seen amidst the smoking ruins."[23] Jackson's treatment of the Seminoles during his invasion of Florida in 1818 was no better. Meanwhile, he seemingly infringed on virtually every rule of international relations and challenged long-held convictions of defensive war by crossing into Spanish territory and executing two British subjects whom he accused of "excit[ing]" the natives.[24]

In all these examples, Jackson ignored Greene's "rules of common justice," instead favoring his own interpretation of Vattel.[25] While focusing on the "ferocious," "savage," and "unprincipled" nature of his enemies, Jackson and his supporters loosely quoted the Swiss philosopher, concluding that when fighting against those who are "guilty" of "a violation of the laws of war," these opponents could be freely "chastised" in order to return them to "the laws of humanity." (Conveniently left out of their argument was Vattel's next line:

"But whenever severity is not absolutely necessary, clemency becomes a duty.")

Jackson's conduct in Florida even sparked the first major formal congressional inquiry, with fierce debate over the ethicality of his deeds. But he was not simply acquitted. Jackson left with his "merits," receiving "applause" and the "thanks of [his] country." Eaton later bragged, "General Jackson appeared better to understand national laws and principles, than members [of Congress] who were in reach of the library."[26]

Five years later Old Hickory stood before the president, receiving an award from the hands of another Revolutionary veteran—an award that had been first granted to General George Washington.[27] Jackson relished his connection to the Revolution. From his own brief service to proudly displaying Washington's pistols on his mantle, Jackson wished to embody the continuation of the Revolution.[28] But he was not Washington. This was a changing country with a changing vision of honor—one in which victory and glory outweighed ethics. His dueling was nonchalantly dismissed simply as "a private reencounter [chance encounter]" or not mentioned at all, his actions against the Creek were remembered for being a "brilliant attack," and his Florida excursion became an "exercise of the law of retaliation . . . necessary to the future safety of his fellow-citizens."[29] But above all, the memory of New Orleans shined like the gold medal in his hand. For his victory (though technically after the war) allowed America to claim, in the words of James Monroe, "that our Union has gained strength, our troops honor, and . . . a character and rank among nations, which we did not enjoy before."[30]

The ever-changing concept of honor had reverted back to one that was pre-Revolutionary in many respects, but one that also allowed diverse groups to plot their ascent in society. Jackson was both a part of and the symbol of the beliefs of a new generation. His admirers cast him at the head of a new pantheon, for, as one wrote to an aged John Adams, "in the generation that follows the Heroes and statesmen of the Revolution, General Andrew Jackson is a most distinguished character."[31] The next generation of youth in America could now look to Jackson, in much the same way that prior ones had viewed the founders. Jackson had "ambition," his 1817 biography proclaimed, "but it rests on virtue." His "ambition" was "regulated by a high sense of honor." For the founders, ambition was dangerous; men like Benedict Arnold and Aaron Burr were ambitious—and they had sacrificed the good of the nation for personal motivations. Now, Eaton continued, "the general, who meets and repeals his country's foes," is entitled to "ambition" and the "nation's gratitude," so long as "his character is marked by virtue" and he was "truly enobled." Ambition was no longer a vice. Honor and virtue remained as ideals of the individual and the nation, but they were no longer synonymous with ethics and morality. They illustrated the wavelike movement and constantly shifting definitions of honor and virtue that would continue for years to come. For Jackson was not alone in this interpretation—with him stood "the well-trained youths of our country, whose bosoms pant for glory."[32]

Notes

BFA	*The Autobiography of Benjamin Franklin*
CA	*The Chesapeake Affair of 1807*
CAF	*The Complete Anti-Federalist*
CMJB	*Proceedings of the General Court Martial Convened for the Trial of James Barron, Captain Charles Gordon, Mr. William Hook, Captain John Hall, of the United States' Ship Chesapeake, in the Month of January, 1808*
DGW	*The Diaries of George Washington*
DJA	*The Diaries of John Adams Digital Edition*
DLTH	*Diary and Letters of Thomas Hutchinson*
FO	"Founders Online: Correspondence and Other Writings of Six Major Shapers of the United States" (FO: [name abbreviation (see above list): AF, BF, AH, TJ, JM, GW])
HKP	Henry Knox Papers
HWC	Hannah Fayerweather Winthrop, Correspondence with Mercy Otis Warren
JBP	James Barron Papers
JCC	*Journals of the Continental Congress*
LDC	*Letters of Delegates to Congress, 1774–1789*
PAH	*The Papers of Alexander Hamilton Digital Edition*
PAJ	*The Papers of Andrew Jackson Digital Edition*
PBF	*The Papers of Benjamin Franklin Digital Edition*
PCL	*The [Charles] Lee Papers*
PGW	*The Papers of George Washington Digital Edition*
PHL	*The Papers of Henry Laurens*
PJA	*Papers of John Adams Digital Edition*
PJM	*The Papers of James Madison Digital Edition*
PNG	*The Papers of General Nathanael Greene*
PTJ	*The Papers of Thomas Jefferson Digital Edition*
WSA	*The Writings of Samuel Adams*
WW	*The Writings of George Washington*

LIBRARIES AND ARCHIVES

BU	John Hay Library, Special Collections, Brown University, Providence, RI
CU	Columbia University Archives, New York, NY
CWF	John D. Rockefeller Jr. Library, Colonial Williamsburg Foundation, Williamsburg, VA
DC	Rauner Special Collections Library, Dartmouth College, Hanover, NH
FSNL	Fred W. Smith National Library for the Study of George Washington, Mount Vernon, VA
HSP	Historical Society of Pennsylvania, Philadelphia, PA
HUA	Archives and Special Collections, Harvard University, Cambridge, MA
HUHL	Houghton Library, Harvard University, Cambridge, MA
LI	Archives, Lincoln's Inn, London, UK

LOC   Library of Congress, Washington, DC
MHS   Massachusetts Historical Society, Boston, MA
MT   Library and Archive, Middle Temple, London, UK
NA   National Archives, Washington, DC
NHM   Whitney Library, New Haven Museum, New Haven, CT
NJHS   New Jersey Historical Society, Newark, NJ
NYHS   New York Historical Society, New York, NY
NYPL   Manuscripts and Archives Division, Astor, Lenox, and Tilden Founda-
          tions, New York Public Library, New York, NY
PURBSC   Rare Books and Special Collections, Princeton University, Princeton, NJ
PUSML   Seely G. Mudd Manuscript Library, Princeton University, Princeton, NJ
RU   Rutgers University Archives, New Brunswick, NJ
SC   Friends Historical Library, Swarthmore College, Swarthmore, PA
SOCDC   Society of the Cincinnati, Washington, DC
UGA   Hargrett Rare Book and Manuscript Library, University of Georgia,
          Athens, GA
UPA   University Archives and Record Center, University of Pennsylvania,
          Philadelphia, PA
USMA   Special Collections and Archives, United States Military Academy,
          West Point, NY
UVA   Albert and Shirley Small Special Collections, University of Virginia,
          Charlottesville, VA
VHS   Virginia Historical Society, Richmond, VA
W&M   Earl Gregg Swem Library at the College of William and Mary, Special
          Collections Research Center, Williamsburg, VA
YUBL   Beinecke Rare Book and Manuscript Library, Yale University,
          New Haven, CT
YUMA   Manuscripts and Archives, Sterling Memorial Library, Yale University,
          New Haven, CT

A general note on spelling: Archaic and irregular spellings have been retained in quotations throughout; [*sic*] has been added to instances in which the variant spelling may
cause confusion for the reader.

Introduction

1. This narrative introduction is compiled from the following: JA to AA, 9 Oct. 1774,
AFC; 5 Sept. 1774, *DJA*; *AJA*, pt. 1; JA, [Notes of Debates in the Continental Congress, 6?
Oct. 1774], FO: AF; JA, [Notes of Debates in the Continental Congress], 8 Sept. [1774],
FO: AF; Godefroy, "Premiere assemblée du congress," [1782], LOC, also in Cresswell,
American Revolution in Drawings and Prints, 81; Peterson, "Carpenters' Hall"; Conti-
nental Congress to BF, William Bollan, Edmund Burke, Charles Garth, Arthur Lee,
Thomas Life, and Paul Wentworth, 26 Oct. 1774, FO: BF; Carpenter's Hall, "Virtual
History Tour"; William Bradford to JM, 17 Oct. 1774, FO: JM; 20 Oct. 1774, *JCC*,

https://memory.loc.gov/ammem/amlaw/lwjc.html, also in Ramsay, *Revolution of South-Carolina*, 1:254; "Declaration of Independence," NA. For an excellent overall account, see Beeman, *Our Lives, Our Fortunes*; elements paraphrased in this section: 41–42, 56, 59, 83–84, 147, 155–57, 161, 163.

2. For more on the European roots of honor and virtue, see Wyatt-Brown, *Southern Honor*; Fischer, *Albion's Seed*; and Bowman, *Honor*.

3. TJ to JA, 28 Oct. 1813, FO: TJ.

4. This book departs from the current historiography's discussions of honor in some notable ways. First, the current framework of the pathology of honor needs reexamination. Bertram Wyatt-Brown's primal honor conveys the violent side of honor. Joanne B. Freeman's discussion of dueling and politics in *Affairs of Honor* (2001) casts a darker view of honor. For Freeman, honor was static, "a source of stability in this contested political landscape" (xv). Both Wyatt-Brown and Freeman focus on the preservation of reputation, underemphasizing the ethics associated with honor and virtue. TJ's exaltation of internalized honor illustrates that there is a substantial gap in the historical literature. This book seeks out the inclusive components of honor, rather than its exclusive, hierarchical, or violent elements.

Second, works such as Charles Royster's *A Revolutionary People at War* (1979), Judith L. Van Buskirk's *Generous Enemies* (2002), and Caroline Cox's *A Proper Sense of Honor* (2004) all support the idea that the Continental army's officers engaged in an overt emulation of European honor and genteel culture, which degraded into a practice of trying to "'out-gentleman' the gentlemen" (Royster, *Revolutionary People at War*, 88, 208; Van Buskirk, *Generous Enemies*, 73–76; Cox, *Proper Sense of Honor*, 23). While correct for a very limited time period, this interpretation fails to address the Revolutionary changes that brought about a new openness of honor to those formerly outside its confines. Lower-class men, women, and African Americans became included in the language of honor as a result of the American Revolution. Simply focusing on the restrictive idea of gentility ignores the growing sense of egalitarian honor that is the basis of *American Honor*.

Third, previous authors have noted changes in the manifestations of honor—but with debatable results and diverse areas of inquiry. Richard L. Bushman's *Refinement of America* (1992) argues for a democratization of gentility (not specifically honor) among the middle class in the nineteenth century, but this view seems to place the change too late in time and only on external appearances, rather than on inner ethics and virtue (31, 61, 63–64). James Bowman also points to this change in the nineteenth century, with the Victorian era as the birth of "modernized" honor. While he notes shifts in honor culture in eighteenth-century Britain and America, he concludes that the Victorian "'Christian gentleman' [was conceived as] a man of honor yet one who owed allegiance to a universal and ethical and not just a local standard" (*Honor*, 5, 75–80). Bowman's Victorian gentleman bears all the same trappings that could be found in the character of GW nearly half a century earlier. The virtue and ethics of honor were of central importance to the American founders, and Bowman's instance on the modernity of Britain, with its monarchy and aristocracy, is puzzling.

Four, the current literature does not accurately define or even note many of the American variants of honor that are in several ways unique to a nonaristocratic Western nation. European studies, such as J. G. Peristiany's *Honour and Shame*, recognize that honor can be "inherited with the family name" (11). As stated previously, Bowman marks Victorian England as reversing this concept, but titles still remain. This directly contradicts BF's concept of ascending honor, which denies the value of such a notion. BF's and TJ's attacks on the ancestral membership of the Society of the Cincinnati, as further discussed in chapter 6, prove that American honor had become something different from its European counterpart. The two founders' ideas cannot be dismissed as mere social climbing or status seeking, as they both had attained eminent rank in the United States and Europe. Finally and most recently, Wyatt-Brown, in *Warring Nation* (2014), notes the continuation of "many versions of honor" and concludes that his book "has covered a limited range, leaving much still to be explored by others" (193). Other disciplines outside history have noted the changing nature of the concept and the links between morality and honor. For more, see Welsh, *What Is Honor?*, especially xv–xvi, 1–5.

5. Google Books' Ngram Viewer enables one to chart the use of words across publications from 1500 to 2008: Google Books Ngram, "ethics," 1500–2008, in American English; Google Books Ngram, "honour, honor, virtue," 1500–2008, in American English; Google Books Ngram, "honour, honor, virtue," 1500–2008, in English—before the 1840s, "honour" is the more common spelling.

6. Paine, *Common Sense*, 76.

7. Seymour, *Documentary Life of Nathan Hale*, xxx.

8. SA to James Warren, 12 Feb. 1779, in *WSA*, 4:124.

9. In Richardson, *Pamela*, Pamela resists the sexual advances of her employer, Mr. B, thus retaining her virtue. Her virtue is ultimately rewarded when they marry. In Richardson, *Clarissa*, Clarissa falls prey to the rakish Robert Lovelace, who rapes her, thereby robbing her of her virtue. She dies disgraced and unmarried.

10. Macaulay, *Immutability of Moral Truth*, 2.

11. Murray, *Selected Writings*, 9, 17, 24, 28–29, 37.

12. Rediker, *Villains of All Nations*, 76–77, 79, 101.

13. Bartram, *Travels*, 24, 113, 213, 490, 518.

14. Carver and Lettsom, *Travels*, 408, 412.

15. Behn, *Oroonoko*, 30.

16. Some of the African American slaves' conceptions of honor have African roots. For more, see Iliffe, *Honour in African History*.

17. Ibid., 119–39; Desch-Obi, *Fighting for Honor*, 111–21.

18. Douglass, *Narrative*, 7; Ball, *Fifty Years in Chains*, 263, 269, 270, 273, 277–78, 298–99.

19. Equiano, *Interesting Narrative*, 152, 267.

20. Douglass, *Narrative*, 102. For more on Frederick Douglass and honor, see Krause, *Liberalism with Honor*, 144–58.

21. Ball, *Fifty Years in Chains*, 224.

22. Linebaugh and Rediker, *Many-Headed Hydra*, 235.

23. Sterling Bland, *African American Slave Narratives*, 2:364, 366.

24. Jacobs, *Life of a Slave Girl*, 13.

25. Sterling Bland, *African American Slave Narratives*, 2:516.

26. James Roberts, *Narrative*, 9–10.

27. TJ to Benjamin Hawkins, 13 Aug. 1786, *PTJ*.

28. Venture Smith, *Narrative*, iii–iv.

29. "Declaration of Independence," NA.

30. 20 Oct. 1774, *JCC*, also in Ramsay, *Revolution of South-Carolina*, 1:254.

31. Wood, "History in Context."

32. For a discussion of the possible revival of the causation narrative, see Hattem, "Return of the American Revolution." For recent interpretations, see Slaughter, *Independence*, and Taylor, *American Revolutions*.

33. For more recent, varied interpretations, see Nash, *Urban Crucible* and *Unknown American Revolution*; Waldstreicher, *Runaway America*; Holton, *Forced Founders*; Breen, *Marketplace of Revolution*; and Jack P. Greene, *Constitutional Origins of the American Revolution*. For an older generation of scholarship, see Wood, *Creation of the American Republic*; Maier, *From Resistance to Revolution*; Bailyn, *Ideological Origins of the American Revolution*; Jensen, *Articles of Confederation*; and Knollenberg, *Origin of the American Revolution*. For examples of consequences, see Holton, *Unruly Americans*; Wood, *Radicalism of the American Revolution*.

34. Noll, *America's God*, 18.

35. Burstein, *Sentimental Democracy*, 23, 27, 86.

36. Beeman, *Our Lives, Our Fortunes*, 156.

37. Bourdieu, *Distinction*; Chabal and Daloz, *Cultural Troubles*; Daloz, *Rethinking Social Distinction*.

38. Hobsbawm and Ranger, *Invention of Tradition*, 1–2, 9–10.

39. Benedict R. O'G. Anderson, *Imagined Communities*, 3, 11.

40. J. L. Austin, *How to Do Things with Words*.

41. Kidd, *God of Liberty*, 8–9.

42. Noll, *America's God*, 3; Nathan O. Hatch, *Democratization of American Christianity*, 5–13.

43. Nathan O. Hatch, *Democratization of American Christianity*, 5; Kidd, *God of Liberty*, ch. 5; Marsden, *Jonathan Edwards*, 278, 464–69; Noll, "Common Sense Traditions," 218–20; Noll, "American Revolution and Protestant Evangelicalism," 619, 622–23; Carney, *Ministers and Masters*; Elder, *Sacred Mirror*; Gaustad, *Dissent in American Religion*, 12–13; James B. Bell, *War of Religion*, ch. 16.

44. Albanese, *Sons of the Fathers*, 5–10; Bellah, "Civil Religion in America"; Kidd, *God of Liberty*, 8–9.

45. Augustine, "Contra Faustum Manichaeum," bk. 22; Aquinas, *Summa Theologica*, pt. 2, question 40; Vattel, *Law of Nations* (1759), bks. 1, 2.

46. Vattel, *Law of Nations* (1759), bk. 1, 83.

47. Appiah, *Honor Code*.

48. See chapter 1.

49. For some British perceptions, see Matthew Carter, *Honor*, 4–5, 10, 14, 19; and Entick, *New Naval History*, 496.

50. JA, "Thoughts on Government," 27 Mar.–Apr. 1776, FO: AF.

51. Mandeville, *Enquiry into the Origin of Honour*, 43. For the connection to BF, see *BFA*, pt. 4.

52. For most of the past century, honor was studied almost exclusively within the framework of Virginia. Following on such representative regional studies as Louis B. Wright's *First Gentlemen of Virginia* (1940), future generations of historians continued this trend of placing honor and its manifestations firmly on Virginian soil. None of these early localized studies engaged honor outside the Chesapeake. What about honor in the rest of the South? How did honor manifest itself in the Northern areas? Thus, though these early studies of honor were effective, they were inherently limited in their reach due to these geographic confinements. A view of honor anywhere beyond Virginia remained unclear.

Wyatt-Brown's *Southern Honor* was the first monograph to explore honor outside the confines of Virginia. His monumental work introduced the concept of "primal honor," which is founded on Indo-European traditions of valor and bravery. Despite the book's title, it does much to transcend a regional framework and draw on European sources; it also marks the first introduction of the Northern colonies into the historiography—albeit indirectly. This initial form of Northern honor is framed by Pennsylvania Quakerism and New England Puritanism. Wyatt-Brown contends that these two religious groups were the "basic moral antithesis to the primal code [of honor]." He further states that Quakers "challenged the tenets of honor" in exchange for the "honor of truth" based on concepts of shame and self-denial (74–75). Thus, while not fully embracing the idea of Northern honor, Wyatt-Brown successfully managed to bring that very concept into the historiographical discussion.

Seven years later, David Hackett Fischer connected honor directly with Puritanism and Quakerism in *Albion's Seed* (1989). He agrees with Wyatt-Brown that Puritan and Quaker honor are fundamentally different from primal honor, but unlike *Southern Honor*, *Albion's Seed* supports the notion of Northern honor. For Fischer, these Northern forms of honor revolve around religion, a feature largely banished from studies of Southern honor. He reveals that Quaker honor is less hierarchical than both Southern and Puritan honor, but he manages to link Quaker, Puritan, and Anglican honor with the defense of reputation and the condemning, exclusionary power of shame associated with a loss of honor (Fischer, *Albion's Seed*, 188, 583–84; Wyatt-Brown, *Southern Honor*, 89–90).

In *Passion Is the Gale* (2008), Nicole Eustace uses honor in Pennsylvania as a subtheme to explore emotion. Her combination of honor and emotion—specifically anger—is comparable to that of Wyatt-Brown's primal honor. Eustace explains, "The mere display of resentment could in some cases be enough to recoup one's reputation. A man who declared that he resented another laid claim to honor." She further argues that honor could be applied to both colonial elites and commoners. In this respect,

Eustace is echoing Wyatt-Brown's declaration that "honor ... applied to all white classes. ... Few could escape it altogether." However, Eustace makes a firm departure from the Southern model and its ingrained concepts of deference and condescension. Instead she finds common ground with the anthropological thesis on Mediterranean honor advanced by Julian Pitt-Rivers that "a man is answerable for his honour only to his social equals." Eustace concludes, "Only an insult from another honorable person could threaten a man of honor." Eustace's Northern version of primal honor, for lack of a better term, seems to refute key principles of Wyatt-Brown's definition of "honor as immortalizing valor," an "opinion of other as an indispensible part of personal identity," and a "defense of male integrity." In part, this may be attributed to the Quaker influence in Pennsylvania, which "opposed anger unequivocally," indirectly contributing a sense of restraint more common to gentility. However, anger was still viewed by many Pennsylvanians as a viable and appropriate reaction to a slight of honor. Thus, honor in Pennsylvania proves interesting on two fronts. First, while others have typically argued that social hierarchy was less rigid in the North, Eustace's supposition that a slight of honor could only come from one of equal or greater rank seems to subvert this idea. Second, the fact that anger (and its outward manifestations) can be justified in defense of honor runs counter to the idea of Northern honor's religious foundation, as alluded to by Wyatt-Brown (Eustace, *Passion Is the Gale*, 160, 163, 164, 167, 189; Wyatt-Brown, *Southern Honor*, 34, 88; Peristiany and Pitt-Rivers, *Honor and Grace*, 31).

53. Ramsay, *History of the American Revolution*, 2:315.

54. National honor is another important concept that has not received adequate attention from the historical community. The prevalence of honor culture in foreign policy highlights the continued importance of national honor and its study. Works such as Donelan's *Honor in Foreign Policy* (2007), Barry O'Neill's *Honor, Symbols, and War* (1999), and *Honor among Nations* (1998), edited by Elliot Abrams and Donald Kagan, have added greatly to the literature on honor, as they have all advanced the idea that relations between states are dependent on an existence and perception of national honor. National honor has been a core value of American society since the eighteenth century. The influence of national honor on foreign policy also appears in Robert Dean's *Imperial Brotherhood* (2003) and Kristin L. Hoganson's *Fighting for American Manhood* (1998), among others, and the authors note the continuity of such a concept over time. Kagan also speaks of national honor as a driving force behind foreign policy since the time of Thucydides. He admonishes those who are dismissive of the role of honor in policy making: "Modern politicians and students of politics commonly call such motives irrational. But the notion that the only thing rational or real in the conduct of nations is the search for economic benefits or physical security is itself a prejudice of our time" (Kagan, "Our Interests and Our Honor," 42–45).

55. BF to Sarah Bache, 26 Jan. 1784, *PBF*; TJ to Peter Carr, 19 Aug. 1785, *PTJ*.

56. Benedict R. O'G. Anderson, *Imagined Communities*, 61. Warner, *Letters of the Republic*, 68; and Evarts B. Greene, "Revolutionary Generation," 324–27, also note the importance of print culture.

57. Shields, *Civil Tongues and Polite Letters*, 249.

58. McKeon, *Origins of the English Novel*, 156.

59. Burlamaqui, *Principles of Natural and Politic Law*, 83.

60. Kenneth S. Greenberg, *Honor and Slavery*, xi.

61. Rutherford, *Institutes of Natural Law*, 361.

62. Richardson, *Pamela*, 180.

63. Grasso, *Speaking Aristocracy*, 80.

64. Mandeville, *Enquiry into the Origin of Honour*, 2–3.

65. Pope, "Epistle II," in *Essay on Man*.

66. Jonathan Edwards [1703–58], *Essay on the Nature of True Virtue*, 1, 2, 44, 45, 48.

67. The concept that the definitions and understanding of honor are constantly changing is accepted in other disciplines. See Welsh, *What Is Honor?*, xv–xvi.

68. Wyatt-Brown, *Southern Honor*, 3, 4, 14, 64, 103.

69. *Essay on the Art of War*, 1.

70. Adam Smith, *Works*, 1:586–87.

71. "Mr. Rind Observe J. D Has Furnished You with Three Paper on the Small-Pox upon My Word, Sir, after Reading the First," *Virginia Gazette*, 15 Feb. 1770.

72. Aristotle, *Nicomachean Ethics*, 6–7, 205, 270.

73. JA to Skelton Jones, 11 Mar. 1809, FO: AF.

74. "For the Pennsylvania Herald: The Gander, No. 1," *Pennsylvania Herald*, 8 Sept. 1787. For other references to American alterations to classical understandings, see Pangle, "Federalists and the Idea of 'Virtue,'" 21–23; and Horwtiz, *Moral Foundations of the American Republic*, 63.

75. For a British acknowledgment of waning British governmental honor, the tendency for the truly honorable to be forced out of government service, and the lack of advancement based on merit, see *Man of Honour*, 3, 4, 8, 11, 12.

76. For an illustration of this point and a discussion of an earlier change in the concept of honor, see Home, *Essays upon Several Subjects*, 31.

77. Samuel Johnson Jr. [1757–1836], *School Dictionary*.

78. The dictionaries used in this section are as follows, in chronological order: Bailey, *Universal Etymological English Dictionary*; Dyche, *New General English Dictionary*; Samuel Johnson [1709–84], *Dictionary of the English Language*, 106; Noah Webster, *American Dictionary of the English Language*; Burstein, *Sentimental Democracy*, 167–68. According to Andrew Burstein, Webster wanted to establish new definitions to separate Americans from the British. This seems very consistent with Americans' adopting new understandings of honor and virtue.

79. Colley, *Britons*, 315–25; Robespierre, "Moral and Political Principles."

80. St. John de Crèvecœur, Letter 3 and Letter 4, in *Letters from an American Farmer*; Evarts B. Greene, "Revolutionary Generation," 340–438. Both sources discuss the creation of an American culture and identity.

81. Noah Webster, *American Dictionary of the English Language*.

82. Tocqueville, *Democracy in America*, ch. 17.

83. JA to TJ, 24 Aug. 1815, FO: AF.

84. Arthur Lee, *Second Appeal*, 21.

Chapter One

1. Livingston, *Franklin and His Press*, v, 1–6.

2. BF to Sarah Bache, 26 Jan. 1784, *PBF*.

3. *DGW*, 6:378; "II. The Diary Account," 14 Dec. 1799, *PGW*; Ellis, *His Excellency*, 269.

4. *BFA*, pt. 1.

5. Ibid.

6. Fischer, *Albion's Seed*, 188; Mather, *Magnalia Christi Americana*, bk. 2, 31–32.

7. Bunyan, *Pilgrim's Progress*, 111.

8. Ibid., 119.

9. Mather, *Essays to Do Good*, 39, 52–53.

10. Wood, *Americanization of Benjamin Franklin*, 30.

11. Mather, *Essays to Do Good*, 80.

12. Mather, *Magnalia Christi Americana*, bk. 3, 14, 32.

13. *BFA*, pt. 2.

14. Plutarch, *Plutarch's Lives*, 270, 41.

15. Ibid., 41.

16. Trolander and Tenger, *Sociable Criticism in England*, 168.

17. *BFA*, pt. 2.

18. Addison and Steele, *Spectator* (1714), 3:195.

19. Ibid., 3:129.

20. Duff, *Plutarch's Lives*, 194.

21. Shields, *Civil Tongues and Polite Letters*, 266–67.

22. Silence Dogood [BF], No. 1, 2 Apr. 1722, printed in the *New-England Courant*, *PBF*.

23. Silence Dogood [BF], No. 2, 16 Apr. 1722, printed in the *New-England Courant*, *PBF*.

24. Silence Dogood [BF], No. 4, 14 May 1722, printed in the *New-England Courant*, *PBF*. For mention of "Ethicks," see Silence Dogood [BF], No. 14, 8 Oct. 1722, printed in the *New-England Courant*, *PBF*.

25. "On Titles of Honor," 18 Feb. 1723, printed in the *New-England Courant*, *PBF*.

26. Addison and Steele, *Spectator* (1714), 3:194.

27. "On Titles of Honor."

28. *BFA*, pt. 1; Wood, *Americanization of Benjamin Franklin*, 22–23.

29. *BFA*, pt. 1.

30. Ibid., pt. 3.

31. Van Doren, *Benjamin Franklin*, 37.

32. *BFA*, pt. 3.

33. Ibid.

34. BF, "Blackamore, on Mollato Gentlemen," 30 Aug. 1733, *Pennsylvania Gazette*, reprinted in BF, *Writings*, 219.

35. *BFA*, pt. 3.

36. Ibid., pt. 4.

37. Van Doren, *Benjamin Franklin*, 51.

38. *BFA*, pt. 6.

39. Ibid.

40. Philadelphia Quaker Monthly Meeting Minutes, microfilm, SC.

41. Fischer, *Albion's Seed*, 583.

42. Edmund S. Morgan, *Benjamin Franklin*, 59.

43. *BFA*, pt. 6; Van Doren, *Benjamin Franklin*, 74–76.

44. Pope, "Epistle III," in *Essay on Man*. For more on Pope, BF, and the Junto, see Eustace, *Passion Is the Gale*, ch. 1.

45. *BFA*, pt. 6.

46. Ibid., pt. 7.

47. Ibid., pt. 9.

48. Ibid., pt. 10.

49. Ibid.

50. 14 Dec. 1742, *Pennsylvania Gazette*.

51. Ibid.

52. Richardson, *Pamela*, xxxv; Lepore, *Book of Ages*, 109–10; BF to Deborah Franklin, 22 Nov. 1757, *PBF*; For more on BF and *Pamela*, see Davidson, *Revolution and the Word*, 118.

53. *BFA*, pt. 10.

54. Ibid., pt. 9.

55. Ibid.

56. Ibid.

57. [BF], "Self Denial Is Not the Essence of Virtue," *Pennsylvania Gazette*, 18 Feb. 1734/5.

58. Ibid.

59. *BFA*, pt. 10.

60. Wyatt-Brown, *Southern Honor*, 14; Wood, *Americanization of Benjamin Franklin*, 36; *Oxford Universal Dictionary on Historical Principles*, s.v. "gentry."

61. On the European origins of honor, see Bowman, *Honor*; Stewart, *Honor*; and Wyatt-Brown, *Southern Honor*. For more on European honor, gentility, and civility, see Arditi, *Genealogy of Manners*.

62. Wright, *First Gentlemen of Virginia*, 5.

63. Longmore, *Invention of Washington*, 9; Isaac, *Transformation of Virginia*, 37.

64. Longmore, *Invention of Washington*, 2.

65. Kolp, *Gentlemen and Freeholders*, 34; Augustine Washington, "Will"; Deed for Ferry Farm, 7 Jul. 1748, *PGW*; Isaac, *Transformation of Virginia*, 131.

66. Isaac, *Transformation of Virginia*, 131; Wright, *First Gentlemen of Virginia*, 81.

67. Ellis, *His Excellency*, 9; GW to Lawrence Washington, 5 May 1749, *PGW*, notes; Isaac, *Transformation of Virginia*, 131.

68. Longmore, *Invention of Washington*, 6; GW, "School Exercises," [ca. 1744–48], in *WW*, 1:1–5, and *PGW*; Jack P. Greene, "Foundations of Political Power," 220.

69. Wright, *First Gentlemen of Virginia*, 81.

70. GW to David Humphreys, 25 July 1785, *PGW*.

71. Chernow, *Washington*, 11.

72. Hale, *Contemplations, Moral and Divine*, 15, 140, 358. Mary Washington and a young GW also interacted with Comber, *Short Discourses upon the Whole Common Prayer, Designed to Inform the Judgment and Excite the Devotion* (1, 7, 20, 27, 55, 152, 157–58, 161), which focuses on the religious links with honor and the supremacy of virtue.

73. Sayen, " 'Compleat Gentleman,' " 23–24; Appleton Griffin, comp., *A Catalogue of the Washington Collection in the Boston Athenaeum* (Boston: Athenaeum, 1897), cited in Longmore, *Invention of Washington*, 8. For more on genteel literature, see John E. Mason, *Gentlefolk in the Making*.

74. Bushman, *Refinement of America*, 32–33; Addison and Steele, *Spectator* (1714), 3:270.

75. Wright, *First Gentlemen of Virginia*, 283; Claude Rawson, introduction to *Tom Jones*, by Fielding, xiv; Wood, *Americanization of Benjamin Franklin*, 36–37; Chesterfield, *Letters*, 100, 114: although this volume was not published until 1774, the letters were being written during GW's youth to Chesterfield's son, who was the same age as GW, as noted in Sayen, "George Washington's 'Unmannerly' Behavior.' " Thus they could have been reflective of the type of advice GW would have received from Lawrence and the Fairfaxes. Bond, *Spectator*.

76. Chesterfield, *Letters*, 100, 114.

77. Ibid., 114.

78. Bushman, *Refinement of America*, 32; Richard Brookheiser, "Founding Father: Rediscovering George Washington," in GW, *Rules of Civility* (2003).

79. GW, *Rules of Civility*, 17.

80. Debate exists over how much influence the *Rules* had on GW, since they may have simply been an exercise in penmanship. See Morison, "Young Man Washington," 166; Longmore, *Invention of Washington*, 7; and Ellis, *His Excellency*, 9. At the very least, the *Rules* show that GW was aware of the genteel literature of the period.

81. Addison and Steele, *Spectator* (1733), 2:21, 72.

82. Fielding, *Tom Jones*, 84.

83. TJ to Robert Skipwith, 3 Aug. 1771, FO: TJ.

84. Fielding, *Tom Jones*, 83.

85. GW, *Rules of Civility*, rule 56, 20.

86. GW to John Augustine Washington, 28 May 1775, *PGW*.

87. *DGW*, 1:4. Thomas Fairfax was the sixth Baron Fairfax of Cameron. William Fairfax was the "crown's collector of customs for South Potomac, presiding justice of the Fairfax court, country lieutenant, and a member of the governor's council of Virginia." Sweig and David, *Fairfax Friendship*, 1. For more, see Kilmer and Sweig, *Fairfax Family in Fairfax County*; Stuart E. Brown Jr., *Virginia Baron*; Kolp, *Gentlemen and Freeholders*; and GW to Ann Fairfax Washington, [Sept.–Nov. 1749], GW to Thomas, Lord Fairfax, [Oct.–Nov. 1749], GW to Robin, [1749–50], *PGW*.

88. Ellis, *His Excellency*, 10.

89. Sweig and David, *Fairfax Friendship*, 2.

90. Addison and Steele, *Spectator* (1714), 3:283; Wyatt-Brown, *Southern Honor*, 99; Morison, "Young Man Washington," 168–72. For a general understanding of Stoicism, see John M. Cooper and J. F. Procopé, general introduction to *Moral and Political Essays*, by Seneca, xxiii–xxiv.

91. For references to Cato, see Fielding, *Tom Jones*, 178–79; and Chesterfield, *Letters*, 20. On the importance of classical scholarship and Roman virtue, see Chesterfield, *Letters*, 20–28; Bond, *Spectator*, 4:503; William Fairfax to GW, 13[–14] May 1756, *PGW*; and Longmore, *Invention of Washington*, 8. A GW-signed copy of Seneca's *Morals* is housed in the George Washington Library Collection, Boston Athenaeum. On GW's love of *Cato*, see Michael Novak and Jana Novak, *Washington's God*, 13; Morison, "Young Man Washington," 169; Longmore, *Invention of Washington*, 173–74; Litto, "Addison's Cato in the Colonies," 440–41.

92. Seneca, *Morals*, 135–36.

93. GW to Bushrod Washington, 15 Jan. 1783, in *WW*, 26:39; GW to Sarah Cary Fairfax, 25 Sept. 1758, *PGW*; Longmore, *Invention of Washington*, 173–74.

94. Seneca, *Morals*, 27–124; Sayen, "'Compleat Gentleman,'" 49; Wood, *Americanization of Benjamin Franklin*, 26; GW to John Augustine Washington, 28 May 1775, *PGW*.

95. Addison and Steele, *Spectator* (1714), 3:282.

96. *DGW*, 1:5; GW, "A Journal of My Journey over the Mountains," 11 Mar. 1747/8 [Mar. 1748], FO: GW; Longmore, *Invention of Washington*, 13. Lawrence Washington was a cofounder of the Ohio Company.

97. Lawrence Washington's position of adjutant general was divided among four districts and officers. Likely the sway of the Fairfaxes and his relation to Lawrence allowed GW to be "graciously" welcomed by the newly appointed Virginia governor, RD, in 1752. *DGW*, 1:34, 114. The Fairfaxes and Lawrence were linked to RD through the Ohio Company, political office, mutual acquaintances, and interactions with relations. Henriques, *Realistic Visionary*, 3.

98. GW originally received the unfavorable Southern District of Virginia, but through petition he gained control of his home district of the Northern Neck. GW to RD, 10 Jun. 1752, *PGW*, 1:50; William Nelson to GW, 22 February 1753, *PGW*, 1:55; Arthur N. Gilbert, "Law and Honour," 75; Fischer, *Albion's Seed*, 384; GW and RD, correspondence from 1754–1757, *PGW*.

99. Wood, *Americanization of Benjamin Franklin*, 59–60.

100. Holderness to RD, 28 Aug. 1753, Public Record Office, CO 5/211, quoted in *DGW*, 1:126; Longmore, *Invention of Washington*, 18; Henriques, *Realistic Visionary*, 3; "Journey to the French Commandant: Narrative, 1753–54," FO: GW; Legardeur de St. Pierre to RD, 31 Oct. 1753, in *DGW*, 1:151. GW delivered RD's letter to the French commandant Jacques Le Gardeur, Sieur de Saint-Pierre, but he was rebuffed.

101. Wyatt-Brown, *Southern Honor*, 46; Cox, *Proper Sense of Honor*, 39.

102. Addison and Steele, *Spectator* (1733), 7:89.

103. Fielding, *Miscellaneous Works*, 1:228; Wright, *First Gentlemen of Virginia*, 77; Wyatt-Brown, *Southern Honor*, 14; William Fairfax to GW, 26[–27] Apr. 1756, *PGW*.

104. Wright, *First Gentlemen of Virginia*, 77; Wyatt-Brown, *Southern Honor*, 14.

105. Royster, *Revolutionary People at War*, 207.

106. GW to Richard Corbin, Mar. 1754, in *WW*, 1:5.

107. Douglass Adair, *Fame and the Founding Fathers*, 10–15, links honor with fame and glory, which is accurate for the traditional connections, but he claims this connection remains throughout the Revolutionary era without any changes.

108. GW to RD, 18 May 1754, in *WW*, 1:50.

109. Ibid.

110. Ibid.; Wood, *Americanization of Benjamin Franklin*, 36, from James Reid, "The Religion of the Bible and Religion of K[ing] W[illiam] County Compared."

111. Journal, 27 May 1754, in *WW*, 1:56.

112. GW to David Humphreys, 25 Jul. 1785, in *WW*, 28:203.

113. Journal, 27 May 1754, in *WW*, 1:58; Henriques, *Realistic Visionary*, 7.

114. Ibid. For varying accounts based on new archival discoveries, see Preston, *Braddock's Defeat*, ch. 1.

115. Cox, *Proper Sense of Honor*, 39–40.

116. Mackay, who signed his name with this spelling, is referred to as Mackay, McKay, and MacKay in GW's letters. Longmore, *Invention of Washington*, 21. For more on Mackay, see Harden, "James Mackay."

117. GW to RD, 10 Jun. 1754, in *WW*, 1:75; GW to RD, 12 Jun. 1754, in *WW*, 1:81; Walne, "Mystery Resolved." On Mackay, see *PGW*, 1:77n6, 210n43, 360n1. For more on the British army dishonoring Americans, see Ramsay, *History of the American Revolution*, 1:196.

118. Longmore, *Invention of Washington*, 24. Regarding another reason for GW's troop movements, it is intriguing that GW chose to advance after receiving news of Colonel James Innes's commission as commander of both the regular and the colonial forces. GW to RD, 10 Jun. 1754, in *WW*, 1:75. It is difficult to imagine that GW was eager to surrender his superior status.

119. Colonel Joshua Fry died, promoting GW to colonel and acting Virginia regimental commander (June 4) until Colonel Innes arrived (June 20). GW to RD, 10 Jun. 1754, in *WW*, 1:75.

120. William Johnson to Goldsbrow Banyar, 29 Jul. 1754, *Papers of William Johnson*, 1:410 quoted in Henriques, *Realistic Visionary*, 6; Longmore, *Invention of Washington*, 24.

121. "II. Articles of Capitulation," [3 Jul. 1754], *PGW*; "I. Account by George Washington and James Mackay of the Capitulation of Fort Necessity," 19 Jul. 1754, *PGW*. Upon gaining a commission, GW instituted his own form of patronage, appointing his former fencing teacher, Jacob Van Braam, as his French interpreter. The "Articles of Capitulation" were poorly translated by Van Braam, proving extremely detrimental to GW's honor. On Van Braam as GW's fencing teacher, see Randall, *George Washington*, 76; Lossing, *The Home of Washington*, 53; "Journey to the French Commandant: Narrative, 1753–54," FO: GW (where he is referred to as Vanbraam); and Flexner, *George Washington: Forge of Experience*, 59 ("a Dutchman, Jacob van Braam, who advertised as a French teacher and whose knowledge of that language was at least attested to by the

badness of his English"). Van Braam's poor translation marked the first time that GW was undone by his personal devotion to patronage. For GW's defense of himself regarding the translation, see "Journal of the March to the Ohio, 1754," 31 Mar. 1754, in *WW*, 1:37n., where he is quoted from a letter, "GW to unknown recipient," as saying, "We were wilfully, or ignorantly, deceived by our interpreter in regard to the word assassination, I do aver, and will to my dying moment.... The interpreter ... called it the death, or the loss, of Sieur Jumonville." Also see "Duquesne to Sieur de Contrecoeur," 8 Sept. 1754, in *DGW*, 1:172; and Ellis, *His Excellency*, 17 (the French Marquis Duquesne calls GW the "epitome of dishonor").

122. Journal, 27 May 1754, in *WW*, 1:57; GW to RD, 29 May 1754, in *WW*, 1:68.

123. Journal, 27 May 1754, in *WW*, 1:57.

124. Flexner, *George Washington: Forge of Experience*, 107; also noted in Henriques, *Realistic Visionary*, 8, and Longmore, *Invention of Washington*, 23.

125. Henriques, *Realistic Visionary*, 8.

126. William Fairfax to GW, 5 Sept. 1754, *PGW*.

127. Henriques, *Realistic Visionary*, 9; Ellis, *His Excellency*, 18; GW to John Robinson, 23 Oct. 1754, GW to John Robinson and the House of Burgesses, 23 Oct. 1754, John Robinson to GW, 15 Sept. 1754, *PGW*.

128. RD to the Earl of Halifax, 25 Oct. 1754, in *WW*, 1:106.

129. GW to Sarah Cary Fairfax, 12 Sept. 1758, *PGW*.

130. Wyatt-Brown, *Southern Honor*, 39.

131. GW to William Fitzhugh, 15 Nov. 1754, *PGW*.

132. *BFA*, pt. 13.

133. Ibid., pt. 10.

134. Ibid., pt. 16.

135. Addison and Steele, *Spectator* (1733), 8:217.

136. Robert Orme to GW, 2 Mar. 1755, Robert Orme to GW, 3 Apr. 1755, *PGW*. For more on the British army in America, see Brumwell, *Redcoats*.

137. GW to William Byrd, 20 Apr. 1755, GW to Robert Orme, 15 Mar. 1754, GW to John Robinson, 20 April 1755, *PGW*.

138. For an excellent account of the battle, see Preston, *Braddock's Defeat*. Preston further illustrates the interconnection between the battle and many notable figures who gained prominence during the Revolution, including GW, BF, CL, Thomas Gage, HG, and Daniel Morgan.

139. GW to Mary Ball Washington, 18 Jul. 1755, *PGW*.

140. Fischer, *Albion's Seed*, 340–44.

141. GW to Robert Orme, 28 Jul. 1755, in *WW*, 1:154, notes.

142. GW to Sarah Cary Fairfax, 25 Sept. 1758, *PGW*.

143. GW to Warner Lewis, 14 Aug. 1755, in *WW*, 1:162.

144. Ibid., 1:163; George W. Fairfax to RD, 4 Sept. 1755, in Neill, *Fairfaxes of England and America*, 80; Longmore, *Invention of Washington*, 32.

145. GW to Augustine Washington, 2 Aug. 1755, *PGW*; Sayen, "'Compleat Gentleman,'" 65.

146. Adam Stephen to GW, 4 Oct. 1755, *PGW*, n. 6.

147. GW to RD, 5 Dec. 1755, *PGW*.

148. GW to RD, 14 Jan. 1756, in *WW*, 1:289. Sharpe supported Dagworthy; GW's claims were supported by many within Virginian society and government. GW to Lieutenant Colonel Adam Stephen, 28 Dec. 1755, in *WW*, 1:262; John Robinson to GW, 16 Dec. 1755, *PGW*.

149. Adam Stephen to GW, 18 Jan. 1756, *PGW*, n. 3; GW to Lieutenant Colonel Adam Stephen, 1 Feb. 1756, in *WW*, 1:294, notes.

150. GW to RD, 2 Feb. 1756, in *WW*, 1:296; GW to Lieutenant Colonel Adam Stephen, 1 Feb. 1756, in *WW*, 1:294.

151. Sayen, " 'Compleat Gentleman,' " 73.

152. William Shirley to GW, 5 Mar. 1756, *PGW*.

153. Lord Loudoun also replaced RD as governor of Virginia. Loudoun never traveled to Virginia, and GW's patron, now lieutenant governor, retained his executive powers in all but name. William Fairfax to GW, 13[–14] May 1756, *PGW*; RD to James Abercromby, 28 May 1756, in *WW*, 1:386, notes; Stuart E. Brown Jr., *Virginia Baron*, 141; William Fairfax to GW, 13[–16] Aug. 1756, *PGW*; GW to John Campbell, Earl of Loudoun, 10 Jan. 1757, *PGW*.

154. Sayen, " 'Compleat Gentleman,' " 99.

155. Henriques, *Realistic Visionary*, 11; Sayen, " 'Compleat Gentleman,' " 99, 97. Sayen questions GW's ability to balance civility with honor, however, for a gentleman, the defense of his rank, and therefore his honor, was of central importance. The loss of honor would have been the most regrettable fate to befall GW. GW to Warner Lewis, 14 Aug. 1755, in *WW*, 1:162; Mandeville, *Enquiry into the Origin of Honour*, 2–3; Pope, "Epistle II," in *Essay on Man*.

156. Seneca, *Morals*, 139.

157. Edmund S. Morgan, *Meaning of Independence*, 36. Morgan links "interest" with "honor."

158. Longmore, *Invention of Washington*, 45; GW, Address, 8 Jan. 1756, *PGW*; [Remonstrance of Officers of the Virginia Regiment to Governor Dinwiddie], 16 Apr. 1757, in *WW*, 2:26–27; Arthur N. Gilbert, "Law and Honour," 84.

159. GW, Address, 8 Jan. 1756, GW to RD, 3 Aug. 1757, *PGW*.

160. Orders, 8 Jan. 1756, in *WW*, 1:271.

161. For more on the changes in merit, see Kett, *Merit*, ch. 1.

162. William Fairfax to GW, 9 May 1756, 13[–14] May 1756, 17 Jul. 1757, 6 Aug. 1757, *PGW*.

163. William Fairfax to GW, 20 May 1756, *PGW*.

164. GW to RD, 17 Sept. 1757, RD to GW, 24 Sept. 1757, *PGW*.

165. Longmore, *Invention of Washington*, 47.

166. Wood, *Americanization of Benjamin Franklin*, 81.

167. BF, *Proposals*, 30.

168. Ibid., 29.

169. BF, "Blackamore, on Mollato Gentlemen."

170. *DGW*, vol. 1; Wood, *Americanization of Benjamin Franklin*, 40. For more on politics, see Kolp, *Gentlemen and Freeholders*; Wright, *First Gentlemen of Virginia*, 85–86; Bushman, *Refinement of America*, 47; and Giordano, *Social Dancing in America*, 72–80.

171. Shields, "George Washington," 148.

172. BF to Mary Stevenson, 25 Mar. 1763, *PBF*.

Chapter Two

1. Wood, *Americanization of Benjamin Franklin*, 18.

2. Roche, *Colonial Colleges*, 1–2, notes the relatively disproportionate ratio of college graduates in the First (one to four) and Second (one to three) Continental Congresses in relation to the general population (one to one thousand). Louis Leonard Tucker, "Centers of Sedition," 17–18, citing Arthur M. Schlesinger's *Birth of a Nation*, notes that roughly five out of six college graduates became patriots.

3. Papers of HUA, HUHL, W&M, YUBL, YUMA, UPA, CU, DC, RU, LI, MT, PUSML, PURBSC, BU, and so on; Waterhouse, *Discourse and Defence*, 112, 134, 148.

4. Opal, *Beyond the Farm*, 100–101.

5. *AJA*, pt. 1.

6. Ibid.

7. Ibid.; JA to Thomas Dawes, 28 Jul. 1821, FO: AF.

8. "To the Honorable, the General Assembly of His Majesty's Colony of Rhode Island," 4 Aug. 1763, Rhode Island College Miscellaneous Papers, BU.

9. Laws, 1783, Corporation Papers, 1:90–91, BU; 24 Sept. 1760, Board of Trustees Records [typescript copies, ca. 1900], PUSML.

10. On the secular perspective, see Roche, *Colonial Colleges*, 10, which notes that historical texts outnumbered theological ones in the Yale library by the Revolutionary era. Broderick, "Pulpit, Physics, and Politics," 55, 57, notes "an unmistakable tendency toward secularization" as early as 1749, and, by 1766, "secular issues predominated" at Princeton. For a connection between the Enlightenment and secularization more generally, see Winterer, *American Enlightenments*, 2, 224.

11. Shaftesbury, *An Inquiry concerning Virtue*, 3, 13.

12. Fiering, "Moral Philosophy in America," 101–5.

13. Hope, *Virtue by Consensus*, 83.

14. Adam Smith, *Theory of Moral Sentiments*, 438–39, 463.

15. Adam Smith, *Works*, 33, 101, 257, 278.

16. Fiering, "Moral Philosophy in America," 106–8.

17. Hutcheson, *Short Introduction to Moral Philosophy*, 1:3, 57.

18. William Beekman, Jr., Notebook, 1773, 11, 35, NYHS.

19. Hutcheson, *Short Introduction to Moral Philosophy*, 1:28.

20. Ibid., 1:28–29, 2:351.

21. Isaac Blauvelt to Rev. Jacob R. Hardenburgh, 7 Nov. 1787, Records of the Queen's College, Rutgers College and Rutgers University Board of Trustees: Manuscript

Minutes, Enclosures, and Subject Files, 1778–1956, RU; 27 Nov. 1800, Senatus Academicus Minutes, UGA.

22. Beekman, Notebook, 1773, 11, 21, 34, 35, Lectures I–V, NYHS.

23. John Witherspoon to Benjamin Rush, 9 Feb. 1768, John Witherspoon Collection, PURBSC; Correspondence, Records of the Queen's College, Rutgers College and Rutgers University Board of Trustees: Manuscript Minutes, Enclosures, and Subject Files, 1778–1956, RU.

24. Beekman, Notebook, 1773, 11, 21, 34, 35, Lectures I–V, NYHS; Noll, *Princeton and the Republic*, 48; Mailer, "Anglo-Scottish Union," 712.

25. Samuel Johnson [1696–1772], *Ethices Elementa*, 46.

26. Humphrey, *From King's College to Columbia*, 180.

27. Samuel Johnson to BF, 10 May 1750, BF to Samuel Johnson, 13 Sept. 1750, BF to Samuel Johnson, 2 Jul. 1752, FO: BF.

28. Humphrey, *From King's College to Columbia*, 178.

29. Green, "Lunatic Apostle," 53.

30. Shaftesbury, *Inquiry concerning Virtue*, 66.

31. Morison, *Three Centuries of Harvard*, 104; Kelley, *Yale*, 75–78; Bush, *Harvard*, 23; Humphrey, *From King's College to Columbia*, 196; Shipton, "Ye Mystery of Ye Ages Solved."

32. Alexander, *Samuel Adams*, 3.

33. Morison, "College Laws of 1655, 1692, and 1762 and College Customs 1734/5," 329.

34. "Orders for the Dining Room," Rhode Island College Miscellaneous Papers [digital versions], BU; "Orders & Customs," 24 Sept. 1760, Board of Trustees Records [typescript copies, ca. 1900], PUSML.

35. Kelley, *Yale*, 75.

36. 9 Sept. 1741, Yale University Corporation Records, YUMA.

37. 9 Nov. 1748, Board of Trustees Records [typescript copies, ca. 1900], 1:16, PUSML.

38. Morison, "Precedence at Harvard College," 373–76.

39. Roche, *Colonial Colleges*, 9.

40. Kathryn McDaniel Moore, "War with the Tutors," examines social status and dissent as the potential causes of student unrest.

41. Thomas Clap, "Some Observations Relating to the Government of Yale College," 1764, Records of Thomas Clap, YUMA.

42. 8 Jan. 1754, Faculty Judgments, YUMA.

43. Samuel Finley to Thomas Clap, 12 Dec. 1764, Records of Thomas Clap, YUMA.

44. Morison, *Three Centuries of Harvard*, 112.

45. 15 Aug. 1768, Faculty Judgments, YUMA; Burroll, William, Beebe, Lewis, Nicolas, James to whom it may concern, 25 May 1770, Rhode Island College Miscellaneous Papers [digital versions], BU.

46. 9 Nov. 1748, Board of Trustees Records [typescript copies, ca. 1900], 1:15, PUSML.

47. 9 Dec. 1763, College of William and Mary Faculty Minutes [transcripts], CWF; 23 Aug. 1775, Board of Trustees Records, DC.

48. "Rules for Conduct of Students," 8 Sept. 1756, Faculty of Yale College Records, YUMA.

49. 12 Sept. 1759, Faculty of Yale College Records, YUMA.

50. Samuel Goodrich to Henry Packer Dering, 13 Mar. 1780, Henry Packer Dering Correspondence, Early Yale Documents, YUBL.

51. "Rules & Ordinances for the Discipline & Good Government of the Students & Scholars," 10 Mar. 1761, Minutes of the Trustees, 1:131, UPA.

52. George Rapalje to the Governors of King's College, 21 Jul. 1774, Columbia College Papers, CU.

53. Student Ledgers, vol. B (1747–64), vol. D (1764–81), MT; Lincoln's Inn Admission Register; "The Judge's Orders, 1664," in *Records of Lincoln's Inn: Black Books*, 3:448–49; *Book of Constitutions and Orders*, no. 30; "18 Jun. 1741," in *Records of the Society of Gentleman*, 5. For more on Americans at the Inns of Court, see Flavell, *When London Was the Capital*, ch. 4.

54. Charter, 1769, Board of Trustees Records, DC.

55. Samuel Seabury to Samuel Johnson, 2 Nov. 1755, Columbia College Papers, CU.

56. Mar.–Aug. 1760, Board of Visitors Records, W&M.

57. "College Intrigues, or The Amours of Patrick [Pagan]," 18 Apr. 1766, Historical Subject Files, CU.

58. "Advertisement: . . . A New Tragic-Comedy Called the Blindman's Bluff or the Art of Abortion . . . ," 18 Apr. 1766, Historical Subject Files, CU; Humphrey, *From King's College to Columbia*, 200–202.

59. Robert Harpur to the Governors of King's College, 21 Jul. 1774, Historical Subject Files, CU.

60. 12 Dec. 1764, College Books, 128, HUA.

61. "Of Misdemeanors and Criminal Offences," 1767, Laws and Statutes of Harvard, HUA.

62. "Orders & Customs," 24 Sept. 1760, Board of Trustees Records [typescript copies, ca. 1900], PUSML; Esther Burr to Lucy Edwards, [ca. 1754], Aaron Burr (1716–1757) Collection, PURBSC; Humphrey, *From King's College to Columbia*, 83.

63. May "19 Thursday," 1756, *DJA*; JA to MOW, 8 Jan. 1776, *PJA*.

64. *DAJA*, 1751–55.

65. Faculty of Arts and Sciences Records, 3:152, 184, 251, HUA; "Duties of Rector," 11 Nov. 1701, Yale University Corporation Records, YUMA; Clap, "Some Observations."

66. Aaron Burr Sr., "Sermon," undated, Aaron Burr to Philip Doddridge, 31 May 1750, Aaron Burr (1716–1757) Collection, PURBSC.

67. Eleazer Wheelock to N. Whitaker, 17 Nov. 1771, Papers of Eleazer Wheelock, DC.

68. Morison, "College Laws of 1655, 1692, and 1762 and College Customs 1734/5," 329; "Concerning a Religious, Moral & Decent Conduct," Corporation Papers, 1:96–97, BU.

69. "April 28 [i.e. 29] Thursday, 1756," *DJA*.

70. Clap, "Some Observations."

71. "Tuesday [January 1759]," *DJA*.

72. Noll, "Common Sense Traditions," 221–22; Noll, *Princeton and the Republic*, 46–48, 51, 53, 58, 64, 66; Roche, *Colonial Colleges*, 2–13; Bailyn, *Education*, 63–66, 89, 106–8; Broderick, "Pulpit, Physics, and Politics," 43–44.

73. Faculty of Arts and Sciences Records, 3:323 [23?], 39, 47, 67, HUA.

74. "Orders for the Dining Room," Rhode Island College Miscellaneous Papers, BU.

75. "To the Honorable Trustees of Dartmouth College," 22 Aug. 1775, Board of Trustees Records, DC.

76. Augusta Academy, present-day Washington and Lee University, in Lexington, Virginia, was founded in 1749. Unfortunately, none of their early records have survived.

77. 10 May 1763, College of William and Mary Faculty Minutes [transcripts], CWF.

78. 15 Apr. 1769, College of William and Mary Faculty Minutes [transcripts], CWF.

79. "Statutes," 1736, College Papers Collection, W&M.

80. 15 Apr. 1769, College of William and Mary Faculty Minutes [transcripts], CWF.

81. 10 May 1763, College of William and Mary Faculty Minutes [transcripts], CWF; Godson et al., *College of William & Mary*, 89.

82. 14 Aug. 1760, Board of Visitors Records, W&M; Godson et al., *College of William & Mary*, 96.

83. Ganter, "William Small, Jefferson's Beloved Teacher," 505–11.

84. *Birmingham Gazette*, 27 Feb. 1773; Nathl. Jefferys to Mathew Bolton, 5 Jul. 1765, William Small Collection, W&M.

85. Article clipping, Folder 1, William Small Collection, W&M.

86. Randall, *Thomas Jefferson*, 22.

87. TJ to John Harvie, 14 Jan. 1760, *PTJ*.

88. Montesquieu, *Spirit of the Laws*, advertisement, 6–9.

89. Blackstone, *Commentaries*, 1:25; J. H. Baker, *Common Law Tradition*, 27.

90. Ronald Hoffman, ed., *Dear Papa, Dear Charley. . . .* 3 vols. (Chapel Hill: Published for the Omohundro Institute of Early American History and Culture, Williamsburg, Virginia, the Maryland Historical Society, Baltimore, and the Maryland State Archives, Annapolis, by the University of North Carolina Press, 2001), 1:1–2, 14, quoted in Flavell, *When London Was the Capital*, 86.

91. Imogene E. Brown, *American Aristides*, 35–36.

92. "Oration Pronounced at the Funeral of George Wythe," *Enquirer* (Richmond, VA), 17 Jun. 1790, George Wythe Collection, W&M.

93. [1758] *AJA*, also in FO: AF.

94. William Munford to John Coalter, 13 Jun. 1790, George Wythe Collection, W&M.

Chapter Three

1. Jonathan Boucher to John James, 10 Sept. 1763, Jonathan Boucher Papers, W&M; HL to Roger Moore, 14 Dec. 1747, HL to James Thomson, 7 Jun. 1748, HL to Grey Elliot, 21 Jan. 1764, in *PHL*, 1:88, 142, 4:140; Alexander Mackie to Col. Theodorick

Bland, 24 Feb. 1758, Bland Family Papers, VHS; Bailey, *Universal Etymological English Dictionary*, s.v. "honor" (one of the definitions for "honor" is credit).

2. GW to Robert Cary and Company, 10 Aug. 1764, *PGW*. For more on merchants and the language of honor, see Smail, "Credit, Risk and Honor."

3. GW to Robert Cary and Company, 10 Aug. 1764, *PGW*.

4. Middlekauff, *Glorious Cause*, 61–62.

5. Wyatt-Brown, *Shaping of Southern Culture*, 37–38; Wyatt-Brown, *Warring Nation*, 64–65.

6. James Otis, *Rights of British Colonies*, 27.

7. "Answer of the House of Representatives of Massachusetts to the Governor's Speech," 23 Oct. 1765, in *WSA*, 1:18–19.

8. "The Advantage of Independence," *Providence Gazette*, 19 Mar. 1768; "For the Pennsylvania Chronicle: The Visitant," *Pennsylvania Chronicle*, 25 Jan.–1 Feb. 1768.

9. Fragmentary Notes for "A Dissertation on the Canon and the Feudal Law," May–Aug. 1765, *PJA*.

10. Thomas Cushing and SA to Rev. G-W-, 11 Nov. 1765, in *WSA*, 1:31.

11. "A Dissertation on Canon and Feudal Law, No. 4," 21 Oct. 1765, *PJA*.

12. [Robert Beverly] to [William] Rind, Oct. 1768, Landon Carter papers, 1763–1774, VHS.

13. For similar findings on emotion "transcend[ing]" traditional "divisions," see Eustace, *Passion Is the Gale*, 387–88.

14. [Draft of a letter to the *Boston Gazette*, May 1761], FO: AF.

15. 23 Dec. 1765, *DAJA*.

16. " 'Cato' Denounces a 'Vile Miscreant,' " *Connecticut Courant*, 26 Aug. 1765, in Edmund S. Morgan and Helen M. Morgan, *Stamp Act Crisis*, 92.

17. Dulany, *Considerations*, 45–47.

18. Ibid. For the boycotts as producing virtue, see Edmund S. Morgan, "Puritan Ethic," 8–9.

19. Edmund S. Morgan and Helen M. Morgan, *Stamp Act Crisis*, 87.

20. Arthur Lee, *Appeal*, 30.

21. Virginia Nonimportation Resolves, 22 Jun. 1770, *PTJ*.

22. Article signed "Populus," *Boston Gazette*, 28 Aug. 1769, in *WSA*, 1:379.

23. James Otis, *Rights of British Colonies*, 4.

24. MOW, *History of the Rise*, 1:68. For more on the connection between women, politics, and economics, see Hartigan-O'Connor, *Ties That Buy*, ch. 6.

25. MOW, *History of the Rise*, 1:68.

26. [Griffitts,] "Patriotic Poesy," 307–8.

27. Dexter, *Literary Diary of Ezra Stiles*, 1:53; "Journal of the Times," *Essex Gazette*, 20 May 1769.

28. Kerber, *Women of the Republic*, 41.

29. MOW, "To the Hon. J. Winthrop, Esq.," [1774], in *Poems, Dramatic and Miscellaneous*, 210.

30. Winterer, *Mirror of Antiquity*, 12–67.

31. Berkin, *Revolutionary Mothers*, 14–25; Middlekauff, *Glorious Cause*, 190–91, 194.

32. Alfred F. Young, *Masquerade*, 37–40.

33. "The Following Agreement . . . ," *Boston Evening Post*, 12 Feb. 1770.

34. Robert Pleasants to Charles Pleasants, 22 Aug. 1774, Robert Pleasants Letterbook, W&M.

35. 29 Apr. 1769, HWC.

36. Bloch, "Gendered Meanings of Virtue," 45; Bloch, *Gender and Morality*, ch. 7.

37. 1 Jan. 1774, HWC.

38. Withington, *Toward a More Perfect Union*, ch. 8, contends that those who failed to comply were viewed as guilty of failing morally and could be subjected to violence.

39. Arthur Lee to Dr. Theodorick Bland, 21 Aug. 1770, Bland Family Papers, VHS.

40. Article signed "Determinatus," *Boston Gazette*, 8 Jan. 1770, in *WSA*, 2:6.

41. GW to Robert Cary and Co., 20 Sept. 1765, *PGW*.

42. Bailyn, *Ordeal of Thomas Hutchinson*, 51.

43. 31 Aug. 1774, *DLTH*, 232.

44. Hosmer, *Life of Thomas Hutchinson*, 3.

45. Bailyn, *Ordeal of Thomas Hutchinson*, 15.

46. Ibid., 12; Jonathan Belcher to Francis Harrison, 27 Jun. 1734, *Collections of the Massachusetts Historical Society*, 6th ser., 1894, 7:77, quoted in ibid.

47. Bailyn, *Ordeal of Thomas Hutchinson*, 258.

48. "Boston, November 11," *Boston Evening Post*, 11 Nov. 1765; "Boston," *Boston Gazette*, 11 Nov. 1765; George P. Anderson, "Ebenezer Mackintosh," 26, 29, 30, 33, 55; Oliver, *Origin & Progress*, 55. Another shoemaker, George R. T. Hewes, was also among the crowd, and his family also possessed a sense of honor. Thatcher, *Traits of the Tea Party*, 17, 68.

49. Gov. Bernard to Lord Halifax, 15 Aug. 1765, in Edmund S. Morgan and Helen M. Morgan, *Stamp Act Crisis*, 106–7. For more on riots and mobs, see Benjamin L. Carp, *Rebels Rising*; and Bourne, *Cradle of Violence*.

50. Andrew Oliver to Thomas Pownall, 19 Sept. 1768, in *DLTH*, 165–66n.

51. Bailyn, *Ordeal of Thomas Hutchinson*, 68–69.

52. TH to Richard Jackson, 30 Aug. 1765, in Edmund S. Morgan and Helen M. Morgan, *Stamp Act Crisis*, 108–9.

53. Chauncy, *Discourse*, 138.

54. HL to Joseph Brown, 22 Oct. 1765, in *PHL*, 5:27.

55. JD, *Address*, i–ii.

56. Eustace, *Passion Is the Gale*, 409–11.

57. JD, *Address*, i–ii.

58. Salem Monthly Meeting, Misc. Papers, 1702–1897, SC; Philadelphia Quaker Yearly Meetings, SC.

59. Fauquier to Lords of Trade, 3 Nov. 1765; House of Lords Manuscripts, 27 Jan. 1766, quoted in Edmund S. Morgan and Helen M. Morgan, *Stamp Act Crisis*, 182, 180–204.

60. Gipson, *Jared Ingersoll*, 233.

61. Roger Sherman to Sheriff of New Haven, 31 Jan. 1766, Teley Blaksele and John Wise [grand jurors] to Roger Sherman, 31 Jan. 1766, Warrant, 3 Feb. 1766, BAP, NHM; Gipson, *Jared Ingersoll*, 234.

62. HL to Joseph Brown, 11 Oct. 1765, in *PHL*, 5:24.

63. HL to Joseph Brown, 28 Oct. 1765, in *PHL*, 5:29.

64. V. "U" to the *Boston Gazette*, 1 Aug. 1763, FO: AF.

65. Zubly, *Stamp Act Repealed*, 21. For more, see Joseph Locke, "Compelled to Dissent."

66. Chauncy, *Discourse*, 138.

67. Article signed "Candidus," *Boston Gazette*, 9 Sept. 1771, in *WSA*, 2:205.

68. JD, *Letters from a Pennsylvania Farmer*, Letter 3, 25, Letter 7, 118.

69. Seabury, *Free Thoughts*, 11–15.

70. MOW, *History of the Rise*, 1:69–70.

71. "Number II," *Essex Journal*, 8 Mar. 1775.

72. Otis, "Advertisement," 4 Sept. 1769, *Boston Gazette*.

73. *Boston Gazette*, 11 Sept. 1769, 2; *Boston Gazette*, 18 Sept. 1769, 1; *Boston Gazette*, 25 Sept. 1769.

74. *Boston Gazette*, 11 Sept. 1769, 2; *Boston Gazette*, 18 Sept. 1769, 1; *Boston Gazette*, 25 Sept. 1769.

75. MOW to James Otis Jr., ca. 10 Sept. 1769, in *Mercy Otis Warren: Selected Letters*, 3–4.

76. Ibid., 4.

77. Article signed "Vindex," *Boston Gazette*, 31 Dec. 1770, in *WSA*, 2:116n2.

78. *Short Narrative*, 17.

79. "Draft Instructions of Boston to Its Representatives in the General Court," 8 May 1769, FO: AF.

80. Quincy, *Memoir of the Life of Josiah Quincy, Junior*, 28.

81. "Adams' Minutes of Josiah Quincy's Opening for the Defense," 29 Nov. 1770, FO: AF.

82. "Josiah Quincy's Argument for the Defense," 3 Dec. 1770, FO: AF.

83. 5 Mar. 1773, *DAJA*.

84. Ramsay, *History of the American Revolution*, 1:92: "The result of the trial reflect great honour on John Adams, and Josiah Quincy . . . and also on the integrity of the jury, who ventured to give an upright verdict."

85. BF to Peter Collinson, 30 Apr. 1764, *PBF*.

86. *The Examination of Doctor Benjamin Franklin* in FO: BF and *Collection of Interesting, Authentic Papers*, 74.

87. Wood, *Americanization of Benjamin Franklin*, 107–8.

88. Ibid., 140.

89. BF to Thomas Cushing, 2 Dec. 1772, *PBF*.

90. Wood, *Americanization of Benjamin Franklin*, 269n93; Bailyn, *Ordeal of Thomas Hutchinson*, 237.

91. TH to Thomas Whately, 20 Oct. 1769, "Appendix: The Hutchinson Letters," *PBF*.

92. TH to Thomas Whately, 20 Jan. 1769, "Appendix: The Hutchinson Letters," *PBF*.

93. *On Wednesday June 16, 1773*, 5–6.

94. TH to Sir Francis Bernard, 9 Mar. 1774, in *DLTH*, 130–31.

95. Andrew Oliver to William Whately, 1 Jun. 1773, in *DLTH*, 83–84.

96. Seitz, *Famous American Duels*, 52–69.

97. "A Letter from London," [ca.] 7 Feb. 1774, in *Boston Gazette*, 25 Apr. 1774, *PBF*.

98. "The Final Hearing before the Privy Council Committee . . . ," 1774, FO: BF.

99. Anthony Todd to BF, 31 Jan. 1774, *PBF*; BF to William Franklin, 2 Feb. 1774, FO: BF.

100. "William Whately's Chancery Suit: II. Franklin's Answer," 19 Apr. 1774, *PBF*.

101. "A Letter from London," [ca.] 7 Feb. 1774, in *Boston Gazette*, 25 Apr. 1774; BF to Thomas Cushing, 15[–19] Feb. 1774, *PBF*.

102. BF to Joseph Galloway, 18 Feb. 1774, *PBF*.

103. "A Letter from London," [ca.] 7 Feb. 1774, in *Boston Gazette*, 25 Apr. 1774, *PBF*; also quoted in *DLTH*, 124.

104. "A Letter from London," [ca.] 7 Feb. 1774, in *Boston Gazette*, 25 Apr. 1774, *PBF*.

105. JA to AA, 6 Jul. 1774, *AFC*.

106. "Extracts . . . Court of Vice Admiralty," in *PHL*, 6:iii; David Duncan Wallace, *Life of Henry Laurens*, 137–49.

107. Middlekauff, *Glorious Cause*, 173.

108. 27 Sept. 1774, HWC.

109. Arthur Lee to JD, 26 Aug. 1769, R. R. Logan Collection of John Dickinson Papers, HSP.

110. Montesquieu, *Spirit of the Laws*, bk. 3. Also see Montesquieu, *Spirit of the Laws* (1762). For more on Montesquieu and honor, see Krause, *Liberalism with Honor*, 32–66; Welsh, *What Is Honor?*, ch. 7. Loyalist honor was linked to loyalty to the king: S. Edward to [Boyce], 8 Nov. 1775, Committee of Safety Papers, CWF. For further use of the language of honor by loyalists, see American Loyalists Collection, NYPL.

111. Montesquieu, *Spirit of the Laws*, bk. 1, 33.

112. Krause, *Liberalism with Honor*, 33.

113. John Locke, *Two Treatises of Government*, secs. 222–23, 237, 239.

114. Kidd, *God of Liberty*, 80.

115. JA to Samuel Osgood, 15 Nov. 1775, *LDC*.

116. Samuel Ward to Samuel Ward Jr., 9 Sept. 1774, SA to the Boston Committee of Correspondence, 14 Sept. 1774, Richard Henry Lee to William Lee, 20 Sept. 1774, Richard Henry Lee to Francis Lightfoot Lee, 21 May 1775, *LDC*.

117. [Notes of Debates in the Continental Congress, 6 September 1774], FO: AF.

118. Duché, *Duty of Standing Fast*, 18.

119. JA to Josiah Quincy Jr., 18 Sept. 1774, *PJA*; Withington, *Toward a More Perfect Union*, 13–17. Examining the Congress's creation of moral laws against vice, Ann Fairfax Withington finds that "the process of abiding by the moral code made colonists aware of themselves as a people, a people with a character" (16).

120. TJ to John Randolph, 25 Aug. 1775, *PTJ*.

121. Vattel, *Law of Nations* (1759), bk. 2, 53; [Lambert], *New System of Military Discipline*, 249.

122. Fischer, *Paul Revere's Ride*, 184–201.

123. "I. Jefferson's Composition Draft," [26 Jun.–6 Jul. 1775], *PTJ*.

124. MOW to Sarah Brown Bowen, Apr. 1775, in *Mercy Otis Warren: Selected Letters*, 47.

125. "III. John Dickinson's Composition Draft," "IV. Declaration as Adopted by Congress," 6 Jul. 1775, *PTJ*. For more, see U.S. Continental Congress, *Declaration by the Representatives*, 9–10.

126. Virginia Resolutions on Lord North's Conciliatory Proposal, 10 Jun. 1775, *PTJ*.

127. Ibid.

128. Petition to the King [Olive Branch Petition], 1775, R. R. Logan Collection of John Dickinson Papers, HSP; Thomas Johnson Jr. to HG, 14 Dec. 1774, *LDC*.

129. U.S. Continental Congress, *Declaration by the Representatives*, 11.

130. Vattel, *Law of Nations* (1759), bk. 1, 23.

131. Kidd, *God of Liberty*, 83. For Anglican loyalism as a matter of honor, see Jonathan Boucher to John James, 7 Jan. 1776, Jonathan Boucher Papers, W&M.

132. Paine, *Common Sense*, 19.

133. Ibid., 35.

134. Ibid., 42.

135. SA to Samuel Cooper, 3 Apr. 1776, in *WSA*, 3:276.

136. Paine, *Common Sense*, 60–61. For a counterpoint, see [Chalmers], *Plain Truth*, 76, 88, which supports a reconciliation with Britain but still argues that honor and virtue "guide" and need to continue shaping the American cause for "the eyes of all Europe are upon us."

137. Robert Morris to Joseph Reed, 21 Jul. 1776, *LDC*.

138. JD to Samuel Ward, 21 Jan. 1775, *LDC*.

139. "Epistle," 9 Sept.–1 Oct. 1774, reprinted in 27 Jun. 1776, Philadelphia Quaker Yearly Meetings, SC.

140. JD, *Letters from a Pennsylvania Farmer*, Letter 3, 28.

141. "John Dickinson's Notes for a Speech in Congress," 1 Jul. 1776, *LDC*.

142. Dexter, *Literary Diary of Ezra Stiles*, 2:182–83.

143. Jacobson, *John Dickinson and the Revolution*, 118; "Appendix V. Mr. Dickinson's Vindication: Of His Career during the Revolution," in Stillé, *Life of John Dickinson*, 364–414.

144. "Declaration of Independence," NA.

145. MOW, *History of the Rise*, 1:310.

Chapter Four

1. MOW to JA, 10 Mar. 1776, *PJA*.

2. AA to JA, 17 Sept. 1775, *AFC*.

3. Vattel, *Law of Nations* (1759), bk. 1, 83.

4. John Adams' Notes on Debates, 27 Oct. 1775, *LDC*.

5. Samuel Chase to James Duane, 5 Feb. 1775, *LDC.*

6. GW to Brigadier General John Thomas, 23 Jul. 1775, in *WW*, 3:359.

7. Fischer, *Albion's Seed*, 397; General Orders, 7 Jul. 1775, in *WW*, 3:314.

8. JA to William Tudor, 14 Nov. 1775, *PJA*; Benjamin Rush's Notes for a Speech in Congress, 1 Aug. 1776, *LDC*; Hitchcock, *Diary of Enos Hitchcock*, 190.

9. William Hooper to Joseph Hewes and John Penn, 6 Feb. 1776, *LDC.*

10. Samuel Ward to Henry Ward, 31 Dec. 1775, *LDC.*

11. For more, see Royster, *Revolutionary People at War*, 25–53.

12. Simes, *Military Guide for Young Officers*, 2:186.

13. HK to Lucy Knox, 7 Jul. 1775, HKP.

14. BA to Major Skene, 11 May 1775, BAP, NHM.

15. Athenian Society, 29 Jun. 1776, Elizabeth R. Boyd Historical Collection on Rutgers University, RU. For more on colleges during the Revolution, see Roche, *Colonial Colleges*; and Louis Leonard Tucker, "Centers of Sedition."

16. GW to MW, 18 Jun. 1775, in *WW*, 3:293–94; GW to the Officers of Five Virginia Independent Companies, 20 Jun. 1775, *PGW.*

17. GW to MW, 18 Jun. 1775, in *WW*, 3:294.

18. Acceptance of Appointment as General and Commander in Chief, 16 Jun. 1775, in *WW*, 3:292–93.

19. GW to Lieutenant General Thomas Gage, 20 Aug. 1775, General Orders, 10 Dec. 1775, *PGW.*

20. GW to John Banister, 21 Apr. 1778, in *WW*, 11:289.

21. Thomas Cushing to James Bowdoin, Sr., 21 Jun. 1775, in *LDC*, 1:531; Fischer, *Albion's Seed*, 396.

22. Richard Henry Lee's Motion for Quitting the Town of Boston, 7–8[?] Oct. 1774, *LDC.*

23. Twohig, " 'That Species of Property,' " 120.

24. GW to Sarah Cary Fairfax, 12 Sept. 1758, *PGW.*

25. GW to Major Christopher French, 26 Sept. 1775, *PGW.*

26. For references to "national honor," see GW to the Secretary for Foreign Affairs, 29 Mar. 1783, in *WW*, 26:267; GW to AH, 31 Mar. 1783, in *WW*, 26:277; GW to the Mayor, Recorder, Alderman, and Common Council of the City of Richmond, 15 Nov. 1784, in *WW*, 27:496; GW to the House of Representatives, 8 Jan. 1790, in *WW*, 30:495; and Edmund S. Morgan, *Meaning of Independence*, 36–37. While Morgan is correct to note that there is a shift toward supporting the nation, he again links interest with honor, but GW's use of the term illustrates a selflessness that would not be consistent with the term. For Morgan, interest, particularly in regard to service, suggests something mutually beneficial. This seems to speak to the older conception of personal honor, which GW would have experienced at the start of the French and Indian War. By the Revolution, to be truly honorable and virtuous was to be disinterested. At this point GW's honor was synonymous with ethics and duty.

27. Phelps, "Republican General," 168.

28. Cox, *Proper Sense of Honor*, 21; Wyatt-Brown, *Shaping of Southern Culture*, 43; GW to Colonel Fisher Gay, 4 Sept. 1776, in *WW*, 6:13; Murrin, "Anglicizing an American Colony," 96.

29. GW to John Hancock, 24 Sept. 1776, GW to a Continental Congress Camp Committee, 29 Jan. 1778, *PGW*.

30. GW to Patrick Henry, 5 Oct. 1776, *PGW*. For a similar sentiment, see GW to Colonel George Baylor, 9 Jan. 1777, *PGW*; and Van Buskirk, *Generous Enemies*, 76.

31. Gruber, *Books and the British Army*, 65. For the British perspective, see ibid.; the book also offers extensive indexes of the libraries of British military officers. Many of the preferred books of Gruber's officers are those discussed in this chapter as influential texts for the Continental army.

32. Waterhouse, *Discourse and Defence*, 101.

33. Stevenson, *Military Instructions for Officers*, 53.

34. Watson, *Military Dictionary*, s.v. "honor."

35. Waterhouse, *Discourse and Defence*, 213.

36. Segar, *Honor Military, and Ciuill [Civil]*, 2.

37. *Antient Policy of War*, 17.

38. Wolfe, *General Wolfe's Instructions to Young Officers*, 54.

39. Stevenson, *Military Instructions for Officers*, 37.

40. Bland, *Treatise of Military Discipline*, 68. For the GW connection, see GW, "An Inventory of the Estate of Lawrence Washington, Esq.," 7–8 Mar. 1753, FSNL. GW would have personally been familiar with Bland for some time, as his brother Lawrence owned a copy. For popularity, see Gruber, *Books and the British Army*, 149–50. Bland's book went through nine editions, and 37.5 percent of the British officers studied owned more than one copy.

41. Middlekauff, *Glorious Cause*, 303–4.

42. Simes, *Military Guide for Young Officers*, 2:237.

43. "Regimental Minutes 1777 under General Gates," 6 Sept. 1777, Larned Family Papers, vol. 3, HSP. For background on the perception of citizen soldiers, see Snyder, *Citizen-Soldiers and Manly Warriors*, 17–32, which examines the linkage between citizens' service as soldiers, virtue, and the common good. Supporting the common good led to "greatness," whereas self-interest was akin to wickedness.

44. [Hanway], *Soldier's Faithful Friend*, 13–14.

45. 1 Aug. 1776, Nathaniel Heard's Brigade, NJ Militia, Record Book, NJHS.

46. Sermon or address to "Gentlemen Soldiers," [Dec. 1775?], Manuscript Collection, FSNL.

47. Apr. 1776, Extracts from the Orderly Book of Colonel Dayton's Battalion, Ebenezer Elmer, Journals, 1776–1785, NJHS.

48. 19 Mar. 1776, Virginia Militia, 5th Regiment, Order Book, 1776, Kept by Capt. George Stubblefield, VHS.

49. See Hitchcock, *Diary of Enos Hitchcock*, 132, 189, 190, 215, for remarks by Wayne and from general orders.

50. Grandmaison, *Treatise on the Military Service*, 24.

51. NG to Deputy Governor Nicholas Cooke, 22 Jun. 1775, in *PNG*, 1:89–90. On religion and morals, see NG to HK, 14 Apr. 1782, in *PNG*, 11:60–62.

52. Gen. Greene's Orders, 4 Jun. 1775, in *PNG*, 1:84–85.

53. Jeney, *Partisan*, 31. For more, see Kidd, *God of Liberty*, ch. 5.

54. Hitchcock, *Diary of Enos Hitchcock*, 106.

55. John Howard to HK, 14 May 1776, HKP.

56. William Hooper to Samuel Johnston, 26 Sept. 1776, *LDC*. For the differences between martial and civilian understanding, see *Essay on the Art of War*, 518.

57. Bland, *Treatise of Military Discipline*, 114; L'Estrange, *Seneca's Morals by Way of Abstract*, 62, which also allows for honor in defeat if the general "dischar'd all the parts of a prudent Commander."

58. Bland, *Treatise of Military Discipline*, 124.

59. North Carolina Delegates to the North Carolina Council of Safety, 18 Sept. 1776, *LDC*.

60. Benjamin Rush to Thomas Morris, 22 Oct. 1776, *LDC*.

61. Frederick the Great, *Instructions for His Generals*, 44.

62. Chernow, *Washington*, 208. For a basis in military texts, see Cavan, *New System of Military Discipline*, 278 ("Nothing proclaims more the reputation of an officer, than a judicious retreat"); and *Essay on the Art of War*, 518.

63. Isaac, *Transformation of Virginia*, 131; GW to the President of the Congress, 24 Sept. 1776, in *WW*, 6:108–9.

64. Petition to HK, 27 Sept. 1776, HKP.

65. GW to Jonathan Trumbull Sr., 18 Jul. 1775, *PGW*.

66. NG to Jacob Greene, 28 Jun. 1775, in *PNG*, 1:92–94.

67. HK to LK, 7 Jul. 1775, HKP.

68. Petition to HK, 27 Sept. 1776, HKP.

69. For example, see the work of Caroline Cox and Charles Royster.

70. JA to NG, 22 Jun. 1776, in *PNG*, 1:238–40; JA to Joseph Ward, 20 Aug. 1776, *LDC*.

71. SA to Elbridge Gerry, 29 Oct. 1775, *LDC*.

72. "A Bill for the More General Diffusion of Knowledge," 18 Jun. 1779, FO: *PTJ*.

73. JA to NG, 22 Jun. 1776, in *PNG*, 1:238–40.

74. For more on Lee and rank, see Lender and Stone, *Fatal Sunday*, 106–9.

75. HK to William Knox, 25 Sept. 1775, HKP.

76. Dr. Benjamin Rush to HK, 30 Jan. 1777, HKP.

77. Cecelia Shee to John Parke, 16 Aug. 1775, 21 Aug. 1775, 30 Sept. 1775, 2 Oct. 1775, 27 Oct. 1775, 13 Dec. 1775, [Jul. 1776?], Shee Family Papers, HSP.

78. Von Steuben, *Regulations*, 129.

79. General Orders, 23 Aug. 1776, *PGW*.

80. Wyatt-Brown, *Shaping of Southern Culture*, 50. For more on GW and slavery, see Philip D. Morgan and Nicholls, "Slave Flight"; Philip D. Morgan, " 'To Get Quit of Negroes' "; Henriques, *Realistic Visionary*, 145–65; Philip D. Morgan, *Slave Counterpoint*; Hirschfeld, *George Washington and Slavery*; Twohig, " 'That Species of

Property'"; Mazyck, *George Washington and the Negro*; Wiencek, *Imperfect God*; Philip D. Morgan and O'Shaughnessy, "Arming Slaves in the American Revolution."

81. Council of War, 8 Oct. 1775, "II. Minutes of the Conference," [18–24 Oct. 1775], General Orders, 12 Nov. 1775, GW to Peter Hog, 27 Dec. 1755, GW to the Continental Congress Camp Committee, 29 Jan. 1778, *PGW*.

82. Hirschfeld, *George Washington and Slavery*, 144; Twohig, " 'That Species of Property,' " 118; Quarles, *Negro in the American Revolution*, 13.

83. Philip D. Morgan and O'Shaughnessy, "Arming Slaves in the American Revolution,"182.

84. Wiencek, *Imperfect God*, 197.

85. "To His Excellency Thomas Hutchinson, Esq; Governor . . . The Humble Petition of Many Slaves, Living in the Town of Boston," [6 Jan. 1773], in *Appendix*, 9–10.

86. Lover of Constitutional Liberty, "Thoughts on Slavery," in *Appendix*, 11–12.

87. Robert Pleasants to John Thomas, 30 May 1775, Robert Pleasants Letterbook, W&M.

88. Force, *American Archives*, 2:762; Hirschfeld, *George Washington and Slavery*, 145.

89. Quarles, *Negro in the American Revolution*, 68–93; Cooley, *Sketches*, 45–46; Quintal, *Patriots of Color*, 175, 178.

90. Hirschfeld, *George Washington and Slavery*, 144; quotation from the Committee of Safety at Cambridge, MA, Resolves, 20 May 1775, in Moebs, *Black Soldiers*, 234.

91. Wiencek, *Imperfect God*, 201.

92. "II. Letter Sent," 10[–11] Jul. 1775, *PGW*; GW to the President of Congress, 10 Jul. 1775, in *WW*, 3:328.

93. GW to Lund Washington, 20 Aug. 1775, GW to Richard Henry Lee, 29 Aug. 1775, *PGW*.

94. GW to Peter Hog, 27 Dec. 1755, GW to the Continental Congress Camp Committee, 29 Jan. 1778, *PGW*.

95. Bland, *Treatise of Military Discipline*, 258.

96. General Orders, 12 Nov. 1775, in *WW*, 4:86; General Orders, 31 Oct. 1775, in *WW*, 4:58.

97. Twohig, " 'That Species of Property,' " 118; Quarles, *Negro in the American Revolution*, 13; Philip D. Morgan and O'Shaughnessy, "Arming Slaves in the American Revolution," 192.

98. Council of War, 8 Oct. 1775, *PGW*; GW to the General Officers, 5 Oct. 1775, in *WW*, 4:8.

99. Force, *American Archives*, 3:1385; Hirschfeld, *George Washington and Slavery*, 142.

100. Hirschfeld, *George Washington and Slavery*, 142; Philip D. Morgan and O'Shaughnessy, "Arming Slaves in the American Revolution," 189; Quarles, *Negro in the American Revolution*, 19–32.

101. Philip D. Morgan and O'Shaughnessy, "Arming Slaves in the American Revolution," 189; Alan Gilbert, *Black Patriots and Loyalists*, 15–37; Edmund Pendleton to James Mercer, 19 Mar. 1776, Robert Williams Daniel Papers, 1776–1882, VHS.

102. Quarles, *Negro in the American Revolution*, 20.

103. Ramsay, *History of the American Revolution*, 1:249.

104. GW to Lt. Col. Joseph Reed, 15 Dec. 1775, *PGW*.

105. GW to Richard Henry Lee, 26 Dec. 1775, *PGW*.

106. GW to John Hancock, 31 Dec. 1775, *PGW*.

107. Mazyck, *George Washington and the Negro*, 44.

108. John Thomas to JA, 24 Oct. 1775, FO: *AP*.

109. Cooley, *Sketches*, 45–46.

110. Copy of Petition of Col. Jona. Brewer, Lt. Col. Thomas Nixon, Col. Wm. Prescott, Lieut. Ephm. Coey, Lieut. Joseph Baker, Lieut. Joshua Read, 5 Dec. 1775, in Quintal, *Patriots of Color*, 175–78.

111. Henriques, *Realistic Visionary*, 161.

112. Mazyck, *George Washington and the Negro*, 44–45.

113. Phillis Wheatley to GW and Enclosure: Poem by Phillis Wheatley, 26 Oct. 1775, *PGW*; Wheatley, *Poems*; Wiencek, *Imperfect God*, 207.

114. Wiencek, *Imperfect God*, 208; Longmore, *Invention of Washington*, 8; GW to Sarah Cary Fairfax, 25 Sept. 1758, *PGW*; William Fairfax to GW, 13–14 May 1756, in *PGW*, 3:125; Michael Novak and Jana Novak, *Washington's God*, 13; Morison, "Young Man Washington," 169; Longmore, *Invention of Washington*, 173–74; Litto, "Addison's Cato in the Colonies," 440–41. For more on Wheatley as a symbol of African American humanity, see Joseph Woods, *Thoughts on the Slavery of the Negroes*, 14.

115. GW to Phillis Wheatley, 28 Feb. 1776, *PGW*; Wiencek, *Imperfect God*, 209; Quarles, *Negro in the American Revolution*, 46.

116. GW to Nicholas Cooke, 2 Jan. 1778, in *WW*, 10:257, also in *PGW*.

117. GW to JL, 10 Jul. 1782, in *WW*, 24:421; Philip D. Morgan and O'Shaughnessy, "Arming Slaves in the American Revolution," 193; Quarles, *Negro in the American Revolution*, 63–65; Nell, *Colored Patriots*, 50–51. For John Hancock's similar support of the Bucks of America, see Nell, *Colored Patriots*, 25. For JL being regarded as "great and good" due to his support of African American soldiers, see Buchanan, *Oration*, 17–18.

118. For numbers and areas of service, see Moebs, *Black Soldiers*, 235, 248, 255–56, 266, 275, 278.

119. Hirschfeld, *George Washington and Slavery*, 167; GW to the Secretary at War, 5 Aug. 1782, in *WW*, 24:467; GW to Governor John Hancock, 31 Oct. 1780, in *WW*, 20:272–73; GW to Jonathan Hobby, 7 Feb. 1783, in *WW*, 26:107–8; Twohig, "'That Species of Property,'" 120; Philip D. Morgan and O'Shaughnessy, "Arming Slaves in the American Revolution," 201.

120. NG to John Matthews, 11 Feb. 1782, in *PNG*, 10:355–56.

121. JM to Joseph Jones, 28 Nov. 1780, FO: *PJM*.

122. Ewing, "Petition of Primus Hall."

123. JM to Joseph Jones, 28 Nov. 1780, FO: *PJM*.

124. GW to Lund Washington, 15 Aug. 1778, *PGW*.

125. GW to JL, 10 Jul. 1782, in *WW*, 24:421.

126. Milch Martha Moore, *Book*, 207.

127. [Reed], "Sentiments of an American Woman," 1; Winterer, *Mirror of Antiquity*, 12–40.

128. Milch Martha Moore, *Book*, 271–72.

129. Kerber, *Women of the Republic*, 31.

130. Mildred Smith to Betsey [Eliza] J. Ambler, [Jun.?] 1780, Elizabeth Jaquelin Ambler Brent Carrington Papers, CWF.

131. MOW to Winslow Warren, 4 Dec. 1779, in *Mercy Otis Warren: Selected Letters*, 118.

132. Ibid., 120.

133. 6 Sept. 1769, HWC.

134. AA to MOW, 28 Feb. 1780, *AFC*.

135. 1 Jan. 1774, 27 Sept. 1774, HWC; MOW to Catherine Macauly, 29 Dec. 1774, MOW to Sarah Brown Bowen, Apr. 1775, in *Mercy Otis Warren: Selected Letters*, 38, 40, 47; AA to John Thaxter, 21 May 1778, *AFC*.

136. 29 Apr. 1769, HWC.

137. 23 Jun. 1775, 17 Aug. 1775, HWC; MOW to HW, 1774, in *Mercy Otis Warren: Selected Letters*, 27.

138. [Reed], "Sentiments of an American Woman," 2.

139. AA to JA, 17 Jun. 1782, *AFC*.

140. MOW to Hannah Quincy Lincoln, 3 Sept. 1774, in *Mercy Otis Warren: Selected Letters*, 34.

141. 20 Jul. 1775, Jane (Bonsall) Clark, Memorandums and Remarks, 22, SC; 7 Nov. 1773, 11 Nov. 1776, Diaries of Susanna Boone, Quaker Women's Diaries, SC.

142. [Reed], "Sentiments of an American Woman," 1.

143. Berkin, *Revolutionary Mothers*, 30.

144. Ramsay, *History of the Revolution of South-Carolina*, 2:124.

145. Oliver Wolcott Sr. to Laura Wolcott, 11 May 1776, Oliver Wolcott Sr. Papers, Connecticut Historical Society, quoted in Winterer, *Mirror of Antiquity*, 40.

146. [Reed], "Sentiments of an American Woman," 1

147. Ibid.

148. Ibid.

149. Mary Morris to Catharine Livingston, 10 Jun. [1780], Ridley Papers quoted in Kerber, *Women of the Republic*, 102; Anna Rawle to Rebecca Rawle Shoemaker, 30 Jun. 1780, Rawle, "Laurel Hill," 398, also quoted in Kerber, *Women of the Republic*, 102.

150. Jane Mecom to Mrs. Richard Bache, [after 18 Aug. 1780], Bache and Wistar Family Correspondence, PURBSC.

151. 5 Jul. 1780, in Dexter, *Literary Diary of Ezra Stiles*, 2:442.

152. [Reed], "Sentiments of an American Woman," 1.

153. Benjamin Rush to JA, 13 Jul. 1780, in *Letters of Benjamin Rush*, 1:253; Kerber, *Women of the Republic*, 102–3.

154. Kerber, *Women of the Republic*, 58–59.

155. JA to AA, 25 Aug. 1776, *LDC*.

156. Benjamin Rush Papers, 1791, Library Company of Philadelphia, quoted in Kerber, *Women of the Republic*, 74.

157. *A New Touch on the Times*, NYHS, in Kerber, *Women of the Republic*, 107.

158. Paine, *American Crisis*, 20.

159. AA to JA, 20 Sept. 1776, *AFC*.

160. *Female Soldier*, 31, 39, 79, 115–17, 147, 168, 170.

161. Mann, *Female Review*, 38.

162. Ibid., 129.

163. Ibid., 109.

164. *New York Gazette*, 10 Jan. 1784.

165. Alfred F. Young, *Masquerade*, 5.

166. Mann, *Female Review*, 129. For biographical information, see Mann, *Female Review*. For biography, analysis, source evaluation, and the biblical connection, see Alfred F. Young, *Masquerade*.

167. Joseph Plumb Martin, *Ordinary Courage*, 87–88; Berkin, *Revolutionary Mothers*, xi, 60, 138–39, 151; Teipe, "Real Molly Pitcher?"; "Sergeant Pitcher," *Time* 7, no. 13 (29 Mar. 1926): 12; Landis, *Short History of Molly Pitcher*; Egle, *Some Pennsylvania Women*, 52–54, 85–86.

168. William H. Cabell to Speaker of the House of Delegates, 28 Jan. 1808, Receipt for Pension for Ann Maria Lane, 20 May 1808, Receipt for Pensions for John Lane and Ann Maria Lane, 6 Feb. 1809, all in Library of Virginia, "Working Out Her Destiny"; Mayer, *Belonging to the Army*, 144–45, 275; Gundersen, *To Be Useful to the World*, 194.

169. Leonard, "Ann Bailey," 1–4; *Pennsylvania Packet*, 25 Jun. 1782; William Barton to [?], 17 Nov. 1788, in "'A Diversion in Newark,'" *New Jersey History* 105 (1787): 75–78; Alfred F. Young, *Masquerade*, 7.

170. Hannah Griffitts, "On the Death & Character of a Late English Nobleman," Mar. 1775, in Milch Martha Moore, *Book*, 242.

171. MOW to HW, 31 Jan. 1774, in *Mercy Otis Warren: Selected Letters*, 23.

172. 15 Apr. 1775, HWC.

Chapter Five

1. New research downplays the role of the battle and suggests that the French entrance into the Revolution had more to do with European relations, but still, the Saratoga victory at least seems to have allowed for a French shift "from secret aid to open conflict." Mapp, "Revolutionary War," 320.

2. General Orders, 4 Sept. 1777, *PGW*.

3. For more, see Lender and Stone, *Fatal Sunday*, 24–32.

4. John Banister to Theodorick Bland, 10 Jun. 1777, VHS.

5. William Tudor to JA, 23 Sept. 1776, *PJA*.

6. JA to AA, 22 Sept. 1776, *AFC*.

7. "Regimental Boston 1777," 22 Jul. 1777, Larned Family Papers, vol. 2, HSP, also in Worthington Chaucey Ford, *General Orders*, 34.

8. HK to William Knox, 25 Sept. 1775, HKP.

9. John Howard to HK, 14 May 1776, HKP.

10. Ibid.

11. Petition to HK [by Wm. Treadwell, Benj. Frothingham, Jonathan Horton, David Allen, Winthrop Sergeant, John Johnston, Thos. Seward, and Benjamin Carpenter], 27 Sept. 1776, HKP.

12. Edmund S. Morgan, in "Puritan Ethic," 19, observes a similar perception after 1776.

13. Randall, *Benedict Arnold*, 243.

14. NG to JA, 7 May 1777, in *PNG*, 2:69–71.

15. Benjamin Rush to Thomas Morris, 22 Oct. 1776, *LDC*.

16. BA to HG, 31 May 1776, in Sellers, *Benedict Arnold*, 103.

17. BA to Mesrs. Campbell and McKenzie, Jan. 1771, BAP, NHM.

18. Randall, *Benedict Arnold*, 262–64; Sellers, *Benedict Arnold*, 101–4.

19. BA to Richard Varick, 30 Oct. 1776, BAP, USMA. However, in 1800, BA was encouraging his son, Edward, to form personal connections and assist superior officers, "for your own Interest is promoted," though he still warned, "I would despise you for being a Sycophant." BA to his son [Edward Shippen Arnold], 7 Sept. 1800, Arnold Family Papers, NYPL.

20. BA to GW, 11 Mar. 1777, *PGW*.

21. HK to Lucy Knox, 23 Mar. 1777, HKP.

22. Benedict Arnold's Commission as Major General from John Hancock, 2 May 1777, Manuscript Collection, FSNL.

23. Arnold, *Life of Benedict Arnold*, 138; 11 and 12 Jul. 1777, Papers of the Continental Congress, no. 162, I, folio 106, 108 in 12 Jul. 1777, *JCC*, n. 1.

24. Nelson, *General Horatio Gates*, 122–25.

25. 20 Sept. 1777, Continental Army Major General Benedict Arnold's Division, Orderly Book, USMA.

26. 26 Sept. 1777, Continental Army Major General Benedict Arnold's Division, Orderly Book, USMA, also in Snow, "American Orderly Books, Saratoga"; Randall, *Benedict Arnold*, 357.

27. Richard Varick to Philip Schuyler, 22 Sept. 1777, in Arnold, *Life of Benedict Arnold*, 179.

28. Ibid.

29. Arnold, *Life of Benedict Arnold*, 179–82.

30. BA to HG, 1 Oct. 1777, in Nelson, *General Horatio Gates*, 31.

31. Randall, *Benedict Arnold*, 368; Brandt, *Man in the Mirror*, 139; Chappel, "Battle of Saratoga."

32. David Griffith to Hannah Griffith, 8 Dec. 1776, David Griffith Papers, VHS.

33. John Harvie to TJ, 18 Oct. 1777, *PTJ*.

34. GW to John Hancock, 24 Oct. 1777, *PGW*.

35. GW to HG, 30 Oct. 1777, *PGW*.

36. *The Thoughts of a Freeman* [enclosure], HL to GW, 27 Jan. 1778, in *PHL*, 12:359.

37. Maj. Gen. John Sullivan to GW, 4 Dec. 1777, *PGW*.

38. HK to GW, 26 Nov. 1777, HKP.

39. GW to Landon Carter, 27 Oct. 1777, *PGW*.

40. Enclosure [copied by HL], GW to Lieutenant Colonel John Fitzgerald, 28 Feb. 1778, *WW*, 10:528–29n.31, originally enclosed in Lieutenant Colonel John Fitzgerald to GW, 16 Feb. 1778, *PGW*.

41. Quoted in GW to Thomas Conway, ca. 5 Nov. 1777, *PGW*.

42. Nelson, *General Horatio Gates*, 157.

43. Thomas Conway to GW, 5 Nov. 1777, *PGW*.

44. GW to Thomas Conway, 30 Dec. 1777, *PGW*.

45. GW to HL, 31 Jan. 1778, *PGW*.

46. HK to GW, 26 Nov. 1777, *HKP*; also in *PGW*.

47. NG to Jacob Greene, 7 Feb. 1778, in *PNG*, 2:277–79.

48. HG to GW, 8 Dec. 1777, *PGW*.

49. Randall, *Benedict Arnold*, 405.

50. U.S. Continental Congress, *Rules and Articles* (1775).

51. Royster, *Revolutionary People at War*, 208–11; Van Buskirk, *Generous Enemies*, 73–76; Cox, *Proper Sense of Honor*, 23. For additional examples of emulation, see Bouton, *Taming Democracy*, 65–68; and Truman, *Field of Honor*, 81, 83. For multiple perspectives on dueling, see Evarts B. Greene, "Code of Honor."

52. U.S. Continental Congress, *Rules and Articles* (1776), 11–12.

53. John Sullivan to GW, 5 Jul. 1777, *PGW*.

54. *New Jersey Gazette*, 17 Mar. 1779, quoted in Royster, *Revolutionary People at War*, 209.

55. Royster, *Revolutionary People at War*, 208.

56. NG to Gen. John Cadwalader, 10 Nov. 1778, in *PNG*, 3:56–58. On NG's opposition to dueling, see NG to GW, 25 Jul. 1776, in *PNG*, 1:262.

57. Gen. John Cadwalader to NG, 5 Dec. 1778, in *PNG*, 3:103–5.

58. For more on civilian-military relations, see Higginbotham, "Civil-Military Tensions, 1777–1778," in *War of American Independence*, 204–25.

59. GW to Thomas Conway, 30 Dec. 1777, *PGW*.

60. NG to Henry Merchant, 17 Nov. 1777, in *PNG*, 2:199–200.

61. AB to GW, 20 Jul. 1777, *PGW*.

62. For more on AB's thinking, see Wood, *Revolutionary Characters*, ch. 8. Gordon S. Wood views AB as being concerned with personal motives and fundamentally going against the principles of the Revolution. For more on AB's understanding of birth status and ambition, see AB to James Monroe, 2 Aug. 1795, AB to Charles Biddle, 20 Jul. 1800, in Burr, *Political Correspondence and Public Papers*, 1:225, 440.

63. Eight Continental Army Field Officers to GW, 4 Sept. 1777, *PGW*.

64. Maj. Gen. John Sullivan to GW, 4 Dec. 1777, *PGW*.

65. GW to a Continental Congress Camp Committee, 29 Jan. 1778, *PGW*.

66. Ibid.

67. Lt. Col. John Brooks to GW, 31 May 1778, *PGW*.

68. GW to Lt. Col. John Brooks, 1 Jun. 1778, *PGW*.

69. GW to Lt. Col. Eleazer Oswald, 14 Oct. 1778, *PGW*.

70. GW to Brig. Gen. Charles Scott, 27 Oct. 1778, *PGW*.

71. Certain General Officers to GW, 31 Jan. 1778, *PGW*.

72. Lender and Stone, *Fatal Sunday*, 105–22; George Henry Moore, *"Mr. Lee's Plan."*

73. CL to GW, 25 Jun. 1778, *PGW*.

74. For instance, in their recent book *Fatal Sunday*, 184–99, Mark Edward Lender and Garry Wheeler Stone place the blame on GW due to "ambiguity," but they do acknowledge that GW intended CL to attack. Ibid., 249–97, 390–403, offers a full account of the battle and court-martial.

75. *Proceedings of a General Court Martial . . . for the Trial of Major General Lee*; Chernow, *Washington*, 340–46; Patterson, *Knight Errant of Liberty*, 200–217; Alden, *General Charles Lee*, 212–27; Thayer, *Making of a Scapegoat*, 36–56; Mazzagetti, *Charles Lee*, 221; Lender and Stone, *Fatal Sunday*, 288–91. Regarding the accuracy of GW's conversation with CL, the authors of *Fatal Sunday* consider GW's calling CL a "damned poltroon" (290) nothing but folklore created when "the fullness of time had ripened and expanded memories" (291). Certainly the two authors make a compelling case for the embellishment of the story. Dominick A. Mazzagetti comes to a similar conclusion, stating that "reports of the confrontation contain less color." But this does necessitate a dismissal of ML's memory. Either way, the legend does seem to have elements of truth or was at least, as Mazzagetti states, "no less dramatic" than traditionally reported. In CL to GW, 30 Jun. 1778, *PGW*, CL wrote to GW complaining about GW's "making use of so very singular expressions" that "implied that I was guilty either of disobedience of orders, of want of conduct, or want of courage." He continued, "But in this instance I must pronounce that he has been guilty of an act of cruel injustice towards a man who certainly has some pretensions to the regard of every servant of this country— And I think Sir, I have a right to demand some reparation for the injury committed." As discussed in the main text, this seems to indicate that GW delivered some comment that CL took as insulting. GW replied by letter (GW to CL, 30 Jun. 1778, *PGW*) that CL made a "shameful retreat." Did GW curse "till the leaves shook on the trees"? Probably not, based on Lender and Stone's convincing analysis of conflicting accounts. Did GW call CL a "poltroon"? ML recalled it in 1824, but the court-martial records don't mention it. Either way, it seems that CL felt that his command and courage were being questioned.

76. Chernow, *Washington*, 343.

77. CL to Richard Henry Lee, 28 [29] Jun. 1778, in *PCL*, 2:430.

78. CL to GW, 30 Jun. 1778, *PGW*.

79. GW to CL, 30 Jun. 1778, *PGW*.

80. CL to GW, GW to CL, 30 Jun. 1778, *PGW*.

81. *Proceedings of a General Court Martial . . . for the Trial of Major General Lee*, 121.

82. CL to Robert Morris, 3 Jul. 1778, in *PCL*, 2:457.

83. *Proceedings of a General Court Martial . . . for the Trial of Major General Lee.*

84. CL to AB, Oct. 1778, in *PCL*, 3:238.

85. Also available in *PCL*.

86. GW to Joseph Reed, 12 Dec. 1778, *PGW*.

87. CL to Miss Rebecca Franks, 20 Dec. 1778, in *PCL*, 3:278–81.

88. NG to Col. Clement Biddle, 20 Jan. 1779, in *PNG*, 3:172–73.

89. Account of a Duel between Major General Charles Lee and Lieutenant Colonel John Laurens [by AH and Evan Edwards], 24 Dec. 1778, *PAH*.

90. Col. Walter Stewart to NG, 29 Jan. 1779, Col. Charles Petit to NG, 13 Apr. 1779, in *PNG*, 3:193–95, 400–402.

91. CL to Miss Sidney Lee, 24 Sept. 1779, CL to General Wayne, 7 Jan. 1779, CL to the President of Congress, 25 Jan. 1780, in *PCL*, 2:366–67, 293, 408; Mazzagetti, *Charles Lee*, ch. 12 and epilogue (p. 197 specifically highlights CL's use of "my Country" as linked with Britain).

92. BA to NG, 10 Nov. 1778, in *PNG*, 3:58–59.

93. Gen. John Cadwalader to [?], 15 Jan. 1777, Cadwalader Family Papers, HSP. For a similar observation, see D. Griffith to Major Leven Powell, 8 Dec. 1776, Leven Powell Papers, W&M.

94. HK to JA, 21 Aug. 1776, *PJA*.

95. Golway, *Washington's General*, 129–32. For more on the connection between honor, officers, and Congress, see E. Wayne Carp, *To Starve the Army*, ch. 6.

96. NG to Catherine Greene, 14 Aug. 1780, in *PNG*, 6:212–13.

97. NG to Col. Jeremiah Wadsworth, 12 Aug. 1780, in *PNG*, 6:201–2.

98. Col. John Cox to NG, 7 Aug. 1780, in *PNG*, 6:186–92.

99. NG to Catherine Greene, 14 Aug. 1780, in *PNG*, 6:212–13.

100. Gen. Alexander McDougall to NG, 24 Mar. 1779, in *PNG*, 3:361–62. For more on military and civilian views on prices, see Carp, *To Starve the Army*, ch. 5.

101. Gen. Alexander McDougall to NG, 30 Oct. 1780, in *PNG*, 6:446–47.

102. NG to Gen. James M. Varnum, 9 Feb. 1779, in *PNG*, 3:223–24.

103. Col. Henry Hollingsworth to NG, 10 Feb. 1779, in *PNG*, 3:229–33.

104. GW to Joseph Reed, 12 Dec. 1778, Letter to the Committee of Conference, 20 Jan. 1779, *PGW*.

105. [?] to Gen. John Cadwalader, 20 Sept. 1780, Cadwalader Family Papers, HSP. For more on civil-martial tension, see Herrera, *For Liberty and the Republic*, 28–29, 42–43, 58.

106. Ramsay, *History of the American Revolution*, 2:172–73. A similar point is made in Ramsay, *History of the Revolution of South-Carolina*, 2:123.

107. Joseph Reed to NG, 2 Sept. 1780, in *PNG*, 6:248–50.

108. Randall, *Benedict Arnold*, 407.

109. Henry Marchant to NG, [25?] Jul. 1778, in *PNG*, 2:470–72.

110. BA to NG, 10 Nov. 1778, Joseph Reed to NG, 5 Nov. 1778, Gen. John Cadwalader to NG, 5 Dec. 1778, in *PNG*, 3:58–59, 40–47, 103–5.

111. Gen. John Cadwalader to NG, 5 Dec. 1778, in *PNG*, 3:103–5. For another, similar opinion, see Silas Deane to NG, 4 Jul. 1779, in *PNG*, 4:199–200.

112. Rutherford, *Institutes of Natural Law*, 365.

113. BA to NG, 10 Nov. 1778, in *PNG*, 3:58–59.

114. Silas Deane to NG, 29 May 1779, in *PNG*, 4:98–100. In contrast, NG refused to use his public position to deal commercially with his brothers. See letters from NG to

Jacob Greene after 24 May 1778, in *PNG*. For more on accusations against BA, see William Kenyon to Josiah Blakely, ca. 1780, BAP, NHM.

115. Silas Deane to NG, 4 Jul. 1779, in *PNG*, 4:199–200.

116. *Proceedings of a General Court Martial . . . for the Trial of Major General Arnold*, 40, 52, 55.

117. General Orders, 6 Apr. 1780, FO: *PGW*.

118. Silas Deane to NG, 4 Jul. 1779, in *PNG*, 4:199–200.

119. Gen. Alexander McDougall to NG, 18 Feb. 1780, in *PNG*, 5:399–400.

120. Gen. Ezekiel Cornell to NG, 19 Sept. 1780, in *PNG*, 6:298–302.

121. NG to BA, 7 Sept. 1780, in *PNG*, 6:268–69.

122. AH to Elizabeth Schuyler, 6 Sept. 1780, *PAH*.

123. BA to NG, 12 Sept. 1780, in *PNG*, 6:281–82.

124. AH to Elizabeth Schuyler, 6 Sept. 1780, *PAH*.

125. HK to NG, 13 Oct. 1780, BAC, NYHS.

126. Lt. Col. Ebenezer Huntington to Andrew Huntington, 7 Jul. 1780, *Letters Written by Ebenezer Huntington*, 87–88. For another pro-military opinion, see Isaac Sears to NG, 25 Oct. 1780, BAC, NYHS.

127. AH to Elizabeth Schuyler, 6 Sept. 1780, *PAH*.

128. Brandt, *Man in the Mirror*, 197. For a completely different perspective and concept of honor, see Ramsay, *History of the American Revolution*, 2:194–95. BA was cast as being in opposition to the "pur[ity] of . . . morals . . . republican principles and patriotism." His "love of pleasure produced the love of money, and that extinguished all sensibility to the obligations of honor and duty." According to David Ramsay, this was solely about money, which was indicative of the acceptance of the new American honor as tied with ethics, independent of self-interest, and wealth. In any event, it illustrates that BA's concept of honor was different from that of other Americans. More recently, Nathaniel Philbrick, in *Valiant Ambition*, 240–41, has similarly concluded that BA's treason was about money. But this seems to ignore the role of honor and represent a more modern sensibility of wealth over reputation.

129. Col. Charles Petit to NG, 5 [and 6] Oct. 1780, in *PNG*, 6:344–47.

130. General Orders, 26 Sept. 1780, FO: *PGW*.

131. AH to Elizabeth Schuyler, 25 Sept. 1780, *PAH*.

132. BA to GW [enclosure], 25 Sept. 1780, *PAH*.

133. Alexander Scammell to Col. Peabody, 3 Oct. 1780, in Royster, *Revolutionary People at War*, 291.

134. General Orders, 26 Sept. 1780, FO: *PGW*.

135. JA to the President of Congress, No. 19, 31 Oct. 1780, *PJA*.

136. AA to JA, 26 Feb. 1780, *AFC*.

137. Col. Charles Petit to NG, 5 [and 6] Oct. 1780, in *PNG*, 6:344–47.

138. Gen. George Weedon to NG, 17 Feb. 1781, in *PNG*, 7:307–9.

139. "The Life and Character of General Arnold Extracted from the New History of the American Revolution," *Continental Journal and Weekly Advertiser*, 18 Oct. 1781, copy in Blackall William Ball Collection, CWF.

140. Alexander Spotswood to TJ, 26 Nov. 1780, *PTJ.*

141. Joseph Reed to NG, 16 Jun. 1781, in *PNG*, 8:395–403.

142. For reactions to Thomas Burke's breaking parole, see NG to Thomas Burke, 21 Jan. 1781, 18 Mar. 1782, 8 Apr. 1782, 31 May 1782, in *PNG*, 10:227–28, 517–21, 11:24–25, 265–66.

143. NG to Jeremiah Wadsworth, 29 Sept. 1782, in *PNG*, 11:711–12.

144. Peter Curtenius to Richard Varick, 19 Oct. 1780, "Proceedings on Court of Inquiry . . . ," 5 Nov. 1780, Richard Varick Papers, NYHS. For HK on Varick, see HK to NG, 13 Oct. 1780, BAC, NYHS.

145. For accounts of the BA-André affair, see *Proceedings . . . respecting Major John André*; Robert McConnell Hatch, *Major John André*; *Proceedings of a General Court Martial for the Trial of Major General Arnold*; Randall, *Benedict Arnold*; Joshua Hett Smith, *Narrative of the Death*; Thacher, *Military Journal*; Van Buskirk, *Generous Enemies*; André, *Journal*; Tillotson, *Beloved Spy*; and John Evangelist Walsh, *Execution of Major André*. For additional accounts from those at West Point, see R. Taft to Lt. Kelley, 29 Sept. 1780, Elijah Warren to Lt. David Kalley, 29 Sept. 1780, West Point Manuscript Collection, USMA.

146. John André to GW, 24 Sept. 1780, in *Proceedings . . . respecting Major John André*, 7; Van Buskirk, *Generous Enemies*, 95.

147. AH to JL, 11 Oct. 1780, *PAH.*

148. AH to HK, 7 Jun. 1782, HKP.

149. Van Buskirk, *Generous Enemies*, 96.

150. Flexner, *Traitor and the Spy*, 83. AH spoke favorably of André.

151. 8 and 11 May 1778, Katharine Farnham Hay Journal, MHS.

152. Journal, 27 May 1754, in *WW*, 1:57.

153. Van Buskirk, *Generous Enemies*, 96.

154. GW to NG, 27 Sept. 1780, in *WW*, 20:98; Robert McConnell Hatch, *Major John André*, 271–72; Van Buskirk, *Generous Enemies*, 101.

155. GW to Lt. Colonel John Jameson, 25 Sept. 1780, in *WW*, 20:86–87.

156. *Proceedings . . . respecting Major John André*, 5, 13; GW to Sir Henry Clinton, 30 Sept. 1780, in *WW*, 20:103–4, also in *Proceedings . . . respecting Major John André*, 15.

157. Van Buskirk, *Generous Enemies*, 100–101.

158. AH to JL, 11 Oct. 1780, *PAH*; AH to HK, 7 Jun. 1782, HKP.

159. John André to GW, 1 Oct. 1780, in *Proceedings . . . respecting Major John André*, 21.

160. Vattel, *Law of Nations* (1759), bk. 2, 51; GW to Robert Cary and Company, 6 Oct. 1773, FO: *PGW.*

161. NG to Elihue Greene, 2 Oct. 1780, in *PNG*, 6:327–28.

162. Evidence of a questionable veracity exists that suggests GW may have been overcome by his notions of gentility, causing him to waver in his decision, even going so far as to consider acquiescing to André's request, but he was thwarted by NG or the board of generals. GW likely felt sympathy for André and probably admired his genteel manners, but he did not allow it to cloud his judgment. The affair illustrates GW's subordination of his personal honor in favor of national honor. For sources for the al-

ternative theory, see Anburey, *Travels*, 2:478; and Joshua Hett Smith, *Authentic Narrative*, 166; also noted in Van Buskirk, *Generous Enemies*, 217.

163. Thomas Paine to NG, 17 Oct. 1780, in *PNG*, 6:404–7.

164. AH to JL, 11 Oct. 1780, *PAH*.

165. MOW to Winslow Warren, 7 Nov. 1780, in *Mercy Otis Warren: Selected Letters*, 142.

166. AH to HK, 7 Jun. 1782, HKP.

167. Isaac Sears to NG, 25 Oct. 1780, BAC, NYHS.

168. For comments on British and loyalist tactics, see James M. Varnum to NG, 17 Sept. 1781, Robert Morris to Jonathan Hudson, 16 Jan. 1781, BAC, NYHS; Samuel Frost Diary, 1–3, Seventeenth- and Eighteenth-Century Manuscript Collection, USMA; St. George Tucker to Mrs. Frances Bland Randolph Tucker, 18 Mar. 1781, Tucker-Coleman Papers, CWF.

169. 30 Apr. 1782, Fort Pitt Orderly Book of Brigadier General William Irvine, CWF.

170. Long, *General Griffith Rutherford and Allied Families*, chs. 2–3, quotation from p. 22.

171. William Moore to Griffith Rutherford, 17 Nov. 1776, Learn NC.

172. NG to Alexander Martin, 9 Oct. 1781, in *PNG*, 9:438–39.

173. Vattel, *Law of Nations* (1759), bk. 3, 63.

174. NG to Alexander Martin, 9 Oct. 1781, in *PNG*, 9:438–39.

175. NG to Griffith Rutherford, 18 Oct. 1781, in *PNG*, 9:452–54.

176. NG to Griffith Rutherford, 20 Oct. 1781, in *PNG*, 9:456–61.

177. Kohn, *Eagle and Sword*, 19, quotation also from "The Address and Petition of the Officers of the Army of the United States," 29 April 1783, *JCC*; "Address at Close of War 1783 Discontent of Soldiers," Larned Family Papers, vol. 6, HSP. Kohn, *Eagle and Sword*, 17–39, is an excellent discussion. Also see Kohn, "Inside History"; Myers, *Liberty without Anarchy*, 1–22; Skelton, *American Profession of Arms*, 69; and Stephen H. Browne, *Ides of War*.

178. Brutus to HK, 12 Feb. 1783, HKP.

179. General Orders, 11 Mar. 1783, in *WW*, 26:208.

180. GW to AH, 12 Mar. 1783, in *WW*, 26:217.

181. GW to Major General Israel Putnam, 2 Jun. 1783, in *WW*, 26:462.

182. GW to Joseph Jones, 12 Mar. 1783, FO: GW.

183. Phelps, "Republican General," 181; GW to the Officers of the Army, 15 Mar. 1783, in *WW*, 26:224.

184. GW to the Officers of the Army, 15 Mar. 1783, in *WW*, 26:227.

185. Saunders, "Origin and Early History," 37; Stephen H. Browne, *Ides of War*, 86–87.

186. Jonathan Trumbell to Richard Varick, 15 Mar. 1783, Richard Varick Papers, NYHS.

187. GW to Joseph Jones, 18 Mar. 1783, in *WW*, 26:232–33.

188. Kohn, *Eagle and Sword*, 34.

189. Washington's Farewell Address to the Army, 2 Nov. 1783, FO: GW.

190. Tallmadge, *Memoir*, 63–64.

191. The narrative of GW surrendering his commission is based on a combination of the following sources: Washington's Address to Congress Resigning His Commission, [23 Dec. 1783], FO: TJ; Report of a Committee on the Response by the President of Congress, [22 Dec. 1783], FO: TJ; Mary (Molly) Ridout to Anne Tasker Ogle, 16 Jan. 1784, Maryland State Archives; Maryland State House, "Old Senate Chamber"; 22 Dec. 1783, 23 Dec. 1783, JCC; George Washington, "Address to Congress"; James Tilton to Gunning Bedford, 25 Dec. 1783, Bryn Mawr College; Chernow, *Washington*, 455–57; Trumbull, "General George Washington."

Chapter Six

1. For more on the Treaty of Paris, see Morris, *Peacemakers*; Schoenbrun, *Triumph in Paris*, 345–90; Hale and Hale, *Franklin in France*; and Hutson, *John Adams*, 117–41.

2. Thomas Johnson Jr. to HG, 14 Dec. 1774, *LDC*.

3. For JA's understanding of the concept, see John Adams, *Letters*, 25.

4. AA to JA, 19 Aug. 1774, *AFC*.

5. William Tudor to JA, 26 Jun. 1775, *PJA*.

6. MOW to JA, Oct. 1775, *PJA*.

7. Cuthbert Harrison to Theodorick Bland, 21 Apr. 1777, Bland Family Papers, VHS.

8. David MacClure to William Knox, 26 Sept. 1776, HKP.

9. AA to Isaac Smith Jr., 30 Oct. 1777, *AFC*.

10. JA to the President of the Congress, 18 Apr. 1780, JA to AA, 17 Jul. 1783, *AFC*.

11. Definitive Treaty of Paris, 3 Sept. 1783, in Morris, *Peacemakers*, 461–65.

12. AH to John Jay in Morris, *Peacemakers*, 444.

13. BF to Joseph Banks, 27 Jul. 1783, *PBF*.

14. JA to the President of the Congress, 18 Apr. 1780, *PJA*.

15. Myers, *Liberty without Anarchy*, 23–24; "The Institution of the Society of the Cincinnati," 13 May 1783, in Myers, *Liberty without Anarchy*, 259–60; "The Institution of the Society of the Cincinnati," 1784, The New York State Society of the Cincinnati Collection, SOCDC.

16. Myers, *Liberty without Anarchy*, 23–24; "The Institution of the Society of the Cincinnati," May 1783; "The Institution of the Society of the Cincinnati," 1784.

17. Brig. Gen. Jethro Sumner to Maj. Gen. William Heath, 28 Oct. 1783, North Carolina Society of the Cincinnati Collection, SOCDC.

18. Winthrop Sargent, "Secret Journal of the Cincinnati," 1784, 93, Proceedings, SOCDC.

19. "The Institution of the Society of the Cincinnati," 13 May 1783, in Myers, *Liberty without Anarchy*, 259.

20. HK to Benjamin Lincoln, 21 May 1783, HKP, cited in Saunders, "Origin and Early History," 67. GW was not involved in its organization, but he played a role in its connections with the French.

21. GW to Major Christopher French, 26 Sept. 1775, in *WW*, 3:522; "The Institution of the Society of the Cincinnati," 13 May 1783, in Myers, *Liberty without Anarchy*, 259.

22. *Synopsis of the Records*, 10–12.

23. Journals of the Society, General Society, ca. 1784, 28, 56, SOCDC.

24. "The Institution," Journals of the Society, General Society, SOCDC; Society of the Cincinnati in the State of New Jersey, *Excerpts of the Proceedings*, 172.

25. 25 Jun. 1789, 13 Jul. 1789, 8 Jul. 1790, Proceedings of the New York State Society of the Cincinnati, SOCDC; "At a Meeting of the Society of the Cincinnati of the State of Rhode Island . . . 4th July, 1789," *New York Daily Gazette*, 15 Jul. 1789.

26. *DGW*, 4:84n.; Saunders, "Origin and Early History," 68; Ellis, *His Excellency*, 158.

27. Burke, *Considerations on the Society*, 6.

28. Ibid., 11.

29. Ibid., 8.

30. Ibid., 7.

31. Ibid., 10.

32. Ibid., 5–6.

33. [Moylan], *Observations on a Late Pamphlet*, 4.

34. "The Institution of the Society of the Cincinnati," 13 May 1783, in Myers, *Liberty without Anarchy*, 259; Burke, *Considerations on the Society*, 13.

35. [Moylan], *Observations on a Late Pamphlet*, 19.

36. Ibid., 19.

37. Ibid., 20.

38. Ibid.

39. GW to ML, 1 Sept. 1778, in *WW*, 12:383.

40. Jun. 1770, in *DGW*, 2:245–46; Shields, *Civil Tongues and Polite Letters*, 175–208. For more on Freemasonry, see Bullock, *Revolutionary Brotherhood*; Hackett, *That Religion*, chs. 1–3.

41. GW to William Barton, 7 Sept. 1788, in *WW*, 30:87.

42. [Moylan], *Observations on a Late Pamphlet*, 18.

43. TJ to James Madison, 28 Dec. 1794, *PTJ*; BF to Sarah Bache, 26 Jan. 1784, *PBF*; Davies, "Society of the Cincinnati," 11; Hünemörder, *Society of the Cincinnati*, 22–55; Myers, *Liberty without Anarchy*, chs. 2–3; Ellis, *His Excellency*, 158–59; Henriques, *Realistic Visionary*, 110; Hume, *George Washington*, 13–15. For a French reaction, see Mirabeau et al., *Considerations*.

44. BF to Sarah Bache, 26 Jan. 1784, *PBF*.

45. TJ to GW, 16 Apr. 1784, *PTJ*.

46. GW to George Washington Parke Custis, 28 Nov. 1796, in *WW*, 35:296.

47. Memo accompanying GW to JL, 30 Jan. 1781, in *WW*, 21:162n53.

48. "I. Observation on the Institution of the Society," ca. 4 May 1784, *PGW*.

49. Ibid.

50. For more on the alterations, see *Circular Letter*.

51. "Instructions to Delegates," 11 Apr. 1787, SOCDC; Massachusetts, "Certification of Delegates and Resolution Concerning Amendment," 9 Oct. 1786, SOCDC; Rhode Island, Correspondence: State Societies, SOCDC; Davies, "Society of the Cincinnati," 15.

52. 6 Jul. 1786, Proceedings of the New York State Society of the Cincinnati, SOCDC.

53. New Hampshire Society to the General Meeting, 3 Feb. 1785, New Hampshire, Correspondence: State Societies, SOCDC.

54. TJ to GW, 7 Jan. 178[6], *PGW*, also in GW to the Secretary at War, 1 Jun. 1786, in *WW*, 28:447n72.

55. GW to James Madison, 18 Nov. 1786, *PGW*; Myers, *Liberty without Anarchy*, 97. GW's interactions with the society became almost exclusively social. *DGW*, 6:130, 137; GW to Edmund Randolph, 28 Mar. 1787, *PGW*.

56. [AH], Circular Letter to the State Societies, 1 Nov. 1786, New York, Correspondence: General Society, SOCDC.

57. Society of the Cincinnati in the State of New Jersey, *Excerpts of the Proceedings*, 179.

58. "Copy of an Account of an Entertainment Given by Major General Nathaniel Greene, Presented by Major Asa Bird Gardner, USA, Asst. Secretary of the Cincinnati Society of the State of Rhode Island to the Cincinnati Society of the State of South Carolina," April 1881, Society of the Cincinnati of the State of South Carolina Collection Proceedings, SOCDC.

59. M. L'Enfant to NY SOC [Society of the Cincinnati], 15 Jul. 1785, New York State Society of the Cincinnati Records, SOCDC. This letter was also read and forwarded in the Proceedings of the New York State Society of the Cincinnati.

60. 6 Jul. 1786, Proceedings of the New York State Society of the Cincinnati, SOCDC.

61. "The Form of Reception," 4 Jul. 1786, Proceedings of the New York State Society of the Cincinnati, SOCDC.

62. BF to Sarah Bache, 26 Jan. 1784, *PBF*.

63. Ibid.

64. "On Titles of Honor," *New-England Courant*, 18 Feb. 1723, *PBF*.

65. BF to Sarah Bache, 26 Jan. 1784, *PBF*.

66. Ibid.

67. TJ to Peter Carr, 19 Aug. 1785, *PTJ*.

68. Ibid.

69. For more, see Richards, *Shays' Rebellion*.

70. "Eastern Convention," *Massachusetts Gazette*, 22 Sept. 1786.

71. "Hampshire County Convention," *Massachusetts Gazette*, 8 Sept. 1786.

72. Joseph Hawley to Ephraim Wright, 16 Apr. 1782, in *American Historical Review*.

73. Holton, *Unruly Americans*, ch. 9.

74. For more on regulation, see Bouton, *Taming Democracy*, ch. 10.

75. Daniel Shays to Benjamin Lincoln, 30 Jan. 1787, in Benjamin Lincoln to GW, 4 Dec. 1786[-4 Mar. 1787], *PGW*.

76. GW to Henry Lee Jr., 31 Oct. 1786, *PGW*.

77. Publicus, "For the Independent Chronicle," *Independent Chronicle and the Universal Advertiser*, 21 Dec. 1786.

78. The Oracle, "For the Centinel," *Massachusetts Centinel*, 11 Aug. 1787.

79. Publicus, "For the Independent Chronicle."

80. "Resolution of the Cincinnati, July 4, 1787," *Massachusetts Centinel*, 17 Jul. 1787.

81. "Extracts of a Letter from a Gentleman in Berkshire County," *Massachusetts Centinel*, 21 Feb. 1787.

82. "Resolution of the Cincinnati, July 4, 1787"; Myers, *Liberty without Anarchy*, 86–87.

83. HK to GW, 19 Mar. 1787, *PGW*. For a public recognition of the society's "perfect equality with all their fellow citizens, who preserve an inviolable attachment to the laws of honor," see "At a Meeting of the Society of the Cincinnati of the State of Rhode Island . . . 4th July, 1789," *New York Daily Gazette*, 15 Jul. 1789.

84. "Boston," *Independent Chronicle and the Universal Advertiser*, 30 Nov. 1786.

85. JM to TJ, 3 Oct. 1785, *PJM*.

86. GW to JJ, 18 May 1786, *PGW*.

87. JM to Edmund Pendleton, 24 Feb. 1787, *PJM*.

88. Essays of Philadelphiensis, *Philadelphia Independent Gazetteer*, Nov. 1787–Apr. 1788, no. 11, in *CAF*, 3:134, 3.9.83.

89. JJ, *Federalist Papers*, no. 2, 33–34.

90. Letters of Centinel, *Philadelphia Independent Gazetteer and Philadelphia Freeman's Journal*, Oct. 1787–Apr. 1788, in *CAF*, 2:202, 2.7.177.

91. "Essay by None of the Well-Born Conspirators," *Freeman's Journal* (Philadelphia), 23 Apr. 1788, in *CAF*, 3:194, 3.15.1.

92. "Letter from a Delegate, Who Has Catched a Cold," *Virginia Independent Chronicle*, 11 Jun. 1788, in *CAF*, 5: 270, 5.19.4.

93. AH, *Federalist Papers*, no. 70, 425.

94. Essays of Philadelphiensis, *Philadelphia Independent Gazetteer*, Nov. 1787–Apr. 1788, no. 6, in *CAF*, 3: 119, 3.9.37.

95. Richard Henry Lee, *Additional Number of Letters*, 61; Cornell, *Other Founders*, 97–98.

96. "Essays by Cato," *State Gazette of South Carolina*, Nov.–Dec. 1787, no. 1, in *CAF*, 5:140, 5.10. 2.

97. AH, *Federalist Papers*, no. 22, 147.

98. JJ, *Federalist Papers*, no. 64, 394.

99. AH, *Federalist Papers*, no. 68, 412.

100. Ibid., no. 31, 190, no. 84, 512.

101. JM, *Federalist Papers*, no. 57, 348.

102. JJ, *Federalist Papers*, no. 64, 396.

103. AH, *Federalist Papers*, no. 36, 220.

104. JM, *Federalist Papers*, no. 40, 247.

105. AH, *Federalist Papers*, no. 69, 419.

106. Ibid., no. 76, 457.

107. Ibid., no. 22, 147.

108. Humphreys, *Miscellaneous Works*, 336.

109. Hull, *Oration*, 13.

110. AH, *Federalist Papers*, no. 12, 85–86.

111. Francis Hopkinson to TJ, 8 Jul. 1787, *PTJ*.

112. Myers, *Liberty without Anarchy*, ch. 5. For more on ratification, see Maier, *Ratification*.

113. TJ to John Banister Jr., 15 Oct. 1785, FO: TJ.

114. 1786, 5 Dec. 1793, Records of the Harvard Faculty and Faculty of Arts and Sciences, 5:223, 6:199, HUA; Columbia College Statutes, Columbia College Papers, CU, 11 Oct. 1790, ch. 1.

115. Rush, "A Plan for Establishing Public School in Pennsylvania," in *Essays, Literary, Moral & Philosophical*, 10. For a similar sentiment, see Bishop James Madison to Joel Barlow, 21 Oct. 1809, Bishop James Madison Papers, W&M.

116. John Bradford Wallace, *Valedictory Oration*.

117. Samuel Stanhope Smith, Moral Philosophy [John R. Witherspoon], 1794, Lecture Notes Collection, PUSML; William R. Hackley, Notebook, 1824, 122, University Archives Bound Volumes Collection, W&M; Commonplace Book of Hector Orr, HUA.

118. *Daily Advertiser*, 25 May 1786.

119. "University of Georgia Charter, 1785."

120. Dr. James Madison to TJ, 28 Dec. 1786, Dr. James Madison Papers, W&M.

121. Linn, *Discourse, Delivered*, 35.

122. 17 Jul. 1799, 16 Jul. 1800, 15 Jul. 1801, Faculty of Arts and Sciences Records, 8:80, 159, 178, HUA. Advocates for a national university also linked education to the creation of national character and honor. See Samuel Knox, *Essay on the Best System*, 15, 18, 41–42, 71.

123. Linn, *Blessing of America*, 18–19.

124. "Rolls of Merit," in *General Regulation for the Army*, 336.

125. "Address to the Students," 17 Sept. 1791, Records of the Faculty Relating to Disorders, HUA.

126. Laws of the College of William and Mary, 1817, College Papers Collection, W&M.

127. *Laws of the College of New Jersey*, three editions: 1794, 1802, and 1813.

128. "Concerning a Religious, Moral & Decent Conduct," Laws, 1783, Corporation Papers, 1:99, BU.

129. William Smith, "Rules for the Good Government & Discipline of the Students & Schools in the University of Pennsylvania," [1791], UPA; 3 Oct. 1825, Transcripts of the Minutes of the Board of Visitors, 1817–1855, UVA.

130. "Class of 1803 Constitution," 14 Sept. 1803, Yale College Records of Classes, YUMA.

131. [At a Public Commencement], 16 Jul. 1800, Records of the Harvard Faculty and Faculty of Arts and Sciences, HUA, 7:159.

132. Daniel Turner, 7 Dec. 1797, Student Essays and Notebooks, BU.

133. "Penalty for Misdemeanors," 11 Sept. 1804, Faculty of Yale College Records.

134. "Address to the Students in General," 13 Mar. 1791, "Address Made to the Freshman Class," 8 Mar. 1805, Records of the Faculty Relating to Disorders, HUA.

135. Opal, *Beyond the Farm*, 111–25.

136. Regulations, 1802–1816, 1216, Nineteenth-Century Manuscript Collection, USMA; *General Regulation for the Army*, 324–25, 330, 334, 336; 17 Dec. 1825, Records, United States Military Academy, March 1814 to February 1838, Nineteenth-Century Manuscript Collection, USMA; A. Partridge to the Gentlemen Cadets of the Military Academy, 24 Nov. 1816, Alden Partridge Papers, Nineteenth-Century Manuscript Collection, USMA.

137. 4 Oct. 1825, Transcripts of the Minutes of the Board of Visitors, 1817–1855, 1:70, UVA.

138. JA, *Defence of the Constitutions*, xvii, xviii, 116.

139. Lowell, *Essay on Hereditary Titles*, 10.

140. [1758] *AJA*, also in FO: AF.

141. JA to Charles Adams, 5 Jun. 1793; JA to JQA, 23 Jan. 1788, FO: AF.

142. JQA, 1 Nov. 1787, *Diary*, FO: AF.

143. "Objections and Answers respecting the Administration of the Government," 18 Aug. 1792, FO: AH.

144. Samuel Morse to TJ, 26 Jun. 1800, FO: TJ, notes.

145. JQA to AA, 6 Jun. 1810, FO: AF; Andrew Ellicot to JM, 2 Jan. 1817, FO: JM.

146. JA to the President of Congress, 5 Feb. 1783 and n. 6, FO: AF.

147. "Report of Commissioners for the University of Virginia to the Virginia General Assembly, [4 Aug.] 1818, FO: JM.

148. "For the Daily Advertiser," *Daily Advertiser*, 19 Jun. 1786.

149. For more, see chapter 7.

150. Aug. 1810, Board of Trustees Records, DC, 349.

151. Richard Dinmore to TJ, 28 Jan. 1802, FO: TJ.

152. JQA to Abigail Adams II, 25 May 1785, *AFC*.

153. Edward Rutledge to TJ, 23 Oct. 1787, *PTJ*.

154. JQA to Abigail Adams II, 25 May 1785, *AFC*.

155. Thomas Mitchell to Francis Jerdone, 9 Jul. 1789, Jerdone Family Papers, W&M.

156. Samuel Stanhope Smith to Elias Boudinot, 27 Jun. 1803, Samuel Stanhope Smith Collection, PURBSC.

157. "Monday; American Franklin; Typographical Association . . .]," *American and Commercial Daily Advertiser*, 21 Nov. 1801.

158. TJ to Pierre Samuel Du Pont de Nemours, 12 Apr. 1800, TJ to Joseph Carr, 28 Apr. 1807, FO: TJ.

159. *BFA*, pt. 7.

160. Benjamin Vaughn to BF, 31 Jan. 1783, *PBF*.

161. "For the Minerva," *American Minerva*, 4 Aug. 1794.

162. BFA, Part 8 and Benjamin Vaughn to BF, 31 Jan. 1783, *PBF*.

163. BFA, Part 7; Benjamin Vaughn to BF, 31 Jan. 1783, *PBF*.

164. BF to Sarah Bache, 26 Jan. 1784, *PBF*.

165. Norton, *Liberty's Daughters*, ch. 8.

166. AA to Elizabeth Cranch, 2 Sept. 1785, *AFC*.

167. AA to Elizabeth Smith Shaw, 19 Jul. 1786, *AFC*; MOW to Janet Livingston Montgomery, Apr. 1785, *Mercy Otis Warren: Selected Letters*, 200.

168. Kerber, *Women of the Republic*, 269–88; Lewis, "Republican Wife"; Margaret A. Nash, "Rethinking Republican Motherhood."

169. Zagarri, "Morals, Manners."

170. Chastity and faithfulness were still associated with honor and virtue. See AA to Mary Smith Cranch, 20 Jan. 1787, *AFC*.

171. Murray, "On the Equality of the Sexes," in *Selected Writings*, 9.

172. Murray, "Observations on Female Abilities," in *Selected Writings*, 15; Murray, *Gleaner*, 217–18.

173. Rowson, *Present for Young Ladies*, 89.

174. Hannah Adams, *Women Invited to War*, 11.

175. Murray, "Observations on Female Abilities," in *Selected Writings*, 24.

176. My sources offer a counterpoint to Bloch, "Gendered Meanings of Virtue"; Jessica Chopin Roney, "'Effective Men' and Early Voluntary Association in Philadelphia, 1725–1775," in Foster, *New Men*, 157–59.

177. Neal, *Essay of the Education*, 33.

178. Rush, *Thoughts upon Female Education*, 76–77.

179. AA to Elizabeth Smith Shaw, 19 Jul. 1786, AFC.

180. Abigail Adams Smith to Lucy Cranch, 15 Oct. 1785, AFC.

181. Lewis, "Republican Wife," 696–702; AA to Mary Smith Cranch, 4 Jul. 1786, AFC.

182. Nelly Custis [Lewis] to Elizabeth Bordley [Gibson], 19 Oct. 1795, 30 May 1797, 3 Feb. 1799, FSNL.

183. Elizabeth Trist to Catharine Wistar Bache, 13 Dec. 1813, Family Letters, Thomas Jefferson's Monticello; Rowson, *Charlotte*, 37–38.

184. Rush, "Plan for Establishing," 19; Cassandra A. Good, *Founding Friendships*, 6, 40, 185. Good states, "Male/female friendships were paragons of central republican values: choice, freedom, equality, and virtue. These were not only political ideals, but also personal ones in a nation where the virtue of the people would sustain the republican political system" (6). These friendships enforced virtue, but Good also notes that friendship was understood as existing between "two equal, virtuous, pious individuals," which further suggests a greater inclusiveness of honor and virtue (40).

185. AA to John Thaxter, 17 Jun. 1782, AFC; Bloch, *Gender and Morality*, 144.

186. Hannah Adams, *Women Invited to War*, 3.

187. Rush, *Thoughts upon Female Education*, 88.

188. Reinier, "Rearing the Republican Child."

189. Rush, "Plan for Establishing," 19. For a similar account, see James Madison [1749–1812], *Discourse Delivered*, 5.

190. "The Petition of Florence Cooke," in Kierner, *Southern Women in Revolution*, 172.

191. AA to JQA, 16 Feb. 1786, 6 Sept. 1785, AFC.

192. Betsy Watts to Sarah C. Watts, 4 Apr. 1807, Sarah C. Watts Papers, W&M. Fathers also played a role. See Henry Tucker to St. George Tucker, 30 Nov. 1771, Tucker-Coleman Papers, CWF; JA to Abigail Adams II, 14 Apr. 1783, 9 Jun. 1783, AFC.

193. AA to JQA, 16 Feb. 1786, AFC.

194. Elizabeth Trist to Nicholas P. Trist, 20 Feb. 1821, Family Letters, Thomas Jefferson's Monticello.

195. For more on female education, see Cott, *Bonds of Womanhood*, ch. 3.

196. Magnaw, *Address*, 8.

197. Rush, *Thoughts upon Female Education*, 76, 87.

198. *Connecticut Gazette*, 13 Feb. 1784.

199. Elizabeth Lee Diary, CWF.

200. Rush, *Thoughts upon Female Education*, 81; Aimwell School Records, Quaker and Special Collections, Haverford College; Dolly Madison to Marie Rivardi, 10 May 1812, *Papers of Dolley Madison*; Nash, "Rethinking Republican Motherhood," 181–85; *Compend of Rhetoric*.

201. Alexander, *Young Gentlemen and Ladies Instructor*, 83.

202. Neal, *Essay of the Education*, 27.

203. *Evening Amusements for the Ladies*, 62.

204. *Rise and Progress*, 37, 95; Mason is also quoted in Zagarri, *Revolutionary Backlash*, 49.

205. Neal, *Essay of the Education*, 17.

206. For continuation of BF's ideas, see Hore Browse Trist to Nicholas P. Trist, 14 Apr. 1820, Family Letters, Thomas Jefferson's Monticello.

207. For a similar opening of American religion, see Nathan O. Hatch, *Democratization of American Christianity*.

208. For more, see Hinks and Kantrowitz, *All Men Free and Brethren*.

209. Hall, *Charge Delivered to the Brethren*, 12. For an abolitionist linking African American military service with good citizenship, see Buchanan, *Oration*, 17–18.

210. Joanna Brooks, "Colonization, Black Freemasonry," 239–40.

211. Marrant, *Sermon Preached*, 18, 22.

212. Joanna Brooks and Saillant, introduction to *"Face Zion Forward,"* 29.

213. Hall, *Charge Delivered to the Brethren*, 3, 12.

214. Marrant, *Sermon Preached*, 20.

215. Hall, *Charge, Delivered to the African Lodge*, 11.

216. "Negro Slavery," "To the New Jersey Society for Promoting the Abolition of Slavery from the Convention of 1798," 6 Jun. 1798, Box 9, Allinson Family Papers, Quaker and Special Collections, Haverford College.

217. Hall, *Charge, Delivered to the African Lodge*, 12.

218. Cooley, *Sketches*, 78; Jonathan Edwards [1703–58], *Essay*, 3.

219. Haynes, *Nature and Importance*, 5, 10, 12–13.

220. [Forten], *Letters*, 2, 8.

221. For a very good account of the politicization of slavery and abolitionism, see Matthew Mason, *Slavery and Politics*, 9–41.

222. Cooper, *Mite Cast into the Treasury*.

223. Lover of Constitutional Liberty, *Appendix*, 4.

224. BF to Benjamin Rush, 14 Jul. 1773, *PBF*. For more on the Pennsylvania society for promoting the abolition of slavery, and the relief of free negroes, unlawfully held in bondage, see "From the Pennsylvania Abolition Society: Constitution," 23 Apr. 1787, *PBF*; Pennsylvania Abolition Society to the United States Congress, 3 Feb. 1790, *PBF*; Pennsylvania Abolition Society to the Pennsylvania Assembly, 24 Nov. 1789, *PBF*. For more on BF and antislavery, see BF to the Editor of the Federal Gazette, 8 Apr. 1788, 23 Mar. 1790, *PBF*.

225. Law, *Extract from a Treatise*, 79.

226. McLeod, *Negro Slavery Unjustifiable*, 18, 42.

227. Cooper, *Serious Address*, 5.

228. Ibid., 4–5, 17.

229. Law, *Extract from a Treatise*, 84.

230. This thesis is central to my future monograph project, "Redemption: The American Revolution, Ethics, and Abolitionism in Britain and the United States." Aspects of this were presented at the 2014 Organization of American Historians Annual Conference as "Redemption: The American Revolution and Abolitionism in Britain and the United States."

231. Antibiastes, *Observations*, 2.

232. Benezet, *Short Observations on Slavery*, 1–4.

233. Cugoano, *Thoughts and Sentiments*, 135. For a similar interpretation of British moral superiority over America, see Price, *Observations on the Importance*, 83–84.

234. ML to GW, 5 Feb. 1783, *PGW*; JM to TJ, 17 Oct. 1784, *PTJ*.

235. Jefferson's Notes from Condorcet on Slavery, [ca. 1788–89], *PTJ*; Condorcet, "Reflections on Negro Slavery," 55–57.

236. Cugoano, *Thoughts and Sentiments*, 61.

237. Clarkson, *Essay on the Impolicy*, 145; Clarkson, *Essay on the Slavery*, 109.

238. Wesley, *Thoughts upon Slavery*, 20.

239. McLeod, *Negro Slavery Unjustifiable*, 16.

240. Truth, *Narrative*, 33.

241. Clarkson, *Essay on the Slavery*, 175. Similar thoughts are present in Clarkson, *Essay on the Impolicy*.

242. *Remarks on a Pamphlet*, 4.

243. Lover of Constitutional Liberty, *Appendix*, 6.

244. Fischer, *Washington's Crossing*, 15; Henriques, *Realistic Visionary*, 155.

245. GW to Lund Washington, 15 Aug. 1778, *PGW*.

246. JM to TJ, 17 Oct. 1784, *PTJ*.

247. 25 Aug. 1787, *Notes of Debates in the Federal Convention of 1787*.

248. Jefferson's "original Rough draught" of the Declaration of Independence, *PTJ*.

249. TJ, *Notes on the State of Virginia*, 161–62, 299–300.

250. JA to TJ, 22 May 1785, *PTJ*.

251. McLeod, *Negro Slavery Unjustifiable*, 34–35.

252. Furstenberg, "Beyond Freedom and Slavery," 1316. For the incompatibility of virtue and slavery, see [Hanway], *Soldier's Faithful Friend*, 15.

253. JM to Joseph Jones, 28 Nov. 1780, FO: JM.

254. On GW's desire to end slavery, see ML to GW, 5 Feb. 1783, GW to ML, 5 Apr. 1783, in *WW*, 26:300n; GW to Lawrence Lewis, 4 Aug. 1797, in *WW*, 36:2. On his reluctance to end slavery, see Ellis, *His Excellency*, 259. For more on GW and antislavery, see Furstenberg, "Atlantic Slavery, Atlantic Freedom."

255. Wyatt-Brown, *Shaping of Southern Culture*, 52; Carter Berkeley to Dr. Robert Carter, 9 Nov. 1804, Shirley Plantation Collection, CWF.

256. GW to Alexander Spotswood, 23 Nov. 1794, in *WW*, 34:47.

257. JM, *Federalist Papers*, no. 42, in FO: JM.

258. TJ to JM, 11 May 1785, *PTJ*.

259. For a good treatment of TJ's concern with public opinion, see Ellis, *American Sphinx*, 86–88.

260. TJ to Brissot de Warville, 11 Feb. 1788, *PTJ*.

261. Matthew Mason, *Slavery and Politics*, 35. For an alternative view, see Helo, *Thomas Jefferson's Ethics*. Helo states that, based on TJ's "ethical thought" centered on "human progress," it was indeed possible to have "consistency in his advocacy of democracy and the rights of man while remaining . . . one of the largest slaveholders in Virginia" (1). He goes on to state that the biggest problem in understanding this stems from "his confusing liberal use of such ethical—or ethically charged—concepts" (2).

262. Humanitas [Edward Darlington], *Reflections on Slavery*, 11.

263. TJ to ML, 2 Apr. 1790, FO: TJ.

264. GW to TJ, 12 Apr. 1793, GW to AH, 12 Apr. 1793, *PGW*.

265. Chernow, *Washington*, 690–91; TJ to Madame d'Enville, 2 Apr. 1790, FO: TJ.

266. TJ to ML, 2 Apr. 1790, FO: TJ.

267. Gouverneur Morris to TJ, 22 Aug. 1792, *PTJ*.

268. Brookhiser, *Gentleman Revolutionary*, 134.

269. Thomas Jefferson's Notes on a Cabinet Meeting, 6 May 1793, *PGW*.

270. Chernow, *Washington*, 690.

271. "Proclamation," *National Gazette*, 24 Apr. 1793.

272. "To the Editor of the National Gazette," *National Gazette*, 18 May 1793.

273. "To the Editor of the National Gazette," *National Gazette*, 22 May 1793.

274. "Citizens Genet, Minister Plenipotentiary from the Republic of France, to the Citizens of Philadelphia," *National Gazette*, 22 May 1793.

275. AH, *Letters of Pacificus*, 6, 7, 14, 17, 18, 32, 33, 35, 38–39, 41–44, 49.

276. JM, *Letters of Helvidius*, 3, 4, 27.

277. BF to HL, 10 Sept. 1783, *PBF*.

278. 12 Jun. 1783, *JCC*.

279. Vertias (No. II) to GW, 3 Jun. 1793, *PGW*.

280. [Nettleton], *Treatise on Virtue and Happiness*, 284. GW's personal copy currently housed at the Boston Athenaeum has the inscription "1792" in the front cover, suggesting that GW was reading this work at virtually the exact same time as he was considering the nature of the French Revolution.

281. Seventh Annual Address, 8 Dec. 1795, in *WW*, 34:388; Draft of GW's Seventh Annual Address to Congress, [28 Nov.–7 Dec. 1795], *PGW*.

282. Farewell Address, 19 Sept. 1796, FO: GW.

283. Col. David Humphreys to MW, 5 Jul. 1800, Julia Bowen, Mary B. Howell, Sarah Halsey, and Abby Chace[?] to MW, 14 Feb. 1800, Martha Washington Papers, FSNL. For GW as a symbol since 1775, see Elizabeth Powel to MW, 7 Jan. 1775, Martha Washington Papers, FSNL.

284. Buckminster, *Religion and Righteousness*, 16.

285. "The Anas," in *Writings of Thomas Jefferson*, 381.

286. "A Development of the Causes of the Disturbances between the American and French Republics: Addressed," *North-Carolina Journal*, 14 Aug. 1797.

287. "The Moralist—No. 283: National Ethics," *Oracle of the Day*, 26 Jan. 1799.

288. Quoted in Grant, *John Adams*, 393.

289. "The Anas," in *Writings of Thomas Jefferson*, 279. For additional views on the character and morals of TJ and AB, see Leven Powell to Burr Powell, 23 Dec. 1800, 12 Jan. 1801, Thomas J. Page to Leven Powell, 5 Feb. 1801, William B. Harrison to Leven Powell, 11 Feb. 1801, Thomas Sims to Leven Powell, 20 Feb. 1801, Leven Powell Papers, W&M; Barnabas Bidwell to AB, 6 Jul. 1801, in AB, *Political Correspondence*, 2:604.

290. "From the New York Evening Post, of June 3," *Washington Federalist*, 11 Jun. 1802; Kett, *Merit*, 41–44.

291. Freeman, *Affairs of Honor*.

292. TJ to JA, 15 Jun. 1813, FO: TJ.

Chapter Seven

1. MOW, *History of the Rise*, 3:339, 396.

2. Freeman, *Affairs of Honor*.

3. The opening narrative is crafted from a combination of the following sources: Chernow, *Alexander Hamilton*, 680–709; Freeman, *Affairs of Honor*, 159–98; AH, [Statement on Impending Duel with Aaron Burr], [28 Jun.–10 Jul. 1804], *PAH*; Alexander Hamilton Collection, NYHS; Van Ness, *Correct Statement*.

4. Philanthropos, *Letter to Aaron Burr*, 22.

5. For example, see *Edict of Statute*; James I, *By the King*; Bacon, *Charge of Sir Francis Bacon*; Despagne, *Anti-Duello*; G. F., *Duell-Ease*; Sewall, *He That Would Keep*; Coleman, *Mr. Coleman's Sermon*; and Pufendorf, *Law of Nature and Nations*. For an example of antidueling fiction, see Tyler, *Algerine Captive*.

6. For personal antidueling views, see GW to ML, 4 Oct. 1778, *PGW*; BF to Thomas Percival, 17 Jul. 1784, *PBF*; "Miscellaneous," *Enquirer*, 21 Jul. 1804, 3; May "19 Thursday," 1756, *DJA*; and AH, [Statement on Impending Duel with Aaron Burr], [28 Jun.–10 Jul. 1804], *PAH*.

7. "Dueling," *Courier of New Hampshire*, 18 Jul. 1797.

8. Wells, "End of the Affair?" Similarly, Wells examines antidueling legislation as a battle between laws and social norms.

9. Chernow, *Alexander Hamilton*, 713.

10. *Weekly Museum*, 14 Jul. 1804; "In Common Council," *American Citizen*, 13 Jul. 1804; *Poulson's American Daily Advertiser*, 16 Jul. 1804.

11. "Mr. Morris' Oration," *Windham Herald*, 2 Aug. 1804.

12. J. M. Mason, *Oration*, 11, 25.

13. Thomas Truxton to Charles Biddle, 26 Jul. 1804, Aaron Burr Letters and Documents, NYPL.

14. "On the Evening of the General's Decease, the Rev. Bishop Moore Addressed the Following Interesting and Pious Letter to the Editor of the New York Evening Post, July 12, 1804," *Jenks' Portland Gazette*, 23 Jul. 1804.

15. Freeman, *Affairs of Honor*, 177–78.

16. "Thoughts on Dueling," *New York Commercial Advertiser*, 3 Jun. 1808.

17. "Duel, Cursitor, Post Obit," *Political Calendar*, 12 Jul. 1804.

18. Chernow, *Alexander Hamilton*, 683.

19. "Duel," *Republican Spy*, 17 Jan. 1804.

20. "From the Balance," *Alexandria Advertiser*, 19 Nov. 1804.

21. "Communication," *United States Gazette*, 20 Jul. 1804.

22. Woodruff, *Danger of Ambition Considered*, 17.

23. Philanthropos, *Letter to Aaron Burr*, 13.

24. Thomas Truxton to Charles Biddle, 18 and 26 Jul. 1804, quoted in Wandall and Minnigerode, *Aaron Burr*, 1: 303–4; "Our Treatment of Aaron Burr," n.d., Aaron Burr (1756–1836) Collection, PURBSC.

25. "From the Trenton Federalist" [ca. 1802], Aaron Burr Letters and Documents, NYPL.

26. AH, [Statement on Impending Duel with Aaron Burr], [28 Jun.–10 Jul. 1804], *PAH*. For an example of its mention in the press, see "Died," *Weekly Museum*, 14 Jul. 1804.

27. "From the Boston Democrat," *Eastern Argus*, 16 Aug. 1804; Richard Bell, "Double Guilt of Dueling." Bell looks at the antidueling movement, which casts dueling and particularly AH's conduct as suicide. He also notes that reformers made sure to point out that dueling was not "true honor" (396).

28. Spring, *Sixth Commandment*, 20.

29. Hopkins, *Hamiltoniad*, vii.

30. Ibid., 31.

31. Abercrombie, *Sermon*, 27; Spring, *Sixth Commandment*, 15; Bell, "Double Guilt of Dueling."

32. Coleman, *Mr. Coleman's Sermon*, 6, 14–15; Sewall, *He That Would Keep*, ii, 6, 10. For more on the 1728 duel, see Henry Phillips, Archive Relating to the Duel on Boston Common in New England, Archives and Manuscripts, British Library, London.

33. "On Duelling," *Enquirer*, 5 Jan. 1805.

34. Woodruff, *Danger of Ambition Considered*, 19.

35. Abercrombie, *Sermon*, 32.

36. "William Ladd," *Maine Library Bulletin* 8, no. 1 (July 1918): 100.

37. Philanthropos, *Letter to Aaron Burr*, 11.

38. Ibid., 12.

39. Abercrombie, *Sermon*, 33–35.

40. Woodruff, *Danger of Ambition Considered*, 5, 6, 21. For more, see Opal, *Beyond the Farm*, viii. Opal shows the connections between ambition, honor, sin, and evil.

41. Hopkins, *Hamiltoniad*, v–vi; Woodruff, *Danger of Ambition Considered*, 15.

42. Abercrombie, *Sermon*, 49.

43. Philanthropos, *Letter to Aaron Burr*, 21.

44. "New-York, August 27," *City Gazette*, 4 Sept. 1804; "Charleston, (S.C.) September 12, 1804," *City Gazette*, 18 Sept. 1804.

45. "Duelling," *Massachusetts Spy*, 10 Oct. 1804; "From the Balance," *Alexandria Advertiser*, 19 Nov. 1804; "Of Dueling," *Alexandria Advertiser*, 24 Sept. 1805.

46. For period proliferation of the Southern dueling connection, see Tyler, *Algerine Captive*, 105.

47. David Ramsay to Benjamin Rush, 27 Sept. 1804, Rush Family Papers, HSP.

48. Spring, *Sixth Commandment*, 15.

49. Byron, "Crime and Punishment," esp. 31.

50. "Duel," *Republican Spy*, 17 Jan. 1804.

51. Hopkins, *Hamiltoniad*, 27.

52. Philanthropos, *Letter to Aaron Burr*, 23.

53. "From the Balance," *Alexandria Advertiser*, 19 Nov. 1804.

54. "On Duelling," *Enquirer*, 5 Jan. 1805.

55. Ibid.

56. Hopkins, *Hamiltoniad*, 39.

57. "On Duelling," *Enquirer*, 5 Jan. 1805.

58. Ibid.

59. Byron, "Crime and Punishment," 7, 26, 28, 32–33.

60. "Domestic: Anti-duelling Association: New-York, August 8, 1809," *Enquirer*, 22 Aug. 1809; "The Address of the Anti-duelling Association," *New York Commercial Advertiser*, 15 Aug. 1809.

61. "Thoughts on Dueling," *New York Commercial Advertiser*, 3 Jun. 1808; Wells, "End of the Affair?," 1820–21 (also notes the links between the AH-AB duel and antidueling, more specifically in the North).

62. Byron, "Crime and Punishment," 6.

63. Appleby, *Inheriting the Revolution*, 30. Appleby discusses dueling's "second life" among the post-Revolutionary generation. Glover, *Southern Sons*, 104–6.

64. "Dueling," *Courier of New Hampshire*, 18 Jul. 1797.

65. Beecher, *Remedy for Duelling*, 9–10.

66. Appleby, *Inheriting the Revolution*, 3 (on the "couscious[ness]" of not having participated in the war); Glover, *Southern Sons*, 2–4, 11–12; Herrera, *For Liberty and the Republic*, 149–50, and Glover, *Founders as Fathers*, 245–47 (on the demands of living up to the Revolutionary generation); Steven J. Novak, *Rights of Youth*, ch. 3.

67. Kett, *Merit*, 40, 50.

68. Barton, *Concise Account*, 3–9.

69. Webster, "Autobiography," [1829], in *Papers of Daniel Webster*, 4–5; Correspondence with John Randolph, Apr. 1816, in *Papers of Daniel Webster*, 197–99; Remini, *Daniel Webster*, 33, 52, 139, 142, 242. For additional examples of sons looking to their fathers, see William Austin, *Selection of Patriotic Addresses*, 103, 185–86.

70. Beecher, *Remedy for Duelling*, 9–10.

71. Opal, *Beyond the Farm*, 1–3, 7.

72. MOW, *History of the Rise*, 3:417, 333. On the concept of diverse notions of masculinity in early America, see Toby L. Ditz, "Afterword: Contending Masculinities in Early America," in Foster, *New Men*, 256: "Several models of masculinity competed with one another throughout the colonial era and would continue to do so after the revolution."

73. Masters of the Grammar School to Trustees, 7 Jan. 1817, Edward Shoemaker to Trustees, Jan. 1817, Trustees of the University of Pennsylvania Records, UPA.

74. Jan [C. Charlton] to Sarah C. Watt, 19 Mar. 1809, Sarah C. Watt Papers, W&M; Samuel Meyers to Moses Meyers, 30 Jan. 1809, Samuel Meyers Papers, W&M; 27 Sept. 1809, Princeton University Commencement Records, PUSML; Glover, *Southern Sons*, 75. Lorri Glover refers to dueling among students as "seldom" taking place. But duels did occur, and, at the very least, violence based on slights to honor were common. In addition, young men carried lessons about the importance of reputation and any proclivities for violence with them when they graduated from school to adulthood.

75. Byron, "Crime and Punishment," 33.

76. "Journal or Log of the Chesapeake," 1807, JBP, W&M; Copy of a Letter from JB to Robert Smith, 23 Jun. 1807, JBP, W&M; Abstract Taken from the US Frigate Chesapeake's Log Book, J. Barron Esq. Commdr., Char. Gordon Esq. Capt., & Samuel Brooke Sailing Master, JBP , W&M; *CMJB*, quotation from 86.

77. "News Story from the *Norfolk Gazette & Public Ledger*," 24 Jun. 1807, in *CA*, 13.

78. Friend of Truth, and of Honorable Peace, *Conduct of Washington*, 20; Cray, "Remembering the USS *Chesapeake*," 447–48. For a discussion of impressment before this event, see Brunsman, *Evil Necessity*.

79. "News Story from the *Norfolk Gazette & Public Ledger*," 24 Jun. 1807, in *CA*, 13.

80. Gaines, "Chesapeake Affair"; Cray, "Remembering the USS *Chesapeake*," 455.

81. "Cavalry Orders," *Norfolk Gazette and Public Ledger*, 29 Jun. 1807, in *CA*, 38.

82. "Division Orders," 1 Aug. 1807, in *CA*, 72–73.

83. Lowell, *Peace without Honor*, "To the Publick" [n.p.].

84. *Voice of Truth*, 13–14.

85. Lowell, *Peace without Honor*, "To the Publick" [n.p.], 22–23.

86. M. Myers to Comm. Barry, 10 Apr. 1798, B. Cocke to JB, 29 Jul. 1806, [John] Rodgers to JB, 23 Jul. 1806, JB to John Rodgers, 29 Jul. 1806, 31 Jan. 1807, JBP.

87. Spencer C. Tucker and Reuter, *Injured Honor*, 84–85.

88. Officers of the Late US Ship Chesapeake to Robert Smith, Secretary of the US Navy, 23 Jun. 1807, JBP.

89. Ibid.

90. Lowell, *Peace without Honor*, 14.

91. Bland, *Treatise of Military Discipline*, 114.

92. Ibid., 124.

93. Alan Taylor also observes similar behavior during the War of 1812. See Taylor, *Civil War of 1812*, 321–24.

94. On Barron's patriotic sentiments, see "Autobiographical Notes by James Barron, with endorsement," n.d., JBP.

95. JB to Capt. Charles Gordon, Jul. 1807, JBP; Spencer C. Tucker and Reuter, *Injured Honor*, 100.

96. Spencer C. Tucker and Reuter, *Injured Honor*, 183.

97. JB to Dr. Bullus, 3 Jul. 1807, JBP.

98. For more on the court-martial, see Latshaw, "Flawed Judgment."

99. *CMJB*, 267–68.

100. Ibid., 286.

101. Ibid., 295–96.

102. Ibid.

103. Spencer C. Tucker and Reuter, *Injured Honor*, 140. For more on TJ's reactions and preparations, see Cogliano, *Emperor of Liberty*, 230–42.

104. Ro. Saunders to JB, 30 Jun. 1808, JBP.

105. *CMJB*, 22. Others were also tried and convicted, including Captain Gordon, Marine Captain John Hall, and Gunner William Hook. On Gordon's verdict, see ibid., 454: he was "guilty of some offense, (although a very slight one)" and sentenced to a private reprimand. On Hall's verdict, see ibid., 476: "No evil has resulted from any of the neglects of duty," and he was sentenced to a private reprimand. On Hook's verdict, see ibid., 496: "Proving that much of his neglect was wilfull; and that the fatal consequences which have in great degree resulted from it," he was dismissed from service. Gordon and Hall escaped with barely a slap on the wrist. It is interesting to note that while Hook suffered by far the harshest penalty, the loss of the *Chesapeake* was never attributed to him in the junior officers' initial charge. In addition, the disgrace of the event was primarily ascribed both publicly and privately only to JB. The fact that only the highest- and lowest-ranking defendants were convicted again shows a democratization of the codes of honor.

106. There were many who believed that JB's conviction was unwarranted, and even some that felt that President TJ would overturn the ruling. Obviously, no such reversal took place. B. Cooke to JB, 30 Jun. 1808, JBP.

107. Cray, "Remembering the USS *Chesapeake*," 473–74.

108. Spencer C. Tucker and Reuter, *Injured Honor*, 192.

109. For examples dismissing economic motivations, see Risjord, "1812"; and Wyatt-Brown, *Warring Nation*, 72–74.

110. For conceptions of the War of 1812 as civil war, see Taylor, *Civil War of 1812*.

111. Report of the Committee on Foreign Relations in the House of Representatives of the United States, 29 Jan. 1813, in Friend of Truth, and of Honorable Peace, *Conduct of Washington*, 21.

112. Eustace, *1812*, 180–81.

113. Google Books Ngram, "personal honor," 1783–2008, in American English.

114. Taylor, *The Civil War of 1812*, 94, 324.

115. Google Books Ngram, "military honor," 1783–2008, in American English.

116. "The Love of Country," quoted in Eustace, *1812*, 53–54.

117. JM, "Proclamation," 19 Jun. 1812, Miller Center.

118. Haynes, *Dissimulation Illustrated*, in Eustace, *1812*, 190–91.

119. Waterhouse, *Journal of a Young Man*, 188, also in Taylor, *Civil War of 1812*, 421. There is debate about whether this source is a work of fiction by Waterhouse or an authentic manuscript written by Babcock (which Waterhouse later edited).

120. JB to William Jones, Secretary of the Navy, 22 Jul. 1813, JBP.

121. Decatur and Barron, *Correspondence*; Allen C. Clark, "Commodore James Barron," 205–8; Long, "William Bainbridge," 49; Waldo, *Life and Character of Stephen*

Decatur, 283–311; Spencer C. Tucker and Reuter, *Injured Honor*, 204–6. On dueling among naval officers, see Budiansky, *Perilous Fight*, 67. Regarding justification of JB's actions and honor, and also for an alternate perspective on the perception of JB's continuing dishonor, see Umphraville, *Oration*, 16; and *Proceedings of a Court of Inquiry*.

122. "Duelling," *Farmer's Museum*, 23 Apr. 1810; *Alexandria Gazette*, 6 Feb. 1810; "Law against Duelling," *Norwich Courier*, 29 Nov. 1809; "Legislature; Georgia; Dueling; Duel," *City Gazette*, 10 Jan. 1810; 3 Feb. 1813, Minutes of the Trustees, UPA; *General Regulation for the Army*, 336; *Laws of Queen's College*, 11.

123. Beecher, *Remedy for Duelling*, 12; Wells, "End of the Affair?," 1821 (argues that antidueling laws failed because they were regulated by those "deeply embedded in the very social practices the laws sought to overturn").

124. TJ to JA, 28 Oct. 1813, FO: TJ.

125. TJ to JA, 12 Oct. 1813, FO: TJ; TJ, *Life and Morals of Jesus of Nazareth.*

126. TJ to Charles Thomson, 9 Jan. 1816, FO: TJ; Helo, *Thomas Jefferson's Ethics*, ch. 3. Ari Helo states that TJ regarded his ethics and focus on the "Philosophy of Jesus" as "moral faith" (80).

127. TJ to JA, 28 Oct. 1813, FO: TJ; JA to TJ, 15 Nov. 1813, FO: AF.

128. TJ to JA, 28 Oct. 1813, FO: TJ.

129. JA, *Defence of the Constitutions*, xvii.

130. JA to TJ, 15 Nov. 1813, JA to Richard Rush, 5 Nov. 1813, MOW to JA, 28 Jul. 1807, JA to John Taylor, 9 Jun. 1814, FO: AF.

131. JA, *Defence of the Constitutions*, 116, 183, 209; "A Bill for the More General Diffusion of Knowledge," 18 Jun. 1779, FO: TJ. For another reference, see New York Ratifying Convention, First Speech of June 21 (John McKesson's Version), [21 Jun. 1788], FO: AH.

132. TJ to JA, 28 Oct. 1813, FO: TJ.

133. JA to John Taylor, 22 Dec. 1814, FO: AF.

134. TJ to JA, 28 Oct. 1813, FO: TJ.

135. JA, *Defence of the Constitutions*, 183, 209.

136. JA to TJ, 15 Nov. 1813, FO: AF.

137. For more, see Larson, *Magnificent Catastrophe*; Newmyer, *Treason Trial of Aaron Burr*; Wheelan, *Jefferson's Vendetta*; Ferling, *Adams vs. Jefferson*; Abernethy, *Burr Conspiracy*.

138. JA to TJ, 15 Nov. 1813, FO: AF.

139. JA to John Taylor, 27 Dec. 1814, FO: AF.

140. Samuel Latham Mitchell to JA, 8 Feb. 1820, FO: AF; G. F. H. Crockett to TJ, 18 Feb. 1823, FO: TJ; Samuel Brown to TJ, 1 Oct. 1812, FO: TJ.

141. For more on the Kappa Lambda Society of Hippocrates and early medical ethics, see Veatch, *Hippocratic, Religious, and Secular*; Baker, *American Medical Ethics Revolution*; Baker, *Before Bioethics*; Ambrose, "Secret Kappa Lambda Society"; and Ambrose, "Historical Importance."

142. G. F. H. Crockett to TJ, 18 Feb. 1823, FO: TJ.

143. Hippocrates, "Oath."

144. John T. J. Wilson, *Address to the [Kappa Lamda] Society*, 4.

145. Percival, *Extracts from the Medical Ethics*, ii, xi, 6, 8.

146. Samuel Latham Mitchell to JA, 8 Feb. 1820, FO: AF.

147. G. F. H. Crockett to TJ, 18 Feb. 1823, FO: TJ.

148. Oath or affirmation in Veatch, *Hippocratic, Religious, and Secular*, 49.

149. G. F. H. Crockett to TJ, 18 Feb. 1823, FO: TJ.

150. Baker, *American Medical Ethics Revolution*, 30; *Minutes of the Medical Society*, 473.

151. *History of the New York Kappa Lambda Conspiracy*, 4.

152. Medical Ethics of New York, 13th sec., in ibid., 19.

153. *History of the New York Kappa Lambda Conspiracy*, 24; " 'Kappa Lambda Society of Hippocrates.' "

154. "Minutes, Board of Visitors, University of Virginia," 3 Oct. 1825, FO: JM.

155. Burstein, *Sentimental Democracy*, 254.

156. Benjamin Waterhouse to JM, 17 Sept. 1834, FO: JM.

Epilogue

1. The opening narrative is crafted from a synthesis of the following sources: AJ to James Monroe, [16 Mar. 1824], AJ to Rachel Jackson, 16 Mar. 1824, *PAJ*; Eaton and Reid, *Life of Andrew Jackson*, vii, 393; AJ to Andrew Jackson Donelson, 16 Mar. 1824, in Parton, *Life of Andrew Jackson*, 3:38; Furst, "Gold Medal Presented to Jackson," [1815–40], LOC; U.S. Congress, *Debates and Proceedings*, 13th Congress, 3rd session, 233–34. For AJ enjoying fame, see Meacham, *American Lion*, 33.

2. Wyatt-Brown, *Shaping of Southern Culture*, 56.

3. Fischer, *Albion's Seed*, 642–44, 755. David Hackett Fischer views AJ as a gentleman (although not of the highest rank) based on the status of his grandfather (in Northern Ireland), his father (in Northern Ireland and America), and his wife and father-in-law (in America) (ibid., 848). Other historians have interpreted AJ as representative of many different classes. For political reasons, John Henry Eaton and John Reid, in *Life of Andrew Jackson*, 10, portray AJ as humbler, with the family inheriting only a "small patrimony" after his father's death. Coinciding with his 1824 presidential campaign, Eaton made AJ even more modest, with no mention of any inheritance, simply stating that children needed to be "provided for by their mother." Eaton, *Life of Andrew Jackson*, 10. For more on the difference between varying editions of this work, see Owsley, *Life of Andrew Jackson*, xvii. The biography was written with political intent. See Meacham, *American Lion*, 11: AJ "chose to remember his upbringing this way," and he "linked" himself and the family with "the common man."

4. Wyatt-Brown, *Southern Honor*, 134.

5. Eaton and Reid, *Life of Andrew Jackson*, 10. For the influence of Old World/Celtic/backcountry honor, see ibid., 38; and Fischer, *Albion's Seed*, 642, 668, 688, 720. For more on Celtic heritage and the Jackson family's connection with Siege of Carrickfergus, see Parton, *Life of Andrew Jackson*, vol. 1, ch. 2.

6. Quincy, *Figures of the Past*, 352.

7. On AJ's using duels to secure his social status, see Cheathem, *Andrew Jackson*, 45.

8. For some examples of his known duels or challenges, see AJ to Waightstill Avery, 12 Aug. 1788, AJ to John Sevier, 10 May 1797, AJ to William Cocke, 25 Jun. 1798, AJ to John Sevier, 3 Oct. 1803, AJ to John Sevier, 9 Oct. 1803, AJ to the Public, 10 Oct. 1803, AJ to John Sevier, 10 Oct. 1803, Thomas Swann to AJ, 12 Jan. 1806, AJ to Thomas Eastin, 10 Feb. 1806, *PAJ*; Cheathem, *Andrew Jackson*, 38–45; Remini, *Andrew Jackson*, 36–37; Burstein, *Passions of Andrew Jackson*, ch. 2.

9. AJ to John Sevier, 10 May 1797, *PAJ*.

10. For a fuller account of the Dickinson-Jackson duel and honor, see Wyatt-Brown, *Shaping of Southern Culture*, 58–61; Brands, *Andrew Jackson*, 139–41. H. W. Brands claims that the duel "was about personal honor more than about public opinion" (139). Wyatt-Brown, in *Southern Honor*, 134, conversely asserts that it was the pressure placed on the duelists by "over a dozen men, some of them at the fringes of male society" that led to "lethal settlement." This would seem to indicate that the spirit of mobility created by honor culture and displayed through dueling was growing in prevalence among varied classes of men.

11. Parton, *Life of Andrew Jackson*, 1:297.

12. Ibid., 1:305.

13. Amy Greenberg, *Manifest Manhood*, 8.

14. For AJ's connection between justice and vengeance, see Opal, *Avenging the People*.

15. "Jackson's Description of His Experiences during and Immediately following the Revolutionary War," [1781], *PAJ*.

16. For more on NG, Rutherford, and the rules of war noted by Emer de Vattel, see chapter 5; William Moore to Griffith Rutherford, 17 Nov. 1776, Learn NC; Vattel, *Law of Nations* (1759), bk. 3, 63; and NG to Alexander Martin, 9 Oct. 1781, NG to Griffith Rutherford, 18 Oct. 1781, NG to Griffith Rutherford, 20 Oct. 1781, in *PNG*, 9:438–39, 452–54, 456–61.

17. Wyatt-Brown, *Southern Honor*, 42.

18. Eaton and Reid, *Life of Andrew Jackson*, 29–34, 42.

19. Ibid., 34.

20. Vattel, *Law of Nations* (1759), bk. 3, 63; NG to Griffith Rutherford, 20 Oct. 1781, in *PNG*, 9:456–61.

21. Eaton and Reid, *Life of Andrew Jackson*, 42.

22. Crockett, *Narrative*, 89.

23. Meacham, *American Lion*, 31; Eaton and Reid, *Life of Andrew Jackson*, 51. While Eaton and Reid don't deny that women and children were "exposed to the general danger," they attempt to justify AJ's conduct, claiming, "Every possible precaution was taken to prevent it." In the 1824 edition, Eaton tries to further exonerate AJ by stating, "In fact many of the women united with their warriors, and contended in battle with fearless bravery." Eaton, *Life of Andrew Jackson*, 54–55.

24. Meacham, *American Lion*, 35–36; Remini, *Andrew Jackson*, ch. 2, 4; Remini, "Jackson Takes an Oath" (AJ seems to have even taken an oath to the Spanish crown in 1789 [in exchange for trading rights], whereby he, "pledging his word of honor," vowed to

"not offend directly nor indirectly conspire against the Spanish nation." This makes AJ's invasion of Florida even more of a departure from an ethical conception of honor.); AJ to Secretary Calhoun, 26 Apr. 1818, in *Correspondence of Andrew Jackson*, 2:363–64.

25. NG to Griffith Rutherford, 20 Oct. 1781, in *PNG*, 9:456–61.

26. For quotations on AJ's and his supporters' views, see [Overton], *Vindication*, 22, 26, 28–29, 33, 36–39, 44–45, 53; AJ to Secretary Calhoun, 26 Apr. 1818, in *Correspondence of Andrew Jackson*, 2:363–64; and Eaton, *Life of Major General Andrew Jackson*, 287–300. No mention of the Seminole War or Vattel exists in the earlier two editions of Eaton's book; Overton and Eaton both cite Vattel, but their quotations seem to be a modification of *The Law of Nations* rather than a word-for-word transcription. For AJ's using similar terminology against the Creek, see Eaton and Reid, *Life of Andrew Jackson*, 42. For Vattel, see Vattel, *Law of Nations* (1797), 348; and Vattel, *Law of Nations* (1805), 416—these period British and U.S. editions differ slightly in terminology in comparison to that of the AJ supporters. Feller, "2009 Catherine Prescott Lecture"; Wilentz, *Andrew Jackson*, 36–41; Rosen, "Wartime Prisoners"; U.S. Congress, *Debates and Proceedings*, 15th Congress, 2nd session, 515–27.

27. Glassman, *Congressional Gold Medals*.

28. For AJ's using this ceremony to link himself to the Revolution and also for political clout in the upcoming 1824 election, see Hay, "American Revolution Twice Recalled." For GW's pistols, see Parton, *Life of Andrew Jackson*, 3:37, 365, 2:660; Meacham, *American Lion*, 37.

29. Eaton and Reid, *Life of Andrew Jackson*, 31; Eaton, *Life of Andrew Jackson*, 34 (Eaton edited out the mention of dueling in the 1824 edition); AJ to Thomas Pinckney, 28 Mar. 1814, in Brannan, *Official Letters*; U.S. Congress, *Debates and Proceedings*, 15th Congress, 2nd session, 527.

30. James Monroe to the Military Committee of the Senate, 22 Feb. 1815, in *Writings of James Monroe*, 321–22.

31. James Ronaldson to JA, 16 Feb. 1820, FO: *AP*.

32. Eaton and Reid, *Life of Andrew Jackson*, 43–44, 395. For AJ's influence on his nephew/ward/"pseudo-son," which is indicative of the passage of his message to younger men, see Cheathem, " 'High Minded Honourable Man.' " For the rise of ambition, see Opal, *Beyond the Farm*, 187.

Bibliography

Unpublished Primary Sources and Archival Collections

Athens, GA
 Hargrett Rare Book and Manuscript Library, University of Georgia
  Abraham Baldwin Papers [microfilm]
  Nineteenth-Century Student Textbooks and Faculty Books
  Senatus Academicus Minutes
Boston, MA
 Boston Athenaeum
  George Washington Library Collection
 Boston Public Library
  Boston Latin School Archives
 Massachusetts Historical Society
  Dana Family Papers
  Hannah Fayerweather Winthrop, Correspondence with Mercy Otis Warren,
   1752–1789
  Henry Knox Papers
   Henry Knox Papers [microform, originals at Gilder Lehrman Institute,
    New York, NY]
   Henry Knox Papers II
    Henry Knox Diary
   Henry Knox Papers III, 1777–1807
  Katharine Farnham Hay Journal, 1778
  Mercy Otis Warren Papers
  Winthrop Family Papers [transcripts], 1630–1741
  Winthrop Family Papers II, 1578–1977
Cambridge, MA
 Harvard University
  Archives and Special Collections
   Class Records of Harvard College, 1788–
   College Books, 1636–1827
   Commonplace Book of Hector Orr, 1789–1804
   Early Records of the Speaking Club, 1770–1813
   Harvard University Societies and Clubs Records, ca. 1795–
   Laws and Statutes of Harvard, 1655–1890
   Records of the Board of Overseers: Minutes, 1707–1932
   Records of the Faculty Relating to Disorders, 1768–ca. 1880s

Records of the Harvard Faculty and Faculty of Arts and Sciences
Houghton Library
  Benedict Arnold Diary: Manuscript, 1775
  Benedict Arnold Papers, 1765–1886
  Jared Sparks Collection of Documents concerning the American Revolution
Carlisle, PA
  Archives and Special Collections, Dickinson College
    John Dickinson Papers
Charleston, SC
  South Carolina Historical Society
    Edward Rutledge, 1749–1800, Letter to "My dear Madam" [1785]
    Records of the Society of the Cincinnati in the State of South Carolina,
      1782–1996
Charlottesville, VA
  Albert and Shirley Small Special Collections, University of Virginia
    Journals of the Chairman of the Faculty Nineteenth-Century Records
    Minutes of the General Faculty
    Transcripts of the Minutes of the Board of Visitors
Hanover, NH
  Rauner Special Collections Library, Dartmouth College
    Alumni Files
    Board of Trustees Records
    [Collection of Manuscripts Relating to the Early History of
      Dartmouth College]
    Papers of Eleazer Wheelock
Haverford, PA
  Quaker and Special Collections, Haverford College
    Aimwell School Records
    Allinson Family Papers
    American Friends Letters
    Henry Drinker Correspondence
London, UK
  Archives, Lincoln's Inn
    Lincoln's Inn Admission Register
  Archives and Manuscripts, British Library
    India Office Records and Private Papers
      Warren Hastings Papers
    Western Manuscripts
      Benedict Arnold, File of Papers Relating to Arnold's Early Trading
        Adventures
      Henry Phillips, Archive Relating to the Duel on Boston Common in
        New England
      Letters from Thomas Burnet to George Duckett

Quebec Siege Diary
William O'Brien, "The Duel! A Comedy"
Library and Archive, Middle Temple
Misc. Administrative Records
Misc. Loose Papers Relating to the Members of Middle Temple
Orders of Parliament
Student Ledgers
Mount Vernon, VA
Fred W. Smith National Library for the Study of George Washington
Manuscript Collection
Benedict Arnold's Commission as Major General from John Hancock,
2 May 1777
Bushrod Washington Family Papers, 1662–1835
Sermon or address to "Gentlemen Soldiers," [Dec. 1775?]
Washington Collection/General Collection
Letters of Nelly Custis Lewis to Elizabeth Bordley Gibson, 1794–1851
[transcripts]
Martha Washington Papers
Newark, NJ
New Jersey Historical Society
Boggs Family Collection, 1737–1942
Ebenezer Elmer, Journals, 1776–1785
Henry Lee General Orders, 1794
Joseph Bloomfield Papers, 1774–1809
Joseph Clark Papers, 1777–1783
Nathaniel Heard's Brigade, NJ Militia, Record Book, 1776–1782
Samuel Baldwin Diary, 1780
Timothy Tuttle Journal, 1775–1776
Van Horne Family Papers, 1707–1827
William Barton Journal, 1779
William Franklin, Governor of NJ, Manuscripts, 1756–1813
William Gould Diary, 1794
New Brunswick, NJ
Rutgers University Archives
Elizabeth R. Boyd Historical Collection on Rutgers University, 1795–1956
Inventory to the Records of the Queen's College, Rutgers College and
Rutgers University Board of Trustees
Peter Kemble Diary, 1780–85
Queen's and Rutgers College Presidents Collection, 1774–1983
Records of the Queen's College, Rutgers College and Rutgers University Board of
Trustees: Manuscript Minutes, Enclosures, and Subject Files, 1778–1956
Rutgers Manuscript Collections
William Leslie Bowles Correspondence, 1792–1797

New Haven, CT
   Whitney Library, New Haven Museum
      Benedict Arnold Papers
   Yale University
      Beinecke Rare Book and Manuscript Library
         Early Yale Documents, 1700–1899
      Manuscripts and Archives, Sterling Memorial Library
         Faculty Judgments
         Faculty Minutes
         Faculty of Yale College Records, 1751–1994 [microfilm]
         Materials concerning Student Discipline at Yale College, ca. 1760–1865
         Materials Documenting Yale Student Unrest, ca. 1774–1991
         Records of Presidents of Yale University, ca. 1718–2002
         Records of Student Courts at Yale, 1763–1766
         Records of Thomas Clap, ca. 1720–1765
         Yale College Records concerning Attendance, Residence, Discipline,
            ca. 1801–1965
         Yale College Records of Classes, ca. 1803–2003
         Yale University Corporation Records, ca. 1714–2007
New York, NY
   Columbia University Archives
      The Black Book of King's College
      Columbia College Papers
         Columbia College Papers
         King's College Papers
      Commencement Collection
      Historical Subject Files
   Manuscripts and Archives Division, Astor, Lenox, and Tilden Foundations,
         New York Public Library
      Aaron Burr Letters and Documents, 1780–1950
      American Loyalists Collection, 1777–1790
      Arnold Family Papers, 1800–1875
      George Clinton Papers, 1776–1819
      Henry Glen Correspondence, 1770–1801
      James Brickett, Orderly Book Kept at Ticonderoga, 1776
      Jedediah Huntington Papers, 1776–1815
      Thomas Grosvenor Papers, 1779–1792
      Webb Family Papers, 1773–1882
   New York Historical Society
      Aaron Burr Papers, 1777–1836
      Alexander Hamilton Collection, 1783–1806
      Alexander Papers, 1668–1818
      Benedict Arnold Collection, 1772–1780

Delaplaine Family Papers, 1762–1966
Jotham Post [Jr.], Diary, 1792–1793
Morgan Lewis Collection, 1781–1791
Richard Varick Papers, 1743–1871
Slavery Collection, 1709–1864
William Beekman, Jr., Notebook, 1773
Philadelphia, PA
Historical Society of Pennsylvania
Cadwalader Family Papers
Gen. John Cadwalader (1742–1786) Papers
Dickinson Family Papers
Edward Hand Papers
Elizabeth Sandwith Drinker Diaries
Fisher Family Papers
Fox Family Papers
Jonathan Potts Papers
Larned Family Papers
Quaker Testimonials and Writings
Rawle Family Papers
R. R. Logan Collection of John Dickinson Papers
Rush Family Papers
Benjamin Rush Correspondence
Shee Family Papers
Shoemaker Family Papers
University Archives and Record Center, University of Pennsylvania
College of Arts and Sciences Records
General Administration Collection
Minutes of the Trustees (also online: http://www.archives.upenn.edu/faids/upa
/upa1/upa1_10online.html)
Office of the Secretary Records
Trustees of the University of Pennsylvania Charters, Statutes, By-Laws and
Rules
Trustees of the University of Pennsylvania Records
Princeton, NJ
Princeton University
Rare Books and Special Collections
Aaron Burr (1716–1757) Collection, 1750–1761
Aaron Burr (1756–1836) Collection, 1778–1831
American Revolution Collection, 1765–1797
Bache and Wistar Family Correspondence, 1777–1895
Fuller Collection of Aaron Burr (1756–1836), 1771–1851
George Simpson Eddy Collection of Benjamin Franklin, 1684–1947
John Witherspoon Collection, 1765–1903

Jonathan Odell Collection, 1750–1780
Princeton Revolution Collection: Documents, 1777
Samuel Stanhope Smith Collection, 1772–1817
Shippen Family Collection, 1750–1810
Signers of the Declaration of Independence Collection, 1765–1813
William Alexander Collection, 1778–1813
Seely G. Mudd Manuscript Library
Board of Trustees Records, 1746–
Historical Subject Files Collection, 1746–2011
Lecture Notes Collection, 1772–1990
Library Records, 1734–2011
Office of Dean of the Faculty Records, 1781–2011
Office of the President Records, 1746–1999
Princeton University Class Records, 1798–2011
Princeton University Commencement Records, 1748–2010
Providence, RI
John Hay Library, Special Collections, Brown University
Anne S. K. Brown Military Collection
Corporation Papers [bound manuscript volume]
James Manning Papers, 1761–1827
Rhode Island College Miscellaneous Papers, 1763–1804
Samuel Jones Papers, 1760–1794
Student Essays and Notebooks
Student Essays and Orations, 1786–1983
Richmond, VA
Virginia Historical Society
Alice (De Lancey) Izard, Letters, 1781–1783
Ball Family Papers, 1716–1983
Barbour Family Papers, 1741–1876
Benjamin Bartholomew Diary, 19 May 1781–30 March 1782
Bland Family Papers, 1713–1825
Cooper Family Papers, 1786–1910
David Griffith Papers, 1742–1789 [photocopies of originals at the Library of
    Congress]
Dunmore Co., VA Committee of Safety, Records, 1775–1776 [photocopies of
    originals at Krauth Memorial Library, Lutheran Theological Seminary,
    Philadelphia, PA]
Fairfax Family Papers, 1756–1787
George Erving, Letter, 15 June 1784
George Washington Fairfax Papers, 1762–1799 [copies of originals at Gunston
    Hall Library and Archives, Lorton, VA]
George William Fairfax, Letter, January 23, 1786

James Breckinridge Papers, 1786–1830

James Gordon Diary, 17 October 1780–6 November 1780

John Banister, Letter, [12 May] 1755

John Banister, Letter, 11 May 1781

John Banister, Letters, 1772, 1778–1783, to Theodorick Bland

John Burgoyne, Letter, 20 October 1777 [copy of original: Baylor Family Papers, Albert and Shirley Small Special Collections Library, University of Virginia, Charlottesville, VA]

John Page, Letter, 12 March 1778

Landon Carter Papers, 1763–1774

Lee Family Papers, 1638–1867

Lee Family Papers, 1761–1882

Randolph Family Papers, 1763–1841

Robert Williams Daniel Papers, 1776–1882

Sally Fairfax Diary, 26 December [1771]–8 January [1772]

Virginia Militia, 5th Regiment, Order Book, 1775, Kept by Capt. George Stubblefield

William Baylies, Letter, 26 September 1779

William Fontaine, Letter, 26 October 1781

William Hawks, Letter, 2 November 1778

Swarthmore, PA

Friends Historical Library, Swarthmore College

Association of Friends for the Free Instruction of Adult Colored Persons Records, 1789–1905

Jane (Bonsall) Clark, Memorandums and Remarks, 1772–1785

Joshua Brown Journals, 1756–1790

Meeting for Sufferings [microfilm, originals at Quaker and Special Collections, Haverford College, Haverford, PA]

Philadelphia Monthly Meeting Minutes

Philadelphia Quaker Yearly Meetings

Quaker Women's Diaries [microfilm]

Diaries of Susanna Boone, 1773–1789

Diary of Susanna Day, 1797–1804

Salem Monthly Meeting, Misc. Papers

Salem Monthly Meeting Records

Washington, DC

Library of Congress

Henley Smith Collection, 1686–1903

Randolph's Vindication, 1795

Papers of Peyton Randolph from ca. 1774

Washington Family Collection

National Archives

Letters Sent and Orderly Book of Brigadier General Edward Hand [microfilm]

Letters Sent by Brigadier General Edward Hand [microfilm]
Letters Sent by Colonel Timothy Pickering [microfilm]
Society of the Cincinnati
Charles C. Pinckney papers [microfilm]
Records of the Society of the Cincinnati
Correspondence
General Society, 1783–1950
French Society, 1783–1888
Pierre Charles L'Enfant, 1783–1793
Société des Cincinnati de France collection
Proceedings
Circular by George Washington, 15 May 1784
General Society, 1783–1902
Journals of the Society
Minutes of the General Society of the Cincinnati
Proceedings with Institution
Winthrop Sargent, "Secret Journal of the Cincinnati"
State Societies, 1783–1933
The New York State Society of the Cincinnati collection
The North Carolina Society of the Cincinnati collection
The Society of the Cincinnati of the State of South Carolina collection
The Society of the Cincinnati in the State of Virginia collection
The Robert Charles Lawrence Fergusson Collection
West Point, NY
Special Collections and Archives, United States Military Academy
Nineteenth-Century Manuscript Collection
Alden Partridge Papers, 1808–1853
Joseph Gardner Swift Memoir, 1807–1865
Joseph Gardner Swift Papers, 1800–1865
Orders for Duties as Cadets, 1804
Records, United States Military Academy, March 1814 to February 1838
Regulations, 1802–1816
Regulations at the Military Academy at West Point, 1 April 1814
Regulations Relative to the Military Academy at West Point, 30 April 1810
Sylvanus Thayer Papers, 1808–1862
United States Military Academy, Orders and Regulations
United States Military Academy Letters, 1812–1824
War Department Letters Relating to the US Military Academy, 1801–1838
Seventeenth- and Eighteenth-Century Manuscript Collection
Elijah Warren, Letter, 1780
Horatio Gates, Letter, 1776
R. Taft, Letter, 1780
Samuel Frost Diary, 1781

Titus Hall, Documents, 1779–1780
West Point Manuscript Collection
Benedict Arnold papers
Continental Army Major General Benedict Arnold's Division, Orderly Book [photocopy, original held at the Connecticut State Library, Hartford, CT]
Williamsburg, VA
Earl Gregg Swem Library at the College of William and Mary, Special Collections Research Center
Bishop James Madison Papers [photostatic copies]
Blair, Banister, Braxton, Horner, Whiting Papers
Board of Visitors Records
Chesapeake-Leopard Affair Letter by George Washington Campbell
College Papers Collection
David Somervill Notebooks
Dr. James Madison Papers
Faculty Minutes
Francis Thornton Turner Letter
George Wythe Collection, 1779–1927
Henry Alexander Wise Letter
Henry A. Washington Papers
Infantry Order Books
Captain James Charlton's Infantry Order Book, 1813–1815
James Barron Papers
James Blair Papers
James Blair Papers (I)
James Blair Papers (II)
Jerdone Family Papers
John Page Memorandum Book
Jonathan Boucher Papers
Joseph Carrington Cabell Papers
Leven Powell Papers [microfilm]
Marie M. and Edith W. Smith Papers
Office of the President Records
James Blair Records, 1701–1747
James Madison Records, 1775–1979
Page Family Collection
Preston Family Papers
Robert Pleasants Letterbook
Samuel Henley Papers
Samuel Myers Papers, 1808–1812
Sarah C. Watts Papers
Student's Commonplace Book

University Archives Bound Volumes Collection
University Archives Publication Collection
William Meade Papers
William Small Collection
John D. Rockefeller Jr. Library, Colonial Williamsburg Foundation
Asa Reddington Revolutionary War Narrative [transcripts, various
    repositories]
Benjamin Henry Latrobe Journals [transcripts, originals at Maryland Historical
    Society, Baltimore]
Blackall William Ball Collection
Capt. George Fleming, Orderly Books
College of William and Mary Faculty Minutes [transcripts, originals at Earl
    Gregg Swem Library at the College of William and Mary, Special
    Collections Research Center, Williamsburg, VA]
Committee of Safety Papers [transcripts, originals at Library of Virginia,
    Richmond, VA]
Cyrus Griffin Papers [transcripts, originals at the Historical Society of
    Pennsylvania, Philadelphia]
Dickinson Family Papers
Elizabeth Jaquelin Ambler Brent Carrington Papers
Elizabeth Lee Diary
Fort Pitt Orderly Book of Brigadier General William Irvine [transcripts,
    originals at the Historical Society of Pennsylvania, Philadelphia]
John Custis Letterbook [transcripts, originals at Library of Congress]
John Graves Simcoe Papers
John Norton and Sons Papers
Joseph Ball Letterbook [transcripts, originals at Library of Congress]
Letters to Fairfaxes [transcripts]
Peyton Randolph Papers
Photocopy Collection
    Williamsburg Lodge of Masons
        Minutes, 1773
        Proceedings, 1774–1779
Robert Carter Letter Books and Day Books [transcripts, originals at David M.
    Rubenstein Rare Book and Manuscript Library, Duke University,
    Durham, NC]
Robert Wormeley Carter Diary
Room by Room Inventories [transcripts, various repositories]
Shirley Plantation Collection
Slavery Manuscripts (Various)
Tucker-Coleman Papers [transcripts, originals at Earl Gregg Swem Library at
    the College of William and Mary, Special Collections Research Center,
    Williamsburg, VA]

Digital Primary Source Collections

"American Founding Era Collection," Rotunda, University of Virginia Press, http:
          //www.upress.virginia.edu/rotunda/collections/american-founding-era/
     The Adams Papers Digital Edition
     The Dolley Madison Digital Edition
     The Papers of Alexander Hamilton Digital Edition
     The Papers of Andrew Jackson Digital Edition
     The Papers of George Washington Digital Edition
     The Papers of James Madison Digital Edition
     The Papers of Thomas Jefferson Digital Edition
"Founders Online: Correspondence and Other Writings of Six Major Shapers of the
          United States," Founders Online, National Archives, http://founders.
          archives.gov/
     The Adams Papers
     The Papers of Alexander Hamilton
     The Papers of Benjamin Franklin
     The Papers of George Washington
     The Papers of James Madison
     The Papers of Thomas Jefferson
Individual/Family Papers
     Adams Papers, http://www.masshist.org/2012/adams/adams-family-papers
          Adams Family Correspondence
          The Adams Papers
          Autobiography of John Adams
          Correspondence between John and Abigail Adams
          The Diary of John Adams
          Papers of John Adams
     Benjamin Franklin, http://www.franklinpapers.org
          The Autobiography of Benjamin Franklin
          The Papers of Benjamin Franklin
     George Washington, http://www.mountvernon.org/educational-resources
          /research-collections/databases
          The Papers of George Washington
     Thomas Jefferson
          The Autobiography of Thomas Jefferson, http://etext.virginia.edu/toc/modeng
               /public/JefAuto.html
          The Correspondence and Writings of Thomas Jefferson, http://founders.archives.gov/
          Family Letters, Thomas Jefferson's Monticello, http://tjrs.monticello
               .org/archive/search/letters?field_tjrs_collection_tid%5B%5D=2353
          Letters of Thomas Jefferson, http://etext.lib.virginia.edu/conditions.html
     Letters of Delegates to Congress, 1774–1789, American Memory: Library of Congress,
          https://memory.loc.gov/ammem/amlaw/lwdg.html

Journals of the Continental Congress, American Memory: Library of Congress, https://memory.loc.gov/ammem/amlaw/lwjc.html

Newspapers

Alexandria (VA) *Advertiser*
American Minerva (NY)
Boston Evening Post
Boston Gazette
City Gazette (SC)
Connecticut Courant
Connecticut Gazette
Continental Journal, and Weekly
    Advertiser (MA)
Courier of New Hampshire
Daily Advertiser (NY)
Eastern Argus (ME)
Enquirer (VA)
Essex (MA) *Gazette*
Essex (MA) *Journal*
Independent Chronicle and the
    Universal Advertiser (MA)
Jenks' Portland (ME) *Gazette*
Massachusetts Centinel
Massachusetts Gazette

National Gazette (PA)
New-England Courant
New York Commercial Advertiser
New York Daily Gazette
Norfolk Gazette (VA) *and Public Ledger*
North-Carolina Journal
Norwich (CT) *Courier*
Oracle of the Day (NH)
Pennsylvania Chronicle
Pennsylvania Gazette
Pennsylvania Herald
Political Calendar (MA)
Poulson's American Daily Advertiser (PA)
Republican Spy (MA)
United States Gazette (PA)
Virginia Gazette
Washington (DC) *Federalist*
Weekly Museum (NY)
Western Reserve Chronicle (OH)
Windham (CT) *Herald*

Published Primary Sources

Abercrombie, James. *A Sermon, Occasioned by the Death of Major Gen. Alexander Hamilton . . . July 22nd, 1804. . . .* Philadelphia: H. Maxwell, 1804.

An Abridgment of the English Military Discipline. London: Charles Bill, Henry Hills, Thomas Newcomb, 1686.

Adams, Hannah. *Women Invited to War, or A Friendly Address to the Honourable Women of the United States.* Boston: Ednes and Son, 1787.

Adams, John. *A Defence of the Constitutions of Government of the United States of America.* London: C. Dilly, 1787.

———. Letters [*by John Adams to Dr. Calkoen of Amsterdam on American Affairs*]. [1786].

Adams, Samuel. *The Writings of Samuel Adams.* 4 vols. Edited by Harry Alonzo Cushing. New York: G. P. Putnam's Sons, 1904–8.

Addison, Joseph. *Cato: A Tragedy.* London: J. Tonson, 1713.

———. *The Miscellaneous Works of Joseph Addison.* London: G. Bell and Son, 1914.

Addison, Joseph, and Richard Steele. *The Spectator.* 8 vols. London: S. Buckley, J. Tonson, 1714.

————. *The Spectator*. 11th ed. 8 vols. London: J. Tonson, 1733.

Alexander, Caleb. *The Young Gentlemen and Ladies Instructor.... Designed as a Reading Book for the Use of Schools and Academies*. Boston: [Samuel Ethebridge] for E. Larking and W.P. & L. Blake, 1797.

[Allestree, Richard]. *The Causes of the Decay of Christian Piety, or An Impartial Survey of the Ruins of Christian Religion Undermin'd by Unchristian Practice*. London: J. H. for E. and R. Pawlet, 1704.

Anburey, Thomas. *Travels through the Interior Parts of America: In a Series of Letters, by an Officer*. 2 vols. London, 1789.

André, John. *Major André's Journal*. New York: New York Times and Arno, 1968.

Antibiastes. *Observations on the Slaves and the Indented Servants, Inlisted in the Army, and in the Navy of the United States*. Philadelphia: Styner and Cist, 1777.

The Antient Policy of War: A Glorious President to the Modern War of Fighting. London: J. How, 1704.

Aquinas, Thomas. *The Summa Theologica*. 2nd ed. (1920). Online ed., edited by Kevin Knight. New Advent, 2016. http://www.newadvent.org/summa/2.htm.

Aristotle. *Nicomachean Ethics*. Edited by Lesley Brown. Translated by David Ross. Oxford: Oxford University Press, 2009.

Augustine of Hippo. "Contra Faustum Manichaeum." In *Nicene and Post-Nicene Fathers, First Series*, vol. 4, edited by Philip Schaff. Buffalo, NY: Christian Literature, 1887. Online ed., edited by Kevin Knight. New Advent, 2009. http://www.newadvent.org/fathers/140622.htm.

Austin, William, ed. *A Selection of Patriotic Addresses to the President....* Boston: John W. Folsom, 1798.

Bacon, Francis. *The Charge of Sir Francis Bacon ... Touching Duells*. London: George Eld, 1614.

————. *The Charge Touching Duells: London 1614*. New York: Da Capo, 1968.

Bailey, Nathan. *An Universal Etymological English Dictionary....* London: E. Bell, J. Darby, A. Bettesworth, F. Fayram, J. Pemberton, etc., 1721.

Bailyn, Bernard, ed. *Pamphlets of the American Revolution*. Vol. 1, *1750–1765*. Cambridge, MA: Belknap Press of Harvard University Press, 1965.

Ball, Charles. *Fifty Years in Chains, or The Life of an American Slave*. New York, 1858.

Bancroft, Aaron. *An Eulogy on the Character of the Late Gen. George Washington, Delivered before the Inhabitants of the Town of Worcester, Commonwealth of Massachusetts, on Saturday the 22d of February 1800*. Worcester, MA: March 1800.

Barclay, Robert. *An Apology for the True Christian Divinity, Being an Explanation and Vindication of the Principles and Doctrines of the People Called Quakers*. Birmingham, UK: John Baskerville, 1765.

Barton, William. *A Concise Account of the Origin and Use of Coat Armour; with Some Observations on the Beneficial Purposes to Which Heraldry May Be Applied in the United States of America*. Philadelphia, 1788.

Bartram, William. *Travels through North & South Carolina, Georgia, East & West Florida*. Philadelphia: James and Johnson, 1791.

Basker, James G., ed. *Early American Abolitionists: A Collection of Anti-slavery Writings, 1760–1820.* New York: Gilder Lehrman Institute of American History, 2005.

Beecher, Lyman. *Remedy for Duelling: A Sermon Delivered before the Presbytery of Long Island . . . April 16, 1806.* Boston: Leavitt and Alden, 1806.

Behn, Aphra. *Oroonoko: or, The Royal Slave.* London: W. Canning, 1688.

Benezet, Anthony. *Short Observations on Slavery, Introductory to Some Extracts from the Writing of the Abbe Raynal, on That Important Subject.* [Philadelphia], [1781?].

Bigelow, Timothy. *An Eulogy on the Life, Character and Services of Brother George Washington, Deceased, Pronounced before the Fraternity of Free and Accepted Masons . . . on Tuesday, Feb. 11, 1800. . . .* Boston, [1800].

Blackstone, William. *Commentaries on the Laws of England . . .* Vol. 1. Oxford: Clarendon Press, 1765.

Blake, George. *A Masonic Eulogy, on the Life of the Illustrious Brother George Washington, Pronounced before the Brethren of St. John's Lodge. . . .* Boston, [1800].

Bland, Humphrey. *A Treatise of Military Discipline.* London: Daniel Midwinter, 1743.

Bland, Sterling Lecater, Jr., ed. *African American Slave Narratives: An Anthology.* 3 vols. Westport, CT: Greenwood Press, 2001.

Bond, Donald F., ed. *The Spectator.* 5 vols. Oxford: Clarendon, 1965.

The Book of Constitutions and Orders of the Honourable Society of Clement's Inn. N.p.: Printed for the Society, 1880.

Boucher, Jonathan. *A View of the Causes and Consequences of the American Revolution; In Thirteen Discourses Preached in North America between the Years 1763 and 1775. . . .* London: G. G. and J. Robinson, 1797.

Boudinot, Elias. *An Oration Delivered at Elizabeth-Town, New Jersey Agreeably to a Resolution of the State Society of Cincinnati, on the Fourth of July MDCCXCIII.* Elizabethtown, NJ: Shepard Kollock, 1793.

Brannan, John, ed. *Official Letters of the Military and Naval Officers of the United States during the War with Great Britain in the Years 1812, 13, 14, & 15.* Washington, DC: Way and Gideon, 1823.

Brooks, John. *An Oration Delivered to the Society of the Cincinnati in the Commonwealth of Massachusetts, July 4th 1787.* Boston: Edmund Freeman, 1787.

[Brown, John]. *An Estimate of the Manners and Principles of the Times.* London: L. Davis and C. Reymers, 1757.

Buchanan, George. *An Oration upon the Moral and Political Evil of Slavery Delivered at a Public Meeting of the Maryland Society, for Promoting the Abolition of Slavery . . . Baltimore, July 4th, 1791.* Baltimore: Philip Edwards, 1793.

Buckminster, Joseph. *Religion and Righteousness the Basis of National Honor and Prosperity: A Sermon, Preached to the North and South Parishes in Portsmouth, Fraternally United in Observance of the 22d February, 1800; the Day Appointed by Congress to Pay Tributary Respect to the Memory of Gen. Washington.* Portsmouth, NH: Charles Peirce, 1800.

Bunyan, John. *The Pilgrim's Progress.* London: Ingram Cooke and Co., 1853. Originally published in 1678.

Burke, Aedanus. *Considerations on the Society or Order of the Cincinnati....* Philadelphia: Robert Bell, 1783.

Burlamaqui, Jean-Jacques. *The Principles of Natural and Politic Law.* Cambridge, MA: Harvard University Press, 1807.

Burr, Aaron. *Political Correspondence and Public Papers of Aaron Burr.* 2 vols. Edited by Mary-Jo Kline and Joanne Wood Ryan. Princeton, NJ: Princeton University Press, 1983.

Caesar, Julius. *Caesar's Commentaries on the Gallic War, and the First Book of the Greek Paraphrase.* New York: Harper and Brothers, 1849.

[Callender, James Thomson]. *British Honour and Humanity; or, The Wonders of American Patience....* Philadelphia: Robert Campbell, 1796.

Carter, Landon, and Peyton Randolph. *A Letter from a Gentleman in Virginia to the Merchants of Great Britain, Trading to That Colony.* London, 1754.

Carter, Matthew. *Honor Rediviuus, or An Analysis of Honor and Armory.* London: E. Coates, 1655.

Carver, Jonathan, and John Coakley Lettsom. *Travels through the Interior Parts of North-America, in the Years 1766, 1767, and 1768.* London: J. Walter, 1778.

Cary, Virginia Randolph. *Letters on Female Character.* Richmond, VA: A. Works, 1830.

Cavan, Richard Lambert, Earl of. *A New System of Military Discipline, Founded upon Principle.* London: J. Almon, 1773.

[Chalmers, James]. *Plain Truth.* Philadelphia: R. Bell, 1776.

Chauncy, Charles. *A Discourse on "the Good News from a Far Country": Deliver'd July 24th [1766]: A Day of Thanks-giving to Almighty God....* Boston: Kneeland and Adams, 1766. Reprinted in John W. Thornton, *Pulpit of the American Revolution,* Boston, 1860. Citations refer to the reprint ed.

Chesterfield, Philip Dormer Stanhope. *Letters Written by the Late Right Honorable Philip Dormer Stanhope to His Son....* 2 vols. Boston and Newburyport, MA: John Boyle and John Douglas McDougall, 1779.

A Circular Letter Addressed to the State Societies of the Cincinnati by the General Meeting Convened at Philadelphia, May 3, 1784. Philadelphia: E. Oswald and D. Humphreys, 1784.

Clarkson, Thomas. *An Essay on the Impolicy of the African Slave Trade.* Philadelphia: Francis Bailey, 1788.

——. *An Essay on the Slavery and Commerce of the Human Species, Particularly the African.* Dublin, 1786.

Coleman, Benjamin. *The Duty and Honour of Aged Women....* Boston: B. Green, 1711.

——. *Mr. Coleman's Sermon after the Late Bloody Duel.* Boston, 1728.

A Collection of Interesting, Authentic Papers, Relative to the Dispute between Great Britain and America; Shewing the Causes and Progress of That Misunderstanding, from 1764 to 1775. London: J. Almon, 1777.

A Collection of the Speeches of the President of the United States to Both Houses of Congress at the Opening of Every Session, with Their Answers; Also, the Addresses to the President, with His Answers from the Time of His Election. Boston: Manning and Loring, 1796.

Comber, Thomas. *Short Discourses upon the Whole Common Prayer, Designed to Inform the Judgment and Excite the Devotion, of Such as Daily Use the Same.* London: J. Nicholson, R. Wilkin, D. Midwinter, B. Cowse, B. Tooke, 1712.

A Compend of Rhetoric in Question & Answer: Compiled for Use of the Young Ladies of the Schenectady Female Academy, Principally from Blair's Lectures. Schenectady, NY: Van Veghten and Sons, 1808.

Condorcet, Marie Jean de Caritat, marquis de. "Reflections on Negro Slavery." In *The French Revolution and Human Rights: A Brief Documentary History*, edited by Lynn Hunt, 55–58. Boston: Bedford, 1996.

Constitution of a Society for Abolishing the Slave Trade, with Several Acts of the Legislatures of the States of Massachusetts, Connecticut, and Rhode Island, for That Purpose. Providence, RI: John Carter, 1789.

Cooley, Timothy Mather. *Sketches of the Life and Character of the Rev. Lemuel Haynes. . . .* New York: Harper and Bros., 1837.

Cooper, David. *A Mite Cast into the Treasury; or, Observations on Slave-Keeping.* Philadelphia: Joseph Crukshank, 1772.

———. *A Serious Address to the Rulers of America on the Inconsistency of Their Conduct Respecting Slavery: Forming a Contrast between the Encroachments. . . .* Trenton, NJ: J. Philips, 1783.

Crockett, Davy. *Narrative of the Life of David Crockett.* Philadelphia: E. L. Carey and A. Hart, 1834.

Cugoano, Ottobah. *Thoughts and Sentiments on the Evil and Wicked Traffic of the Slavery and Commerce of the Human Species. . . .* London, 1787.

Cunningham, William. *An Eulogy Delivered at Lunenburg, on Saturday the 22d of February 1800, the Day Recommended by Congress to Commemorate the Unequalled Virtues and Preeminent Services of Gen. George Washington: First President of the United States of America, and Commander in Chief of the Revolutionary War.* Worcester, MA: March 1800.

Decatur, Stephen, and James Barron. *Correspondence, between the Late Commodore Stephen Decatur and Commodore James Barron, Which Led to the Unfortunate Meeting on the Twenty Second of March.* Boston: Russell and Gardner, 1820.

"Declaration of Independence: A Transcription." National Archives. Last updated June 26, 2017. https://www.archives.gov/founding-docs/declaration-transcript.

Defoe, Daniel. *Essays upon Several Projects.* London, 1702.

———. *A Tour thro' the Whole Island of Great Britain.* London: S. Birt, T. Osborne, D. Browne, J. Hodges, J. Osborn, A. Milar, and J. Robinson, 1748.

Despagne, John. *Anti-Duello: The Anatomie of Duells. . . .* London: Thomas Harper, 1632.

Dexter, Franklin Bowditch, ed. *The Literary Diary of Ezra Stiles.* 3 vols. New York: Charles Scribner's Sons, 1901.

Dickinson, John. *An Address to the Committee of Correspondence in Barbados.* Philadelphia: William Bradford, 1766.

———. *Letters from a Pennsylvania Farmer.* Philadelphia: David Hall and William Sellers, 1768.

Douglass, Frederick. *Narrative of the Life of Frederick Douglass, an American Slave.* Dublin: Webb and Chapman, 1845.

Drinker, Elizabeth. *The Diary of Elizabeth Drinker.* 3 vols. Edited by Elaine Forman Crane. Boston: Northeastern University Press, 1991.

Duché, Jacob. *The Duty of Standing Fast in Our Spiritual and Temporal Liberties: A Sermon, Preached in Christ-church, July 7th, 1775, before the First Battalion of the City and Liberties of Philadelphia; and Now Published at Their Request.* Philadelphia: J. Humphreys Jr., 1775.

Dulany, Daniel. *Considerations on the Propriety of Imposing Taxes in the British Colonies.* Annapolis: Jonas Green, 1765.

Dyche, Thomas. *A New General English Dictionary....* London: Catherine and Richard Ware, 1765.

Eacker, George I. *An Oration, Delivered at the Request of the Officers of the Brigade of the City and County of NY.... on the Fourth of July 1801.* New York: William Durrell, 1801.

Eaton, John Henry. *The Life of Andrew Jackson....* Philadelphia: Samuel F. Bradford, 1824.

———. *The Life of Major General Andrew Jackson ... Addenda ... History of the Seminole War....* Philadelphia: McCarty and Davis, 1828.

Eaton, John Henry, and John Reid. *The Life of Andrew Jackson: Major General in the Service of the United States....* Philadelphia: M. Carey and Son, 1817.

An Edict of Statute Lately Set Forth by the French King. London: William Hall and Richard Boyle, 1609.

Edwards, Jonathan [1703–58]. *An Essay on the Nature of True Virtue.* London: W. Oliver, 1778. Originally published 1765.

Edwards, Jonathan [1745–1801]. *The Injustice and Impolicy of the Slave-Trade, and of the Slavery of the Africans: Illustrated in a Sermon....* Providence, RI, 1792.

Entick, John. *A New Naval History; or, Compleat View of the British Marine....* London: R. Manby, W. Reeve, W. Bizet, P. Davey and B. Law, and J. Scott, 1757.

Equiano, Olaudah. *The Interesting Narrative of the Life of Olaudah Equiano, or Gustavus Vassa, the African.* London, 1789.

Essay on the Art of War, in Which the General Principles of All the Operations of War in the Field Are Fully Explained. London: A. Millar, 1761.

Establishment of the Society of the Cincinnati. Charleston, SC: J. Miller, 1783.

Evening Amusements for the Ladies; or, Original Anecdotes Intended to Promote a Love of Virtue in Young Minds: A Series of Letters. Boston: Manning and Loring, 1796.

Ewald, Johann. *Diary of the American War: A Hessian Journal.* Translated by Joseph P. Tustin. New Haven, CT: Yale University Press, 1979.

Ewing, John. "Petition of Primus Hall, Alias Trask." 4 January 1838. Committee on Revolutionary Pensions. House document number H.rp.275, serial vol. 333, sessional vol. 1.

The Examination of Doctor Benjamin Franklin, before an August Assembly, Relating to the Repeal of the Stamp Act, &c. Philadelphia: Hall and Sellers, 1766.

Extracts from a Letter Written to the President of the Congress by the Honorable Arthur Lee in Answer to a Libel Published in the "Pennsylvania Gazette," of the Fifth of December, 1778 by Silas Deane, Esq.... Philadelphia: Francis Bailey, 1780.

The Female Soldier; or, The Surprising Life and Adventures of Hannah Snell. London: R. Walker, 1750.

Fidfaddy, Frederick Augustus. *The Adventures of Uncle Sam, in Search after His Lost Honor.* Middletown, CT: S. Richards, 1816.

Fielding, Henry. *The History of Tom Jones: A Foundling.* New York: Alfred A. Knopf, 1991. Originally published 1748.

———. *The Miscellaneous Works of Henry Fielding in Four Volumes.* New York: H. W. Derby, 1861.

———. *Tom Jones.* New York: W. W. Norton, 1995.

Fisher, Samuel Rowland. *Journal of Samuel Rowland Fisher of Philadelphia, 1779–1781.* Philadelphia, 1917.

Force, Peter, ed. *American Archives.... A Documentary History of the English Colonies in North America...* 4th series, 6 vols. Washington, DC: M. St. Clair Clarke and Peter Force, 1837–53.

Ford, Paul Leicester, ed. *The Writings of John Dickinson.* Philadelphia: Historical Society of Pennsylvania, 1895.

Ford, Worthington Chaucey, ed. *General Orders Issued by Major-General Israel Putnam when in Command of the Highlands in the Summer and Fall of 1777.* Brooklyn: Historical Printing Club, 1893.

[Forten, James]. *Letters from a Man of Colour, on a Late Bill before the Senate of Pennsylvania.* [Philadelphia?], 1813.

Franklin, Benjamin. *Proposals Relating to the Education of Youth in Pennsylvania.* Philadelphia: Franklin and Hall, 1749.

———. *Writings.* New York: Library of America, 1987.

Frederick the Great. *Instructions for His Generals.* New York: Dover, 2005.

A Friend of Truth, and of Honorable Peace. *The Conduct of Washington, Compared with That of the Present Administration, in a Series of Letters and Official Documents, with Notes.* Boston: True and Rowe, 1813.

Frisbie, Levi. *An Eulogy on the Illustrious Character of the Late General George Washington... on the 7th day of January, 1800....* Newburyport, MA, 1800.

Furst, Moritz. "Gold Medal Presented to Jackson by Congress." [1815–40]. Library of Congress, http://www.loc.gov/pictures/resource/cph.3b15566/.

G. F., defendour of Christian valoure. *Duell-Ease: A Worde with Valiant Spiritts Shewing the Abuse of Duells....* [London]: Imprinted by Ann Griffin London, 1635.

Gaines, Edwin M. "The Chesapeake Affair: Virginians Mobilize to Defend National Honor." *Virginia Magazine of History and Biography* 64, no. 2 (April 1956): 131–42.

[Gallatin, Albert]. *An Examination of the Conduct of the Executive of the United States, towards the French Republic.* Philadelphia: Francis and Robert Bailey, 1797.

General Regulation for the Army.... Philadelphia: M. Carey and Sons, 1821.

Gifford, John. *A Letter to the Hon. Thomas Erskine; Containing Some Strictures on His View of the Causes and Consequences of the Present War with France.* Philadelphia: William Cobbett, 1797.

Godefroy, Francis. "Premiere assemblée du congress." [1782]. Library of Congress. http://www.loc.gov/pictures/item/2004670031/.

Grandmaison, de. *A Treatise on the Military Service, of Light Horse, and Light Infantry, in the Field, and in the Fortified Places. . . .* Translated by Lewis Nicola. Philadelphia: Robert Bell, 1777.

Greene, Nathanael. *The Papers of General Nathanael Greene.* 12 vols. Chapel Hill: University of North Carolina Press, 1976–2015.

Greenman, Jeremiah. *Diary of a Common Soldier in the American Revolution, 1775–1783.* Edited by Robert C. Bray and Paul E. Bushnell. DeKalb: Northern Illinois University Press, 1978.

[Griffitts, Hannah]. "Patriotic Poesy." ["The Female Patriots," 1768]. *William and Mary Quarterly* 34 (1977): 307–8.

Hale, Matthew. *Contemplations, Moral and Divine.* London: W. Shrowsbury, 1705.

Hall, Prince. *A Charge, Delivered to the African Lodge, June 24, 1797, at Menotomy.* Boston: Benjamin Edes, 1797.

———. *A Charge Delivered to the Brethren of the African Lodge on the 25th of June, 1792, at the Hall of Brother William Smith, in Charlestown.* Boston: T. and J. Fleet, 1792.

Hamilton, Alexander. *Letters of Pacificus: Written in Justification of the President's Proclamation of Neutrality.* Philadelphia, 1796. Originally published 1793.

———. *Writings.* New York: Library of America, 2001.

Hanson, Thomas. *The Prussian Evolutions in Actual Engagements: Both in Platoons, Sub, and Grand-Divisions. . . .* Philadelphia: J. Douglas M'Dougall, [1775].

[Hanway, Jonas]. *The Soldier's Faithful Friend; Being Prudential, Moral, and Religious Advice to Private Men in the Army and Militia.* 2 vols. London: J. Dodsley, J. Rivington, N. Young, 1766.

Harte, Walter. *The History of the Life of Gustavus Adolphus, King of Sweden.* 2 vols. London: J. Hinton and R. Baldwin, 1767.

Hawkins, Francis. *Youths Behavior, or Decency in Conversation amongst Men.* London: printed by W. Wilson for W. Lee, 1651. Electronic reproduction. Ann Arbor: University Microfilms International, 1999.

Hawley, Joseph. Joseph Hawley to Ephraim Wright, 16 April 1782. In "Documents: Shay's Rebellion," *American Historical Review* 36, no. 4 (July 1931): 776–78.

Haynes, Lemuel. *Dissimulation Illustrated: A Sermon Delivered at Brandon, Vermont February 22, 1813. . . .* Rutland, VT: Fay and Davison, 1814.

———. *The Nature and Importance of True Republicanism: With a Few Suggestions, Favorable to Independence: A Discourse, Delivered at Rutland, (Vermont,) the Fourth of July 1801.* Rutland, VT: William Fay, 1801.

Heath, William. *Memoirs of Major-General Heath.* Boston: I. Thomas and E. T. Andrews, 1798.

Hippocrates. "The Oath." Internet Classics Archive, Massachusetts Institute of Technology. Accessed August 27, 2017. http://classics.mit.edu/Hippocrates/hippooath.html.

The History of a Schoolboy. New York: W. Durell, 1792.

A History of the New York Kappa Lambda Conspiracy. . . . New York: W. Stuart, 1839.

Hitchcock, Enos. *Diary of Enos Hitchcock, D.D., a Chaplain in the Revolutionary Army.* Edited by William B. Weeden. Providence: Rhode Island Historical Society, 1899.

Home, Henry, Lord Kames. *Essays on the Principles of Morality and Natural Religion.* Edinburgh: R. Fleming, 1751.

———. *Essays upon Several Subjects, concerning British Antiquities.* . . . Edinburgh: T. Maccliesh, 1797. Originally published 1745.

Hopkins, Joseph R. *Hamiltoniad, or, The Effects of Discord: An Original Poem: With an Appendix, Containing a Number of Interesting Papers Relative to the Late Unfortunate Duel.* Philadelphia, 1804.

Hopwood, Charles Henry, ed. *Middle Temple Records.* London: Masters of the Bench, 1904–5.

[Horry, Charles]. *A Five Minute Answer to Paine's Letter to Genl. Washington.* London: L. F. J. Gransart, Moorfields, 1797.

Hull, William. *An Oration Delivered to the Society of the Cincinnati in the Commonwealth of Massachusetts, July 4, 1788.* Boston: Benjamin Russell, 1788.

Humanitas [Edward Darlington]. *Reflections on Slavery: with Recent Evidence of Its Inhumanity.* . . . Philadelphia, 1803.

Humphreys, David. *The Miscellaneous Works of Colonel Humphreys.* New York: Hodge, Allen, and Campbell, 1790.

Huntington, Ebenezer. *Letters Written by Ebenezer Huntington during the American Revolution.* New York: C. F. Heartman, 1915.

Hutcheson, Frances. *A Short Introduction to Moral Philosophy.* 2 vols. Glasgow: Robert and Andrew Foulis, 1764.

Hutchinson, Peter Orlando, ed. *Diary and Letters of Thomas Hutchinson.* London: Sampson, Low, Marston, Searle and Rivington, 1883.

Hutchinson, Thomas. *The Diary and Letters of His Excellency Thomas Hutchinson.* . . . Boston: Houghton Mifflin, 1884–86.

———. *Hutchinson Papers.* Albany, NY: printed for the Society by J. Munsell, 1865.

Jackson, Andrew. *Correspondence of Andrew Jackson.* Vols. 1–2. New York: Kraus Reprint, 1969.

———. *The Papers of Andrew Jackson.* Vol. 1. Knoxville: University of Tennessee Press, 1980.

———. *The Papers of Andrew Jackson.* Vol. 5. Knoxville: University of Tennessee Press, 1996.

Jacobs, Harriet A. *Incidents in the Life of a Slave Girl.* Boston, 1861.

James I. *By the King: A Proclamation against Private Challenges and Combats.* . . . London: Robert Baker, 1614.

Jefferson, Thomas. *The Life and Morals of Jesus of Nazareth.* Washington, DC: Government Printing Office, 1904. Electronic Text Center, University of Virginia Library. http://web.archive.org/web/20110110200407/http://etext.lib.virginia.edu/etcbin/toccer-new2?id=JefJesu.sgm&images=images/modeng&data=/texts/english/modeng/parsed&tag=public&part=all.

———. *Notes on the State of Virginia.* Paris, 1784.

———. *The Writings of Thomas Jefferson.* Vol. 1. Washington, DC: Thomas Jefferson Memorial Association of the United States, 1905.

Jeney, de. *The Partisan; or, the Art of Making War in Detachment... Translated from the French of Mr. de Jeney, by an Officer in the Army.* London: R. Griffiths, 1760.

Johnson, Samuel [1696–1772]. *Elementa Philosophica: Containing Chiefly, Noetica, or Things Relating to the Mind or Understanding: And Ethica, or Things Relating to the Moral Behaviour.* Philadelphia: B. Franklin and D. Hall, 1752.

———. *Ethices Elementa, or The First Principles of Moral Philosophy....* Boston: Rogers and Fowle, 1746.

Johnson, Samuel [1709–84]. *A Dictionary of the English Language....* London, 1777.

———. *Johnson's Dictionary of the English Language, in Miniature....* London: C. Whittingham, 1800.

Johnson, Samuel, Jr. [1757–1836]. *A School Dictionary, Being a Compendium of the Latest and Most Improved Dictionaries....* New Haven, CT: Edward O'Brien, [1797 or 1798].

Jones, E. Alfred. *American Members of the Inns of Court.* London: St. Catherine, 1924.

Jones, John Paul. *Life and Correspondence of John Paul Jones....* New York: D. Fanshaw, 1830.

Journal of the Proceedings of the Convention Held at Richmond, in the County of Henrico on the 20th Day of March, 1775. Williamsburg, VA: J. Dixon and W. Hunter, 1775.

Kane, Richard. *A System of Camp-Discipline, Military Honours, Garrison-Duty, and Other Regulations for the Land Forces.* London: J. Millan, 1757.

" 'The Kappa Lambda Society of Hippocrates'—Who Are They?" *American Medical Gazette* 10 (1858): 381–87.

Kimber, Isaac, ed. *London Magazine; or, Gentleman's Monthly Intelligencer.* 4 vols. London: Charles Ackers, John Wilford, Thomas Cox, John Clarke, Thomas Astley, 1732–35.

Kimber, Isaac, and Edward Kimber, eds. *London Magazine; or, Gentleman's Monthly Intelligencer.* 37 vols. London: Richard Baldwin Jr., 1747–83.

[Kippis, Andrew]. *Considerations on the Provisional Treaty with America, and the Preliminary Articles of Peace with France and Spain.* London: T. Cadell, 1783.

Kline, Mary-Jo, and Joanne Wood Ryan, eds. *Political Correspondence and Public Papers of Aaron Burr.* 2 vols. Princeton, NJ: Princeton University Press, 1983.

Knox, Henry. *A Plan for the General Arrangement of the Militia of the United States.* [New York, 1786].

Knox, Samuel. *An Essay on the Best System of Liberal Education, Adapted to the Genius of the Government of the United States.* Baltimore: Warner and Hanna, 1799.

Laurens, Henry. *The Papers of Henry Laurens.* 16 vols. Edited by David C. Chesnutt and C. James Taylor. Columbia: University of South Carolina Press, 1968–2002.

La Valiere, Chevalier de. *The Art of War, Containing, the Duties of All Military Officers, in Actual Service; the Duties of Soldiers in General, in Actual Service; the Rules and Practice of the Greatest Generals, in the Manoeuvres.* Philadelphia: Robert Bell, 1776.

Law, William. *An Extract from a Treatise on the Spirit of Prayer . . . and Considerations on Slavery.* Philadelphia: Joseph Crukshank, 1780.

Laws of Queen's College. New Brunswick, NJ: Abraham Blauvelt, 1810.

Laws of the College of New Jersey. Trenton, NJ: Isaac Collins, 1794.

———. Philadelphia: R. Aitken, 1802.

———. Trenton, NJ: George Sherman, 1813.

Lee, Arthur. *An Appeal to the Justice and Interests of the People of Great Britain, in the Present Disputes with America.* London: J. Almon, 1775.

———. *An Essay in Vindication of the Continental Colonies of America: From a Censure of Mr. Adam Smith, in His Theory of Moral Sentiments. . . .* London: printed for the author, 1764.

———. *A Second Appeal to the Justice and Interests of the People, on the Measures Respecting America.* London: J. Almon, 1775.

———. *A Speech Intended to Have Been Delivered in the House of Commons: In Support of the Petition from the General Congress at Philadelphia.* London: J. Almon, 1775.

Lee, Charles. *The Lee Papers.* 4 vols. New York: New York Historical Society, 1871–75.

Lee, Richard Henry. *An Additional Number of Letters Prom [sic] the Federal Farmer to the Republican: Leading to a Fair Examination of the System of Government. . . .* [New York], 1788.

Lengel, Edward G., ed. *This Glorious Struggle: George Washington's Revolutionary War Letters.* New York: HarperCollins, 2007.

L'Estrange, Roger, ed. *Seneca's Morals by Way of Abstract.* 15th ed. London, 1746.

Library Company of Philadelphia. *A Catalogue of the Books Belonging to the Library Company of Philadelphia: To Which Is Prefixed a Short Account of the Institution with the Charter, Laws, and Regulations.* Philadelphia: Zachariah Poulson Jr., 1789.

Linn, William. *The Blessing of America. A Sermon.* New York: Thomas Greenleaf, 1791.

———. *A Discourse, Delivered on the 26th of November, 1795.* New York: T. and J. Swords, 1795.

———. *A Discourse on National Sins: Delivered May 9, 1798.* New York: T. and J. Swords, 1798.

Locke, John. *An Essay concerning Human Understanding.* Blacksburg: Virginia Tech, 2001.

———. *Two Treatises of Government.* London: A. Millar et al., 1764.

Lover of Constitutional Liberty. *The Appendix, or Some Observations. . . .* Boston: E. Russell, 1773.

Lowell, John. *An Essay on Hereditary Titles, and University Degrees; Particularly Doctorates in Divinity.* Boston: Manning and Loring for Caleb Bingham, 1798.

———. *Peace without Honor—War without Hope: Being a Calm and Dispassionate Enquiry into the Question of the Chesapeake, and the Necessity and Expediency of War.* Boston: Greenough and Stebbins, 1807.

Macaulay, Catherine. *A Treatise on the Immutability of Moral Truth.* London, 1783.

Madison, James [1749–1812]. *A Discourse Delivered at the Funeral of Mrs. Ann C. Semple, June 25, 1803.* Richmond: John Dixon, 1803.

———. *A Discourse on the Death of General Washington*. Richmond: Thomas Nicolson, 1800.

———. *Manifestation of the Providence towards America: A Discourse Delivered . . . 19th Feb. 1795. . . .* Richmond: Thomas Nicolson, 1795.

———. "An Oration in Commemoration of William and Mary College . . . , August 15, 1772." *Bulletin of the College of William and Mary in Virginia* 31, no. 7 (November 1937): 7–13.

Madison, James [1751–1836]. *Letters of Helvidius: Written in Reply to Pacificus, on the President's Proclamation of Neutrality, Published Originally in the Year 1793*. Philadelphia, 1796.

———. *Notes of Debates in the Federal Convention of 1787*. Athens: Ohio University Press, 1985.

———. "Proclamation of a State of War with Great Britain." 19 June 1812. Miller Center, University of Virginia. https://millercenter.org/the-presidency /presidential-speeches/june-19-1812-proclamation-state-war-great-britain.

Magnaw, Samuel. *An Address, Delivered in the Young Ladies Academy, at Philadelphia, on February 8, 1787. . . .* Philadelphia: Thomas Dobson, 1787.

The Man of Honour. London, 1737.

Mandeville, Bernard. *An Enquiry into the Origin of Honour and the Usefulness of Christianity in War*. London: John Brotherton, 1732.

Mann, Herman. *The Female Review, or, Memoirs of an American Young Lady. . . .* Dedham, MA: Nathaniel and Benjamin Heaton, 1797.

The Manuel Exercise as Ordered by His Majesty in 1764. . . . Boston: T. and J. Fleet, [1774].

Marrant, John. *A Sermon Preached on the 24th Day of June 1789, Being the Festival of St. John the Baptist, at the Request of the Right Worshipful the Grand Master Prince Hall, and the Rest of the Brethren of the African Lodge of the Honorable Society of Free and Accepted Masons in Boston*. Boston: Thomas and John Fleet, 1789.

Martin, Joseph Plumb. *Ordinary Courage: The Revolutionary War Adventures of Joseph Plumb Martin*. Oxford: Wiley-Blackwell, 2013.

Mason, J. M. *An Oration Commemorating the Late Major General Alexander Hamilton . . . 31st July, 1804*. New York: Hopkins and Seymour, 1804.

Mather, Cotton. *Essays to Do Good*. Lexington, KY: Thomas T. Skillman, 1822. Originally published in 1710.

———. *Magnalia Christi Americana*. London: T. Parkhurst, 1702.

Mauduit, Israel. *Franklin before the Privy Council, White Hall Chapel, London, 1774. . . .* Philadelphia: J. M. Butler, 1860.

———. *The Letters of Governor Hutchinson, and Lieut. Governor Oliver. . . .* London: J. Wilkie, 1774.

McIntosh, Lachlan. *A Historical Duel; a Letter Written by Brigadier General Lachlan McIntosh to Colonel John Laurence . . . Three Days after the Death of Button Gwinnett, Being a True Relation of the Duel, of the Events That Caused It and of Its Consequences: After One Hundred and Sixty Years the Authentic Story of the Historical Duel*. [Merion Station, PA]: American Autograph Shops, 1937.

McLeod, Alexander. *Negro Slavery Unjustifiable: A Discourse.* New York: T. and J. Swords, 1802.

A Military and Sea Dictionary. London: J. Morphew, 1711.

Minutes of the Medical Society of the County of New York. Vol. 1. New York: Medical Society of the County of New York, 1878.

Mirabeau, Honoré-Gabriel de Riquetti; Sébastien-Roch-Nicolas Chamfort; Samuel Romilly; Anne-Robert-Jacques Turgot, baron de l'Aulne; and Guy-Jean-Baptiste Target. *Considerations on the Order of Cincinnatus; to Which Are Added, as Well Several Original Papers Relative to That Institution. . . .* London: J. Johnson, 1785.

Monroe, James. *The Writings of James Monroe.* Vol. 5. New York: G. P. Putnam's Sons, 1901.

Montesquieu. *Spirit of the Laws.* New York: D. Appleton and Company, 1912. Electronic Text Center, University of Virginia Library. http://web.archive.org/web /20110216183948/http://etext.lib.virginia.edu/etcbin/toccer-new2?id=MonLaws .xml&images=images/modeng&data=/texts/english/modeng/parsed&tag =public&part=all.

———. *The Spirit of the Laws.* Edinburgh: A. Donaldson, 1762.

Moore, Milch Martha. *Milch Martha Moore's Book: A Commonplace Book from Revolutionary America.* Edited by Catherine La Courreye Blecki and Karin A. Wulf. University Park: Pennsylvania State University Press, 1997.

Moore, William. William Moore to Griffith Rutherford, 17 November 1776. Learn NC, University of North Carolina, School of Education. http://www.learnnc.org /lp/editions/nchist-revolution/4291.

Morison, Samuel Eliot, ed. "College Laws of 1655, 1692, and 1762 and College Customs 1734/5." In *Publications of the Colonial Society of Massachusetts.* Vol. 31. Boston: Published by the Society, 1935.

[Moylan, Stephen]. *Observations on a Late Pamphlet, Entitled "Considerations upon the Society of Order of the Cincinnati." . . .* Philadelphia: Robert Bell, 1783.

Muenchhausen, Friedrich von. *At General Howe's Side, 1776–1778.* Monmouth Beach, NJ: Philip Freneau, 1974.

Murray, Judith Sargent. *The Gleaner: A Miscellaneous Production in Three Volumes.* Boston: I. Thomas and E. T. Andrews, 1798.

———. *Selected Writings of Judith Sargent Murray.* New York: Oxford University Press, 1995.

Neal, J. A. *An Essay of the Education and Genius of the Female Sex; to Which Is Added, an Account, of the Commencement of the Young Ladies' Academy of Philadelphia, held the 18th of December 1794. . . .* Philadelphia: Jacob Johnson, 1795.

[Nettleton, Thomas]. *A Treatise on Virtue and Happiness.* London: T. W., 1736.

The New Whole Duty of Man: Containing a Clear & Full Account the Faith as Well as Practice of a Christian. London: only for Alex Hogg, [1785?].

New York State Society of the Cincinnati. *The Institution of the Society of the Cincinnati Formed by the Officers of the Army of the United States, for the Laudable Purposes Therein Mentioned; Published by Order and for the Use of the Members in the the [sic] State of New-York.* New York: Samuel Loudon, 1784.

North, Louise V., Janet M. Wedge, and Landa M. Freeman. *In the Words of Women: The Revolutionary War and the Birth of the Nation, 1765–1799.* Lanham, MD: Lexington Books, 2011.

Oliver, Peter. *Peter Oliver's Origin & Progress of the American Revolution: A Tory View.* Palo Alto, CA: Stanford University Press, 1961.

On Wednesday June 16, 1773, the House of Representatives by a Very Large Majority Came into the Following Resolves, upon the Letters that Had Been Laid Before Them on Wednesday the Second of the Same Month.... [Boston: Ednes and Gill, 1773].

Otis, Harrison Gray. *Eulogy on General Alexander Hamilton, Pronounced at the Request of the Citizens of Boston, July 26, 1804.* New York: Isaac Collins and Son, 1804.

Otis, James. *The Rights of British Colonies Asserted and Proved.* Boston: Edes and Gill, 1764.

[Overton, John]. *A Vindication of the Measures of the President and His Commanding Generals, in the Commencement and Termination of the Seminole War.* Washington, DC: Gales and Seaton, 1819.

Paine, Thomas. *The American Crisis.* London: Daniel Isaac Eaton, 1776.

———. *Common Sense.* Philadelphia: R. Bell, 1776.

Percival, Thomas. *Extracts from the Medical Ethics....* Lexington, KY: T. Smith, 1821.

Philanthropos [William Ladd]. *A Letter to Aaron Burr, Vice-President of the United States of America: On the Barbarous Origin, the Criminal Nature and the Baneful Effects of Duels Occasioned by His Late Fatal Interview with the Deceased and Much Lamented General Alexander Hamilton.* New York: John Low, William Barlas, and John Reid, 1804.

Pickering, Timothy, Jr. *An Easy Plan of Discipline for a Militia.* Salem, MA: Samuel and Ebenezer Hall, 1775.

Plutarch. *Plutarch's Lives.* London: T. Hodgkin and J. Tonson, 1683–86.

Pope, Alexander. *Essay on Man.* Reprint of the 1891 London edition published by Cassell, Project Gutenberg, 2007. https://www.gutenberg.org/files/2428/2428-h /2428-h.htm.

Price, Richard. *Observations on the Importance of the American Revolution and the Means of Making It a Benefit to the World.* London, 1784.

———. *Observations on the Nature of Civil Liberty, the Principles of Government, and the Justice and Policy of the War with America....* Philadelphia: Reprinted by John Dunlap, 1776.

Proceedings of a Board of General Officers, Held by Order of His Excellency Gen. Washington, Commander in Chief of the Army of the United States of America; Respecting Major John André, Adjutant General of the British Army, September 29, 1780. Philadelphia, 1780.

Proceedings of a Court of Inquiry Held at the Navy Yard, Brooklyn, New York, upon Captain James Barron ... May 1821. Washington, DC: J. Gideon, 1822.

Proceedings of a General Court Martial for the Trial of Major General Arnold. New York: printed privately, 1865.

Proceedings of a General Court Martial ... for the Trial of Major General Arnold, June 1, 1779. Philadelphia: F. Bailey, 1780.

Proceedings of a General Court Martial . . . for the Trial of Major General Lee. Cooperstown, NY: J. H. Prentiss, 1823.

Proceedings of the General Court Martial Convened for the Trial of James Barron, Captain Charles Gordon, Mr. William Hook, Captain John Hall, of the United States' Ship Chesapeake, in the Month of January, 1808. [Washington, DC]: J. Gideon Jr., 1822.

Proceedings . . . respecting Major John André, Adjutant General of the British Army, September 29, 1780. Philadelphia, [1780].

Pufendorf, Samuel Freiherr von. *The Law of Nature and Nations; or, A General System of the Most Important Principles of Morality, Jurisprudence, and Politics. . . .* London: J. and J. Bronwicke, 1749.

Quincy, Josiah. [1802–82]. *Figures of the Past from the Leaves of Old Journals.* Boston: Roberts Brothers, 1883.

Ramsay, David. *The History of the American Revolution.* 2 vols. Philadelphia: R. Aitken and Son, 1789.

————. *The History of the Revolution of South-Carolina from a British Province to an Independent State.* 2 vols. Trenton, NJ: Isaac Collins, 1785.

Randolph, Edmund. *An Oration in Commemoration of the Founders of William and Mary College, Delivered on the Anniversary of Its Foundation, August 15, 1771.* Williamsburg, VA: William Rind, 1771.

————. *Political Truth; or, Animadversions on the Past and Present State of Public Affairs with an Inquiry into the Truth of the Charges Preferred against Mr. Randolph.* Philadelphia: Samuel Harrison Smith, 1796.

————. *A Vindication of Mr. Randolph's Resignation.* Philadelphia: Samuel H. Smith, 1795.

Records of the Connecticut State Society of the Cincinnati, 1783–1804. Hartford: Connecticut Historical Society, 1916.

The Records of the Honorable Society of Lincoln's Inn: Admissions. 2 vols. [London]: Lincoln's Inn, 1896.

The Records of the Honorable Society of Lincoln's Inn: The Black Books. 4 vols. [London]: Lincoln's Inn, 1897–1902.

The Records of the Society of Gentleman Practisers in the Courts of Law and Equity Called the Law Society. London: Incorporated Law Society, 1897.

[Reed, Esther De Berdt]. "The Sentiments of an American Woman"/ "I D E A S, Relative to the Manner of Forwarding to the American Soldiers the Presents of the American Women," 1780 Humanities Center Resource Toolbox, Making the Revolution: America, 1763–1791, Library of Congress. http://americainclass.org /sources/makingrevolution/war/text7/reedsentimentsamerwoman.pdf.

Remarks on a Pamphlet, Written by the Rev. James Ramsay, M.A. under the Title of Thoughts on the Slavery of the Negroes, in the American Colonies. London: J. P. Bateman, 1784.

Richardson, Samuel. *Clarissa; or, The History of a Young Lady: Comprehending the Most Important Concerns of Private Life. . . .* London: A. Millar, J. and Ja. Rivington, J. Osborn, and J. Leake, 1748.

———. *Pamela; or, Virtue Rewarded.* . . . London: C. Rivington and J. Osborn, 1741.

Ridout, Mary (Molly). Mary (Molly) Ridout to Anne Tasker Ogle, 16 January 1784. Maryland State Archives. http://msa.maryland.gov/megafile/msa/speccol/sc3500 /sc3520/016800/016812/images/ridoutletter_transcription.pdf.

The Rise and Progress of the Young-Ladies' Academy of Philadelphia. . . . Philadelphia: Stewart and Conchran, 1794.

Roberts, James. *The Narrative of James Roberts, a Soldier under Gen. Washington in the Revolutionary War, and under Gen. Jackson at the Battle of New Orleans, in the War of 1812.* . . . Chicago: printed for the author, 1858.

Roberts, Richard Arthur, ed. *A Calendar of the Inner Temple Records.* London: Geo. Barber and Sons, 1933.

Robespierre, Maximilien. "On the Moral and Political Principles of Domestic Policy," 1794. Fordham University, Modern History Sourcebook. http://sourcebooks .fordham.edu/mod/robespierre-terror.asp.

Rogers, William. *An Oration, Delivered July 4, 1789: At the Presbyterian Church, in Arch Street, Philadelphia.* Philadelphia: T. Dobson, 1789.

Rossiter, Clinton, ed. *The Federalist Papers.* New York: Signet Classic, 2003.

Rowson, Susanna. *Charlotte: A Tale of Truth.* Philadelphia: D. Humphreys, 1794.

———. *A Present for Young Ladies: Containing Poems, Dialogues, Addresses, &c., &c., &c., as Recited by the Pupils of Mrs. Rowson's Academy at the Annual Exhibitions.* Boston: John West, 1811. Microform.

Rules and Articles for the Better Government of His Majesties Land-Forces in Pay. London: Charles Bill, Henry Hills, and Thomas Newcomb, 1688.

Rush, Benjamin. *Essays, Literary, Moral & Philosophical.* Philadelphia: Thomas & Samuel F. Bradford, 1798.

———. *Letters of Benjamin Rush.* 2 vols. Edited by Lyman Henry Butterfield. Princeton, NJ: Published for the American Philosophical Society by the Princeton University Press, 1951.

———. *Thoughts upon Female Education* . . . . *Addressed to the Visitors of the Young Ladies' Academy in Philadelphia, 28th July, 1787.* . . . Philadelphia: Prichard and Hall, 1787.

Rutherford, Thomas. *Institutes of Natural Law; Being the Substance of a Course of Lectures on Grotius de Jure Belli et Pacis Read in S. John's College, Cambridge.* Cambridge, UK: J. Archdeacon, 1779. Originally published 1754.

St. John de Crèvecœur, J. Hector. *Letters from an American Farmer: Describing Certain Provincial Situations, Manners, and Customs . . . and Conveying Some Idea of the Late and Present Interior Circumstances of the British Colonies in North America / Written for the Information of a Friend in England.* London: T. Davies, 1782. http://avalon.law .yale.edu/subject_menus/letters.asp.

Seabury, Samuel. *Free Thoughts on the Proceedings of the Continental Congress, Held at Philadelphia, Sept. 5, 1774.* . . . New York [?], 1774.

Segar, Sir William. *Honor Military, and Ciuill [Civil], Contained in Foure Books.* London: Robert Barker, 1602.

Seneca, Lucius Annaeus. *Moral and Political Essays.* Edited by John M. Cooper and J. F. Procopé. Cambridge: Cambridge University Press, 1995.

———. *Seneca's Morals of a Happy Life, Benefits, Anger, and Clemency.* Chicago: W. B. Conkey, 1902.

Serle, Ambrose. *The American Journal of Ambrose Serle.* Los Angeles: Ward Ritchie, 1940.

Sewall, Joseph. *He That Would Keep God's Commandments....* Boston: B. Green, 1728.

Seymour, George D. *Documentary Life of Nathan Hale: Comprising All Available Official and Private Documents Bearing on the Life of the Patriot.* Whitefish, MT: Kessinger, 2006.

Shaftesbury, Earl of (Anthony Ashley Cooper). *An Inquiry Concerning Virtue....* London: A. Bell, E. Castle, and S. Buckley, 1699.

A Short Narrative of the Horrid Massacre in Boston. Boston: Edes and Gill, 1770.

Simes, Thomas. *A Military Course for the Government and Conduct of a Battalion: Designed for Their Regulations in Quarter, Camp, or Garrison....* London: Almon, Hooper, Richardson, Urquhart, and Walter, 1777.

———. *The Military Guide for Young Officers.* Vol. 2. Philadelphia: Humphreys, Bells, and Aitken, 1776.

———. *The Military Guide for Young Officers, Containing a System of the Art of War....* London, 1781.

Smith, Adam. *Theory of Moral Sentiments.* London: A. Millar, 1759.

———. *The Works of Adam Smith, LL.D. and F.R.S. of London and Edinburgh: One of the Commissioners of His Majesty's Customs in Scotland....* London: T. Cadell and W. Davies, 1811–12.

Smith, Joshua Hett. *An Authentic Narrative of the Causes Which Led to the Death of Major Andre.* London: Matthews and Leigh, 1808.

Smith, Venture. *A Narrative of the Life and Adventures of Venture, a Native of Africa: But Resident above Sixty Years in the United States of America, Related by Himself.* New London, CT: C. Holt, 1798.

Smith, William. *Discourses on Several Public Occasions during the War in America: Preached Chiefly with a View to the Explaining the Importance of the Protestant Cause, in the British Colonies, and the Advancement of Religion, Patriotism, and Military Virtue.* London: R. Griffiths and G. Keith, 1759.

———. *A Sermon on Temporal and Spiritual Salvation: Delivered in Christ-Church, Philadelphia, before the Pennsylvania Society of the Cincinnati.* Philadelphia: T. Dobson, 1790.

[Smollett, Tobias George]. *The Adventures of Peregrine Pickle: In Which Are Included, Memoirs of a Lady of Quality.* 2 vols. Dublin: Robert Main, 1751.

Snow, Dean R., ed. "American Orderly Books, Saratoga, September 15 to October 17, 1777." http://global.oup.com/us/companion.websites/fdscontent/uscompanion/us /static/companion.websites/9780190618759/PDF/America_Orderly_Book.pdf.

Society of the Cincinnati in the State of New Jersey. *Excerpts of the Proceedings of the Society of the Cincinnati in the State of New Jersey from May 13th, 1783, to July 4, 1906.* [Brooklyn, NY?]: W. T. B. S. Imlay, for the Society, 1908.

Spring, Samuel. *The Sixth Commandment Friendly to Virtue, Honor and Politeness: A Discourse in Consequence of the Late Duel.* . . . Newburyport, MA: E. W. Allen, 1804.

Statutes of the University of William & Mary. Richmond: Augustine Davis, 1792.

Stevenson, Roger. *Military Instructions for Officers Detached in the Field.* . . . Philadelphia: R. Alpeen, 1764.

Stiles, Ezra. *The United States Elevated to Glory and Honour: A Sermon Preached before His Excellency Jonathan Trumbull . . . and the Honourable the General Assembly of the State of Connecticut, Convened at Hartford, at the Anniversary Election, May 8th, MDCCLXXXIII.* Worcester, MA: Isaiah Thomas, 1785.

Storing, Herbert J., ed. *The Complete Anti-Federalist.* 7 vols. Chicago: University of Chicago Press, 1981.

Sweig, Donald M., and Elizabeth S. David, eds. *A Fairfax Friendship: The Complete Correspondence between George Washington and Bryan Fairfax, 1754–1799.* Fairfax County, VA: Fairfax County History Commission, 1982.

A Synopsis of the Records of the State Society of the Cincinnati of Pennsylvania. Philadelphia: State Society of the Cincinnati of Pennsylvania, 1891.

Tallmadge, Benjamin. *Memoir of Col. Benjamin Tallmadge.* New York: T. Holman, 1858.

Temple, William. *Miscellanea: The Second Part.* London: R. A. Simpson, 1705.

Thacher, James. *Military Journal of the American Revolution.* New York: Arno, 1969.

Thatcher, Benjamin Bussey. *Traits of the Tea Party: Being a Memoir of George R. T. Hewes.* . . . New York: Harper, 1935.

Tilton, James. James Tilton to Gunning Bedford, 25 December 1783. Bryn Mawr College. http://www.brynmawr.edu/library/speccoll/guides/tilton.pdf.

Tocqueville, Alexis de. *Democracy in America.* From the Henry Reeve translation, 1899. American Studies Programs, University of Virginia, 1997. http://xroads .virginia.edu/~hyper/detoc/toc_indx.html.

Trumbull, John. "General George Washington Resigning His Commission." Oil on canvas, 1824, Rotunda, U.S. Capitol, Washington, DC. https://www.aoc.gov/art /historic-rotunda-paintings/general-george-washington-resigning-his -commission.

Truth, Sojourner. *The Narrative of Sojourner Truth.* Boston: published by the author, 1850.

Turpin de Crissé, Lancelot. *An Essay on the Art of War.* 2 vols. Translated by Captain Joseph Otway. London: A. Hamilton, 1761.

Tyler, Royall. *The Algerine Captive.* Walpole, NH, 1797.

Umphraville, Angus. *An Oration on the Death of Commodore Stephen Decatur of the United States Navy: Who Was Killed in a Duel by James Barron, Formerly Commander of the Chesapeake.* Pittsburg, 1820.

"The University of Georgia Charter, 1785." Transcribed by E. Merton Coulter and John O. Eidson. Hargrett Rare Book and Manuscript Library, University of Georgia. Last updated May 30, 2017. http://www.libs.uga.edu/hargrett/archives /exhibit/charter/chartertranscription.html.

U.S. Congress. *The Debates and Proceedings in the Congress of the United States.* 13th Congress, 3rd session. Washington, DC: Gales and Seaton, 1854.

———. *The Debates and Proceedings in the Congress of the United States.* 15th Congress, 2nd session. Washington, DC: Gales and Seaton, 1854.

U.S. Continental Congress. *A Declaration by the Representatives of the United Colonies of North America Now Met in General Congress at Philadelphia.* Philadelphia: William and Thomas Bradford, 1775.

———. *Rules and Articles for the Better Government of the Troops . . . of the United States of America.* Philadelphia: John Dunlap, 1776.

———. *Rules and Articles for the Better Government of Troops Raised, or to Be Raised, and Kept in the Pay by and at the Joint Expence of the Thirteen United English Colonies of North America.* Philadelphia: William and Thomas Bradford, 1775.

[U.S. Department of State]. *A Letter from Mr. Pickering, Secretary of State to Mr. Pinckney, Minister Plenipotentiary at Paris, in Answer to the Complaints Communicated by Mr. Adet, Minister of the French Republic, against the United States of America.* Richmond: T. Nicholson, 1797.

Van Ness, William P. *A Correct Statement of the Late Melancholy Affair of Honor between General Hamilton and Col. Burr. . . .* New York: G. and R. Waite, 1804.

Vattel, Emer de. *The Law of Nations; or, Principles of the Law of Nature: Applied to the Conduct and Affairs of Nations and Sovereigns. . . .* London: J. Newbery, J. Richardson, S. Crowder, T. Caslon, T. Longman, B. Law, J. Fuller, J. Coote, and G. Kearsly, 1759.

———. *The Law of Nations; or, Principles of the Law of Nature: Applied to the Conduct and Affairs of Nations and Sovereigns. . . .* London: G. G. and J. Robinson, 1797.

———. *The Law of Nations; or, Principles of the Law of Nature: Applied to the Conduct and Affairs of Nations and Sovereigns. . . .* Northampton, MA: Thomas M. Pomroy for S. and E. Butler, 1805.

The Voice of Truth, or, Thoughts on the Affair between the Leopard and Chesapeake: In a Letter from a Gentleman at New York to His Friend. New York: J. Osborn, 1807.

Von Steuben, Freidrich Wilhelm. *A Letter on the Subject of an Established Militia, and Military Arrangements: Addressed to the Inhabitants of the United States.* New York: J. M'Lean, 1784.

———. *Regulations for the Order and Discipline of the Troops of the United States.* Philadelphia: Styner and Cist, 1779.

Waldo, Samuel Putnam. *The Life and Character of Stephen Decatur. . . .* Hartford, CT: P. B. Goodsell, 1821.

Wallace, John Bradford. *Valedictory Oration . . . at the College of New Jersey . . . Class of 1794.* Albany, NY: Munsell, 1874.

Warren, Mercy Otis. *History of the Rise, Progress and Termination of the American Revolution: Interspersed with Biographical, Political and Moral Observation. . . .* 3 vols. Boston: Manning and Loring, 1805.

———. *Mercy Otis Warren: Selected Letters.* Edited by Jeffrey H. Richards and Sharon M. Harris. Athens: University of Georgia Press, 2009.

———. *Poems, Dramatic and Miscellaneous.* Boston: I. Thomas and E. T. Andrews, 1790.

Washington, Augustine. "Will." 11 April 1743. George Washington Papers at the
Library of Congress, 1741–1799: Series 4, General Correspondence, 1697–1799.
https://www.loc.gov/item/mgw441960/.

Washington, George. "Address to Congress on Resigning His Commission."
[23 December 1783]. Maryland State Archives. http://msa.maryland.gov/msa
/stagser/s1259/131/html/gwresign.html.

———. *The Diaries of George Washington.* 6 vols. Edited by Donald Jackson and
Dorothy Twohig. Charlottesville: University Press of Virginia, 1976.

———. *The Papers of George Washington.* 63 vols. Charlottesville: University Press of
Virginia, 1983–2016.

———. *Rules of Civility and Decent Behavior in Company and Conversation.* Bedford,
MA: Applewood Books, 1988.

———. *Rules of Civility and Decent Behaviour in Company and Conversation.* Edited by
Richard Brookhiser. Charlottesville: University of Virginia Press, 2003.

———. *The Writings of George Washington.* 39 vols. Edited by John C. Fitzpatrick.
Washington, DC: Government Printing Office, 1931–44.

Washington, George, and Marvin Kitman. *George Washington's Expense Account.*
New York: Simon and Schuster, 1970.

Washington, Martha. *Worthy Partner: The Papers of Martha Washington.* Edited by
Joseph E. Fields. Westport, CT: Greenwood, 1994.

Waterhouse, Benjamin, ed. *A Journal of a Young Man of Massachusetts. . . .* By Amos G.
Babcock. Milledgeville, GA: Reprinted by S. and F. Grantland, 1816.

Waterhouse, Edward. *A Discourse and Defence of Arms and Armory. . . .* London:
Samuel Mearne in Little Britain, 1660.

Watson, J. *A Military Dictionary.* London: T. Read, 1758.

Webster, Daniel. *The Papers of Daniel Webster.* Vol. 1. Hanover: published for
Dartmouth College by the University of New England, 1974.

Webster, Noah. *An American Dictionary of the English Language. . . .* New York:
S. Converse, 1828.

Wesley, John. *Thoughts upon Slavery.* London, 1774.

Wharton, Charles Henry. *A Poetical Epistle to His Excellency George Washington. . . .*
Annapolis, 1779; London: reprinted for C. Dilly, 1780.

Wheatley, Phillis. *Poems.* Alexandria, VA: Chadwyck-Healey, 1996.

Whitaker, Nathaniel. *An Antidote against Toryism, or, The Curse of Meroz in a Discourse
on Judges 5th 23.* Newburyport, MA: John Mycall, 1777.

Wilmer, James Jones. *An Address to the Citizens of the United States on National
Representation; with a Sketch of the Origin of Government, and the State of Public
Affairs.* Baltimore: William Pechin, 1796.

Wilson, John Lyde. *The Code of Honor; or, Rules for the Government of Principals and
Seconds in Dueling.* Charleston, SC: James Phinney, 1858. Originally published 1838.

Wilson, John T. J. *An Address to the [Kappa Lamda] Society of Hippocrates: Delivered
January 6th, 1823.* Lexington, KY: Thomas T. Skillman, 1823.

Wolfe, James. *General Wolfe's Instructions to Young Officers. . . .* London: J. Millan, 1768.

Wollstonecraft, Mary. *A Vindication of the Rights of Woman with Strictures on Political and Moral Subjects.* London: Joseph Johnson, 1792.

Woodruff, Hezekiah North. *The Danger of Ambition Considered: A Sermon, Preached at Scipio, N.Y., Lord's Day, August 12, 1804; Occasioned by the Death of General Alexander Hamilton, Who Fell in a Duel with Aaron Burr, Vice-President of the United States of America: On the 11th July, 1804.* Albany, NY: Charles R. and George Webster, 1804.

Woods, Joseph. *Thoughts on the Slavery of the Negroes.* London: James Phillips, 1784.

Young, William. *Manoeuvers, or Practical Observations on the Art of War.* London: J. Milan, [1771?].

Zubly, John Joachim. *The Stamp Act Repealed, a Sermon. . . .* Savannah: James Johnston, 1766.

Secondary Sources

Abernethy, Thomas Perkins. *The Burr Conspiracy.* New York: Oxford University Press, 1954.

Abrams, Elliot, and Donald Kagan, eds. *Honor among Nations: Intangible Interests and Foreign Policy.* Washington, DC: Ethics and Public Policy Center, 1998.

Adair, Douglass. *Fame and the Founding Fathers: Essays by Douglas Adair.* Indianapolis: Liberty Fund, 1974.

Albanese, Catherine L. *Sons of the Fathers: The Civil Religion of the American Revolution.* Philadelphia: Temple University Press, 1976.

Alden, John Richard. *General Charles Lee: Traitor or Patriot?* Baton Rouge: Louisiana State University Press, 1951.

———. *Robert Dinwiddie: Servant of the Crown.* Charlottesville: University Press of Virginia, 1973.

Alexander, John K. *Samuel Adams: America's Revolutionary Politician.* Lanham, MD: Rowman and Littlefield, 2002.

Ambrose, Charles T. "The Historical Importance of Transylvania University's Medical Department (1799–1859). . . ." *Microbiology, Immunology, and Molecular Genetics Faculty Publications,* paper 62 (2011). http://uknowledge.uky.edu /microbio_facpub/62.

———. "The Secret Kappa Lambda Society of Hippocrates (and the Origin of the American Medical Association's Principles of Medical Ethics)." *Yale Journal of Biological Medicine* 78, no. 1 (January 2005): 45–56.

Anderson, Benedict R. O'G. *Imagined Communities: Reflections of the Origin and Spread of Nationalism.* London: Verso, 2006.

Anderson, Fred. *A People's Army: Massachusetts Soldiers and Society in the Seven Years' War.* Chapel Hill: University of North Carolina Press, 1984.

Anderson, George P. "Ebenezer Mackintosh: Stamp Act Rioter and Patriot." *Publications of the Colonial Society of Massachusetts* 26 (1927): 15–64, 349–61.

Appiah, Kwame Anthony. *The Honor Code: How Moral Revolutions Happen.* New York: W. W. Norton, 2010.

Appleby, Joyce. *Inheriting the Revolution: The First Generation of Americans.* Cambridge, MA: Belknap Press of Harvard University Press, 2001.

Archer, Jayne Elisabeth, Elizabeth Goldring, and Sarah Knight, eds. *The Intellectual and Cultural World of the Early Modern Inns of Court.* Manchester: Manchester University Press, 2011.

Archer, Richard. *As if an Enemy's Country: The British Occupation of Boston and the Origins of Revolution.* New York: Oxford University Press, 2010.

Arditi, Jorge. *A Genealogy of Manners: Transformations of Social Relations in France and England from the Fourteenth to Eighteenth Century.* Chicago: University of Chicago Press, 1998.

Arnold, Isaac Newton. *The Life of Benedict Arnold: His Patriotism and Treason.* Chicago: Jansen, McClurg, 1880.

Austin, J. L. *How to Do Things with Words.* Cambridge, MA: Harvard University Press, 1962.

Bailyn, Bernard. *Education in the Forming of American Society: Needs and Opportunities for Study.* New York: W. W. Norton, 1960.

———. *The Ideological Origins of the American Revolution.* Enlarged ed. Cambridge, MA: Belknap Press of Harvard University Press, 1992. Originally published 1967.

———. *The Ordeal of Thomas Hutchinson.* Cambridge, MA: Harvard University Press, 1974.

Baker, J. H. *The Common Law Tradition: Lawyers, Books, and the Law.* London: Hambledon Press, 2000.

Baker, Robert, ed. *The American Medical Ethics Revolution: How the AMA's Code of Ethics Has Transformed Physicians' Relationships to Patients, Professionals, and Society.* Baltimore: Johns Hopkins University Press, 1999.

———. *Before Bioethics: A History of American Medical Ethics from the Colonial Period to the Bioethics Revolution.* New York: Oxford University Press, 2013.

Beeman, Richard R. *Our Lives, Our Fortunes, and Our Sacred Honor: The Forging of American Independence, 1774–1776.* New York: Basic Books, 2013.

———. *Plain, Honest Men: The Making of the American Constitution.* New York: Random House, 2010.

Bell, James B. *A War of Religion: Dissenters, Anglicans, and the American Revolution.* New York: Palgrave Macmillan, 2008.

Bell, Richard. "The Double Guilt of Dueling: The Stain of Suicide in Anti-dueling Rhetoric in the Early Republic." *Journal of the Early Republic* 29, no. 3 (Fall 2009): 383–410.

Bellah, Robert N. "Civil Religion in America." *Daedalus* 96, no. 1 (Winter 1967): 1–21.

Bennetton, Norman A. *Social Significance of the Duel in Seventeenth-Century French Drama.* Baltimore: Johns Hopkins University Press, 1938.

Berkin, Carol. *First Generations: Women in Colonial America.* New York: Hill and Wang, 1997.

————. *Revolutionary Mothers: Women in the Struggle for America's Independence.* New York: Alfred A. Knopf, 2005.

Billacois, Francois. *The Duel: Its Rise and Fall in Early Modern France.* New Haven, CT: Yale University Press, 1990.

Bloch, Ruth H. *Gender and Morality in Anglo-American Culture, 1650–1800.* Berkeley: University of California Press, 2003.

————. "The Gendered Meanings of Virtue in Revolutionary America." *Signs* 13, no. 1 (Autumn 1987): 37–58.

Bolton, Charles Knowles. *The Private Soldier under Washington.* Port Washington, NY: Kennikat, 1962.

Booraem, Hendrik. *Young Hickory: The Making of Andrew Jackson.* Dallas: Taylor Trade, 2001.

Bourdieu, Pierre. *Distinction: A Social Critique of the Judgment of Taste.* Oxon: Routledge, 2010.

Bourne, Russell. *Cradle of Violence: How Boston's Waterfront Mobs Ignited the American Revolution.* Hoboken: John Wiley and Sons, 2006.

Bouton, Terry. *Taming Democracy: "The People," the Founders, and the Trouble Ending the American Revolution.* New York: Oxford University Press, 2007.

Bowman, James. *Honor: A History.* New York: Encounter Books, 2006.

Bradburn, Douglas. *The Citizenship Revolution: Politics and the Creation of the American Union.* Charlottesville: University of Virginia Press, 2009.

Brands, H. W. *Andrew Jackson: His Life and Times.* New York: Doubleday, 2005.

Brandt, Clare. *The Man in the Mirror: A Life of Benedict Arnold.* New York: Random House, 1994.

Breen, T. H. *The Marketplace of Revolution: How Consumer Politics Shaped American Independence.* New York: Oxford University Press, 2005.

————, ed. *Shaping Southern Society: The Colonial Experience.* New York: Oxford University Press, 1976.

————. *Tobacco Culture: The Mentality of the Great Tidewater Planters on the Eve of Revolution.* Princeton, NJ: Princeton University Press, 1985.

Broderick, Francis L. "Pulpit, Physics, and Politics: The Curriculum of the College of New Jersey, 1746–1794." *William and Mary Quarterly* 6, no. 1 (January 1949): 42–68.

Brookhiser, Richard. *Founding Father: Rediscovering George Washington.* New York: Free Press, 1996.

————. *Gentleman Revolutionary: Gouverneur Morris, the Rake Who Wrote the Constitution.* New York: Free Press, 2003.

Brooks, Joanna. "Colonization, Black Freemasonry, and the Rehabilitation of Africa." In *Messy Beginnings: Postcoloniality and Early American Studies,* edited by Malini Johar Schueller and Edward Watts, 237–50. Piscataway, NJ: Rutgers University Press, 2003.

Brooks, Joanna, and John Saillant. Introduction to *"Face Zion Forward": First Writers of the Black Atlantic, 1785–1798,* edited by Joanna Brooks and John Saillant, 3–34. York, PA: Maple, 2002.

Brown, Christopher Leslie. *Moral Capital: Foundations of British Abolitionism*. Chapel Hill: published for the Omohundro Institute of Early American History and Culture, Williamsburg, VA, by the University of North Carolina Press, 2006.

Brown, Christopher Leslie, and Philip D. Morgan, eds. *Arming Slaves: From Classical Times to the Modern Age*. New Haven, CT: Yale University Press, 2006.

Brown, Gregory. *A Field of Honor: Writers, Court Culture, and Public Theater in French Literary Life from Racine to the Revolution*. New York: Columbia University Press, 2005.

Brown, Imogene E. *American Aristides: A Biography of George Wythe*. Rutherford, NJ: Fairleigh Dickinson University Press, 1981.

Brown, Kathleen M. *Foul Bodies: Cleanliness in Early America*. New Haven, CT: Yale University Press, 2009.

Brown, Stuart E., Jr. *Virginia Baron: The Story of Thomas 6th Lord Fairfax*. Berryville, VA: Chesapeake Book Company, 1965.

Browne, Stephen H. *The Ides of War: George Washington and the Newburgh Crisis*. Columbia: University of South Carolina Press, 2016.

Brumwell, Stephen. *Redcoats: The British Soldier and War in the Americas, 1755–1763*. Cambridge: Cambridge University Press, 2002.

Brunsman, Denver. *The Evil Necessity: British Naval Impressment in the Eighteenth-Century Atlantic World*. Charlottesville: University of Virginia Press, 2013.

Bryson, Frederick Robertson. *The Point of Honor in Sixteenth-Century Italy: An Aspect of the Life of the Gentleman*. New York: Columbia University Press, 1935.

———. *The Sixteenth-Century Italian Duel: A Study in Renaissance Social History*. Chicago: University of Chicago Press, 1938.

Budiansky, Stephen. *Perilous Fight: America's Intrepid War with Britain on the High Seas, 1812–1815*. New York: Alfred A. Knopf, 2010.

Bullock, Steven C. *Revolutionary Brotherhood: Freemasonry and the Transformation of the American Social Order, 1730–1840*. Chapel Hill: published for the Omohundro Institute of Early History and Culture by the University of North Carolina Press, 1998.

Burstein, Andrew. *The Passions of Andrew Jackson*. New York: Alfred A. Knopf, 2003.

———. *Sentimental Democracy: The Evolution of America's Self-Image*. New York: Hill and Wang, 1999.

Bush, George Gary. *Harvard: The First American University*. Boston: Cupples, Upham, 1886.

Bushman, Richard L. *The Refinement of America: Persons, Houses, Cities*. New York: Alfred A. Knopf, 1992.

Byron, Matthew A. "Crime and Punishment: The Impotency of Dueling Laws in the United States." PhD diss., University of Arkansas, 2008.

Carney, Charity R. *Ministers and Masters: Methodism, Manhood, and Honor in the Old South*. Baton Rouge: Louisiana State University Press, 2011.

Carp, Benjamin L. *Rebels Rising: Cities and the American Revolution*. New York: Oxford University Press, 2007.

Carp, E. Wayne. *To Starve the Army at Pleasure: Continental Army Administration and American Political Culture, 1775–1783.* Chapel Hill: University of North Carolina Press, 1984.

Carpenter's Hall. "Virtual History Tour." Accessed ca. October 18, 2016. http://www.carpentershall.org/visit/virtualtour.htm.

Carr, Lois Green, Philip D. Morgan, and Jean B. Russo, eds. *Colonial Chesapeake Society.* Chapel Hill: University of North Carolina Press, 1988.

Chabal, Patrick, and Jean-Pascal Daloz. *Cultural Troubles: Politics and the Interpretation of Meaning.* Chicago: University of Chicago Press, 2006.

Chappel, Alonzo. "Battle of Saratoga, General Arnold Wounded in the Attack on the Hessian Redoubt." Engraving, 1860. New York Public Library Digital Collections. http://digitalcollections.nypl.org/items/510d47e0-f5cc-a3d9-e040-e00a18064a99.

Cheathem, Mark R. *Andrew Jackson, Southerner.* Baton Rouge: Louisiana State University Press, 2013.

———. "'The High Minded Honourable Man': Honor, Kinship, and Conflict in the Life of Andrew Jackson Donelson." *Journal of the Early Republic* 27, no. 2 (Summer 2007): 265–92.

Chernow, Ron. *Alexander Hamilton.* New York: Penguin, 2004.

———. *Washington: A Life.* New York: Penguin, 2010.

Clark, Allen C. "Commodore James Barron, Commodore Stephen Decatur: The Barron-Decatur Duel." *Records of the Columbia Historical Society, Washington, D.C.* 42/43 (1940/1941): 189–215

Clark, J. C. D. *The Language of Liberty, 1660–1832: Political Discourse and Social Dynamics in the Anglo-American World.* Cambridge: Cambridge University Press, 1994.

Cogliano, Francis D. *Emperor of Liberty: Thomas Jefferson's Foreign Policy.* New Haven, CT: Yale University Press, 2014.

Colley, Linda. *Britons: Forging the Nation, 1707–1837.* New Haven, CT: Yale University Press, 2012.

Cornell, Saul. *The Other Founders: Anti-federalism and the Dissenting Tradition in America, 1788–1828.* Chapel Hill: University of North Carolina Press, 1999.

Cott, Nancy. *Bonds of Womanhood: Women's Sphere in New England, 1780–1835.* New Haven, CT: Yale University Press, 1997.

Cox, Caroline. *A Proper Sense of Honor: Service and Sacrifice in George Washington's Army.* Chapel Hill: University of North Carolina Press, 2004.

Cray, Robert E., Jr. "Remembering the USS *Chesapeake*: The Politics of Maritime Death and Impressment." *Journal of the Early Republic* 25, no. 3 (Fall 2005): 445–74.

Cresswell, Donald H. *The American Revolution in Drawings and Prints.* Washington, DC: Library of Congress, 1975.

Cunliffe, Marcus. *Soldiers and Civilians: The Martial Spirit in America, 1775–1865.* Boston: Little, Brown, 1968.

Daloz, Jean-Pascal. *Rethinking Social Distinction.* Basingstoke, UK: Palgrave Macmillan, 2013.

Dandridge, Danske. *American Prisoners of the Revolution.* Baltimore: Genealogical, 1967.

Davidson, Cathy N. *Revolution and the Word: The Rise of the Novel in America.* New York: Oxford University Press, 2004.

Davies, Wallace Evan. "The Society of the Cincinnati in New England, 1783–1800." *William and Mary Quarterly* 4, no. 1 (January 1948): 3–25.

Davis, David Brion. *The Problem of Slavery in the Age of the Revolution, 1770–1823.* Ithaca, NY: Cornell University Press, 1975.

Dean, Robert D. *Imperial Brotherhood: Gender and the Making of Cold War Foreign Policy.* Amherst: University of Massachusetts Press, 2003.

Desch-Obi, T. J. *Fighting for Honor: The History of African Martial Art Traditions in the Atlantic World.* Columbia: University of South Carolina Press, 2008.

Donelan, Michael. *Honor in Foreign Policy.* New York: Palgrave Macmillan, 2007.

Douthwaite, William Ralph. *Gray's Inn: Notes Illustrative of Its History and Antiquities.* London: Benson and Page, 1876.

Duff, Tim. *Plutarch's Lives: Exploring Virtue and Vice.* Oxford: Clarendon, 1999.

Durnin, Richard G. "The Role of the Presidents in the American Colleges of the Colonial Period." *History of Education Quarterly* 1, no. 2 (June 1961): 23–31.

Egle, William Henry. *Some Pennsylvania Women during the War of the Revolution.* Harrisburg, PA: Harrisburg, 1898.

Elder, Robert. *The Sacred Mirror: Evangelicalism, Honor, and Identity in the Deep South, 1790–1860.* Chapel Hill: University of North Carolina Press, 2016.

Ellis, Joseph J. *The American Sphinx: The Character of Thomas Jefferson.* New York: Vintage, 1998.

———. *Founding Brothers: The Revolutionary Generation.* New York: Alfred A. Knopf, 2000.

———. *His Excellency: George Washington.* New York: Alfred A. Knopf, 2004.

Ellison, Julie K. *Cato's Tears and the Making of Anglo-American Emotion.* Chicago: University of Chicago Press, 1999.

Elting, John R., ed. *Military Uniforms in America: The Era of the American Revolution, 1755–1795.* San Rafael, CA: Presidio, 1974.

Emmerson, John C., Jr. *The Chesapeake Affair of 1807. . . .* Portsmouth, VA, 1954.

Eustace, Nicole. "The Cornerstone of Copious Work: Courtship, Love, and Power in Eighteenth-Century Philadelphia." *Journal of Social History* 34, no. 3 (Spring 2001): 517–46.

———. *1812: War and the Passions of Patriotism.* Philadelphia: University of Pennsylvania Press, 2012.

———. *Passion Is the Gale: Emotion, Power, and the Coming of the American Revolution.* Chapel Hill: published for the Omohundro Institute of Early History and Culture by the University of North Carolina Press, 2008.

———. "Vehement Movements: Debates on Emotion, Self, and Society during the Seven Years War in Pennsylvania." *Exploration in Early American Culture* 5 (2001): 79–117.

Feller, Dan. "2009 Catherine Prescott Lecture—The Seminole Controversy Revisited: A New Look at Andrew Jackson's 1818 Florida Campaign." *Florida Historical Quarterly* 88, no. 3 (Winter 2010): 309–25.

Ferling, John. *Adams vs. Jefferson: The Tumultuous Election of 1800.* New York: Oxford University Press, 2004.

———. *John Adams: A Life.* Newtown, CT: American Political Biography, 1996.

———. *Setting the World Ablaze: Washington, Adams, Jefferson, and the American Revolution.* New York: Oxford University Press, 2002.

Fiering, Norman Sanford. "Moral Philosophy in America, 1650 to 1750, and Its British Context." PhD diss., Columbia University, 1969.

Fischer, David Hackett. *Albion's Seed: Four British Folkways in America.* New York: Oxford University Press, 1989.

———. *Liberty and Freedom: A Visual History of America's Founding Ideas.* New York: Oxford University Press, 2004.

———. *Paul Revere's Ride.* New York: Oxford University Press, 1994.

———. *Washington's Crossing.* New York: Oxford University Press, 2004.

Fischer, David Hackett, and James C. Kelly. *Bound Away: Virginia and the Westward Movement.* Charlottesville: University Press of Virginia, 2000.

Flavell, Julie. *When London Was the Capital of America.* New Haven, CT: Yale University Press, 2010.

Fleming, Thomas. *Duel: Alexander Hamilton, Aaron Burr, and the Future of America.* New York: Basic Books, 1999.

Flexner, James Thomas. *George Washington: Anguish and Farwell.* Boston: Little, Brown, 1969.

———. *George Washington: The Forge of Experience (1732–1775).* Boston: Little, Brown, 1965.

———. *The Traitor and the Spy: Benedict Arnold and John Andre.* New York: Harcourt, Brace, 1953.

Foner, Philip S. *Blacks in the American Revolution.* Westport, CT: Greenwood, 1975.

Foote, Lorien. *The Gentlemen and the Roughs: Manhood, Honor, and Violence in the Union Army.* New York: New York University Press, 2010.

Foster, Thomas, ed. *New Men: Manliness in Early America.* New York: New York University Press, 2011.

Freeman, Joanne B. *Affairs of Honor: National Politics in the New Republic.* New Haven, CT: Yale University Press, 2002. Originally published 2001.

Frevert, Ute. *Men of Honour: A Social and Cultural History of the Duel.* Cambridge, UK: Polity Press, 1995.

Furstenberg, Francois. "Atlantic Slavery, Atlantic Freedom: George Washington, Slavery, and Transatlantic Abolitionist Networks." *William and Mary Quarterly* 68, no. 2 (April 2011): 247–86.

———. "Beyond Freedom and Slavery: Autonomy, Virtue, and Resistance in Early American Political Discourse." *Journal of American History* 89, no. 4 (March 2004): 1295–1330.

———. *In the Name of the Father: Washington's Legacy, Slavery, and the Making of a Nation.* New York: Penguin Books, 2007.

Gallup-Diaz, Ignacio, Andrew Shankman, and David J. Silverman, eds. *Anglicizing America: Empire, Revolution, Republic.* Philadelphia: University of Pennsylvania Press, 2015.

Galvin, John R. *The Minute Men: The First Fight: Myths and Realities of the American Revolution.* New York: Pergamon-Brassey's, 1989.

Ganter, Herbert L. "William Small, Jefferson's Beloved Teacher." *William and Mary Quarterly* 4, no. 4 (October 1947): 505–11.

Gaustad, Edwin Scott. *Dissent in American Religion.* Chicago: University of Chicago Press, 1973.

Gilbert, Alan. *Black Patriots and Loyalists: Fighting for Emancipation in the War for Independence.* Chicago: University of Chicago Press, 2012.

Gilbert, Arthur N. "Law and Honour among Eighteenth-Century British Officers." *Historical Journal* 19, no. 1 (March 1976): 75–87.

Giordano, Ralph G. *Social Dancing in America: Fair Terpsichore to the Ghost Dance, 1607–1900.* Vol. 1. Westport, CT: Greenwood, 2007.

Gipson, Lawrence Henry. *Jared Ingersoll: A Study of American Loyalism in Relation to British Colonial Government.* New Haven, CT: Yale University Press, 1920.

Glassman, Matthew Eric. *Congressional Gold Medals, 1776–2010.* Washington, DC: Congressional Research Service, March 2011.

Glover, Lorri. *Founders as Fathers: The Private Lives and Politics of the American Revolutionaries.* New Haven, CT: Yale University Press, 2014.

———. *Southern Sons: Becoming Men in the New Nation.* Baltimore: Johns Hopkins University Press, 2007.

Godson, Susan H., Ludwell H. Johnson, Richard B. Sherman, Thad W. Tate, and Helen C. Walker. *The College of William & Mary: A History.* Vol. 1, *1693–1888.* Williamsburg, VA: King and Queen Press, 1993.

Golden, James L., and Alan L. Golden. *Thomas Jefferson and the Rhetoric of Virtue.* Lanham, MD: Rowman and Littlefield, 2002.

Golway, Terry. *Washington's General: Nathanael Greene and the Triumph of the American Revolution.* New York: Owl Books, 2006.

Good, Cassandra A. *Founding Friendships: Friendships between Men and Women in the Early American Republic.* New York: Oxford University Press, 2015.

Goodwin, Lorinda B. R. *An Archaeology of Manners: The Polite World of the Merchant Elite of Colonial Massachusetts.* New York: Kluwer Academic/Plenum, 1999.

Google Books. "Ngram Viewer." Accessed ca. October 5–8, 2013. https://books.google .com/ngrams.

Grant, James. *John Adams: Party of One.* New York: Farrar, Straus and Giroux, 2005.

Grasso, Christopher. *A Speaking Aristocracy: Transforming Public Discourse in Eighteenth-Century Connecticut.* Chapel Hill: University of North Carolina Press, 1999.

Gray, Edward G., and Jane Kamensky, eds. *The Oxford History of the American Revolution.* New York: Oxford University Press, 2013.

Green, Dominic. "The Lunatic Apostle: The Life and Times of Lord George Gordon (1751–1793)." PhD diss., Brandeis University, 2012.

Greenberg, Amy. *Manifest Manhood and the Antebellum American Empire*. New York: Cambridge University Press, 2005.

Greenberg, Kenneth S. *Honor and Slavery*. Princeton, NJ: Princeton University Press, 1996.

Greene, Evarts B. "The Code of Honor in Colonial and Revolutionary Times, with Special Reference to New England." *Publications of the Colonial Society of Massachusetts* 26 (1927): 367–88.

———. "The Revolutionary Generation, 1763–90." In *A History of American Life*, edited by Mark C. Carnes and Arthur M. Schlesinger Jr., 298–408. New York: Scribner, 1996.

Greene, George Washington. *The Life of Nathanael Greene: Major-General in the Army of the Revolution*. 3 vols. New York: Hurd and Houghton, 1871–78.

Greene, Jack P. *The Constitutional Origins of the American Revolution*. Cambridge: Cambridge University Press, 2010.

———. "Foundations of Political Power in the Virginia House of Burgesses, 1720–1776." In *Shaping Southern Society: The Colonial Experience*, edited by T. H. Breen, 215–31. New York: Oxford University Press, 1976.

Gruber, Ira D. *Books and the British Army in the Age of the American Revolution*. Chapel Hill: University of North Carolina Press; Washington, DC: Society of the Cincinnati, 2010.

Grundset, Eric G., ed. *Forgotten Patriots: African American and American Indian Patriots in the Revolutionary War*. Washington, DC: National Society Daughters of the American Revolution, 2008.

Gundersen, Joan R. *To Be Useful to the World: Women in Revolutionary America, 1740–1790*. Chapel Hill: University of North Carolina Press, 2006.

Hackett, David G. *That Religion in Which All Men Agree: Freemasonry in American Culture*. Berkeley: University of California Press, 2014.

Hale, Edward E., and Edward E. Hale Jr. *Franklin in France*. Boston: Roberts Brothers, 1888.

Hammond, John Craig, and Matthew Masons, eds. *Contesting Slavery: The Politics of Bondage and Freedom in the New American Nation*. Charlottesville: University of Virginia Press, 2011.

Harden, William. "James Mackay, of Strathy Hall, Comrade in Arms of George Washington." *Georgia Historical Quarterly* 1, no. 2 (June 1917): 77–98.

Hartigan-O'Connor, Ellen. *The Ties That Buy: Women and Commerce in Revolutionary America*. Philadelphia: University of Pennsylvania Press, 2009.

Harvey, Tamara, and Greg O'Brien, eds. *George Washington's South*. Gainesville: University Press of Florida, 2004.

Hatch, Nathan O. *The Democratization of American Christianity*. New Haven, CT: Yale University Press, 1989.

Hatch, Robert McConnell. *Major John André: A Gallant in Spy's Clothing*. Boston: Houghton Mifflin, 1986.

Hattem, Michael D. "The Return of the American Revolution." *The Junto: A Group Blog on Early American History*, May 27, 2013. https://earlyamericanists.com/2013 /05/27/the-return-of-the-american-revolution/.

Hay, Robert P. "The American Revolution Twice Recalled: Lafayette's Visit and the Election of 1824." *Indiana Magazine of History* 69, no. 1 (March 1973): 43–62.

Hayes, Kevin J. *The Road to Monticello: The Life and Mind of Thomas Jefferson.* New York: Oxford University Press, 2008.

Helo, Ari. *Thomas Jefferson's Ethics and the Politics of Human Progress: The Morality of a Slaveholder.* New York: Cambridge University Press, 2014.

Henriques, Peter R. *Realistic Visionary: A Portrait of George Washington.* Charlottesville: University of Virginia Press, 2006.

Herman, Daniel Justin. *Hell on the Range: A Story of Honor, Conscience, and the American West.* New Haven, CT: Yale University Press, 2010.

Herrera, Ricardo A. *For Liberty and the Republic: The American Citizen as Soldier, 1775–1861.* New York: New York University Press, 2015.

Higginbotham, Don, ed. *George Washington Reconsidered.* Charlottesville: University Press of Virginia, 2001.

———. *The War of American Independence: Military Attitudes, Policies, and Practice, 1763–1789.* New York: Macmillan, 1971.

Hinks, Peter P., and Stephen Kantrowitz. *All Men Free and Brethren: Essays on the History of African American Freemasonry.* Ithaca, NY: Cornell University Press, 2013.

Hirschfeld, Fritz. *George Washington and Slavery: A Documentary Portrayal.* Columbia: University of Missouri Press, 1997.

Hobsbawm, Eric, and Terrence O. Ranger. *The Invention of Tradition.* Cambridge: Cambridge University Press, 1992.

Hoffer, William James Hull. *The Caning of Charles Sumner: Honor, Idealism, and the Origins of the Civil War.* Baltimore: Johns Hopkins University Press, 2010.

Hofstadter, Richard. *America at 1750: A Social Portrait.* New York: Random House, 1971.

Hoganson, Kristin L. *Fighting for American Manhood.* New Haven, CT: Yale University Press, 1998.

Holton, Woody. *Abigail Adams.* New York: Free Press, 2009.

———. *Forced Founders: Indians, Debtors, Slaves, and the Making of the American Revolution in Virginia.* Chapel Hill: published for the Omohundro Institute of Early American History and Culture by the University of North Carolina Press, 1999.

———. *Unruly Americans and the Origins of the Constitution.* New York: Hill and Wang, 2007.

Hope, V. M. *Virtue By Consensus: The Moral Philosophy of Hutcheson, Hume and Adam Smith.* Oxford: Clarendon Press, 1989.

Hopper, Andrew. *"Black Tom": Sir Thomas Fairfax and the English Revolution.* Manchester: Manchester University Press, 2007.

Horwitz, Robert H. *The Moral Foundations of the American Republic.* Charlottesville: University Press of Virginia, 1979.

Hosmer, James Kendall. *The Life of Thomas Hutchinson.* New York: Da Capo, 1972.

Hume, Edgar Erskine. *George Washington and the Society of the Cincinnati.* Washington, DC: George Washington Bicentennial Commission, 1933.

Humphrey, David C. "Colonial Colleges and English Dissenting Academies: A Study in Transatlantic Culture." *History of Education Quarterly* 12, no. 2 (Summer 1972): 184–97.

———. *From King's College to Columbia, 1746–1800.* New York: Columbia University Press, 1976.

Hünemörder, Markus. *The Society of the Cincinnati: Conspiracy and Distrust in Early America.* New York: Berghahn Books, 2006.

Hutson, James H. *John Adams and the Diplomacy of the American Revolution.* Lexington: University Press of Kentucky, 1980.

Iliffe, John. *Honour in African History.* Cambridge: Cambridge University Press, 2005.

Isaac, Rhys. *The Transformation of Virginia: 1740–1790.* Chapel Hill: University of North Carolina Press, 1982.

Jacobson, David L. *John Dickinson and the Revolution in Pennsylvania, 1764–1776.* Berkeley: University of California Press, 1965.

Jensen, Merrill. *The Articles of Confederation: An Interpretation of the Social-Constitutional History of the American Revolution, 1774–1781.* Madison: University of Wisconsin Press, 1959.

Johnson, Laurie M., and Dan Demetriou, eds. *Honor in the Modern World.* Lanham, MD: Lexington Books, 2016.

Johnson, Walter. *Soul by Soul: Life Inside the Antebellum Slave Market.* Cambridge, MA: Harvard University Press, 1999.

Kagan, Donald. "Our Interests and Our Honor." *Commentary,* April 1997, 42–45.

Kane, John. *Between Virtue and Power: The Persistent Moral Dilemma of US Foreign Policy.* New Haven, CT: Yale University Press, 2008.

Kelley, Brooks Mather. *Yale: A History.* New Haven, CT: Yale University Press, 1974.

Kelly, James. *"That Damn'd Thing Called Honour": Dueling in Ireland, 1570–1860.* Cork: Cork University Press, 1995.

Kerber, Linda K. *Women of the Republic: Intellect and Ideology in Revolutionary America.* Chapel Hill: University of North Carolina Press, 1980.

Ketchum, Richard M. *The Winter Soldiers.* New York: Doubleday, 1973.

Kett, Joseph F. *Merit: The History of a Founding Ideal from the American Revolution to the Twenty-First Century.* Ithaca, NY: Cornell University Press, 2013.

Kidd, Thomas S. *God of Liberty: A Religious History of the American Revolution.* New York: Basic Books, 2010.

———. *The Great Awakening: The Roots of Evangelical Christianity in Colonial America.* New Haven, CT: Yale University Press, 2007.

Kiernan, Victor Gordon. *The Duel in European History: A Study of the Aristocratic Ascendancy.* Oxford: Oxford University Press, 1988.

Kierner, Cynthia A. "Genteel Balls and Republican Parades: Gender and Early Southern Civic Rituals, 1677–1826." *Virginia Magazine of History and Biography* 104, no. 2 (Spring 1996): 185–210.

———. *Scandal at Bizarre: Rumor and Reputation in Jeffersonian America*. New York: Palgrave Macmillan, 2004.

———. *Southern Women in Revolution, 1776–1800*. Columbia: University of South Carolina Press, 1998.

Kilmer, Kenton, and Donald Sweig. *The Fairfax Family in Fairfax County: A Brief History*. Fairfax, VA: Fairfax County Office of Comprehensive Planning, 1975.

Knollenberg, Bernhard. *Origin of the American Revolution: 1759–1766*. New York: Macmillan, 1960.

Knott, Sarah. *Sensibility and the American Revolution*. Chapel Hill: published for the Omohundro Institute of Early History and Culture by the University of North Carolina Press, 2009.

Kohn, Richard H. *Eagle and Sword: The Federalists and the Creation of the Military Establishment in America, 1783–1802*. New York: Free Press, 1975.

———. "The Inside History of the Newburgh Conspiracy: America and the Coup d'Etat." *William and Mary Quarterly* 27, no. 2 (April 1970): 188–220.

Kollmann, Nancy Shields. *By Honor Bound: State and Society in Early Modern Russia*. Ithaca, NY: Cornell University Press, 1999.

Kolp, John Gilman. *Gentlemen and Freeholders: Electoral Politics in Colonial Virginia*. Baltimore: Johns Hopkins University Press, 1998.

Koontz, Louis Knott. *Robert Dinwiddie: His Career in American Colonial Government and Westward Expansion*. Glendale, CA: Arthur H. Clark, 1941.

Krause, Sharon R. *Liberalism with Honor*. Cambridge, MA: Harvard University Press, 2002.

Landis, John B. *A Short History of Molly Pitcher, the Heroine of the Battle of Monmouth*. Carlisle, PA: Cornman, 1905.

Larson, Edward J. *A Magnificent Catastrophe: The Tumultuous Election of 1800, America's First Presidential Campaign*. New York: Free Press, 2008.

Latshaw, K. Michael. "Flawed Judgment: The Court-Martial of Commodore James Barron." *Virginia Magazine of History and Biography* 105, no. 4 (Autumn 1997): 377–408.

Lee, Wayne E. *Crowds and Soldiers in Revolutionary North Carolina*. Gainesville: University Press of Florida, 2001.

———. "From Gentility to Atrocity: The Continental Army's Ways of War." *Army History* 62 (Winter 2006): 4–19.

Lemmings, David. *Professors of the Law: Barristers and English Legal Culture in the Eighteenth Century*. London: Oxford University Press, 2000.

Lender, Mark Edward, and Garry Wheeler Stone. *Fatal Sunday: George Washington, the Monmouth Campaign, and the Politics of Battle*. Norman: University of Oklahoma Press, 2016.

Lengel, Edward G. *General George Washington: A Military Life*. New York: Random House, 2005.

Leonard, Patrick J. "Ann Bailey: Mystery Woman of 1777." *Minerva: Quarterly Report on Woman and the Military* 11, nos. 3–4 (1993): 1–4.

Lepore, Jill. *Book of Ages: The Life and Opinions of Jane Franklin.* New York: Alfred A. Knopf, 2013.

Leverenz, David. *Honor Bound: Race and Shame in America.* New Brunswick, NJ: Rutgers University Press, 2012.

Lewis, Jan. "The Republican Wife: Virtue and Seduction in the Early Republic." *William and Mary Quarterly* 44, no. 4 (October 1987): 689–721.

Library of Virginia. "Working Out Her Destiny: Women's History in Virginia, 1600–2004." http://www.lva.virginia.gov/exhibits/destiny/index.htm.

Linebaugh, Peter, and Marcus Rediker. *The Many-Headed Hydra: Sailors, Slaves, Commoners, and the Hidden History of the Revolutionary Atlantic.* Boston: Beacon, 2001.

Lipsett-Rivera, Sonya, and Lyman L. Johnson, eds. *The Faces of Honor: Sex, Shame, and Violence in Colonial Latin America.* Albuquerque: University of New Mexico Press, 1998.

Litto, Frederic M. "Addison's Cato in the Colonies." *William and Mary Quarterly* 23, no. 3 (July 1966): 431–49.

Livingston, Luther S. *Franklin and His Press at Passy.* New York: Grolier Club, 1914.

Locke, Joseph. "Compelled to Dissent: The Politicization of Rev. John Joachim Zubly, 1760–1776." *Georgia Historical Quarterly* 94, no. 4 (Winter 2010): 453–78.

Lombard, Anne S. *Making Manhood: Growing Up Male in Colonial New England.* Cambridge, MA: Harvard University Press, 2003.

Long, David F. "William Bainbridge and the Barron-Decatur Duel: Mere Participant or Active Plotter?" *Pennsylvania Magazine of History and Biography* 103, no. 1 (January 1979): 34–52.

Longmore, Paul K. *The Invention of Washington.* Berkeley: University of California Press, 1988.

Lossing, Benson J. *The Home of Washington or Mount Vernon and Its Associations....* Hartford, CT: A. S. Hale, 1870.

Low, Jennifer A. *Manhood and the Duel: Masculinity in Drama and Culture.* New York: Palgrave Macmillan, 2003.

Maier, Pauline. *From Resistance to Revolution: Colonial Radicals and the Development of American Opposition to Britain, 1765–1776.* New York: W. W. Norton, 1992. Originally published 1972.

———. *Ratification: The People Debate the Constitution, 1787–1788.* New York: Simon and Schuster, 2010.

Mailer, Gideon. "Anglo-Scottish Union and John Witherspoon's American Revolution." *William and Mary Quarterly* 67, no. 4 (October 2010): 709–46.

Mapp, Paul W. "The Revolutionary War and Europe's Great Powers." In *The Oxford Handbook of the American Revolution,* edited by Edward G. Gray and Jane Kamensky, 311–26. New York: Oxford University Press, 2013.

Marsden, George A. *Jonathan Edwards: A Life.* New Haven, CT: Yale University Press, 2003.

Martin, James Kirby. "Political Elites and the Outbreak of the American Revolution: A Quantitative Profile in Continuity, Turnover, and Change, 1774–1777." PhD diss., University of Wisconsin, 1969.

Martin, James Kirby, and Mark Edward Lender. *A Respectable Army: The Military Origins of the Republic, 1763–1789*. Arlington Heights, IL: Harlan Davidson, 1982.

Maryland State House. "The Old Senate Chamber: Where Washington Resigned His Commission." Accessed ca. April 15, 2017. http://msa.maryland.gov/msa /mdstatehouse/html/old_chamber.html.

Mason, John E. *Gentlefolk in the Making: Studies in the History of English Courtesy Literature and Related Topics from 1531 to 1774*. New York: Octagon Books, 1971. Originally published by the University of Pennsylvania Press, 1935.

Mason, Matthew. *Slavery and Politics in the Early Republic*. Chapel Hill: University of North Carolina Press, 2006.

Maurer, Maurer. "Military Justice under General Washington." *Military Affairs* 28, no. 1 (Spring 1964): 8–16.

Mayer, Holly A. *Belonging to the Army: Camp Follower and Community during the American Revolution*. Columbia: University of South Carolina Press, 1996.

Mazyck, Walter H. *George Washington and the Negro*. Washington, DC: Associated Publishers, 1932.

Mazzagetti, Dominick A. *Charles Lee: Self before Country*. New Brunswick, NJ: Rutgers University Press, 2013.

———. *Thomas Jefferson: The Art of Power*. New York: Random House, 2012.

McAleer, Kevin. *Dueling: The Cult of Honor in Fin-de-Siècle Germany*. Princeton, NJ: Princeton University Press, 1994.

McConville, Brendan. *The King's Three Faces: The Rise and Fall of Royal America, 1688–1776*. Chapel Hill: University of North Carolina Press, 2006.

McKeon, Michael. *The Origins of the English Novel, 1600–1740*. Baltimore: Johns Hopkins University Press, 2002. Originally published 1987.

Meacham, Jon. *American Lion: Andrew Jackson in the White House*. New York: Random House, 2008.

Metzger, Charles H. *The Prisoner in the American Revolution*. Chicago: Loyola University Press, 1971.

Middlekauff, Robert. *The Glorious Cause: The American Revolution, 1763–1789*. New York: Oxford University Press, 2007.

———. *Washington's Revolution: The Making of America's First Leader*. New York: Alfred A. Knopf, 2015.

Moebs, Thomas Truxton. *Black Soldiers—Black Sailors—Black Ink: Research Guide on African-Americans in US Military History, 1526–1900*. Chesapeake Bay, VA: Moebs, 1994.

Moore, George Henry. *"Mr. Lee's Plan—March 29, 1777"; The Treason of Charles Lee. . . .* New York: Scribner, 1860.

Moore, Kathryn McDaniel. "The War with the Tutors: Student-Faculty Conflict at Harvard and Yale, 1745–1771." *History of Education Quarterly* 18, no. 2 (Summer 1978): 115–27.

Morgan, Edmund S. *Benjamin Franklin*. New Haven, CT: Yale University Press, 2002.

———. "Ezra Stiles: The Education of a Yale Man, 1742–1746." *Huntington Library Quarterly* 17, no. 3 (May 1954): 251–68.

———. *The Meaning of Independence: John Adams, George Washington, Thomas Jefferson*. Charlottesville: University of Virginia Press, 1976.

———. "The Puritan Ethic and the American Revolution." *William and Mary Quarterly* 24, no. 1 (January 1967): 3–43.

Morgan, Edmund S., and Helen M. Morgan. *The Stamp Act Crisis: Prologue to Revolution*. Chapel Hill: University of North Carolina Press, 1953.

Morgan, Philip D. *Slave Counterpoint: Black Culture in the Eighteenth-Century Chesapeake and Lowcountry*. Chapel Hill: University of North Carolina Press, 1998.

———. " 'To Get Quit of Negroes': George Washington and Slavery." *Journal of American Studies* 39, no. 3 (December 2005): 403–29.

Morgan, Philip D., and Michael L. Nicholls. "Slave Flight: Mount Vernon, Virginia, and the Wider Atlantic World." In *George Washington's South*, edited by Tamara Harvey and Greg O'Brien, 197–222. Gainesville: University Press of Florida, 2004.

Morgan, Philip D., and Andrew Jackson O'Shaughnessy. "Arming Slaves in the American Revolution." In *Arming Slaves: From Classical Times to the Modern Age*, edited by Christopher Leslie Brown and Philip D. Morgan, 180–220. New Haven, CT: Yale University Press, 2006.

Morison, Samuel Eliot. "Precedence at Harvard College in the Seventeenth Century." *Proceedings of the American Antiquarian Society* 42 (October 1932): 371–431.

———. *Three Centuries of Harvard, 1636–1936*. Cambridge, MA: Belknap Press of Harvard University Press, 2001. Originally published 1936.

———. "The Young Man Washington." In *By Land and by Sea: Essays and Addresses*, 161–80. New York: Alfred A. Knopf, 1953.

Morris, Richard B. *The Peacemakers: The Great Powers and American Independence*. New York: Harper and Row, 1965.

Murrin, John M. "Anglicizing an American Colony: The Transformation of Provincial Massachusetts." PhD diss., Yale University, 1966.

Myers, Minor, Jr. *Liberty without Anarchy: A History of the Cincinnati*. Charlottesville: University Press of Virginia, 1983.

Nash, Gary. *Race and Revolution*. Madison, WI: Madison House, 1990.

———. *The Unknown American Revolution: The Unruly Birth of Democracy and the Struggle to Create America*. New York: Penguin, 2005.

———. *The Urban Crucible: Social Change, Political Consciousness, and the Origins of the American Revolution*. Cambridge, MA: Harvard University Press, 1981.

Nash, Margaret A. "Rethinking Republican Motherhood: Benjamin Rush and the Young Ladies' Academy of Philadelphia." *Journal of the Early Republic* 17, no. 2 (Summer 1997): 171–91.

Neill, Edward D. *The Fairfaxes of England and America*. Albany, NY: Joel Munsell, 1868.

Nell, William C. *The Colored Patriots of the American Revolution. . . .* Boston: Robert F. Wallcut, 1855.

Nelson, Paul David. "Citizen Soldiers or Regulars: The Views of the American General Officers on the Military Establishment, 1775–1781." *Military Affairs* 43, no. 3 (October 1979): 126–32.

———. *General Horatio Gates: A Biography*. Baton Rouge: Louisiana State University Press, 1976.

Newmyer, R. Kent. *The Treason Trial of Aaron Burr: Law, Politics, and the Character Wars of the New Nation*. Cambridge: Cambridge University Press, 2012.

Noll, Mark A. "American Revolution and Protestant Evangelicalism." *Journal of Interdisciplinary History* 23, no. 3 (Winter 1993): 615–38.

———. *America's God: From Jonathan Edwards to Abraham Lincoln*. New York: Oxford University Press, 2002.

———. "Common Sense Traditions and American Evangelical Thought." *American Quarterly* 37, no. 2 (Summer 1985): 216–38.

———. *Princeton and the Republic, 1768–1822*. Princeton, NJ: Princeton University Press, 1989.

———. "Princeton in the Revolutionary Era, 1757–1815." *Journal of Presbyterian History* 85, no. 2 (Fall/Winter 2007): 89–101.

Norton, Mary Beth. *Liberty's Daughters: The Revolutionary Experience of American Women, 1750–1800*. Ithaca, NY: Cornell University Press, 1996. Originally published 1980.

Novak, Michael, and Jana Novak. *Washington's God: Religion, Liberty, and the Father of Our Country*. New York: Basic Books, 2006.

Novak, Steven J. *The Rights of Youth: American Colleges and Student Revolt, 1798–1815*. Cambridge, MA: Harvard University Press, 1977.

Nye, Robert A. *Masculinity and Male Codes of Honor in Modern France*. New York: Oxford University Press, 1993.

O'Neill, Barry. *Honor, Symbols, and War*. Ann Arbor: University of Michigan Press, 1999.

Opal, J. M. *Avenging the People: Andrew Jackson, the Rule of Law, and the American Nation*. New York: Oxford University Press, 2017.

———. *Beyond the Farm: National Ambitions in Rural New England*. Philadelphia: University of Pennsylvania Press, 2008.

Owsley, Frank L., Jr., ed. *The Life of Andrew Jackson*. Tuscaloosa: University of Alabama Press, 2007. Originally published 1974.

Pace, Robert F. *Halls of Honor: College Men in the Old South*. Baton Rouge: Louisiana State University Press, 2004.

Pagan, John Ruston. *Anne Orthwood's Bastard: Sex and Law in Early Virginia*. New York: Oxford University Press, 2003.

Palmer, John McAuley. *General Von Steuben*. Port Washington, NY: Kennikat, 1966.

Pangle, Thomas L. "Federalists and the Idea of 'Virtue.'" *This Constitution: A Bicentennial Chronicle* 5 (Winter 1984): 19–25.

Parton, James. *Life of Andrew Jackson*. 3 vols. New York: Mason Brothers, 1860.

Patterson, Samuel White. *Horatio Gates: Defender of American Liberties*. New York: Columbia University Press, 1941.

———. *Knight Errant of Liberty: The Triumph and Tragedy of General Charles Lee.* New York: Lantern, 1958.

Peach, Bernard. *Richard Price and the Ethical Foundations of the American Revolution: Selections from His Pamphlets, with Appendices.* Durham, NC: Duke University Press, 1979.

Peltonen, Markku. *The Duel in Early Modern England: Civility, Politeness, and Honour.* Cambridge: Cambridge University Press, 2003.

Pennypacker, Morton. *General Washington's Spies on Long Island and in New York.* New York: Long Island Historical Society, 1939.

Peristiany, J. G., and Julian Pitt-Rivers, eds. *Honor and Grace in Anthropology.* Cambridge: Cambridge University Press, 1992.

———. *Honour and Shame: The Values of Mediterranean Society.* Chicago: University of Chicago Press, 1966.

Peterson, Charles E. "Carpenters' Hall." *Transactions of the American Philosophical Society* 43, no. 1 (1953): 96–128.

Phelps, Glenn A. "The Republican General." In *George Washington Reconsidered,* edited by Don Higginbotham, 165–97. Charlottesville: University Press of Virginia, 2001.

Philbrick, Nathaniel. *Valiant Ambition: George Washington, Benedict Arnold, and the Fate of the American Revolution.* New York: Viking, 2016.

Pocock, J. G. A. *Virtue, Commerce, and History: Essays on Political Thought and History, Chiefly in the Eighteenth Century.* Cambridge: Cambridge University Press, 1985.

Potts, Louis W. *Arthur Lee: A Virtuous Revolutionary.* Baton Rouge: Louisiana State University Press, 1981.

Prest, Wilfrid. *William Blackstone: Law and Letters in the Eighteenth Century.* Oxford: Oxford University Press, 2008.

Preston, David L. *Braddock's Defeat: The Battle of the Monongahela and the Road to Revolution.* New York: Oxford University Press, 2015.

Quarles, Benjamin. *The Negro in the American Revolution.* Chapel Hill: University of North Carolina Press, 1961.

Quincy, Josiah. *Memoir of the Life of Josiah Quincy, Junior, of Massachusetts: 1744–1775.* Boston: Press of J. Wilson, 1874.

Quintal, George, Jr. *Patriots of Color: "A Peculiar Beauty and Merit"; African Americans and Native Americans at Battle Road and Bunker Hill.* Boston: Division of Cultural Resources, Boston National Historical Park, 2004.

Randall, Willard Sterne. *Benedict Arnold: Patriot and Traitor.* New York: William Morrow, 1990.

———. *George Washington: A Life.* New York: Henry Holt, 1997.

———. *Thomas Jefferson: A Life.* New York: Henry Holt, 1993.

Rawle, William Brooke. "Laurel Hill and Some Colonial Dames Who Once Lived There." *Pennsylvania Magazine of History and Biography* 35, no. 4 (1911): 385–414.

Reddy, William M. *The Invisible Code: Honor and Sentiment in Postrevolutionary France, 1814–1848.* Berkeley: University of California Press, 1997.

Rediker, Marcus. *Villains of All Nations: Atlantic Pirates in the Golden Age*. Boston: Beacon, 2005.

Reinier, Jacqueline S. "Rearing the Republican Child: Attitudes and Practices in Post-Revolutionary Philadelphia." *William and Mary Quarterly* 39, no. 1 (January 1982): 150–63.

Remini, Robert V. *Andrew Jackson: A Biography*. New York: Palgrave Macmillan, 2008.

———. *Daniel Webster: The Man and His Time*. New York: W. W. Norton, 1997.

———. "Jackson Takes an Oath of Allegiance to Spain." *Tennessee Historical Quarterly* 54, no. 1 (Spring 1995): 2–15.

Richards, Leonard L. *Shays' Rebellion: The American Revolution's Final Battle*. Philadelphia: University of Pennsylvania Press, 2002.

Risjord, Norman K. "1812: Conservatives, War Hawks and the Nation's Honor." *William and Mary Quarterly* 18, no. 2 (April 1961): 196–210.

Robinson, Paul. *Military Honour and the Conduct of War: From Ancient Greece to Iraq*. London: Routledge, 2006.

Roche, John F. *The Colonial Colleges in the War for American Independence*. Millwood, NY: Associated Faculty, 1986.

Rosen, Deborah A. "Wartime Prisoners and the Rule of Law: Andrew Jackson's Military Tribunals during the First Seminole War." *Journal of the Early Republic* 28, no. 4 (Winter 2008): 559–95.

Rotundo, E. Anthony. *American Manhood: Transformations in Masculinity from the Revolution to the Modern Era*. New York: Basic Books, 1994.

Royster, Charles. "The Nature of Treason: Revolutionary Virtue and American Reactions to Benedict Arnold." *William and Mary Quarterly* 36, no. 2 (April 1979): 163–93.

———. *A Revolutionary People at War: The Continental Army and American Character, 1775–1783*. Chapel Hill: University of North Carolina Press, 1979.

Saunders, Richard Frank, Jr. "The Origin and Early History of the Society of the Cincinnati: The Oldest Hereditary and Patriotic Association in the United States." PhD diss., University of Georgia, 1970.

Sayen, William Guthrie. " 'A Compleat Gentleman': The Making of George Washington, 1732–1775." PhD diss., University of Connecticut, 1998.

———. "George Washington's 'Unmannerly' Behavior: The Clash between Civility and Honor." *Virginia Magazine of History and Biography* 107, no. 1 (Winter 1999): 2–36.

Schoenbrun, David. *Triumph in Paris: The Exploits of Benjamin Franklin*. New York: Harper and Row, 1976.

Seitz, Don C. *Famous American Duels. . . .* Freeport, NY: Books for Libraries Press, 1966.

Sellers, Charles Coleman. *Benedict Arnold: The Proud Warrior*. New York: Minton, Balch, 1930.

Shaw, Peter. *American Patriots and the Rituals of Revolution*. Cambridge, MA: Harvard University Press, 1981.

Shields, David S. *Civil Tongues and Polite Letters in British America*. Chapel Hill: University of North Carolina Press, 1997.

———. "George Washington: Publicity, Probity, and Power." In *George Washington's South*, edited by Tamara Harvey and Greg O'Brien, 143–54. Gainesville: University Press of Florida, 2004.

Shipton, Clifford K. "Ye Mystery of Ye Ages Solved, or, How Placing Worked at Colonial Harvard and Yale." *Harvard Alumni Bulletin* 57 (December 1954): 258–63.

Shy, John. *A People Numerous and Armed: Reflections on the Military Struggle for Independence*. New York: Oxford University Press, 1976.

Simkin, Richard. *Uniforms of the British Army*. Exeter, UK: Webb and Bower, 1982.

Skelton, William B. *An American Profession of Arms: The Army Officer Corps, 1784–1861*. Lawrence: University Press of Kansas, 1992.

Slaughter, Thomas P. *Independence: The Tangled Roots of the American Revolution*. New York: Hill and Wang, 2014.

Smail, John. "Credit, Risk, and Honor in Eighteenth-Century Commerce." *Journal of British Studies* 44, no. 3 (July 2005): 439–56.

Smith, Craig Bruce, and Dan Demetriou. *George Washington's Lessons in Ethical Leadership*. Mount Vernon, VA: George Washington's Mount Vernon, 2016.

Smith, Jay M. *Nobility Reimagined: The Patriotic Nation in Eighteenth-Century France*. Ithaca, NY: Cornell University Press, 2005.

Smith, John Howard. *The First Great Awakening: Redefining Religion in British America, 1725–1775*. Madison, NJ: Fairleigh Dickinson University Press, 2015.

Smithers, Peter. *The Life of Joseph Addison*. Oxford: Clarendon, 1968.

Snyder, Claire R. *Citizen-Soldiers and Manly Warriors: Military Service and Gender in the Civic Republican Tradition*. Lanham, MD: Rowman and Littlefield, 1999.

Sorley, Lewis. *Honor Bright: History and Origins of the West Point Honor Code and System*. Boston: McGraw Hill Learning Solutions, 2009.

Spierenburg, Pieter, ed. *Men and Violence: Gender, Honor, and Rituals in Modern Europe and America*. Columbus: Ohio State University Press, 1998.

Steffen, Charles G. *From Gentlemen to Townsmen: The Gentry of Baltimore County, Maryland 1660–1776*. Lexington: University Press of Kentucky, 1993.

Stevens, William Oliver. *Pistols at Ten Paces: The Story of the Code of Honor in America*. Boston: Riverside, 1940.

Steward, Dick. *Duels and the Roots of Violence in Missouri*. Columbia: University of Missouri Press, 2000.

Stewart, Frank Henderson. *Honor*. Chicago: University of Chicago Press, 1994.

Stillé, Charles J. *The Life of John Dickinson, 1732–1808*. Philadelphia: Historical Society of Pennsylvania, 1891.

Streatfeild, George Sidney. *The Mind of the Spectator under the Editorship of Addison & Steele*. New York: Henry Holt, 1923.

Taylor, Alan. *American Revolutions: A Continental History, 1750–1804*. New York: W. W. Norton, 2016.

———. *The Civil War of 1812: American Citizens, British Subjects, Irish Rebels, & Indian Allies*. New York: Alfred A. Knopf, 2010.

———. *The Internal Enemy: Slavery and War in Virginia, 1772–1832*. New York: W. W. Norton, 2013.

Teipe, Emily J. "Will the Real Molly Pitcher Please Stand Up?" *Prologue Magazine* 31, no. 2 (Summer 1999): 118–26.

Thayer, Theodore. *The Making of a Scapegoat: Washington and Lee at Monmouth*. Port Washington, NY: Kennikat, 1976.

Tillotson, Harry Stanton. *The Beloved Spy: The Life and Loves of Major John Andre*. Caldwell, ID: Caxton, 1948.

Tillson, Albert H., Jr. *Gentry and Common Folk: Political Culture on a Virginia Frontier, 1740–1789*. Lexington: University Press of Kentucky, 1991.

Trolander, Paul, and Zynep Tenger. *Sociable Criticism in England, 1625–1725*. Newark: University of Delaware Press, 2007.

Truman, Ben C. *The Field of Honor: Being a Complete and Comprehensive History of Duelling in All Countries. . . .* New York: Fords, Howard, and Hulbert, 1884.

Tucker, Louis Leonard. "Centers of Sedition: Colonial Colleges and the American Revolution." *Proceedings of the Massachusetts Historical Society* 91 (1979): 16–34.

Tucker, Spencer C., and Frank T. Reuter. *Injured Honor: The Chesapeake-Leopard Affair, June 22, 1807*. Annapolis: Naval Institute Press, 1996.

Twohig, Dorothy. " 'That Species of Property': Washington's Role in the Controversy over Slavery." In *George Washington Reconsidered*, edited by Don Higginbotham, 114–40. Charlottesville: University of Virginia Press, 2001.

Ultee, Maarten, ed. *Adapting to Conditions: War and Society in the Eighteenth Century*. Ann Arbor, MI: University Microfilms International, 1999. Originally published by the University of Alabama Press, 1986.

Van Buskirk, Judith L. *Generous Enemies: Patriots and Loyalists in Revolutionary New York*. Philadelphia: University of Philadelphia Press, 2002.

Van Doren, Carl. *Benjamin Franklin*. New York: Viking, 1938.

Veatch, Robert M. *Hippocratic, Religious, and Secular Medical Ethics: The Points of Conflict*. Washington, DC: Georgetown University Press, 2012.

Volk, Kyle G. *Moral Minorities and the Making of American Democracy*. New York: Oxford University Press, 2014.

Waldstreicher, David. *Runaway America: Benjamin Franklin, Slavery, and the American Revolution*. New York: Hill and Wang, 2004.

Wallace, David Duncan. *The Life of Henry Laurens*. New York: Russell and Russell, 1967.

Walne, Peter, ed. "A Mystery Resolved: George Washington's Letter to Governor Dinwiddie, June 10, 1754." *Virginia Magazine of History and Biography* 79, no. 2 (1971): 121–44.

Walsh, James J. *Education of the Founding Fathers of the Republic: Scholasticism in the Colonial Colleges*. New York: Fordham University Press, 1935.

Walsh, John Evangelist. *The Execution of Major André*. New York: Palgrave, 2001.

Walsh, Lorena S. *Motives of Honor, Pleasure, and Profit: Plantation Management in the Colonial Chesapeake, 1607–1763.* Chapel Hill: published for the Omohundro Institute of Early History and Culture by the University of North Carolina Press, 2010.

Wandall, Samuel H., and Meade Minnigerode. *Aaron Burr: A Biography . . .* 2 vols. New York: G. P. Putnam's Sons, 1927.

Warner, Michael. *The Letters of the Republic: Publication and the Public Sphere in Eighteenth-Century America.* Cambridge, MA: Harvard University Press, 1990.

Weintraub, Karl J. "The Puritan Ethic and Benjamin Franklin." *Journal of Religion* 56, no. 3 (July 1976): 223–37.

Wells, C. A. Harwell. "The End of the Affair? Anti-dueling Laws and Social Norms in Antebellum America." *Vanderbilt Law Review* 54, no. 4 (2001): 1805–47.

Welsh, Alexander. *What Is Honor? A Question of Moral Imperatives.* New Haven, CT: Yale University Press, 2008.

Weslager, C. A. *The Stamp Act Congress: With an Exact Copy of the Complete Journal.* Newark: University of Delaware Press, 1976.

Wheelan, Joseph. *Jefferson's Vendetta: The Pursuit of Aaron Burr and Judiciary.* New York: Carroll and Graf, 2005.

Wiencek, Henry. *An Imperfect God: George Washington, His Slaves, and the Creation of America.* New York: Farrar, Straus and Giroux, 2003.

Wilentz, Sean. *Andrew Jackson.* New York: Times Books, 2005.

"William Ladd." *Maine Library Bulletin* 8, no. 1 (July 1918): 98–105.

Williams, Jack K. *Dueling in the Old South.* College Station: Texas A&M University Press, 1980.

Wills, Garry. *Cincinnatus: George Washington and the Enlightenment.* Garden City, NY: Doubleday, 1984.

Winterer, Caroline. *American Enlightenments: Pursuing Happiness in the Age of Reason.* New Haven, CT: Yale University Press, 2016.

———. *The Mirror of Antiquity: American Women and the Classical Tradition, 1750–1900.* Ithaca, NY: Cornell University Press, 2007.

Withington, Ann Fairfax. *Toward a More Perfect Union: Virtue and the Formation of American Republics.* New York: Oxford University Press, 1991.

Wood, Gordon S. *The Americanization of Benjamin Franklin.* New York: Penguin, 2004.

———. *The Creation of the American Republic, 1776–1787.* Chapel Hill: University of North Carolina Press, 1998. Originally published 1969.

———. *Empire of Liberty: A History of the Early Republic, 1789–1815.* New York: Oxford University Press, 2009.

———. "History in Context: The American Vision of Bernard Bailyn." *Weekly Standard* 20, no. 23 (February 23, 2015). http://www.weeklystandard.com/history-in-context/article/850083.

———. *The Radicalism of the American Revolution.* New York: Vintage Books, 1991.

———. *Revolutionary Characters: What Made the Founders Different.* New York: Penguin, 2006.

Woods, Michael E. *Emotional and Sectional Conflict in the Antebellum United States.* Cambridge: Cambridge University Press, 2014.

Wright, Louis B. *The First Gentlemen of Virginia: Intellectual Qualities of the Early Colonial Ruling Class.* San Marino, CA: Huntington Library, 1940.

Wyatt-Brown, Bertram. *Honor and Violence in the Old South.* New York: Oxford University Press, 1986.

———. *The Shaping of Southern Culture: Honor, Grace, and War, 1760–1880s.* Chapel Hill: University of North Carolina Press, 2001.

———. *Southern Honor: Ethics and Behavior in the Old South.* New York: Oxford University Press, 1982.

———. *A Warring Nation: Honor, Race, and Humiliation in America and Abroad.* Charlottesville: University of Virginia Press, 2014.

Yarbrough, Jean M. *American Virtues: Thomas Jefferson on the Character of a Free People.* Lawrence: University Press of Kansas, 1998.

Young, Alfred F. *Liberty Tree: Ordinary People and the American Revolution.* New York: New York University Press, 2006.

———. *Masquerade: The Life and Times of Deborah Sampson, Continental Soldier.* New York: Alfred A. Knopf, 2004.

———. *The Shoemaker and the Tea Party: Memory and the American Revolution.* Boston: Beacon, 1999.

Young, Alfred F., Gary Nash, and Ray Raphael, eds. *Revolutionary Founders: Rebels, Radicals, and Reformers in the Making of the Nation.* New York: Vintage, 2012.

Zagarri, Rosemarie. "Morals, Manners, and the Republican Mother." *American Quarterly* 44, no. 2 (June 1992): 192–215.

———. *Revolutionary Backlash: Women and Politics in the Early Republic.* Philadelphia: University of Pennsylvania Press, 2007.

Index